GOVERNING DYNAMICS:
How to Uplift
SCHOOL PERFORMANCES,
Raise Employees' Productivity & Attract Prosperity
Vol I

By

Festo Michael Kambarangwe

KAMBARANGWE INSTITUTE OF LEADERSHIP & INNOVATION
Dar es Salaam, Tanzania EA

Festo Michael Kambarangwe

GOVERNING DYNAMICS: HOW TO UPLIFT SCHOOL PERFORMANCES, RAISE EMPLOYEE'S PRODUCTIVITY & ATTRACT PROSPERITY

By
Festo Michael Kambarangwe

All Rights Reserved
Copyright © 2016 by Festo Michael Kambarangwe

ISBN: 978-9987-9976-8-8

No part of this publication may be reproduced, stored in a retrieval system, or transmitted in any form or by any means, electronic, mechanical, photocopying, recording, scanning, or otherwise, except for a few short quotations, without either the prior written permission of the Publisher, or authorization of the Copyright holder.

While the publisher and author have used their best efforts in preparing this book, they make no representations or warranties with respect to the accuracy or completeness of the contents of this book. Besides, they also understand that the advices or strategies contained herein may not be suitable for every person's or organization's situation.

Printed in the United States of America

Other books by Festo Michael Kambarangwe:

How Universities Under Develop You!

What Business Leaders Should Know
but They Don't

What Makes People Rich and Nations Powerful

Festo Michael Kambarangwe

"Small is the number (of people)
That sees with their own eyes,
And feels with their own hearts;
But it is their strength,
That will decide whether,
The human race must relapse
Into that state of stupor,
Which a deluded multitude
Appears today to regard as the ideal…"

—Albert Einstein

"Welcome or unwelcome,
Agreeable or disagreeable;
Whether this shall be an entire slave nation,
Is the issue before us!"

—A. Lincoln

Festo Michael Kambarangwe

Festo Michael Kambarangwe

For the Glory of God and my Country

Festo Michael Kambarangwe

In delightful memories of you Michael Junior—our son—and a dedication to all parents who have lost their beloved ones in circumstances that could otherwise be avoided. Son, we thank you! We thank you for though you couldn't live long enough, the nine moons of our personal communication and that one last day when we physically got in touch at TMJ Hospital—where you were born and died—remain as intact as if you are right here with us today. Though your life faded so fast, it gave us a great gift of fathering and mothering you. We thank you for the lessons of humility and submission to the natural law you taught us so well in just one day; much as you taught us not to give up on life; but to accept situations we can't change—and to always be thankful in all things.

Festo Michael Kambarangwe

ACKNOWLEDGEMENTS

Here're a couple of compliments I've, very humbly, received over the years. They are from people who are closest to me. The paraphrased notes read thus:

"I might not have told you that it was through your support that I'm where I'm today. You have dedicated your precious resources giving up your personal desires to support my education. It is with your devotion that today my life is filled with joy. We often take such favors from family members for granted. I think it is wrong. Without your support, today I wouldn't be in my present station in life. Thanks for being there when I needed you most."

The second note read thus: "I've thought of the perfect words to express how grateful I'm, but I've not found any. I'm indeed thankful more than words can convey. Thank you so much and may God bless you!" The third note arrived on 27 of October 2009 at 11.36. 06 PM. It read thus: "You may never see how much I care for you. You may never hear how much I treasure you. You may never feel how much I appreciate you; because only right here in my heart you can feel them true..."

Looking back, learning from the magnitude of the gratitude embedded in the words from these three great persons, I realize fully how I haven't been as grateful to the people who have been there for me—over the years. I recognize thereof, that, I couldn't have accomplished anything worthwhile, if other people didn't support me materially and morally. Such is how I find myself obliged to thank my parents, brothers, sisters, my teachers, superiors, co-workers and friends without whose support I would not have accomplished anything noteworthy. Today I realize yours have been invaluable sacrifices and priceless devotion.

I thank you because I realized that I was warm, well fed and dressed only because you were such selfless individuals who went through the cold nights and endured a day's heat under hard labor and often without food; poorly dressed or inadequately provided for that I could fair better. You tirelessly gave me courage to take my first steps in whatever I wanted to do. You never gave up on me.

As I pass to you the three notes of gratitude above, let me say to the three persons who took their time to express their appreciation to me that I cannot thank you more! I would also like to thank my good children, Princess, Priscilla, Patricia and Prince; for putting up with me during those grim times when I was writing and thus not being there for them. To all of you I would like say that you all have been a blessing to me. To all of you let me say: "It was kind of you to share my troubles. And you... sent me help now and again (Philippians 4.14-23)!" And indeed because of what you have been to me, "I've loved you with an everlasting love (Jer. 31:3)!"

May God bless you and add unto you—abundantly.
Lastly, but not least, I'm grateful for the transgenerational wisdom—wisdom passed down by a pen or word of mouth.

Finally, but not in the order of importance, as the author of this book, I truly know that God is the primary author of everything we do. I know that truly such an endeavor of writing and eventually publishing a book like this one requires very hard choices. Truly an accomplishment of this magnitude isn't an exclusive work of man! Surely I have accomplished this work with the benefaction of the Supreme Power. It is for this reason that I whisper: "Dear Lord," I whisper, "Our Father in heaven, I thank Thee, I thank Thee, I thank Thee[1]"

—Author

---

[1] Borghild Dahl in I wanted to See in How to Stop Worrying and Start Living by Dale Carnegie p.152.

ABOUT THE AUTHOR

Festo Michael Kambarangwe is the third born to Pudensiana Kambarangwe (also known as Mama Julius, daughter to Mathias and Theresa Mkaka). The author is thirteenth to Michael Kambarangwe who left behind 50 minus four children and 70 grand and great grand children when he was laid to eternal rest in 2009 in Biharamulo not very far from Bukililo, Bushubi, a small village where he was born during the German rule in the then Tanganyika. An only son to Augustine Kambarangwe, one of the first prominent earliest converts to Christianity and a teacher in the colonial Biharamulo district; which prompted Michael Kambarangwe, the author's father to pursue education at the junior seminaries of Rutabo and Katoke before he studied at Rubya seminary and later preferred family life to priesthood. Brother to Kigenza and Rwaburundi, Augustine was the son of Ndabikunze, one of many sons and daughters of King Rwabigimba, who reigned in the place of his father Kibogora, ruler of the kingdom of Bushubi (A HINDA STATE FALLING Within the Zinza-Ha sphere (*journals.cambridge.org/production/*) thus closely linked with Karagwe and Biharamulo from which it split). Bushubi, one of the now ancient Hinda States that thrived in the *Great Lakes Region* long before the white men set their boots on the mainland soil; time when even names like Tanganyika or Tanzania, Kenya or Uganda existed, thrived to its pinnacle under Kibogora, whom the American explorer Henry Morton Stanley, writes about meeting seeking permission to cross the country on his way to Ujiji before that famous greeting *"Dr. Livingstone, I presume,"* on meeting Dr. Livingstone at the bank of one of the deepest rivers in the whole world, River Tanganyika in 1840s in his book *The Sources of the Nile* (www.amazon.com*)*.

Bushubi fell under German East Africa in 1890s. According to E. K. Lumley, the first British district officer in the kingdom in his book *Forgotten Mandate* (www.amazon.com), Bushubi remained fairly independent because both Germans and British were stationed in the colonial Biharamulo district until during the reign of King Nkundabagore—Augustine Kambarangwe's cousin brother—when the British first started ruling directly from within the kingdom. Bushubi was unified with other pre-colonial states in 1961 on independence forming independent Tanganyika which later in 1964, united with Zanzibar to form the modern day Tanzania before kingdoms were abolished under Tanzania's first president, Julius Kambarage Nyerere.

Based in Dar es Salaam, Tanzania in the East Africa, the author resides in Mbezi Louis, a few miles from the coastline of the Sea of Dar es Salaam also known as Indian Ocean. He is happily married to Nafro daughter of Mzee Miki Nassoro Magetta (RIP) and Mwalimu Moshi Mikidadi Magetta daughter of Mzee Pakomu and Mwana Mhawila. The author and his wife God graciously blessed with precious children Princess Felista, Priscilla Sasha, Michael Junior (RIP), Patricia Cleopatra and Prince Kennedy Ruhinda.

TRIBUTES TO FESTO MICHAEL KAMBARANGWE—AUTHOR OF "WHAT MAKES PEOPLE RICH AND NATIONS POWERFUL," AND AUTHOR, EDUCATOR & TRAINER OF "HOW TO UPLIFT SCHOOL PERFORMANCES AND RAISE EMPLOYEES' PRODUCTIVITY" PROGRAM

"You know what! You never stop encouraging, inspiring, and motivating me! Thank you for the insights. Can't explain the way this helps me multiply and grow bigger and bigger! You give me the pressure—you encourage me to move forward!" —Maria Mwakasege; university graduate and one time author's coworker

"Finally, I've stumbled upon a book that bespeak what I consider as right solutions to our problems." —Michael Ogwari John; a HR director and (at the time) acting principal secretary for the Ministry of health

"I congratulate you for a book with so much useful insights." —Dr. Alawi Shaaban Swabury, Member of the UN Business Sector Steering Committee on Finance for the Development-New York; CEO of ESSB Berlin

"I'm deeply pleased and inspired to read your work. Well done. This is an incredible achievement. I truly appreciate your efforts for coming up with such a work to benefit all. I assure you of my support. I'm currently out of the country when I return I'll definitely contact you! Indeed to say I'm proud of you, will be understatement!!" —Helen Michael; former author's co-worker who has served in different capacities among several world-class international organizations

"By the way I've always been an admirer of your writing skills and style! It's like watching Mikel Arteta playing football! You just sit back and enjoy it to the last drop! It's incredible!"—Emmanuel Kanagisa; marketing professional and of course a great fan of Arsenal Football Club

"Congratulations, Festo. This is a great work! Surely, Africans should enumerate on what you have accomplished...this is a tremendous achievement." —Alex Modest; communication specialist

"Quite appealing!" — Dr. Alphoncina Nanai

"You truly are contributing to The Making of a Nation" —Leonard C. Kitoka; prominent entrepreneur, consultant and managing partner with Innovex Development Consulting Limited

"Inspirational indeed!" —Benedict Emmanuel; thinker, economist and one time author's classmate

"Oh, yeah, he is an inspiration indeed!" —Cyrus Gabone; top finance professional, with education and work skills from both in Tanzania and the UK

"Felicitations!" —Chelaus Rutta; a University of Dar es Salaam and Makerere learned economist serving with IMF in Dar es Salaam

"Happy is the person who will put you to use!" —Julius Mitinje; A finance professional

"I'm sure people will benefit a lot from you. Festo is a blessing and an inspiration to us! I've said this several time. I repeat..." —Francis Nanai; CEO, Mwananchi Communication (a Nation Media Company)

"You have proved the old adage as Arthur Gordon put it 'The real measure of commitment is action'. You have set yourself on a greatness journey in which you are soon achieving. You inspire people by unveiling unto them their own riches; that being the greatest good you can do for another person which is not just sharing your riches but to reveal to them their own... Indeed you are headed for greatness. Bravo!! —James Tapela; a Zimbabwean consultant and one time author's coworker

"I'm proud of your accomplishment after you decided to quit a very lucrative job at Celtel in Dar es Salaam and go "to the street" to write. Once again, congratulations.., you have made us all proud. Hope you will manage to get these books in the East and Southern African bookstores. It's a great work and I feel especially like I am part of it. Your works is truly very relevant to our people. Salutes..." —Laurean Rugambwa Bwanakunu; CEO-MSD

"Hats off! Congratulations are in order even though it has not come to me as a surprise! I remember you during secondary school debating sessions; you were simply superb. This is just a continuation of what you could do...I advise you again to really think of what more you can do in the future (considering that the vengeance of the economic crisis is still ongoing and social and economic disorders at their peaks). Yes; indeed; Festo did make us all proud." —Edward (John) Munyangabe

"I'm proud of your achievement. And thank you for this gift.... Given the response I see...I suggest that the priority now should be to make these books available."—Respicius Didace, Didace & Co. Advocates, Dar es Salaam, Tanzania

"I like your emphasis on common sense—a commodity which is often short in supply!"— Phillip Parham (referring to the original idea of this work at the time when he was British High Commissioner to Tanzania)

"Congratulations Mr. Kambarangwe. I must say we share a lot regarding education and how to advance this country." —Anonymous billionaire, lawyer, businessman and politician

"You know what, you are very gifted my brother. I am impressed. Congratulations! I must say you are in another league. You have exceeded my expectations. "You know what, you are very gifted my brother. I am impressed. Congratulations! I must say you are in another league. You have exceeded my expectations. Now I believe that for a nation to break from underdevelopment and move to prosperity, it needs a group of few individual thinkers, local as well as international, as its growth Think Tank. And it is in this RARE CLASS that you, the author, belong. —Kiteja Ntobela Mayunga; graphics designing entrepreneur

"Being your brother, I may possibly take your accomplishment so lightly, you know! Quite frankly, if I didn't know you I would say, "Wow! This guy is a genius! Truly this is something out of ordinary. Congratulations." —The author's sibling

"This is a great piece of work!" —John Ernest Kitoka; intellectual columnist and consultant based in Dar es Salaam, Tanzania

"You have made a very big difference. Your work is an answer to those who doubt that ordinary individuals like me and you can make a big difference. Knowing that you were quietly accomplishing a splendid work for humanity, i have waited endlessly for this book. NOW THAT your work has finally brought out its face, I am sure people will give it the pledge of allegiance." —Vitalis Michael, graduate of Mass Communication

"It is always great to link up with you. You are a very carefully selected talent yourself. You refused to take droplets of dollars coupled with tiny favors from without yourself and decided to harness many facets of riches from within your own self and discovered a YOU—a wonderful approach indeed! You refused to accept small principles of money - making from working for which you were not born to do and entered a red hot tunnel which delivered you the other side as a new and pure person! You are an example to all who still labor in the process of self discovery. Congratulations comrade!" —Zephrine Galeba; intellectual, attorney, entrepreneur and Managing Partner GRK Advocates

"This is not just a book. It is the philosophy of life." — Albert M.M, Principal Editor in Dar es Salaam

"Very powerful indeed! Like a religious sermon." —Doctor Solomon Aclaus Mlau

"I believe no ordinary human means can accomplish this magnitude of feat without the intercession of the Higher Powers." —Alex William Rwabitara Bwanakunu

"With the accomplishment of this magnitude, now you can die!" —Daudi Michael Kambarangwe; author's sibling.

Festo Michael Kambarangwe

"Fallen, fallen is Babylon the great! She has become a dwelling place of demons and a prison of every tainted spirit, and a prison of every dirty and vile vulture. For all the nations have drunk of the wine of the passion of her immorality, and the kings of the earth have committed sin with her, and the merchants of the earth have become rich by the wealth of her body...
Come out of her, my people, lest you take part in her sins, lest you share in her plagues..." —Revelation of John 18:2-4

Festo Michael Kambarangwe

Table of Contents

PREFACE...xxiii

PERSONAL REFLECTION: THE LIFE OF THE EDUCATED
MEDIOCRE...xxvii

1. THERE IS A HIDDEN TREASURE IN YOU:
HOW I BEGAN PACKAGING AND SELLING HUMANS AT A
PREMIUM PRICE..1

2. A SICK NATION: IDEALISTIC OR REALISTIC.......................15

3. DIAGNOSIS OF A SICK NATION: SYMPTOMS OF A SICK
NATION..23

XENOPHOBIA, KING ZWELETINI, OF THE ZULU
AND THE SICK SOCIETY...48

4. THE DEATH OF A NATION:

THE FATE OF A SICK NATION..56

5. PERSONAL SELF EVALUATION..76

6. THE YOUTH: A LOST GENERATION....................................91

7. SIGNIFICANCE OF THE YOUTH: THE YOUTH AND THE
FUTURE OF THE NATION..104

8. ENTERTAINMENTATION OF THE NATION AND THE FATE OF
THE NATION..122

9. WHAT SHOULD WE TRANSFORM: THE YOUTH OR
EDUCATION?...134

10. LOW GRADUATE SELF EMPLOYMENT—THE DARK SCAR
IN OUR TRADITIONAL COLLEGE EDUCATION....................154

11. WHO IS TO BLAME?..168

12. THE FEAR OF UNKNOWN: THE REASON WHY WE HAVE
FAILED TO MOVE FORWAR..187

13. GOING BACK TO THE BASICS: THE PRINCIPLED UNIVERSE
AND THE RAW LAW OF NATURE..203

14. GOVERNING DYNAMICS: HUMAN ECONOMIC FACTOR..*253*

15. A GLIMMER OF HOPE: NARROWING THE BASICS DOWN TO SPECIFICS..*267*

EPILOGUE: HOW TO BUILD THE IDEAL CITIZEN, UPLIFT SCHOOL PERFORMANCES, RAISE EMPLOYEES PRODUCTIVITY AND ATTRACT PROSPERITY..*294*

REFERENCES AND ENDNOTES RETRIEVED DURING THE WRITING PERIOD UP TO JULY 2015..*323*

PREFACE

On Saturday of April 21, 2012 at 11:05 PM, I received an email note from a person known to me personally. His name is Benedict Emanuel. In his own words, he warned of sad tidings if we didn't address the problem our nation was facing. Recognizing that Napoleon Bonaparte was right when he said: "The world suffers a lot; not very much because of the violence of bad people but rather because of the silence of good people," Benny chose not to complain but to do something about it.

Below is that email. In its unofficial paraphrased version I have interpreted into English from Kiswahili, it read thus: "My dear friends, hello. It is long since I had the privilege of writing to you. I'm writing this note because I've had a persistent hunch that something in our society is pervasively going wrong," he began. *"Though, surprisingly,* I cannot explain what exactly that problem is, though I cannot precisely lay down what exactly that problem is or how it's brought to my attention, but my instincts lead me to believe that somewhere, somehow, something is eating into the fiber of our society and I fear there's a profound crisis on the cards.

"Without necessarily going into the description of my hunch, let me say we shouldn't keep quiet and do nothing when we fear our society is on the brink of crumbling. Now though in a summary form, I know one Mr. Kambarangwe, a person who has attempted to describe what I consider to be the problem we face and the alternative solutions through his work *Building Ideal Graduates: How to Uplift School Performances, Raise Employees' Productivity and attract prosperity*. Mr. Reverend—and every one of you—if you would, you would please find it in your heart to support this gentleman's efforts. How? You could assist him by listening to him. By simply doing so, by giving him audience, you would be led to the deeper insights into the problems our nation—or the world as a whole—is facing today.

About his contacts, you can find his email address in the list above. Ask him questions. Share your inputs. Deliberate on alternative solutions. Help him to reach out to as many people as possible both in the country and beyond in the Diaspora. You can support his efforts in as many favorable ways as you see it fit and as it is revealed to you! Together we can derail the crisis and lift up the nation from its knees and lead her back to prosperity and thereof bring dignity to our people and the nation once again. I know you can do something about it. I am certain you are going to do something.

All of you! For after all, doing so, you help to make life better for yourselves, your families and the nation as a whole. By doing so, you help to make the world a better place! May God bless you!"

By those words: *May God bless you*; he had concluded his note which he undersigned with his same-same good names: Benedict Emanuel Bugufi.

Now because this great thinker referred to the author, let me say something beforehand. I feel truly privileged for my efforts to have finally brought out the face to the surface such as to attract the attention of some important persons like Benny and co. Notwithstanding how privileged I feel, I bear witness to the fact that I have not had the privilege of personally meeting this other recipient he only introduced as Mr. Reverend. But I must admit I feel highly privileged to have had my work introduced to such a personality; for surely no average man ever became a reverend—excepting of the fishermen among those Jesus himself handpicked in Galilee. I also, finally fill gratified knowing that my sacrifice has not been in vain. We are, moreover, flattered especially by the magnitude of confidence he has had in what we do. Not once though. He has not only always, but indeed constantly, been there supporting, encouraging and engaging others to join this platform.

We thank Benny for voicing the problem and having encouraged others to see and getting engaged into seeking more relevant solutions to our problems than simply complaining. By sharing the problem with the wider audience, you do a noble duty of warning them. Besides, letting them ponder about the imminent problem and placing the burden of finding answers to the public, you do the society a greater service. Benny has also helped us to learn the significance of honoring relevant local efforts in addressing chronic problems our societies are facing. We congratulate Benny for such a gifted foresight—and thank him so much for that.

Learning from Benny, using the words of the German philosopher Wolfgang von Goethe: "I have come to a frightening conclusion that I am a decisive element. It is my personal approach that creates climate. It is my daily mood that makes weather. I possess tremendous power to make life miserable or joyous. I can be a tool of torture, or instrument of inspiration; I can humiliate or humor, I can hurt or heal. In all situations, it is my response that decides whether a crisis is escalated or deescalated, and a person is humanized or dehumanized."

You and I can indeed be the tools of torture or instruments of inspiration. You and I can humiliate or humor. You and I can hurt or heal. In all situations, it is our response that decides whether a crisis is escalated or deescalated, and a person is humanized or dehumanized. It is indeed toward this end that this book has been written.

—Author

Festo Michael Kambarangwe

PERSONAL REFLECTION: THE LIFE OF THE EDUCATED MEDIOCRE

"The plain fact is that the planet does not need more "successful" people. But it does desperately need more peacemakers, healers, restorers, Storytellers, and lovers of every shape and form. It needs people who Live well in their places. It needs people of moral courage (and) willing To join the fight to make the world habitable and humane. And these needs have little to do with success as our culture Has defined it."—David Orr[2]

You are driving your old used car with two hundred thousand kilometers on it; a car you acquired through the credit facility your employer organized for you thanks to your degree in economics and your position as an assistant bank branch manager. The traffic is heavy. Your windows are open even though the heat outside in threatening to murder you because you can't afford air condition.

You cannot replace it. And you want to economize fuel usage. You call yourself a prudent economist. You take out a worn-out besoiled handkerchief from your long pocket and brush your red face. The traffic is satanically static. There is nothing holy about it. The heat is homicidal.

Then you hear people shouting: Mwizi, Mwizi which is Thief, Thief...The caravan forms as it turns towards whence the yell had come from. The audience is typical jobless goons from the drug loaded streets of Kinondoni. You can't stop it. A smile. It forms on your face. The events happening on the outside belie you. You forget your troubles for a moment. You count your blessings. The mob is passing by chasing a couple of shabby blood stained human forms running to save their souls as blood was still gushing out.

---

[2] What Is Education For? Six myths about the foundations of modern education, and six new principles to replace them by David Orr

You say to hell. Let natural justice triumph. As your lane moves on you smell blood and gasoline and s you turn you see rings of the smoking cloud forming as the agonizing sounds of a groaning man remind you what has just transpired to the unfortunate boys.

You glance at the inside of the car. Beer cans, cigarette butts—and lo! The 6-pack prize is still untouched. Only its neighbor, another pack—a 3-pack rubber contraceptive seems to have been un-abandoned! It is a mess. I mean your car.

Your job too! All your life is a shit. You are a mess. You admit. You look at the used contraceptives and ponder at the event a night before—young, innovative, energetic! What a catch that was!

A little crooked smile blossoms again. Then you give a little prayer of thanksgiving your wife didn't spy on you. The events in the back seat wouldn't make her happy one bit. Because of the traffic jam, fuel, heat and the present state of your car you are forced to run away from your own car.

But what would people think of you! Pride comes in. You sit back. You ponder at your crooked necktie. You crave to look executive—to impress people around you! You fix it! I mean your tie. You peer a mile ahead. The cars are still static. Probably there is an accident! You curse!

You desire a cold longneck of Kilimanjaro or Serengeti Lager brand to extinguish dryness in your throat and certainly counter the hangover—and hunger—for you often eat liquid lunch. With hang over, the alcoholic dinner that comes in a beer bottle is the most preferable.

Two in one! You smile at your creativity. For thirty more minutes—reading from your cheap marred wrist watch—the traffic is still heavy.

The little hot springs of sweat are now flowing from every "water table" in your body. Ubiquitous traffic policemen sparkling with twinkling buzzing walkie-talkies and guns in their hands pass by demonstrating every sign of real combat as if you are on the battle field in Kosovo or somewhere in Afghanistan.

Soon it is after seven in evening and the sun is setting back from where it came. The convoy of motor bikes passes by hooting speeding along Ali Hassan Mwinyi Road.

They move toward the opposite direction. Then a convoy of expensive cars follows and you recognize the national flag and a presidential flag fly with no specific direction as the winds sweep the air above the ground. It was the top personality in the country passing by speeding toward an unknown destination—for an unidentified mission.

And you don't care. It doesn't bother you. What matters to you now is a cold beer with or without president. To hell with all presidents! That's a title you will never assume.

You are alone in the car—and without air condition, you begin to perspire in the heat of car. But now conscious that in your adjacent lane a young lady is behind the wheel.

And you cannot miss that hers is a brand new car you also cannot miss that radiates prosperity and self confidence. As you pry, you notice an old man with graying hair and an old woman seated beside her.

You recognize for sure they were her parents. As the traffic jam seems to be endless, and your interest around the three persons in the car in the adjacent lane, you conclude by the body language and their respective ages that the older persons were a reserved couple and the younger person behind the wheel was their daughter.

You also conclude that as reserved as she was, and the self confidence she exuded, she must be a well educated graduate from the High Profile University. She also must have graduated in the recent past few years.

The rest are the assumptions you have attempted to jig-saw-fit: the car is hers and only newly imported from Japan; she has just picked her parents from their nice home somewhere in Masaki; she is driving toward Serena Hotel for the evening ambiance—as you are heading for any lousy outfit. She is grateful to her parents—that you cannot miss—she adores them. They have been so loving and caring to her since her childhood. She cannot forget it.

They seem like persons who would sell any household items at throw away price to send her back to school starving themselves saving for her school fees when the situation was tough back then. They are people who made her who she is today. You look at her car.

It is a brand new 4x4 car from Japan. Her destination is a 5 Star hotel and you can visualize her under the umbrellas in a beach hotel across from the waters of the Sea of Dar es Salaam they call Indian Ocean. Yours is a cheap lousy roadside outfit. Your life is a complete contrast—you conclude. You feel little troubled by shrug it off. You say your time will come.

The traffic is long and the sun falls fully behind the clouds over the ocean. You don't know where you are going. You are a person who is trying to live a large life and impress whomsoever he meets. But deep inside you is a person who has been wounded.

You are wounded by your education, wounded by your job, wounded by your employer, wounded by your nagging and spiteful wife. You have got children. They are a set of unfortunate children—you admit.

They are four of them. You curse the day you got yourself into that mess they call wedlock. It is a prison cell. The fact that there is a toddler your wife is still nursing and a couple of them in the off-the-record relationships don't do much to help your situation.

You look at the public bus with too many passengers burning in the heat and look down on them imagining you are far better off. You switch off the car to save fuel. Around 33 degrees Celsius the heat is about to kill you. Suddenly to your relief the traffic policeman beckons your lane of cars. You switch on and the battery doesn't respond.

The cars behind you start hooting angrily. Luckily finally the ignition responds and you start driving but you follow the road to nowhere. You find yourself crossing around the Leader's Club grounds and you drive along the Container Pub, opposite French embassy. It is almost already dark. You say let me try Leaders Club; there could be some live music show or any entertainment you so much crave.

You need to soothe your wounded ego. You want some fun. But no sooner as you cross the Heart Institute than you see a shadow. It is a female shadow. That you cannot miss.

This shadow on the road ahead catches your attention. She is another girl—quite an opposite number of the one who was driving the brand-new car in the adjacent lane during the traffic jam, a few minutes back. They are a contrast to each other.

xxx

Then suddenly something dramatic happens that determines your state of affairs in the next couple of hours—and many years to come. She has literally thrown herself at your feet and you scarcely drive over her. You slow down! She is now at the open window screen of your car.

Things happen so fast. You try to ponder about the situation. But while you are contemplating your next move she disrobes and displays her wares emphasizing she is still very young but that she is experienced enough to pack you with all worldly pleasures you desire.

How profitable a transaction that is!

Cautiously you watch through the side mirrors and see no car coming. You want an affair with her and you still crave some reputation—nonetheless. You could do with privacy!
You park the car and bid her enter. She or you become a victim of another's passionate and beastly desire for adventure but indeed of conquest—the sheer desire of having somebody under your spell. The passion right in the car is raw and therefore irresistible. Inevitable. Unavoidable.
You say after all my wife nags every time. And she nurses. Suddenly you are entangled. Two things are imminent now! You realize you didn't use condoms and she didn't need any. You are drunk but just mildly. To her credit and true to her word she quite pleases you. And thus you don't care much about VIH or SDIA. You assert in your state of drunkenness that the pleasure was yours.

Economist yourself, you judge that it has been a fair return on your investment. You don't care. After all, all men shall die at one or another point in time. What's the use of self denial? Or self pity? Time for religion isn't yet due. Let the seventies come. What is this disease they call VIH or SDIA? In your wantonness and half-witted mind you ask yourself belittling the virus. You laugh at the virus. How minute it is! It's a joke. It cannot kill he-men like you.

You are drunk which is why you reversed the initials of the epidemic. HIV!? No! That can't be possible.

She is so young and heavenly—you have just witnessed on firsthand account how youthful and magical she is. Soon you are in a club with her again. Tracing your ATM card and promise her big monies for her sweet things and a wonderful company. She wantonly surrenders head over heels at your desires. Now you are in a club. You are chatting as you caress.

The waitresses serve you with drinks and bites. The atmosphere is superb for your little raw satanic adventure. It is semi dark in your cabin just for the love birds somewhere deep in Kinondoni. And it is dark. Soft lounge music furnishes your little picnic and any needed extras. The sofa settee is large enough. It feels home. And after all, home is where the heart is. And you forget it. I mean your home.

You comfort and serve yourself. In that darkness no eye of man or virus is capable of watching anything. It is total dark. Not even God can see you. You throw all cautions to the four winds. You are after all avoiding nothing. You have just had her. You justify your actions. And to hell with your nagging wife!

And you laugh at your catch! You laugh at your audacity! You laugh at your luck—and bravely. And you laugh at the grocery in your neighborhood deep in Mbagala where you live. You laugh at the shabby waitresses back there.
You laugh at your nagging aging wife! You sit back and wash your sins away with a crazy golden drink and begin to socialize.
You learn from your catch that she was brought up by a single mother who had dropped out of school and started on her own in the streets where she made lots of money enough for their modest living.

Her mother was another case study: dropped out of school at nine, raped at eleven, loaded with a bastard at your side at eleven, ran away at twelve and had a baby on the street at twelve. Then the same child found herself on her mother's lap and back at Fire or Surrender Bridge in the city surrendering to manly desires for her insane world or survival.

You learn principally that your new catch grew sexually since long ago understudying her mother who died a couple of years back when she was only around ten—you guess. The girl beside you didn't attend not only the school but also the church! And she didn't know how to read or write. Her mother died of HIV and AIDS later leaving her on the streets. That's part of her books of account.

On your part the books of account read as follows: graduating in accounts—a discipline you didn't choose or love; studied—by the grace of your relatives—and without purpose; you ended up as a C—student; got any first lousy job in an Indian factory and took it; running away from the village and from your poor parents and relatives; married. And what's more, a woman beside you carries your baby in her womb. It is two hours old now. Your wallet is slimmer. And you have contracted HIV.

FINAL THOUGHT
As we come to the end of this heartrending episode, I ask you to take a little break. And during this little break, in the meditation of your heart, by the word of your mouth and works of your hands, hand on heart, promise yourself to be truthful to yourself as you analyze and record down the true feelings and little resolutions propping up in your heart from this self censorship exercise.

With little meditation, now you realize that you and I could be one of the individual people above! You can be this pitiful man driving along the road—the road to nowhere. Or you could be the nagging wife that repels her husband, or even the motherly lady of grace above. You could also choose to be that pregnant young girl, or create the kind of the child in her womb.
You could be the parents in the opposite car driving toward Serena Hotel; a happy couple whose child had graduated from the university and now on your way to the Serena Hotel reaping from your balanced life and devotion through giving and making life better for others. Probably you realize you or your daughter could even be that girl who in a very short period of time had almost accomplished her dreams and already setting higher ones—goals that aren't self-centered but ones that shower blessing to people and society around her—blessing to her family, the neighborhood, the nation and humanity as a whole.

Notice also that you could be one of the secret service policemen with buzzing walkie-talkies and guns or the traffic policeman directing cars under the overhead sun in hot Dar air or the chauffeur driving a Benz with a presidential flag on it. Surprisingly you could even be the he-man such as a writer, the author of a book like this one, or the one in the dark-blue Mercedes Benz speeding past as armed men and traffic policemen wait on him—a Mr.(or Ms.) President! Why not!

But that requires work. Dedication. Commitment! Determination. Devotion. You recognize as an individual, you are not any safer. Are we—as a society? You, the reader, are not different from the unfortunate person above. You are not any safer anymore.

Nine out of ten people you meet on the streets today could fall into this category. What is the nation are we building? These are the same-same people we see in schools. We see them in workplaces. We see them in every profession. They are ubiquitous in politics. We see them in places of worship. They are the same-same people in all high places. They are our teachers.

They are our fiancés or fiancées. They are the future parents—the future nation. We see them far and wide in the ubiquitous pubs and bars in the country. We see them—nine out of 10—in night clubs and whorehouses. They, like ants, are lining up everywhere in our society today. Nine out of 10! A staggering figure, huh!

As a nation we must recognize that there is more, much more work to do. Indeed, "Therefore he who thinks he stands let him take heed lest he fall." *But we have hope. And our hope is genuine.* "Our greatest glory," aptly said Ralph Waldo Emerson, "Our greatest glory is in never falling, but in rising up every time we fall."

Luckily, there is a remedy. And it is within your reach; it is on your lap as you read this book. Little over 200 years ago Professor William James remarked that "The greatest discovery of my generation," he said, "is that a human being can alter his life by altering his attitudes... his thinking." It follows therefore that if one human being can alter his or her life by altering his or her attitudes, his thinking, that person can therefore alter his life and that of his family for better. It follows therefore that if majority of individual persons in any society can alter their lives by altering their attitudes, their thought patterns, those individual persons can alter, or transform their own lives as well as the lives of their families for better. If many households in a country can change or transform their lives for better, that country can transform itself into a self reliant and prosperous nation.

We know that probably the reader will question why we seem to have addressed the changes almost entirely on the individual person's level. It doesn't really matter at all. For after all, according the principles of economics, national income—or the wealth of a nation—is a sum total of the income or wealth of each individual household in an economy or nation. Indeed, "There is no such a thing as society," so aptly said Margaret Thatcher. "There are individual men, and women, and families." By addressing the problems and mindset of these individual men and women, we transform them and their families. By transforming their families, we transform the whole society.

The American Dream for many individuals and America herself, or the success stories of modern day China, Malaysia, Botswana or respectively histories of either the post-Amin Uganda or the post-genocide Rwanda speak loud for themselves. And in the end, in the end, try much as i can, there are things i can't say with words—at least for now. May i plead therefore, that as goes the ancient prayer, "can you please just listen through my heart?"

Here we go....

Festo Michael Kambarangwe

1. THERE IS A HIDDEN TREASURE IN YOU: HOW I BEGAN PACKAGING AND SELLING HUMANS AT A PREMIUM PRICE

"Those of you who are graduating with high honors and distinctions, Well done! And I would also like to tell the C—students: You too can become presidents!"—George W. Bush

THE HIDDEN TREASURE IN YOU
In every little boy, in the young Prince, there's a hero. In every failed man, there's a potential Julius Kambarage Nyerere. In him there a potential Abraham Lincoln, a Mandela or an Obama! In every failed student, there's a Newton, an Einstein or a Gandhi; in him there's a Professor Mukandala, a Dr. Kimei, a Professor Maliyamkono, a Mustapha Sabodo, a Dr. Reginald Mengi, an Abu Bakar, or a Saint Peter or Saint Paul! In any young Princess, in every Priscilla, in little Patricia; in any baby girl, there's a Hillary Clinton, a Rosa Parks, a Dr. Asha-Rose Migiro, a Michelle Obama, an Anna-Kilango Malechella, a Professor Wangari Mathai, a Pudensiana alias Mama Julius or even—a Mother Teresa!

What's more, it also so astonishes me, how in any organization—an organization of any size—there's in it a City Group, a Vodafone, a Coca Cola Group etc. In every writer of any status there is a Shaban Robert, a Shakespeare, a Ben Carson or a Dale Carnegie or Napoleon Hill, a Nelson Mandela or a Museveni. In every kindergarten; in every school, an institute or college of any size there's a University of Dar es Salaam, a Princeton, a Cambridge, an Oxford, a Harvard or Yale. In every person there's a "special" talent. Indeed in every poor or mediocre performer, there's the best performer.

Probably at this point in time, you will have realized that therefore in every troubled society there's a United Republic of Tanzania—and that too in every indebted and underdeveloped state or nation there's a China, a Japan, Germany, Denmark, Sweden or even the United States!

This, however, is only the beginning. Identifying first the strengths and weaknesses, opportunities and threats and then nurturing and harnessing these strengths or talents together form the challenge we are facing. You realize I have begun this chapter with a success story, a good ending.

But you notice that this success story, a good ending I assert is only possible if that person, school, business organization, society or nation is nurtured and guided to identify its own strength or talent and to leverage and optimize the potentials so identified. Did I say *optimize*? Yes, that's the right word. Dictionary.cambridge.org defines Optimize as, *to make something as good as possible.* Here is an example of the use of the word Optimize. *We need to optimize our use of the existing technology.*

Therefore to reclaim, unearth and indeed optimize this hidden potential, develop it and actually put it to use, that person, organization or society must be ready to scan and identify his or her own weaknesses. This chapter and the book you are now reading shoulders this burden. It is because of this burden that the author chose to resign from work to write books, create and develop training programs addressing this challenge.

Reclaiming a hero that there's in every little boy or girl; recovering a winner in every failed man; transforming a failing matrimony and a family unit; rejuvenating a failing organization or society—one way or another—is the noble goal the author had in mind when writing this book.

I hope, sir or madam, you probably have already begun recognizing that you are engaged in something of major significance to your life. You are through this book engaged in an endeavor that shall impact not only your life but that of your family so significantly, lead to the prosperity of your business and affluence of the people around you!

HOW I BEGAN PACKAGING, BRANDING, MARKETING AND SELLING HUMANS AT A PREMIUM PRICE

Love it or hate it, but we have got a mountain of work ahead of us. What I mean is that if we have to see meaningful change, we have got to rebuild the fabric of our society. But unfortunately we cannot work with tools we don't have. This is the challenge I faced most when I began working on the call to transform first myself, the people around me, and then society as a whole. Yet I'd no other major training or source or books of reference on the subject. Why? Before this book was written, the book and training like this one were yet unborn. Really! If there is one, certainly it had never crossed my path. That is why I had to start from somewhere. And that somewhere was not a very inspiring spot. Why? Because I had to start from the scratch! Luckily though, I knew what I wanted and I wanted it so badly. I was also deeply convinced I could do something about the situation. So what was I going to do?

Here is not only what I could do, but exactly what I did. And this is what I did. I dug deep and drew out from my own observation, experience and intuition. Yes I had no prior understanding of the training. Yes I had no prior education on the subject of healing a sick nation, which was the situation I feared would come to pass if we didn't do something about it—but I'd my own experience and intuition to fall back on. This is the major source of learning, of education and of knowledge. Remember education comes from *Educo* a Latin word for *Educe* or to draw out, to develop from within. It is probably what Ornstein and Hunkins called: *To retrieve old information.*[1]

This is in other words known as *to educe*. Mark the word for you shall hear much about it. That is the major scope of the challenge I had thrown myself into. I had to find, from my own experience, how to transform and make the mediocre people and a crumbling society into a money maker.

HOW DO COMPANIES SELL PRODUCTS FOR PROFIT?

Considering the disadvantageous position we in the so called third world are in, I had to find, from my own experience, how to transform and make the mediocre people, a crumbling society into a money making machine. Simply put, from my experience as a professional seller and marketer of products and services—products and services such as beer, drugs, telecoms and banking —I had sold before and experienced at that, I realized for the first time that humans were products or services, yes, depending on your choice. And as products, they had services to offer to other people and could therefore be improved and sold at premium price. That's how I began trading in humans—selling people.

Was I a slave trader? No! I was far from getting inspired by Tip Tippu the notorious slave trader! No! I was an improver of humans. I was going to look at what they have in themselves that can potentially be marketed and sold. I was going to make them draw from the deep wells of their own inner resources to turn themselves—with my support of course—into more useful individuals—useful to themselves and the world around them—and therefore make money in the process of rendering such useful services to humanity. That's how I was going to turn them into money making persons.

I created this business model based on the existing business theory by transferring my skills and experiences in selling products and services into building an education that would make it possible to sell what a person's character can offer. Being a graduate of economics and marketing myself, I readily transformed the knowledge such as why the American dollar is worth than our shilling, or why generally one currency appreciates while another depreciate, and used it to appreciate a person's value and thus have their services sold at premium prices; and so making them acquire value in the process as the other party gets useful services in the process of making money, and me make a profit in the process—as money changers do; making everyone happy.

In this process you realize that these individuals would as a result thrive personally as humans and their families, the business entities would bloom once again employing many people at high rates and tossing money around in the economy thereby generating various linkages—vertically and laterally—transforming the nation in the process. This is an extension of the economics I named Festo Michael Kambarangwe Economics, or Michael economics romantically named Michonomics as you can find in the book What Makes People Rich and Nations Powerful. So if you thought I was talking about packaging, branding and marketing and selling human flesh or that I was engaged in human trafficking, you are way off beam. I'm not into that. I'm not a cannibal or even in anyway dealing with human trafficking. Even the ancient Arab and European slave traders have civilized and since ceased trading in slaves anymore. How can I? I'm not into that. I'm into advancing humans.

DO WE NEED NEW EDUCATION?

Following social economic changes in a dynamic society like ours, disorientation in our society is raging, and it effects on people's livelihood so dreadful and rambling. The recent economic crisis, revelations behind its occurrence and its effects call for fine-tuning our education—what we teach, how, and why we teach what we teach and breathtaking revolution in ICT coupled with globalization, all necessitate to reorganize every aspects in the society—if we should remain abreast with the rapidity of change in the human society today. With this disadvantageous position in which we find ourselves unfortunately, the need for new ideas has quite so dramatically outstripped supply. Surely, we can attempt to adapt ourselves to changes. Indeed we can as well try to transform our old ways to suit the challenges we face. Yet the lasting solutions can only be found in hunting for, and building new ideas from completely new timber. In words of Allan C. Ornstein and Francis P. Hunkins in their book Curriculum Foundations, Principles and Issues (3rd edition p.51): *"(the) Society is always changing, and the curriculum has to change*; students and teachers must be change agents. (And as such) A curriculum based on social issues and services is ideal."[2]

In order to respond to the need for a curriculum based on social issues and services, we the reorientation of thought pattern or the mindset of our people, and the society as a whole, the need for transformation is almost an emergency. It is because of the foregoing pressing challenges that made the author to find himself packing and leaving his job to concentrate with research and writing. It is in the same emergency that the program Benedict referred to—*Building Ideal Graduates: How to Uplift School Performances, Raise Employees' Productivity and attract prosperity*—was conceived.

It is from constructing this program that we realized the greatest weakness in our education namely the failure to establish the DNA of the ideal society, that of the education we need today, and indeed the core values of the ideal scholar—the scholar we need to produce. It is from this program that we found it was important to redefine the meaning of education. It is in it that we set out to identify the qualities, core values or the DNA of the ideal graduate or scholar. It is in this process that we found we had to lay down the core values of the ideal citizen, the ideal employee and the ideal society we intend to build. If we fail to establish these aspects, we shouldn't expect to change, and as such, we will fail to change or transform the society, beginning with our education, to match socio-economic environment in which we live.

Also what is probably most important discovery from this entire study is that we realized we cannot move forward if we don't first understand where we are now, our true position as a society when compared to the ideal station where we ought to be. It is in this realization that we arrived at a shocking revelation that indeed not every country is indeed healthy or sound. We discovered that there is indeed a country that could be unhealthy, indeed a sick nation!

Here is a quick sample analysis we ought to have done. Fifty years after the independence, is indeed a sufficient amount of time to re-examine ourselves as individuals and society, identifying and accepting where we went right or wrong. With this analysis we could then learn from both our positive experiences and mistakes thereby drawing a map of where we are and where we want to go as individuals and the society as a whole.

Today larger numbers of young men graduate from different schools and colleges annually. Others in growing numbers drop out of schools and choose to begin on their own. Yet the economy cannot generate sufficient employment for our people. Do the demand and supply chains offer ample employment opportunities and facilities or good environment for the self employed? With traditional education and lack of self advancement among adult employees within the formal employment circles experience their skills fast becoming obsolete even before they approach retirement.

On the other hand, without creation of employment many young graduates retire even before they get dignified jobs. And as a result families are bewildered. They don't know what to do with their adult children. The expectations they had that for instance the hope that as they age the children would support them has vanished through thin air. Today it is the aging parents who find themselves forced to support their adult youth—timelessly.

There's a rising dependence ratio at the time when the income earners experience shrinking incomes among individual households, organizations and the government coffers. The business sector especially the middle class is dwindling and shrinking. The life of most start ups never goes beyond infancy. Many people witness their businesses subside right before their eyes. All these people need answers as they seek new beginnings. Likelihood for millions of people to get quality education or jobs is so slim and as a result many have lost hope. Such people need confidence to start all over again for otherwise they will surrender to hopelessness and depravity thereof. The society needs a new moral fabric. We need to open eyes to the truth that wealth began with mere ideas. Such a population could do with the knowledge of how to turn the ideas into actionable plans that can turn around the tables—with or without financial capital. Is it possible? We shall see to that through the proceeding chapters but suffice here to say that: "If a man can build a better mousetrap," aptly Said Ralph Waldo Emerson, "If a man can build a better mousetrap, the world will beat a path to his door."

Truly the situation at hand calls for open-mindedness if we have to be able to analyze where we, as individuals, and the society as a whole went wrong. And this is not all. They have got to know how to remedy the situation. In a situation where hopes are shattered, our people badly need courage—and therefore our encouragement. Is encouragement necessary? Yes sir! Very much? Very much so!

Discouragement breeds various negative effects such as the danger of prolonging the economic crisis—and helplessness. As a generation, we have endured the economic crisis from which psychological and social crises are very imminent and their effects far reaching.

All these circumstances demand immediate and viable explanations. The people need answers. The answers must be transformational, genuine and relevant to our society. They must therefore be from within. Why? Yes you ask why? Is it important that answers must come from within?

Here is your answer.

The economic crisis leaves us with nowhere to turn to. We can no longer go overseas to the West or East to have our problems solved. We must turn but to ourselves. The West and the East have problems of their own to bear. We cannot keep pointing fingers.

We are to blame for the mess we find ourselves in. If there's anything we need as society today, if we should reverse the situation, we need a set of books and training programs that stimulate the mind and create environment and processes that address these problems. We need a shift in our people's mindset and priorities.

If we can create such programs and back them up with incentives, we would be certain that we have provided lasting solutions to problems we face as individual persons, households, schools or academic institutions, corporations and society as a whole.

Though we all demand these blessings we naturally face huddles when pursuing recovery and prosperity. Why? Hard work and superior character—two among top things which attract prosperity—are unnatural. On the other hand, negative practices such as anarchy and partying hand in hand with vices such as envy, jealousy, hatred and laziness, greed, pride, dishonesty, lust and quick fix instead of order, hard work and innovation are unfortunately natural—like weeds. These negatives tend to stifle any hope of lasting prosperity. To transform your life and be able to attain meaningful life, you have got to keep these negative inclinations constantly under your control. Hard work, positive mindset, persistence and superior character must be sown, watered and accorded constant attention. That is how we constantly kept my mother's farm clean and neat long ago when I was a teenager back in the village of Kifuye Katera in Kyerwa Karagwe.

ROLE OF LEADERSHIP: LESSONS FROM MY MOTHER

For such a dramatic change to take shape, you need a certain kind of leadership. Such leadership is the one that recognizes that we need change. It must be a kind of leadership that is willing to scan the society and the situation on the ground ready to accept the weaknesses therein. When I was writing this chapter, I tracked down some of our leaders in the process of analyzing the weaknesses in our society. In this analysis I realized that our leaders don't tell us the truth.

They do so either to appease their superiors—local or foreign—or the voters who unfortunately prefer such cheap lies out of their ignorance. This isn't gainful to anyone for in the long run it works against the leaders and system they genuinely endeavored to preserve. The ideal leadership must be intrapersonal as well as interpersonal. Is this that important? But how do I know all this? When I was young back in the village we faced a similar situation. We would have grounded in chaos if it wasn't for my mother's leadership.

Mother loved us but she never made it her end. Her love for us made her to seek to provide more for us. She set high standards. She planned a great future. That's why somehow she had to have an iron hand. She knew there was time for love for her children but love cannot persist if there was no livelihood. For life to be sustainable, for her expectations from life and us to be real, we had to work and work so hard. That's why she stubbornly woke us up early in the morning every single other working day. Did I say morning? No sir! It was still dark.

Forget the twenty four hour clock. It was still night in the traditional twelve hour clock. In the latter system, there was a day and night. So no matter whether the weather was unfriendly, we still had to get to work. And what a work! We had to get rid of weeds from our plantation constantly come rain, come shine. In it we grew coffee, banana, beans and maize. Now see what happened.

Because mummy knew the secret that hard work and persistence and superior character were unnatural, and that they were the factors attracting prosperity, she forced us to wake up every day we were on leave including holidays and weekends. This becomes more dramatic when you draw the mind picture of my mother's peers next door. These were our neighbors and of course my father's other wives who pulled the bed sheets covering their heads and closing their eyes in order to cover up the fact that the sun was already up.

The drama gets so amusing when you consider that we had never done any menial work all our lives. Servants served all our needs. But now that dad had retired and returned home to the village back in Ngara and Karagwe, coupled with the fact that my father's huge family had become a thorn into his purse, such that less and less supplies were all we could expect. Mother realized that we had to change the pattern of our thoughts and of our lives if we had to live happily and with dignity. She believed we had had more than enough rest to last the whole of our lives. To be brief she realized it was time to work.

Now the first harvest came out. Mummy had had a hundred measures of grain and of beans and maize as the bananas and coffee flourished extremely well. Soon she was earning more money than the rest of the family and dad put together. Mother even began saving and serving some produces for the rest of dad's huge family.

Was she, I mean the author's mother, different from the others by birth? Well, being my mother, I might have such ideas. But those are mere wishes. So was she really different from the others by birth? No madam! I am sorry to disappoint myself but that's a fact. Was she more educated than most? Yes! Relatively! But that doesn't explain why she really flourished than the others.

The reason why she flourished was that they didn't know the secret of prosperity which she knew and observed to the letter. It is no wonder too often too many people end up in deep poverty despite many years they wasted receiving useless education.

Yet how the number of people plunged into deep poverty is on a sharp rise by the day is so saddening. Superior character does always reward its possessor so deservingly. But such an estate must be prepared, seeds sown and watered, and weeds removed constantly. Doing same things that after all brought us where we are now is pure insanity.

"Insanity," aptly said Albert Einstein, "Insanity is doing the same thing over and over again and expecting different results." naturally I should be enthusiastic to shower praises on my mother, but that's not why I wrote this book. Suffice to say therefore that whereas everybody else didn't know where the shoe pinched, mother did and did the right thing however hard choice that was. That's how she stood tall and alone in the cloud of her peers who remained on the receiving end—and she, on the giving end—beefing up material and lessons for anyone who craved life and prosperity.

LESSONS FROM BRAND MANAGEMENT

Brands are created as a result of the pressing need to address specific needs of certain specific group or consumer interests. With the need to address specific needs, the brand management team finds that deliberate efforts are required and therefore a certain specific investment if the brand has to meet—and where possible exceed—the needs or expectations of its target consumers. Having served as brand manager for Carlsberg, doubtless one of the top brands in the world, I know how even before the birth of a brand, or its campaigns, the brand management team makes sure they have the ground prepared.

Such is why they have the market scanned and the gaps in addressing consumer needs identified, and brand DNA established. Then the product test is done and improvement based on the feedback from the actual consumers is done. Then the roll-out plan is established with prelaunch activities based on adequate information and support required in terms of the human resources, facilities and finances required to be in place.

The team must as well have in place a comprehensive *Who-Does-What*, and this program should indicate clear cut when and how activity plans established are to be discharged before it is signed off as a token. Thus the introduction plan is made and growth plan prepared and followed up almost religiously, like the Roman holidays! If the plans are followed to the letter and there is constant support and amendments are done only when necessary to address unforeseeable factors, or troubleshooting, the brand has no way but to succeed.

You want to know the secret of success? It is purpose, shrewdness, deliberate effort, persistence and constant surveillance—an empowering, delegating and friendly but constant eye. What can I say to summarize the secret of success? Well, through their various works, Ralph Waldo Emerson, Professor William James, Bob Proctor, Wallace D. Wattles, Zig Ziglar, Earl Nightingale and Napoleon Hill (inter alia) have however separately and somehow differently written about this secret so magnificently.

But put plainly, when one has a purpose to achieve in life, and is religiously committed to achieving it, forces of nature seem to conspire to make it happen! What's astonishing is that, though he is the sower and *nourisher* of these forces, but once they take on their true force, they will work to bring stupendous results that will even astonish the *sower*!

Circumstances we face today as individual persons, schools, households, corporations or institutions and nations force each of us to do things differently. Thus you and I do have to do either of the following: do same things but only differently; doing different things the same way we used to do; or to completely do different things in a very different way.

This includes bringing in new people into your workforce; seeking new suppliers; pursuing new markets and new usages and thus innovation. In the whole, these changes suggest that we must reform how we learn, relate and work if we have to turn tables around. It is also of great significance to widen and deepen empowerment of our youth and the staff. To pave the way for transformation, thus once again enhancing the condition *'sine quo non'* for prosperity can best be done by listening to the people, and placing more attention to the traditionally overridden groups: *The youth, the employees, the customers, the* students, your family (your spouse and children), your constituencies and the public you serve.

If you have to succeed in transforming yourself, your family, your organization or institution and community or nation in general you have got to pursue new ideas and encourage individual persons, institutions or corporations that endeavor to seek and put new ideas to use. Well, did I say encourage? That's not good enough. Reward is the word.

Let there be free flow of, and putting, new ideas to use. Most important is to develop self expression among our youth and the society as a whole. An individual person therefore, institution, business organization or human society must seek and identify own character or DNA.

By doing so they will be able not only to identify but also leverage on own strengths, contain weaknesses, ward off threats and maximize opportunities as they present themselves. Indeed "This changed world in which we live," aptly observed Napoleon Hill, "is demanding new ideas, new ways of doing things, new leadership, new inventions, new methods of teaching, new methods of marketing, new books, new literature, new features for radio, new ideas for moving pictures…and (definitely), definiteness of purpose!"

Probably through the above pages you have stumbled upon some new ideas to enable you to do that. Whether you accept these ideas religiously or not doesn't matter at all. Use them in your way to meet and conquer the amounting challenges our society faces today. Commit to memory that you were not born to fail. Have a goal and make sure to follow it. If you do so, you have almost succeeded already.

What this chapter presents, certainly doesn't cover all the required conditions needed as insurance against failure. We know that. That's why the proceeding chapters will further help to prepare you to do just that. In the final analysis the book and programs thereof help to empower you the individual to desire the most and best and how to plan and acquire that what you have always desired. Before we end this opening chapter, let me tell you how.

THE CHAPTER'S LAST WORD

One day, Apostle Peter—the Chief Apostle and first Archbishop of Rome—and his company met a poor disabled person begging at the temple's doorsteps. I love this event. The bible talks so much about it. One thing, though, is not clarified as dramatic as it should be. Yes, Peter and the apostles felt compassion for the beggar.

Yes they wanted to give him money as was his plead. The intensity of their compassion was however heightened because they didn't have hard cash to stash in every needy person's wallet—if they had one anyway.

They could, of course, go round tossing money around for everybody in need to pick—if they wanted to. But they had lived enough with Jesus to comprehend that however invaluable money can be, still the checkbook couldn't solve all human problems.

And when I say they could stash money into this beggar's wallet it is not a joke, mind you? Jesus had of course granted that ability to them. I know they could from the event that I recall so well. And this is how it happened. Because of his criticism of the system, the men from the ancient Jewish Revenue Authority—and remember the authority men can be crooks! So because he criticized them so often, cunningly knowing he didn't carry money for he didn't do any business, they set a trap for him.

When he crossed the city on his way from the temple, the men from the Revenue Authority accompanied by the Italian secret servicemen, they told him: *we know you and your company have not yet paid the head tax.* Peter expected him to defy for he knew he was above human jurisdiction or law therefore. Peter was besides him. Peter looked at him of course asking him to defy.

A passionate and professional fisherman himself, Peter had a sinker with him almost every time. And of course Jesus knew that. Instead of defying the law of the land Jesus asked him to set a hook in the waters of Jordan River across. He picked a very big Jordanian fish but it couldn't bring in enough cash to pay the head tax for the lord and his apostles.

As he brought the only catch to Jesus who was in a situation very close to what you could call *custody,* he thought the order was ridiculous. As he returned with the fish, Peter felt like an idiot. What were they going to do if Jesus had no money? He knew that was his principle. Jesus let him suffer for a moment. At the same time, he gave the men of authority the moment of pride.

Then he asked Peter pointing to the fish that he held awkwardly in his hands saying: *Open the Mouth of the Big Fish and Pay the Head Tax.* And obediently, Peter opened the mouth of the fish. And like a human wallet, a silver coin worth to pay in full the due head tax lay safely there in the mouth of the dancing fish—the animal I suppose was returned into the Jordan—for no one need fish but trouble.

And of course the reader is a grown up man to know I wasn't there at the scene. So if you are going to ask me the source of the narrative that you may quote it, this is my own description of the situation. It isn't real pattern of events. Grown men and women ourselves now, we know enough that charity or philanthropy from without has never, can never, and will never bring change or transform the society when the beneficiaries don't have plan or purpose in life.

Such charity or philanthropy will remain fruitless if the local boys have no reason or the desire to transform their own lives. Do I have to substantiate this assertion?

The experience from decades of the constant inflow of grants and economic assistances from the west to the developing world does more than testify in favor of the foregoing assertion. What the needy people need and deserve therefore, is inspiration and guidance. They need to know that it is possible to be wealthy, healthy, free and happy! They need to know how to get there—on their own. So no matter how desperate you are, like Peter and co. we won't give you a blank check!

We shall, however like Apostle Peter, give you what we have which is more important than cash; and that is to make you stand up on your own feet and be able to reach out to the bounty of life so you can enjoy whatever you have always desired to accomplish for yourself, your family, business and the nation as a whole.

That's why we believe with this training program, the big moment for you personally, your family, business and your nation as a whole has just arrived!

2. A SICK NATION: IDEALISTIC OR REALISTIC

"You ask me why life is so unfair; why is death lurking everywhere? Man it is hard for me to tell you. But I will because I care. You should listen to those words." —Lyrics from misconceptions track two: Goddessa 6[3]

I am certain you have met these strange people someone chose to call doctors. Not doctors of philosophy though? No. I mean medical doctors. You will distinguish them effortlessly. The doctors I talk about prefer to wear gloves. They hang little strange apparatus they call stethoscope over their white overcoats. The Stethoscope is a piece of medical equipment which doctors use to spy on your heart and lungs. They also prefer thermometers, instruments that are seemingly constantly looming quite close to their recliners. I call these people strange for they act strangely. But that's what they call professionalism. Here now is how my problem with medical doctors began—and ended. One day I went to see one. I'd malaria. I knew that. I was positive about it. I could bet my life on it. And I had reason to be sure about it. I've lived in the tropics for decades to know it when I carry in my body the unfriendly parasites someone called plasmodia.

Do I know what this term means? No. I don't know or care. I only know what they do to your body when they get there—welcome or unwelcome. These are the emotional and physical effects they cause to your body. The medics call it symptoms. Now, notice that I just went there to get his permission to buy some medicines he must prescribe and scrawl his signature on a piece of paper before I can be allowed to pay for them. Some other strange and uncalled-for bureaucracy! When he did bid me enter, I told him straight to his face that I'd malaria. That was quite obvious. I was also in a rush. So why meander. I am not a *meanderer* anyway. Besides, I am not a preacher. And I'd a tight schedule on that day. Common sense is indeed not common. with my clear description, while he should have just picked up a ball point pen and scribbled some names of some tough drug nomenclature so that the drug store may allow me to get into my possession the medication prescribed needed.

I was there in front of him and he saw me breathing alright. But you know his reaction? He was stunned! Shocked! I knew later that he had been shocked by my bold announcement. I had announced that I had malaria—outright. Why not? Now despite my announcement, and this time to my shock, he surprisingly consulted his stethoscope. It was uncalled-for—I was dead certain. He placed it on my chest. Then he placed some fancy thing called thermometer in my armpits. I didn't worry about the latter action for I normally clean them. To be sure, mine are as clean as an eggshell. That's why I didn't care supplying my armpits. For me that was wastage of time. My illness was quite obvious. Why then waste my time as well as his? I didn't know some people find fun in wasting time. He was one of the people whose hobby was to waste time. Besides, what he did was not only uncalled-for but also meddling into my private domain anatomically—and it has never tasted well with me.

Well, back to my doctor, I judged that he was one of the greatest time wasters I have had the misfortune of ever meeting. Stethoscope? Heart beat? Thermometers? What for? Indeed doctors were time wasters. I felt all symptoms. I had fever. I felt cold. I was shivering. I didn't have appetite. I felt pain in my joints. That wasn't enough for this strange man. He sent me to a laboratory and a little man in a white overcoat, a man who seemingly had a hobby of watching blood gushing out of its natural traffic, pierced my finger. Unlike his boss, I established his hobby as that of piercing people and watching blood gushing out and experiencing people suffer in deep pain. As blood began oozing, a big smile formed on the little face. He squeezed my finger a few more times before he collected my blood with great enthusiasm as Satan would collect souls of fallen saints. On my part, I fear blood. I loathe it. As for my career or vocation, as you are going to see in this series in these volumes, medicine, army and certainly terrorism are out.

Now forget the whole thing. Here is the message: I've never before believed in the whole thing, thinking it was a tactic to collect cash from patients. On the day I recall that I cursed these men under my teeth and waited nonetheless. Then the results were out. And yes I'd malaria. Strange as it is, in his profession he had to make sure he treated the right disease. That is how they work. They diagnose the patient and after diagnosis, they determine which tests they should do. Then after they compare the results with the symptoms, that's when they are able to determine the disease, and the full proof prescription thereof. That is how medical doctors work. I am not a medic myself but now I know that's how we should all work—thanks to my time-wasting doctor and his cohorts.

A SICK NATION

I bear witness that I've never read anywhere that nations go sick. I have never been tipped that there were nations that were sick—sick nations! It just came to me as a surprise as I am about to expound hereafter. It is also surprising that I am myself a graduate of economics yet despite reading all theories of national as well as international economics, nothing like this ever crossed my path. We are told there're developed as are developing countries. But I fear that that is not enough.

Provided nations are made up of individual persons, if people go sick, nations can be sick too. But here is another level of analysis. If a healthy nation is one with healthy humans, it must as well be a healthy land, air, the waters, and a secure habitat where vegetations and animals thrive. Without this condition, that country is not healthy.

That's why I wrote this book. That's why I developed the symptoms of a sick nation. That's why I would like you to read this book so closely. That's why I want you to determine whether your community or nation is a sick or a healthy society. Then, after that analysis, do I have to tell you what to do? You tell me.

No! Having laid down the diagnosis, analyzed the symptoms and tested the results; and having developed alternative prescription in this very book, I leave the rest into your hands. I leave the rest into your hands because after all, it is your life—not mine—that is under the microscope. It is your life you are messing with, and the lives of your children that are at stake unless you want to run away seeking asylum somewhere overseas. And that is one of the top symptoms I'm underlining hereafter.

Well, did I say it was your life and the lives of your children that were at stake unless you wanted to run away seeking asylum somewhere overseas? Even so, very few arrive on the other side of the shore alive. And it is really one of the reasons why this book was written.

We have been witnesses of the thousand souls that in different occasions have drowned off the Italian shores of Lampedusa and Malta respectively—en route to Europe running away from home.

THE MALADY OF NATIONS: CASE STUDIES OF SOMALIA AND HAITI

But before we launch into real symptoms of a sick nation, let's first consider case studies of both Somalia and Haiti. I do so intending to demonstrate that what you are reading is not mysticism or mere fairy tales. I also bring this analysis to send a message home that we shouldn't relax today and now when we think we are doing better.

Times change, don't they? How do we cope with the pace of change? The rapidity with which social economic and technological changes are ensuing is so astonishing!

What we used to count as valuable resources, no longer count the same way anymore. The facts we had over different subjects, no longer amount to sufficient knowledge—or even the subject itself no longer any weighty. It is even almost distressing to realize all we worked hard to learn and earn considering them as invaluable resources, become obsolete over a short period of time.

And here is another sad lesson I have stumbled upon. Unless we transformed our perception or mindset, to allow ourselves to review our priorities in order to keep abreast with the pace of change through education in the broader sense, we are doomed to find ourselves in the position we find Haiti or Somalia today.

Yet I know there are those of my readers who are hard core indifferent about anything excepting of life of course. Such people will say: what for? Why bother? So what? For them here is my message: As long as sick people die, sick nations die too. So their confidence and clinging to life as lifeless as it is, is groundless.

At the end of the chapter, we are going to discuss the fact that if we don't work hard to restore the situation, the sick will eventually *pass out!*

Truly, with the prevalence and escalation of social economic crises, and the rapidity of pace of change, and regularity and ubiquity of the symptoms we are going to discuss shortly, we realize that indeed even the wealthy nations of the North-West aren't any safer anymore. And this is not something I am attempting to craft.

Addressing his fellow Americans recently, Dr. Ben Carson warned America that she is not herself the first pinnacle nation. We know that before America, there were such pinnacle nations such as Greece, Rome, the Ottomans, or simply Turkey, Spain, the Great Britain etc.

But where are they now? We also know Germany, USSR and Japan were heading there save for notoriety of Hitler, red-tape and economic crisis respectively. Each one of these nation states saw themselves backsliding to mediocrity, giving way to another pinnacle nation, unprepared and therefore bewildered. We know Greece is now a nation state that only a nation on the papers, a nation that can be said to be in ICU!

I am writing this analysis to forewarn any person or nation that assumes that he or she is above the failures we talk about based on the present economic performance, or cohesion in the society etc. The maladies of nations are stronger than those of the individual humans. They know no limit.

SOMALIA: THE PATHWAY TO STATE FAILURE

Everybody knows that Somalia is the typical failed state—defined as a state which has failed to provide political, social and economic goods to the citizenry—which it is required to do. According to Ahmad Rashid Jamal,[4]"...the Somali state is recognized as having failed in 1991."

This is somewhat baffling, since Somalia is one of the most homogenous countries in Africa in terms of ethnicity (85 percent Somali), religion (99 percent Sunni Muslim), and language (85 percent Somali). The primary divisions in Somalia are along clan and sub clan lines.

The main clan families in Somalia are Darod, Dir, Issaq, Hawiye, and Digil-Mirifle. Within these major clans are numerous sub clans. It is along these clan and sub clan identities that sub national tension or hostility occurs in Somalia (Clarke and Godsende 2003: 132).

"Somalia gained independence in June, 1960 when British and Italian colonies were combined to form the Somali Republic". The problem was this nation state was not one. It had to be united first after independence. The country had brief period of democratic governance. A national constitution was adopted by referendum in 1961 and a National Assembly created to represent the various clans...the National Assembly elected Abdirashid Ali Shermarke as the president of the country...

By October of the same year, president Shermarke was assassinated by one of his body guards and Major General Mohammed Siad Barre took control of the apparatus of government in a military coup (Zartman 2005: 77). After the coup, General Barre took all executive and legislative powers in the Supreme Revolutionary Council, which was chaired by him. General Barre then stopped the constitution. Barre nationalized access to land, water, banks, and other productive assets. Much of the nationalized assets were redistributed to General Barre's own clan and supporters. This, coupled with the poor economic policies implemented by General Barre, hurt the Somalia economy so significantly that, by early 1990, the country was on the edge of collapse. Barre was overthrown by rival clans in 1991 and the central government subsequently collapsed.

Numerous factions tried to take control of the government but failed and what enhanced was a civil war. After this, the international community has attempted numerous interventions, including one leading by the United States in 1993... Barre's violent regime accommodated to fuel mistrust among clans in Somalia. Finally, many clan groups decided that they could not trust central government but had to depend only on their own clan for security and economic and social development.

Consequently, numerous clan-based warlords emerged to fight for control of the apparatus of government. Civil war soon enhanced, but none of the warlords was capable to take full control of the territory. The civil war in 1991 and 1992 ruined the country's economic competence, killed about 250,000 people, brought about a shocking famine, and shaped a serious refugee problem. In the case of Somalia, the terms are used to refer to an essential state failure, it exists on a map but the physical reality of security, sovereignty and a centralized government does not exist." With reference to the above account, I have no doubt whatsoever that most of the readers have the same opinion that Somalia is a failed state. Yet only very few recognize that the above situation doesn't only end up in toppling one leader replacing him with another. For them, the concern begins and ends with the failed state context. They forget that in the end the whole situation works to stifle the spirit of fight left in a person one by one and in the end the whole nation gives way, escalating into a *Sick Nation* in as far as the mental health or their mindset of the masses is concerned. You realize there is a circle in which the failure of the government institutions was caused by both historical and internal situation in the Somali society—beginning with the ethos of the Somalis at the family level aside from the fact that there was no Somalia per se but two nations that were immediately at their independence, forced into a single state that was prone to failure.

And Haiti provides us with yet another best analogy of the net result we describe in the foregoing statements. Indeed it seems to me that there is no better country that illustrates the *sick-nation-situation* better than Haiti. That's why I found it to be important to talk about the Haitian problem albeit in summary.

WHY IS HAITI POOR

"The story of Haiti is heavy and depressing;" thus Bob Corbett began his article Why Is Haiti So Poor. "Haiti," continued Bob Corbett, "once called The Jewel of the Antilles, was the richest colony in the entire world. Economists estimate that in the 1750s, Haiti provided as much as 50% of the Gross National Product of France. The French imported sugar, coffee, cocoa, tobacco, cotton, the dye indigo and other exotic products. In France they were refined, packaged and sold all over Europe. Incredible fortunes were made from this tiny colony on the island of Hispaniola.

"How could Haiti have once been the source of such wealth and today be the poorest country in the Western Hemisphere? How could this land that was once so productive today be semi-barren? How did "The Jewel of the Antilles" become the Caribbean's hell-hole?

WHAT IS THE SOURCE OF THE PROBLEM?

Is it important to trace and analyze the true source of the demise the countries like Somalia or Haiti are facing? It is more than important. With knowledge of what was the source of problem, we can be able to solve the problem by marshalling our resources or attention toward the right area. So what is the source of the Somali or Haitian demise? "The ultimate causes of Haiti's misery;" thus responds Bob Corbett, "The ultimate causes of Haiti's misery are human. They are rooted in greed and power. Both the international community and Haiti's rulers have continuously assured the destruction of Haiti's colonial wealth and the creation and continuance of her misery."[5] Though this book is not mainly about historical causes or sources of the problems nations face but here are, briefly, what Bob Corbett summed up as causes of the poverty of the country that was once called The Jewel of the Antilles. Among what he identified as Root causes of Haitian misery are the international community's role and the role of Haiti's rulers.

These include: French colonial contribution(assimilation as a policy and its net result of disintegrating the unity of the Haitian society), the international boycott of the new nation of 1804, the French debt of 1838,the United States occupation of 1915-1934 and post World War II United States domination. Others include: slave-like labor systems in the early republic, the elite's protection of its wealth, Haitian corruption and human rights violations as a tool of oppression.

Others which the author called immediate causes of Haitian misery include: language as an oppressor, ignorance and illiteracy, the system of education (or miseducation) , soil erosion, export crops vs. local food crops, the lack of a social infrastructure: inadequate roads, water systems, sewerage, medical services, schools, unemployment and underemployment, underdevelopment in an age of international economic competition and the Haitian self-image. Now let us forget the causes. We know that Haitian problem is so acute. We know that the Haitians cannot sustain themselves as individuals or households. We know that Haiti is a nation whose wealth benefits only a few elites and their families.

We know that Haiti is country where people are on the run, running away from the state machinery. And thus because of oppressive nature of the state machinery, Haitians run from social as well as economic goods and therefore away from infrastructure and fertile valleys and low lands. We know that Haitians spirit to fight back has given way. We know that the Haitians have lost hope and a sense of dignity. In the end we come to a realization that there is a very fine line between causes for, and symptoms of the poor country.

But in the end, a poor nation cannot run itself and therefore runs the risk of sliding back into domination and neocolonialism. It runs the risk of sliding back into mystifying forms of contemporary slavery for the nation in its entirety on one hand, and heartrending pitiful miseries to its people on the other. I am writing this introduction to sensitize the people against indifference to poverty and the state of a Failed State to their government. It is still possible to recreate and rebuild a strong Haitian state but it will take long before the real Haitian problem is solved. And this is true because Haitian problem isn't only about a failed state. In the end, Haiti is a sick nation!

3. DIAGNOSIS OF A SICK NATION: SYMPTOMS OF A SICK NATION

"What you are stands over you the while and thunders, that I cannot see what you say to the contrary."—Ralph Waldo Emerson

We ended the previous chapter by asking whether, and thereby introducing the remedy to the maladies of a sick nation. We cannot however heal a nation without first establishing which sickness it is suffering from—thanks to my time wasting medical doctor. You probably now realize why I made that talk so tall! Here now are the symptoms of a sick nation. To begin with, let's bring the Haitian place to the microscope. With this analogy, you will identify a sick nation by a government that has persistently failed to meet its responsibilities, to provide necessary conditions for security and growth—that a sovereign government should.

You will identify a sick nation by a government that has persistently failed, and yet the people are indifferent about it. And what so astonishes me, is that the problem of this country really is not solely economic or lack of resources: not even lack of physical infrastructure per se. It is more about the people themselves—the mindset. Take Haiti for instance. The same country could produce and export various products to France only a few decades back, then it is not the question of infrastructure. Concerning natural resources, according to the *Transcript of Haiti the Failed State*,[6] Haiti shares the island of Hispaniola with the Dominican Republic. Yet Haiti is soooo poor whereas the Dominican Republic is prosperous such that there is a huge wave of illegal immigration of Haitians seeking work in the Dominican Republic. The Dominican Republic gains cheap labor in areas such as cutting of sugar canes and mixing concrete, but Haiti loses its manpower and consumers or market for its locally produced products.[7]

A sick nation is a country home to crippled social and economic infrastructure therefore. If the people cannot hold their government responsible—for whatever reasons—you shouldn't expect anything less, should you? What I have come to realize, finally, is that there is a very fine line between causes for, and symptoms of a sick nation. In other words, there is a very fine line between a failed state and a sick nation. I believe the theme of a sick nation is bigger than that of a failed state. A failed state can enhance a sick nation situation, yes. Yet, what intrigues me is that not all sick nations are failed states. To be brief, a notion of a sick nation is about the people, whereas the failed state is about the government malfunction. Thus a sick nation and failed state notions are closely related but not one and same thing.

Notice also that a sick nation will eventually lead to a failed state while a failed state doesn't necessarily mean that that country is a sick nation. With recent economic downturn we experienced even most developed nations such as the Greece and Portugal almost succumb to near failed state situations. Kenya and Zimbabwe offer another example. Whereas these countries aren't necessarily sick nations, but they experienced situations typical to a failed state during the post 1997 election in Kenya, and the economic embargo of the Zim. respectively. Such is the case of the pre genocide-Rwanda. The nation had healthy state machinery but was already sick long before the crush of the presidential plane. The crush was only an immediate effect that was apt to happen anyway—one way or the other. The information we have on what was going on in that society, and works of the news media in Rwanda, prove our assessment to be affirmative. What is tantalizing is that, the two situations, have their balance hanging on the edge of a knife. South Africa is another country that offers another good example of the balance between a failed state and a sick nation situation. Whereas the apartheid South Africa had strong government machinery, she was a sick nation deep in its national fiber. The two latter countries prove the role of people in getting the nation sick and also in healing the nation—tackling the problem by the roots.

Is belonging to a sick nation a simple matter that we should tolerate it? Let us see. We have indicated that in this country, a country which is a sick nation, its government has failed to provide necessary services that a sovereign state should. That is why in that country livelihood and sanitation are pitiably far below bearable standards. And the problem, we indicated, is not solely economic or lack of natural or human resources. It is more about the people themselves—the mindset. This is the break from the failed state situation.

Here is a heartrending account of how belonging to a sick nation is a tragedy. Whereas the two countries stretch out side by side, and therefore safe to assume the two countries have equal or homogenous soils and other natural resources, yet Haiti cannot provide for its people and thus they flee the country crossing the border to the Dominican Republic. Whereas Haiti loses it's much needed manpower Dominican Republic gains cheap labor and market for its cheap products. Besides, the Dominican Republic gains cheap labor in areas such as cutting of sugar canes and mixing concrete, as Haiti loses its manpower and market for its locally produced products having taken refuge from the maladies back home. Indeed there is nothing romantic about a sick nation.

Here is a story we adapted from *Transcript of Haiti the Failed State* by Elsa Chase et al. It is an account of the life of one woman only identified as Selemene.

"Selemene lives in Ouanaminthe, Haiti, a border town in the north, separated from Dajabón, Dominican Republic by the Massacre River. She lives with her three young sons. Her husband went to the Dominican Republic to work in construction and send money back to Haiti to support his family. It is a great sacrifice to live apart, but it is the only way to support a family. As a single parent, Selemene lives in a small hut with a latrine for sanitation.

Her children go to school but are often sick with diseases from mosquitoes or bacteria from the latrine. She cooks on charcoal (and that's not the most heartrending point. The point is, she cooks on charcoal only) when there is money to buy food! The lack of public sanitation leads to illness and premature deaths from illnesses such as cholera. Her household farm cannot produce anything since it is no longer fertile due to soil erosion and deforestation for firewood. Because they cannot grow anything on it, they have to buy everything even when they cannot earn any monies. In the market place, fruits are in an open air market, on the ground, where they are easily infected by fecal material from animals and people. The market place is unhygienic and people relieve themselves anywhere as the animals relieve themselves of their droppings wherever they are. The little canals around have human waste. The flies carry bacteria from latrines (scattering on) to food..."[8]

You realize that such a country is not only a failed state but indeed it is a sick nation, don't you?

Here are more symptoms in summary:

This country is home to an education system that is crippled. With reference to the analysis of Haiti, the handicap in education escalates until when half the population cannot read or write—in the 21st century! Recent indices indicated that only 52.9% of Haitians are literate. Education is not free; public schools only are 20% of total schools. Education is expensive; most educated children go to private schools. Only the wealthy can afford education. Many schools lack basic utilities. There are no enough books, textbooks, teachers, classroom space, and learning materials.

In this country, generally speaking, education system is dependent on foreign structure and curricula and teaching material etc. Scholars and learned people in this country are running off into politics—if they can't make it to the overseas. There are ubiquitous educated slaves and illiterate graduates in this country: people who don't know who they are and aren't really educated despite their many years of being instructed. In Haiti or instance 40.6 percent of people over 15 are unemployed. Most of the country's educated and professionals have fled the country in search of opportunities abroad and they never return.[9]

In that society people seldom read or write books. Indeed there is very minimum self advancement and low reading and writing culture with too much dependence on foreign authors for its reading and teaching material etc. In this country, asking university students to buy or read any kind of book would be seen as punitive. Students in this country, not surprisingly, would rather be anywhere else but in class. And that's not all.

Writing a book—particularly choosing writing as a vocation—is scandalous such that it requires the mind that sits perilously on the edge of insanity to engage yourself in books—reading, writing or selling. (Mwalimu Nyerere, gravely, once said that writing, publishing and reading the *Arusha Declaration* i.e. a book he had written which endeavored to build ideals and model Tanzanian society—speaking in Kiswahili said—required *Roho Ya Mwenda Wazimu*; literally meaning *The Heart of a madman*.

He sadly didn't know that writing and reading not only the Arusha declaration, but any other worthwhile book would be considered as something that scandalously sits very close to insanity only a few decades later!)

Here is a piece of writing I read very recently and I must admit I don't like one bit. I have to bring it here, nonetheless. Writing under the title *Someone Save Myampala's Manuscripts from Rot*, this author's compatriot, Emanuel Ntabaye, wrote thus: *Sometime in the early 1960s, a lecturer at the University of Nairobi, Mr. Taban Lo Liyong described East Africa as a literary desert owing to the paucity of literary works it had produced. At this time…East Africa stood out as barren prompting Liyong to remark that the region was:* "A literary wasteland, a dry, desolate, barren stretch of wilderness where literature simply refused to sprout." Mr. Ntabaye added that: "Unfortunately, it seems the rains fertilized the literary seeds in Kenya and Uganda more than they did in Tanzania…in spotting and nurturing budding writers."

Is really reading and writing such an important set of twin qualities for a nation's health? Let us examine the records—records based on conclusions from distinguished personalities. From deep observation, Joseph Stalin said: *Writers are the engineers of the human souls*. Thomas Carlyle—from in-death scrutiny—said: *Literature is the thought of the thinking men*. John Wolfgang von Goethe—from wide research—concluded that: *The decline of literature indicates the decline of the nation!* Need I say more?

You recognize we are still engaged in the analysis of the symptoms of the sick nation. In a sick nation, tribalism and sectarian sentiments, and therefore frictions, are rampant; tribal, racial or religious fanaticism isn't only tolerated but encouraged for personal or group interests. In this country, a country home to a sick nation, there is a large gap between the privileged minority, and the deprived majority. Politically, fewer people from the same club contest and win elections as majority turn out to be politically lifeless and as a result only a few turn out for elections whether to elect or get elected. Very few people know or care how the government is run and the leadership is happy and does nothing about it.

In this country nepotism is deep-rooted to the extent that even national leadership or the government and all the spicy jobs are in—or left to—the hands of the few members of the same family or small group of elite families as if it were a monarchy. I suppose that many who will try to analyze this statement, will typically point fingers to Pyongyang or Damascus, I presume, they may be wrong nonetheless. Indeed look around you. And then the issue of major concern is this: if they are voted into power back to back, does it mean that the whole country doesn't have alternative minds?

And if so, why? If they persistently manipulate the voting through bribes or rigging, why is possible? Why are people so tame when in frustration everything is weeping for rescuing? In the case of Haiti, one percent of the population owns an estimated 50 percent of the country's wealth. Only around a third of the population has access to sanitation and access to clean water. 70 percent of the people are unemployed—and certainly a larger population is unemployable—among which population is in the public and private sectors payrolls. Coup d'états are rampant ousting the popularly elected leaders. The country is generally poor with a corrupt government.

In this country there is uncalled-for unchecked mystifying form of atypical consumerism. People don't care about saving or investing. And of course you cannot blame them. They make very little—if any monies.

But what surprises me is that in that country, there is soaring desire to buy anything foreign and therefore high rate of importation of goods and services partly because they don't produce anything at home.

In that country, you will nonetheless be amazed how there is soaring rate of importation of *Mitumba:* the secondhand cloths, hand-me-down cars, hand-me-down cast-off aircrafts, recycled machines, used undergarments, cast-off books, out-of-date syringes, watered-down expatriates and tryout medication etc. The youth in that country are what we could describe as crippled. Not physically though?

They are persons who are physically strong but mentally and spiritually imponderably weak. There is low patriotism; they are fans of foreign football clubs; there is great airtime and love for foreign music and culture. The people and especially youth in this country have towering appetite for music, modeling, art and all sports.

Quick fix or middle-man-ship is the love of the nation. Industry, agriculture or farming, sciences and technology or even professions are astonishingly disgraced.

Surprisingly, music, art and modeling and beauty contests attract bigger financing and airtime from the leadership, the business sector and mass media and therefore creating typical role models and short-lived millionaires. In this country professionals and graduates are brainwashed by the outside and disillusioned by the inside and thus emigration into foreign countries legally or especially illegally and denouncing their real citizenship is a way of life.

Is the foregoing assertion only a myth? Well, the author also hopes it were so. But sadly it is not. Sorry to disappoint you! Can we prove it? Let's see. If you audit the number of passports in the hands of its citizens—not people—in that country, the number of passports in the hands of its citizens is far less than the actual number issued—with exception to the rule of course. And this is true, excepting of the Swedish scenario of course. The Swedish passports are sold and bought on the black-markets because of their high demand from illegal immigrants and credibility they afford the holder over the borders and entry points into the foreign countries such as airports as compared to blacklisted nations. Why the number of passports issued in the sick nation is less than the actual number held in hands of its citizens? That's the question. That's the concern.

These passports are burnt down first thing once one finally sets foot on the foreign soil. Having done so, one shamelessly claims he (—well, he or she—but let me say this right from the beginning that the two, he or she, mean nothing. Human is human. He or she will be used together or interchangeably. They stand for the third person singular man or woman and that's all. Male or female, as Michael Jackson said: it doesn't matter) is an asylum seeker running from war-torn country such as Somalia; or fleeing genocide or sectarian cleansing from somewhere else. In this country self pity is rising by the day much as the loyalty to the self and country is falling by the same magnitude. Indeed a great number of people in that country wish that they had better been born overseas as swines, mice or dogs than live as humans back home. This is a people that have lost personal dignity or even the meaning of life itself.

There is as a result rampant suicide in this country besides drug addiction and rampant alcoholism. People have lost hope on life. The levels of unhappiness have soared and the inflicted find no reason to live any more. Call it anything, loyalty or religious fundamentalism, which is only nomenclature, in this country people seem to be great followers of the religious leader and religions that preach them to take sanctuary from life than to love and live it. The truth be told: People in this country, take away their lives because they find no meaning in it rather than the romanticism for the afterlife. On the other hand, excessive *consumerism* and unprecedented accumulation of toys especially among the marginalized communities in the west is a corresponding symptom of a sick society. Not every gold glistering obese men and women in these communities represent happiness or affluence. Indeed there are fatty and stuffy children starving in some sick parts of America. There is too much bragging and of flying your own kite in this country whereas in fact most affluent and happy individuals rarely show off.

Remember we are still engaged in the analysis of the sick nation. The question is this: Is yours a healthy society or sick nation? Just read on.

If there's excessive mindless rural-urban migration, in a country, that country is a sick nation.

We must substantiate this point.

Though especially there is even a great shift of the economic framework from manual to automation, and therefore less and less people or hands on the farm and more in factories and industry; and so excessive migration to the cities, if the above condition is not fulfilled and there is more hand hoes in the land than tractors and still there is rural urban migration, that country is a sick nation.

Did we talk about democracy? In that nation democracy is sham. The nation is not necessarily a dictatorship but democracy is just on the papers. There's no civic education or attempt to encourage the masses to pursue their civic and human rights—they don't vote or getting themselves voted for.

A country is also a sick nation when either the people or the government is indifferent or doesn't hold the other party accountable or responsible. If that happens such that whatever one does goes, that country is a sick nation.

The people in that country don't hold the administration or government responsible in executing its duties.

The government in this country works to hinder its people from progressing; it hinders the masses from enjoying their human and civil or civic rights. The government doesn't seem to help its masses in pursuing their rights to life, wealth, liberty and happiness.

Remember? We are still engaged in the analysis of the symptoms of the sick nation. If there is high rate of black-market or informal economy, that nation is sick. There is staggering tax evasion and avoidance—and money paid under the table.

There is staggering siphoning of money outside the country into Swiss banks or offshore accounts in the no man's lands. There is autocracy; and the administrative institutions are inadequate.

This country is dependent on foreign aid. Surprisingly, though this country is dependent on foreign aid there is a chain of events and cohorts engaging in the embezzlements of public funds. National, regional and municipal leaders abuse aid money and channel it into their private properties or home areas.

There is high unemployment side by side with discriminatory procurement processes whether of human or material resources. There is staggering corruption in that country. Despite ubiquitous cases and proof of corruption, no sentencing is forthcoming. Why? There is no will or machinery to do so—and there is fear of stamping on the feet of the big boys.

Because of the popular "10 percent clause" and almost legalizing of stashing public funds in offshore tax free private bank accounts when they cut deals or on signing contracts locally or internationally, there are ubiquitous counterfeit goods and poor infrastructures in this country. What I mean is that the shelf life of roads, machinery, etc is very low in this country. Electricity is a luxury and flowing water a vocabulary in this country. Large population of people still use water contaminated by feces.

Technology in this country is not only low, but indeed it is still very raw, and the use of internet and ICT is very low. In this country therefore the society is far much behind time—and the government is happy to domesticate its citizenry.

In this country there is a very low ratio of social services to population such as the ratio of physicians, hospital beds etc. per 1,000 people.

Abuse of human rights is the order of the day: execution without trial, no free speech, police brutality, overcrowded prisons, poverty, violence, corruption, etc.

The budget on education and health is very low; and as a result we have schools without education, and hospitals without medication. The banks in this country are banks without funds and there is astonishing minimum access to funds by the masses.

The national budget focuses on the administrative tasks with meager funds allocated on development projects.

Prostitution, armed robbery, drugs, embezzlement of public funds, kidnapping, bribes and money changing hands under the table are other forms of industry. In this country, yes, there are courts of law. But they are courts without laws; and laws without justice.

In such a society, there are long court procedures and the poor people are victims and scapegoats. There is also indifference to justice as the convicts spend decades behind bars before justice is discharged.

Probably you recognize the magnitude of the problem: justice delayed is justice denied. BBC reported how in Haiti, criminality: kidnapping, burglary, sabotage, bank raiding, abductions, drugs, and blackmail have become an industry; and after spending very short time behind bars, the convicts are back in the streets engaged in the same criminal activities once again.

In that country there is a saddening collapse of family institution. And the foregoing is one of the major symptoms of a sick nation. In that society there is low or complete lack of chastity; and talking about fidelity in such a society is a joke.

It is from the same reasons that there are excessive cases of second and third secret matrimonies—the secret satellite families thereof. Whether from ignorance or hopelessness, people have thrown all cautions to the four winds and as a result promiscuity and STDs are very high in this country.

Domination of one gender by another is very high and gender and sexually based violence is lofty and neither the people nor the government gives a damn about it. They are indifferent.

There is towering cohabitation and amplified levels of single mothers in that society as a result. There is great self-neglect and surrender to HIV and AIDS pandemic and deaths of youth and spouses and therefore a rising number of street children.

In such a society, street children and orphanages are rampant and ubiquitous—themselves legalized as industry. In this country they have legalized a rising nation of street children—a nation within a nation—due to gross neglect.

The street child has become a traded product and a mushrooming money making industry.

Following the foregoing statement, is it then no more astounding that there is very low labor to leisure ratio, which is high rate of preference of leisure to labor. Doesn't it then follow that there is too much gossip in this country? In this country there is too much talk and surprisingly talk is industry and people are hired because they can talk.

It is no wonder in this society excessive middle-man-ship, *mission town* and quick fix take the place of industry and innovation. In this country, the extent of quick fix and money mindedness are so high such that people begin valuing money and people with it regardless of how it was made.

There is unwarranted veneration for—and both political and social respect bestowed on—the wealthy people in every other sector without questioning how they made that money.

In this country, it doesn't matter whether someone made millions by stealing, prostitution, witchcraft and selling of human body portions as potion, gambling, swindling, pick pocketing or drug trafficking. It really doesn't matter. What is important, is the feel-good element and the immunity the money gives its possessor.

Did we talk about lack of innovation and rampant quick fix? There are ubiquitous beer bars everywhere in this country. Guest houses have mushroomed as a money maker and liquor and sex are hot traded goods or services—goods or services sold anywhere, anyhow and anytime to anyone in the residential neighborhood.

The casual commercial sex therefore—now regarded as any traded merchandise—is is rampant and sold to anyone: a family man, student, doctor, teacher, judge, politician, cleric, an old man or woman, child or teenager—and it is appreciated. And it doesn't matter for somehow it is taxed?

In short everything is legal and everything is business. People have opted for prostitution, drugs or crime as vocation.

There is little incentive to work hard or earn a dignified livelihood. Many have surrendered, have given up saying come what may. Such a herd says: *I'd better live comfortable today and die tomorrow than live in hardships waiting for the bright tomorrow.*

they have no or have very minimum and inadequate life goals, people in this country have a great love for a drink and of course, ubiquitous bars are everywhere and as such in this country and bars and clubs are a popular rendezvous and reference points (the author has heard a TV and radio commercial advertising hospital and a church location as being adjacent so and so bar). Alongside addiction to drugs, there is a high rate of insanity in this country—as a result.

When in a society there's very low level of punctuality and indifference to hard work, that country is a sick nation. And this symptom should have been at the head. The trend of slothfulness then goes on and on until when sloppiness among people of all age and ranks becomes a culture and as result there are low levels of quality and productivity. It is a people who believe they cannot do anything and that in order to prosper or finance national budgets—as a nation—you must beg and therefore this country accepts certain attached conditions and thus a country with lesser national dignity but more so, lower personal liberties, dignity and self esteem.

Did we talk about self neglect? Low self esteem? People in this country say they had better live well for only a few years and then die than live long while struggling to make the ends meet. We mentioned earlier on that in this society, there is excessive mania for sports and entertainment such as beauty contests and modeling or art while they debase industry, agriculture and professions—and that they praise and sanctify embezzlement of funds as clever and artists as role models—they therefore promote quick fix in this society.

With low productivity, and mania for quick fix and preference for leisure against labor, there is therefore staggering influx of watered down expatriates! There is also and therefore very low rate of creativity and self employment hand in glove with weak and scanty middle class.

And this is no fiction. In a sick country democracy is a joke. Only a few people see why they should vote or contest for leadership. In Haiti the masses even seem to be on the constant run where a community is almost running away, avoiding any association with the government. In short the few elite families will rule—whether you vote for them or not. The rulers are often autocrats, elected or not.

The children and offspring of the ruler tend to step into the shoes or offices of their fathers. This trend is almost a tradition and the republic in no less a sultanate or a monarchy. Don't the same few families also diffuse in all key organizations and institutions in the country—qualified or not?

Indeed, "Power tends to CORRUPT and ABSOLUTE power corrupts ABSOLUTELY!" Lord Acton was right.

That's indeed the danger—the real danger of a system such as ours—a system where few yes innocent men and women have access to the secret of success, and therefore to the right education and character.

The military oppression by the ruling elite is one of the tools to perpetuate domination. The law of the jungle applies in all forms of life.

Corruption is ubiquitous and the gap between the rich and the poor is at an industrial scale. The country is home to ethnic and religious discord and crime is rampant.

Internal strife and revolts, ethnic or religious, are rampant in this country.

Provision of health care and education is not a priority. Democracy is a luxury. Lawlessness and crime are rampant.

The nation is consumed by internal violence. Dialogue in this country is impossible because of intolerance. It follows therefore that whatever contention or misunderstanding, the two parties resort to fistfights or the gun.

We definitely talked about political indifference? There are unstable and short term coalition governments, themselves neither of the people , nor for the people.

This society is generally a dependent economy. Take Haiti for instance. Over 80 percent of people—in the 21st century—are under the poverty line, and 54 percent live in abject poverty.

GDP is very low and normally lower than the GNP—if you know what I mean. There is gross misappropriation of public funds. In Haiti remittances are 20 percent of GDP. Over half of annual budget is from outside sources. The country is donor dependent and therefore there is donor fatigue and the nation experiences extreme poverty.

It follows therefore that when natural hazards or vagaries of weather happen, hazards such as drought, flood or earthquakes, the economy is ravaged, and rarely heals up.

Many times there are many assassinations, and disappearance of people—and no one is held responsible. There is almost complete disarray amongst pillars of the government and the country can be said to be going without a government. There are many IDP's or the Internally Displaced Persons—refugees in their own country—living in tent cities. There are rampant epidemics such as cholera outbreaks. Girls and women along with some groups of people are kidnapped for political, religious, economic or superstitious reasons. Such is the case of albinos. There is serious gender inequality and discrimination such as in areas of inheritance or education. There are also rampant forced marriages and slave wives besides the Taliban style of justice according to The Daily Mail of 10th of November 2014.

ISIS has recently—as a good gesture—released a group of hundreds of elderly men and children of the abducted Yazidi community in the country they now control falling between Syria and Iraq. But they retained the girls and women whom they redistributed among their soldiers as gifts or slave wives.

Boko Haram abducted and retained over two hundred Chibok schools girls and have remarried them among themselves—under what they call their religious law—Mohammedan or not—by force. We recently learned of an Indian woman who was stripped bare, and naked, and paraded through the village on a donkey for trifles but ones considered so grievous in the radical brainwashed mind. Human trafficking, and slave labor or something in its proximity still exists in this country. In this country there is instability, insecurity, chaos and therefore anarchy. There arises a group of terrorists, warlords and gangs of looters who regard robbery, abduction or piracy as an industry.

Life expectancy in this country, following all these reasons, is very low. As such *teenagers* are elders in this country. Life expectancy in such a country is so low and therefore more than two thirds of the population can be said to literally be underage. It follows therefore that in this country seldom you can find adults or aging population.

There is complete disarray in the country or society. Authority, law, and order in the country are in shambles. The financial infrastructures are almost inexistent or are shaky and favor the wealthy money launderers. Physical infrastructure such as roads drainage system city planning and enforcers of the same laws are nonexistent such that when the rains hit, due to poor infrastructure, in words of John Ernest Kitoka, "the shambolic city is under the siege."

Order and discipline are therefore almost a vocabulary in this Godforsaken land. And there's decay of the moral fiber. In this country everything goes. They haven't drawn a line between what is good and what is not. They have no a set of major goals or established vision, mission and values or virtues. These are the same values that ought to pervade the households, organizations and nations as a whole. In a sick nation—a nation with no ideals or values—the people have thrown all cautions to the four winds. The society has no values or virtues and it has not laid down a set of ideals as its guiding philosophy, and so there is anarchy and anything is permissible; and therefore everybody does what is good in his own eyes. Unlimited freedom is no good to anyone. The deprived beggar shouldn't sit around and celebrate his irresponsibility. Like Lord Acton, Wayne Price was right too. "…it is also true that 'powerlessness corrupts!'" The lack of power of the exploited and oppressed leads to mass demoralization, defeatism, emotional dysfunction, and cynicism. Those who are currently on the bottom of society need to win power—on a radically democratic basis." And that's why this book has been written. It has been written to empower the powerless.

In this country people spit, piss, throw material wastes and human droppings on every corner around the streets or highway, and—what's more—it is okay before the on lookers. It is a serious problem because it displays the heaps of rubbish inside that manifests on the outside. Such a society is a sick nation.

There is rampant anarchy in that country and no one cares. And when I say this I am not concocting a fiction story here. Only recently, the Indian civil servant has been fired after taking leave 25 years ago and never returned to work, reported the Express (www.express.co.uk/news/world/550913). How often have we heard of ghost workers who are on the public payroll and no one is held responsible?

There are no virtues in this sick nation such that a manager and his subordinate are free to leave the office at ten in the morning for a nearby hotel room for bed, beer and breakfast in the beginning of the working day! Senior government officials or company executives divide the cake amongst themselves, and it is okay. There is anarchy in this country such that the employee in retaliation—almost instinctively—steals or rather picks up the stationary as the medical practitioner lifts up and sells the monthly medical kit to the nearby private hospital and it is okay.

This trend or anarchy goes on and on until it is almost legal to steal and sell stolen items. The anarchy is so prevalent that almost there are legalized bazaars or supermarkets for stolen goods in the middle of the city where ads on television and radio lead you to these bazaars where everybody can get premium goods at throw away prices—a setting that makes everybody happy. Luckily this is not something that will cost the author so dearly to prove. You, the reader, don't have to get a passport to witness this scenario if you are in Dar es Salam or any major such cities. You only have to go to Gerezani market in Kariakoo. Then the trend, the curve, shifts in its balance.

In this country, the farmer burns down the bush for fresh pasture of his flock, and it is okay; the employees don't work and they demand salary increments and they get it even when it cannot help them for the money is worthless. The foregoing analysis then leaves the human resources department in this country therefore, because there are no values or principles, the most languid and good-for-nothing department where the most cunning idlers are not only safer, but they are highly praised too.

In this lawless country, a wealthy man buys out the public land and fences it for his own use or future prospects, and you nobody cares. You will be certain a country is seriously sick when few racketeers and their benefactors in the government collude with the investors and besiege a national park and mercilessly abduct animals, kill elephants and rhinos chopping off the horns and tusks from the innocent rhinos and elephants, and bag the tusks along the a caravan of breathing lively animals out of the country and they are cleared at the exit points by the government institutions.

When in a country the children are turned into drug addicts and walking cocaine stockpiles and no one cares, that is country is a sick nation. There is breathtaking anarchy in this country: it is lawless such that the official gang up and steal from the public coffers and both the swindlers and the funds leave no trace. It is also surprising that the embezzlers and criminals in this country are never brought before justice.

But there is also another trend if there is pressure on the law officials to convict the murderers and embezzlers of government funds.

They are put behind bars only temporarily not for the good of the public but for the victim's own good until when the atmosphere cools down on the outside, and only the next day, they are back on the streets trading in the same merchandize that threw them in the custody in the first place. Indeed there an incentive to loot and steal in this godforsaken country. And you can't blame them.

There are no laws and no standard or benchmark to follow. And not only that, sir! Such lifters, wealthy male and female gold-diggers whose doctrine is "the dog-eat-dog, crawl your way to the top; anything for a buck, baby" mentality, are praised as futuristic and focused role models.

They are role models for in this country money is praised no matter whether it is dirty or bleeding money.

The trend goes on and on until when the obvious, the worst, happens.

Because of anarchy and incentive to steal money and votes, these clever individuals don't stop in their tracks—since there is no one to stop them. They, then, pass on to buy votes and become politicians not for the good of the people but to defend not only their financial interests but their souls, their lives.

The foregoing is another thing that the author doesn't have to struggle to evidence. The recent *election-related corruption Saga* coming from many countries has helped to put this assertion into perspective.

It is no wonder from henceforth, half or more of government funds then, go unaccounted for, and no one is concerned! It is not surprising when seventy five of businesses goes unlicensed; 80 percent of revenues unaccounted for as big boys enjoy the tax holiday, and thus over fifty percent of potential government revenues through taxes and levies untraceable—and declared lost—as the country's leadership goes out on official begging trips!

Surprisingly, there is no shame among the people and their leaders in that country! And that is an understatement.

It is an understatement because a country that is rich ending up playing the role of a beggar is not a laughing matter!

In the end, this is a nation divided against, and at war with itself. And such as a nation is divided against itself, there can be nothing to make it stand—not even the donor funds.

Again, the recent good gesture from the donors who cancelled a billion worth of debts for many of the highly indebted countries puts the foregoing assertion into perspective.

That's why it doesn't matter anymore whether a country is mineral wealthy or has greater tourist attractions or other natural resources potential.

Its resources are siphoned and channeled outside the country benefiting the foreigners and a handful of local mercenaries or cohorts in the administrative roles; and surprisingly the people vote them back in their positions, or, to be more objective, they let them rig elections each and every time.

And this is an easy thing for them to do for the masses are no longer concerned with what happens counting it as fate and their afflictions as destiny—and still no one cares!

The people are timid and have low self esteem while self confidence lacks so deeply from grass roots to the top that the nation trembles in the sight of other nations. This can be proved by simple analysis. For instance, analyze a country's performance in local and regional tourneys.

How many times have we won manly games against our neighbors? What are the games we win? How do we stand up and get voted for in the elections or offices in the regional blocs?

In this society the fear of the unknown is so rampant such that people cannot talk or discuss the things that really matter to their lives. With this knowledge a local radio in Somali, as its slogan, chose to declare, quoting from Dr. Martin Luther King J.R., that: "Our lives begin to end the day we become silent about things that matter(to our lives)." Al-Shabab didn't like it. They leveled the building to the ground and gunned down the dedicated free speech agents.

DO WE NEED TO ATTEND TO THESE WEAKNESSES?

We have laid down a number of symptoms of the sick nation. If you look closely at your society, you will be able now to establish if yours is a sick nation and so if it needs to see the doctor. Notice also that the major difference between the failed state and a sick nation is that the latter is more about the people than the physical resources or institutions.

Talking about the health of a nation, the country needs to see the doctor when she triumphs only in some dark games such as gambling, dancing competitions, modeling, beauty contests, and the likes while she fails to make a mark in *manly* competitive sports such as athletics in the Olympics, football or boxing—let alone intellectual works such as research, writing, sciences and technology.

It, I think following the foregoing assessment, is fair to say that though everybody has right and duty to follow his calling and ambition, and so whatever he chooses he should rest assured that no one will condemn him or criminalize his actions. But he should also know that there is a certain social value the children or even infants attach to a strong man in athletics or boxing career, than another person with the same gifts who works as a barman, waiter, *Machinga* or one demonstrating his body and the cloth lines in a fashion show. This innocent judgment is what I talk about—an ambition or calling for its full value minus dollars attached to it. Is this analysis necessary? Indeed it is more than necessary especially in the world today where everything is tolerable before law whereupon killing and selling elephants' and rhinoceros horns, drugs, prostitution, gay marriages or transgender operation—behind which there is a profit or business motive much as how there is a business syndicate in sorcery and therefore business in body potion of the humans with albinism can attract more money than men and women who are in farming, industry or professions and other callings.

And these aren't the author's insinuations. Here is an article written in response to the failure we have just laid down—the failure to do better in some lines of professions and sports and instead celebrate the victory in reality shows.

"So the Big Brother Africa is over," he began, "and the Tanzanian "representative", Mr. Richard Bizubenhout, is declared a winner. Well, the amount of dough, $100,000 is not a cheap change....

What prompted me to write this article is what Richard said in a press conference following his victory. Fred Ogot, the Guardian writer, quoted Richard as saying that he has made Tanzanians proud by winning the BBA top prize. Well, maybe he has made other Tanzanians proud, but not me...a product meant for folks ... unable to evaluate values imparted ... through a television tube.

I can only presume the show was another soft pornography transmitted for unaware Tanzanian minds to wholeheartedly consume. And they did....

Folks, television and movie producers will always tell that their work is only capturing life. Well, I got news for you. Movie and television producers want you to see life through their own eyes. In other words, television producers communicate their values through their work. Well, let's just look at the mind behind the Big Brother show, for instance.

According to wikipedia, Big Brother reality television show is a brainchild of Johannes Del Mol. Del Mol, not surprisingly, happened to be a native of one of the most liberal countries in the world, Netherlands. It shouldn't come as a surprise then that sex and alcoholism is the cornerstone of the Big Brother show.

I know, I know, I sound like a grandpa. Nevertheless, I would rather sound like grandpa than being stupid. You know, sometimes wisdom is needed in discerning what is good from what is a bunch of crap. Television, just like any other medium of communication, could be used both positively and negatively. Television could be used either to build or to destroy values. I wonder if average folks understand how imagery could distort our understanding of life and even who we are.

So for any Tanzanian who is soooo proud that Richard became a winner of the BBA show, just be informed of this: you just made Mr. de Mol a few bucks richer, while consuming his personal values and convictions. And I am not very sure if those values align well with conservative, Tanzania values.

There are plenty of Tanzanian folks out there, doing meaningful things that I am definitely proud of. Richard, unfortunately, does not make that list. Then there fol.lod comments as follows: in response Anonymous said: "…that was nasty! Did the show go live in TZ too? …I am certainly not proud of him and he did not represent me as Tanzanian either. Shame goes to those ladies too drinking that much and let loose of their valves. Why do they call this show big brother anyway? Who are they big brother to? He is not my kinda' of big brother…i hope the wife (ex) did not open the door for him… shame! Shame!"

Jaduong Metty said: "…I also wonder who these people are Big Brothers to. But I am sure I have absolutely nothing to admire from the show."

Stephen replied saying: "Metty I respect your views and like you said you did not watch the entire show. The show which went on for three months was, in my view, very very entertaining….."

In response Jaduong Metty said: "…..Entertainment should (not) be an excuse for compromising one's values!"

Anonymous said: "Metty I couldn't agree with you more …."

Timmy said: "Metty, you have spoken like a true African. This big brother thing is nowhere in line with our culture and values as Africans. I am Nigerian and the way Richie conducted himself is being viewed worldwide as an African thing and the misguided young man in response to allegations of sexual misconduct was quoted as saying 'this is Africa'. Well, Richie I agree with you, this is Africa!

And that is precisely why we will not stand for this alien show of shame. Winner indeed, I would only agree if the contest was for the most disgusting, uncultured, unscrupulous and indecent 'wanna-be African' who has the misfortune of being alive in an age where he can display all his shameful attributes globally.

Thumbs up Metty! Down with Richie and his kind! As for those who say he was the favorite, I suggest YOU hang your head and cry over Africa, if we have come to the day when Africans would prefer pigs and he-goats to human beings![10]

Following yet another recent triumph by another Tanzanian Idris Sultan in the 2014 Reality TV Show, Big Brother Africa Hotshots competition staged in South Africa after good showing by Mwisho Mwampamba and co., before Richard's victory, a Tanzanian congratulating the nation rather than Idris himself, for winning for us yet another victory bagging and coming home with some 300,000 dollars from the BBA this countryman wrote a message that read thus:

"Congratulations. But (don't you think) it is time Tanzanians brought home trophies from other competitions—more manly sports!"

Another one responded saying, "We need more David Rudishas, more Kiprotiches, more Usain Bolts, more of Malala Yousafzai, more Lionel Messis, more James Ngugis, more Chinua Achebes, more Shaban Roberts, more Obamas, more Ben Carsons, more Zuckerbergs, more Julius Nyereres, etc!"

This author person says: yes in a nation like ours you cannot have all the people behaving or living in a certain uniform way.

But yes it is true that we need more of one kind of character or vocation than the other.

CHRONIC SELFISHNESS, ENVY AND THE CULTURE OF "UNAMWAGA UGALI NAMWAGA MBOGA"

Chronic selfishness, envy and excess hatred against one another as individual and communities in a society is another symptom of a sick society. How? Why? We already know that humans are social animals—that we are interdependent. That is to say if we have to grow and sustain through the harshness of life and conquer nature, we must at work together. The future of a society that cannot work together is in jeopardy but that of a society in which people are not only ready to help one another but to sabotage one another's efforts is a society that is *articulo mortis*: a society that is at the point or moment of death (or extinction).

If in a nation there is tendency to get in the way of other people's efforts only is a culture that has been put it into perspective by the recent elections slogan 'Ukimwaga Ugali, Namwaga Mboga,' literally meaning because I have lost, I cannot let you win. We see so much of that tendency in the Simba-Yanga football politics. Simba and Yanga are the two most popular football teams in Tanzania. When one loses and another is on its way to win the trophy, the other team chooses to lose a game to any other weak opponent or use any other means possible to get into the way of the potential winner. Azam football club in Dar es Salaam has been a beneficiary in this tag of war.

The point I am trying to make is this: When in the country, there is too much envy, jealousy and distrust, When in that nation *All are not for One and One is not for All,* and when to get or acquire something, you must take it from someone else; a country where generally the motto seems to be *Everybody For Himself and God for us All*; that nation needs to see the doctor—immediately.

Is this spirit—one for all, and all for one (Un pour tous, tous pour un; also inverted to *All for one, and one for all)* —any important to a nation? Let's see. This motto is traditionally associated with the titular heroes of the novel *The Three Musketeers* written by Alexandre Dumas Père, first published in 1844. In the novel, it was the motto of a group of French musketeers named Athos, Porthos, Aramis and d'Artagnan who stayed loyal to each other through thick and thin. On November 30, 2002, in an elaborate but solemn procession, six Republican Guards carried the coffin of Dumas from its original interment site in the Cimetière de Villers-Cotterêts in Aisne to the Panthéon. The coffin was draped in a blue-velvet cloth inscribed with the motto.

EARLIER USE

In a meeting in 1618 between leaders of the Bohemian Catholic and Protestant communities, which resulted in the defenestration of Prague, a representative of the Protestants read a letter affirming that, "As they also absolutely intended to proceed with the execution against us, we came to a unanimous agreement among ourselves that, regardless of any loss of life and limb, honor and property, we would stand firm, with all for one and one for all... nor would we be subservient, but rather we would loyally help and protect each other to the utmost, against all difficulties.[11]

When the gap between the wealthy and poor is so dramatic, and the rich dwellings in the city are like heaven surrounded by very poor while a messy neighborhood dominates the whole country; when the poor masses have lost hope and surrendered to their situation as fate and have resorted to dissociate with the state as is the case of Haiti; when the masses don't even see why they should struggle for a better livelihood or political reforms; when the people have lost appetite to work hard or transform their lives through imagination or the ballot box, one must realize that the situation is thus getting out of hand and that soon it is going to be impossible for such a nation which has reached this state to reverse its situation on its own—or be rescued. It is at point in time that immediately someone must take this country to the doctor. And you recognize that, that someone who should take the country to the doctor—is you, yes you, the immediate reader!

When the country is not environment-friendly, as a tradition, that country is a sick nation and it needs to see the doctor urgently.

When in the country too often, short term gains are praised over long term prosperity, and the people and leaders fail to look beyond the next day, that country is a sick nation and it needs to see the doctor right away.

It is logical to seek medical advice if the foregoing is true because as a result, the national economic base will collapse. And if the economic base collapses, in that country people lose a sense of humanity, which more than anything else is the pulse of the nation.

When in the country the future is not part of its agenda, neither the family nor are the children, or the environment, someone must take this nation to the doctor—even when the leaders or their doctored statistics say otherwise!

Did I say don't relax and imagine everything is ok? Didn't Benny—not I—say to analyze if your society is okay, then *ask questions*? These are further areas of concern or questions you must ask yourself: What attention is the nation exerting on education?

And when I say education I do not mean education-education, if you know what I mean. What are we doing in as far as the preserving ecosystem or the natural environmental balance is concerned?

When animals struggle to adapt to such human activities as excessive lumbering or felling of trees for charcoal fuel and poaching, this isn't a good indicator at all. Mahatma Gandhi said, *"The greatness of a nation and its moral progress can be judged by the way its animals are treated."* *It therefore is safer to say* the greatness of a nation *and* its moral progress can be judged by the way its citizens treat environment.

Now before we move on, let me say that I didn't write this book as some sort of sport for myself, or an entertainment package to the reader. I wrote it because I am so much concerned about the future of a nation that doesn't regenerate itself? On July 4 at 7:22 P.M, Kamaleki Nicolaus Mutalemwa posted on the facebook wall that; "Ekitezaile Kichweeka,"[12] a Kihaya saying meaning that anything that doesn't regenerate itself goes extinct.

And that's not Mutalemwa's speculation or this author's theory. In the Zambezi valley, elephants are now reproducing mono-horned infants or even completely hornless calves as a result of poaching. Just like these Zambezian elephants, if humans and nations don't evolve and adapt to changing environment, they surely will become extinct!

Much as we value the environment, we must as well be able to conclude that if therefore the greatness of a nation and its moral progress can be judged by the way its animals are treated, isn't it logical or prudent therefore to say that a country where personal freedoms—within limits of course—and democracy are infringed and people are coerced is a sick nation?

If a nation creeps far deep into poverty and dependence a century after its independence, doesn't it then follow that it is prudent for someone in such a nation to take it to the doctor?
 Notice however that not one symptom can lead to the conclusion that a person, organization or a nation is sick.

A great good number of individual persons, organizations and nations have one or a couple of these symptoms for one reason or another.

However, nothing can be far from the truth that a nation is no longer safer when most of these symptoms pervade her systems—and especially her people.

When that happens, you must really halt and ponder about what future a nation chooses for itself—if there is any left.

And I say if any because really for such a society there is no future. Such a mediocre society gives way and will soon perish if its illness is not well reported and diagnosed so that the right medication or prevention of such maladies is discharged.

But sadly, *"Health is not valued,"* rightly said Thomas Fuller, *"Health is not valued till sickness comes."*

And if these symptoms are ignored and the causative is not tackled, like how the bandwagon down a steep mountain will naturally gain momentum and crush, so it will be for a nation with many of these symptoms.

Now as we finalize this chapter, I know someone who questions the above assertions still needs some kind of testimony. Is my context realistic?

Is my message urgent? In the theories of *State Failure*, we know that states may cease to exist. Such are cases of Czechoslovakia, Yugoslavia and USSR in our recent history.

But we can talk of Libya, Syria, Iraq, Sudan etc, besides Haiti and Somalia of course. Sick nations may pass on to death if not healed.

We know human communities which have become, or which are becoming extinct until as I write. We also know that human communities have become extinct through history.

Is it speculation or cynicism on the part of this author? Far from that!

Let us, together, examine the records, lest ours becomes a sick society beyond rescue—a society that will soon pass on and become extinct!

XENOPHOBIA, KING ZWELETINI, OF THE ZULU AND THE SICK SOCIETY

We have highlighted the fact that yes, Somalia arrived at its present state following the failure of the state which began with the toppling of the first democratically elected president hand in hand with mismanagement of the economy and the nation in general under general Siad Barre.

We have also indicated that it is possible to recreate and rebuild a strong Haitian state but that it will take long before the real Haitian problem is solved. We have underscored the fact that both the Haitian and Somali problems aren't about a failed state—per se! The truth is that, both countries are sick nations!

It is important therefore that the reader—and the leader of the future—recognize that the Somali and Haiti problems are deep rooted—and so you cannot heal such a malady by patting, stroking or laying a hand on the drying leaves or the weak branches. You cannot heal such a tree by wetting its branches or leaves. A tree whose sickness springs from the roots, has to be healed by the roots.

The collapse of the Somali or Haitian state, began in the decay of "humanity" —call it civilization or compassion—beginning with the birth of the Somali state, a state that was though homogenous by tribe and religion, but heterogeneous by ethos of the two Somali states.

That's why in turn Somalis turned to hard core radicalism and piracy as ways of life. That's what paved way to al Shabab. In a situation like that, the people stop trusting not only their own government but one another. In the end, we come to a realization that the escalation of Somali division and worsening of the mental and then economic and social health was inevitable.

Mental or intellectual collapse also resulted in spiritual decay and total collapse of the human nature among the Somali men and women.

And what I speak of Somali man and woman, I speak of the Haitian man and woman. You notice that in this vicious circle of collapse, mental and spiritual collapse alongside piracy killed the incentive to think and do. The net result is that the people stopped valuing work or to work hard. They ceased becoming responsible not only to the government or to one another, but also to themselves.

When a nation reaches this state, not the physical human resources, rich natural resources—such as the discovery of gold, diamonds, oil and gas, not even hard cash and material wealth will heal this nation—though this cannot create a scapegoat or an alibi for the politicians, or even Jack Warner and his cohorts in the court of justice.

The problem among these societies is already embedded deep in its ethos: its culture or traditions and especially the philosophy on which a society governs itself. The recent homecoming of xenophobia in South Africa evidences the foregoing statement. Once such a malady of the nation is deep deep-seated and ingrained in the society, no quick fix approaches can heal it. Civil wars and xenophobia are like homing pigeons. They always come again unless you heal such a malady by the roots.

In retrospect, it wasn't the Zulu king, King Zweletini, who triggered xenophobia in South Africa. It wasn't his comments didn't trigger it. They just added fuel on a flame that was already alight. The South African problem is deep rooted in the society's beliefs, ethos and values. No! I, for one, cannot stoop so low as to allow myself to put blame on the poor king, or the recent generation of South Africans!

The South African problem, the malady of South Africa as a nation springs from its history. It is its history that we saw the rise of Shaka Zulu. It was in the rise of Shaka Zulu that the Mfetsane wars erupted and a large section of the Zulu or South African society migrated and among them settled in Tanzania forming the Ngoni tribe we recognize as one of our communities today.

But the recent scar in the history of South Africa stems from the day when Jan van Riebeck set his boots on the Cape of Good Hope. It was that very moment —the moment itself and no man—that robbed South Africa with a good hope implanting xenophobia in the mind of the South African as we see today.

It is in South African history, beginning with Jan van Riebeck setting his foot on the South African soil that the British set their boots on the continent. It was the British setting of their boots in South African that set the conflict and eventual war and the defeat of the Boers was perfected which then set in motion the trekking further north thereby robbing the black South African of his land and his heart. With this loss, the loss of the land and the way of life of the South African., xenophobia began to take deep roots.

The whole thing was climaxed by the loss of mind. But it began with the foregoing inconceivable loss of the land and his way of life, and as a result the South African lost his mind. Is the foregoing allegation a mere insinuation on the part of this author? Oh, no! No any one of my countrymen was massacred in the recent wave of xenophobia and the only 23 Tanzanians living in South Africa were safely lifted into the country according to our foreign minister Membe.

So having no grudges to nourish, malice to nurture or scores to settle, I can then go on to lay down how the whole thing took roots. The question of the loss of mind on the part of the South African we talk about is made foolproof by the indiscriminate massacre of the fellow black man who liberated him from the sharp claws of his real enemy—the apartheid regime. It was from the Great Trek and discovery of gold as results of Jan van Riebeck and the British settlement that apartheid set in motion which furthered erosion of the South African mental health. The mental health then transcended itself into spiritual decay or the malady of the soul: loss of personal and national identity, low self esteem, self hate, loathing of work, surrender, hopelessness, helplessness and total erosion of humanity: kindness, civilization, compassion, sympathy, charity, reasoning, common sense.

AN OPEN LETTER TO THE SOUTH AFRICAN YOUTH AND LEADERSHIP

Here is a shocking revelation—a revelation that is self explanatory—something that explains the deep problem within the South African society. And notice that this open letter goes to the South African youth and especially the leadership—not Zweletini.

"My name is Lovelyn Chidinma Nwadeyi. I am a Nigerian. Born in Nigeria to two Nigerian parents. Raised in Queenstown, Eastern Cape by those same Nigerian parents right up until I completed my Bachelors at Stellenbosch. ... I speak fluent Xhosa, Igbo, Afrikaans and English. I can make sense of Tswana and Sotho. ..." that's how this—I must say—a delightfully brilliant Nigerian lady began the account of her incredible experience of South Africa's Xenophobia.

She then picks up from here by highlighting the vast ethos of the South African society in this abridged account—an account in which she shares how she has unbelievably managed to blend into the diverse South African society over the years—an incredible feat she accomplished almost from the scratch—only because she was out of place and everybody told her so. "But my ability to navigate all these spaces," she continued, "did not just happen (like that). Learning to blend into all these spaces was a matter of survival for me. You see ….What nobody knew was that for the first three years of my life in South Africa, my little brother and I barely saw my dad more than twice a month… selling pillowcases, duvets and bed sheets, from door to door on foot through the streets, villages and side roads of the old Transkei and Ciskei…

"My father would leave the house on Monday mornings and after him my mom got us ready for school, and he would be gone for days and weeks, selling the few pillowcases and bed sheets he had from door to door. On foot. We were never sure when he would return. But when he did, we were always more grateful for his safety and aliveness than anything else.

"From Queenstown to Cala, Umtata, Qumbu, Qoqodala, Whittlesea, Mount Fletcher, King Williamstown, Mdantsane, Bhisho, Indwe, Butterworth, Aliwal North and even as far as Matatiele and Kokstad. There are so many other places he went to that I do not even know. That is how my parents put us through school, until they saved up enough money to open their own little shop where they then started selling sewing machines, cotton and then community phones. Then sweets and chips and take-aways; and then hair products and the list goes on and on. It was on this that I was able to go through primary school, high school, and university. My parents have no tertiary education; it was only in their late 40s that both of them decided to register for part-time studies at Walter Sisulu to get their Diplomas. Note: Diplomas. It took them four years, because they were busy trying to keep their kids in school, and keep selling their sweets and sewing machines while attempting to dignify their efforts with a degree.

"My story is not unique (though) —it is the story of most foreigners in South Africa. Very few foreigners come into SA with skills that make them employable here. Unless you are a medical doctor, an academic and maybe an engineer or well-established businessman before coming here, your chances of getting meaningful employment in SA are as limited as…almost impossible. Most foreigners come to SA with the ability to braid hair, carve wood, or sell fruits, veggies, clothes, fizz pops, carpets and soap before they can find their feet here. Some are graduates…but what can another African degree do for you in SA? And any foreigner in SA will tell you that this is the truth. All of us started from below the bottom…

"I can bet you that there is not up to 10% of South Africans who would be willing to do the menial and embarrassing work my parents and other foreigners did .... Let's discuss this: Arachnophobia—the fear of spiders (for instance).... (as is) Xenophobia—the fear of foreigners. However individuals who are afraid of spiders do not go around killing spiders, rather they avoid spiders....

"What is happening in SA is ... fuelled by a deep-seated hatred for which no single foreigner is responsible. .... This is not the first wave of attacks of this nature in South Africa. In fact, the 2008 attacks were much worse in terms of raw numbers of casualties suffered than these have been so far. The issue of xenophobia is not a new one in SA. However, the differentiator in 2015 is that this wave is backed by a strong ideology; that somehow these attacks can be and are justified.

"An ideology that sees merit in the argument that foreigners are stealing the jobs of locals, that they are stealing their women, that these "makwerekwere" are the cause of most ills in South African society... is a shame how uninformed and how baseless these arguments are. Foreigners do not and CANNOT steal jobs in SA. Do you know how hard it is to get South African papers, just to get into the country—not to talk of getting a work permit and convincing any company to take on the cost of employing you as a foreigner? Unless you have some freaking scarce skills in the country—it just does not happen like that...There is a disgusting entitlement that is attached to this notion that jobs can be stolen. This implies that there are jobs waiting for you – of which there are none. There are no freaking jobs waiting for anyone.

"Pick up a bucket and start washing cars. Put on your shoes and walk through your streets, sell tomatoes, eggs and tea—anything people eat, they will buy. Or pick up a book, hustle your way into university, work for a scholarship and get yourself an education. But stop this senselessness. Nobody is stealing your jobs. I got my first job when I was 11-years-old. I worked on the school bus in my town. I collected money for the bus driver, wrote out receipts and kept order on the bus. I didn't get paid much, but it helped me learn first that nothing comes easy; I learnt to be responsible and accountable to someone else. Secondly, it helped me pay for little extramural expenses I did at school which were not the priority for my parents at the time (and rightly so). In 'varsity, even though I had a tuition bursary, I worked two part-time jobs and one contract job for the entire three years at Stellenbosch so I could pay for my good, clothes and some additional materials etc. Yes my parents supported me as best they could, but naturally, part of growing up is that you don't bother your parents for every Rand you need.

"So people see me and my family now, several years later driving a decent car and living in an average house and they say, "Ningama kwekwere, asinifuni apha. Niqaphele, aningobalapha." "You are foreigners; we do not want you here. You better watch out, you are not of this place,"—unaware of and unwilling to hear of the years of struggle and hustle that came with the decent car and the average house. (Which, by the way, you can never fully own as SA law now restricts ownership of property by foreigners – but that is another discussion.) And what has been the government's response to the worsening unemployment and crime situation in the cities and suburbs that incites this violence and dissatisfaction amongst its people? To tighten immigration laws, border controls and any little room the foreigner may have had ...as if that is where the problem began.

"Is it not the way our economy is structured? That there is limited room for unskilled labor in the workforce? That those who are not vocationally trained must then settle for employment outside of their existing areas of knowledge such as artisans, plumbers and electricians—whereas these skills are equally needed in a developing economy? That we have this thing called BEE which in practice just ensures that the Black bourgeoisie get wealthier by hook or by crook while still protecting and cushioning the impact of democracy on old, white money and big business? Is it really the little Ethiopian man with his spaza shop that is threatening your progress na Bhuthi? Is it really the Nigerian woman who braids hair and sells Fanta that is stealing your job and place in your own land na Sisi? I can't deal.

"If none of these arguments have merit for you, then think of the fact that during apartheid, Nigeria (or Tanzania for that matter) spent thousands of dollars on the ANC protecting and moving its members across borders; Angola, Mozambique, Tanzania, Burundi, Zambia, Zimbabwe, Botswana, Kenya, Rwanda, Uganda all housed, supported and/or trained struggle heroes with open arms and with no strings attached. How dare South Africans forget how much Africans did for them during apartheid? How dare you! South Africans, go and learn your history. When you have read your history, then please teach the correct version to your children. Let them know that Africa helped put SA where it is now.

"Let them know that all blacks are not Xhosa or Zulu, but that that is irrelevant to the amount of dignity you accord to another human being. Teach your children that they must work for everything they want to have except your love as a parent. Teach your children that they are nothing without their neighbor—stop being selective about who *Ubuntu*[13] applies to and does not. Teach them the truth about you. The greatest enemy of the black man has always been himself. Not the colonialists. Not the apartheid architects. Only himself. And as long as you refuse to take responsibility for where you are now, you will remain there. Kill us foreigners or not, it actually makes very little difference to your fortunes in life, people of *Mzansi!"*

"Lovelyn Nwadeyi,

20 April 2015."

It is probably why shocked, Joseph Baguma wrote on his facebook wall a day before the author had his hands on the lovely email from Lovelyn Nwadeyi, on April 19 that, "it's only in South Africa where an illiterate...thinks a qualified medical doctor from another African country stole his job!"

CONCLUSION

In the year 1998, I served as a dedicated sales representative for Smithkline Beecham in Tanzania. On this good chilly evening, I was driving home from a sales trip in Tabora and Shinyanga. Aziz, my driver, was behind the wheel.

We had crossed Shinyanga town and as we approached Hungumarwa, a small town along the highway, I saw the road block ahead of us and a road sign indicating that the roadwork was in progress. That part of the highway was impassable therefore. A shorter distance ahead I saw a diversion and that's the direction I had expected Aziz to take. He didn't.

Trusting him believing that he was watching, and he knew better what he was doing, I remained cool, calm. But suddenly, I saw the Toyota heading for the hurdles. That's when I shouted "Aziz. Aziz, Aziz".

He didn't listen. I shouted one more time: Aziz, *Stop the car, or change the direction.* Fortunately he heard my voice. Then intuitively, he wheeled the car towards the bush. He struggled with the Toyota but in the end managed to control her. Finally—one way or the other—Aziz or the car in defiance, managed to land us in a roadside diversion.

We got out immediately. I checked all around me and my driver, and we were both okay. I went on my knees and closed my eyes in prayer. We had avoided the accident. Even though the car was damaged but the worst had been avoided. Think of what would happen if I shut up? Such is a sense of responsibility we advocate. Concerning this accident, you realize that this is the analogy of the moment we find ourselves in today. Unless we change direction we are heading for the rocks. You probably are on the highway and find it to be the only right direction. Some of the times it is safer to lead away from the clear highway toward the bush as Aziz or the car did.

The final question is this. Did Aziz see it; I mean the accident, coming? Here is the truth. Like an innocent infant, he was sound asleep and probably in the middle of a very sweet dream lightly snoring over his fatty lunch behind the wheel driving in coma. I probably couldn't hear him snore under the thundering engine of the car.

What is it that stops you from seeing or hearing the snoring man behind the wheels of your household, organizational, academic or political vehicle? Look around you. Ask questions. Observe. It could be something you and I could avert. In the end, *we come to a realization that accepting everything is that which John Dewey called "erecting silence as a virtue."*

It really doesn't make me a villain by trying to help; nor should it make me a victim of the noble service I have rendered for the glory of God and my country. "He," said the Holy Prophet (SAW); "He is my dearest friend who points out my drawbacks to me, and gives me a gift by doing so!

At last, as I told Aziz, I'm boldly telling you now: *Stop the car, or change the direction.*

4. THE DEATH OF A NATION: THE FATE OF A SICK NATION

"And now, look, your house is abandoned and desolate."
—Matthew 23:38

Man, beware. Sick nations die. Did I say die? Is it true that sick nations die? well, let's paraphrase this question. Is it true that sick nations can die? Or rather, can sick nations die? And again, forget the terminology that I have used. And it doesn't matter. It is just nomenclature. What is definite is that sick nations may become extinct.

Through the immediate previous chapter, we saw that if the health of your country is questionable, if your country is a sick nation, if that malady or infirmity is not healed, just like how when cancer for instance isn't cured a sick person gives the ghost up, that nation or society may give its ghost and go extinct.

Is this claim matter-of-fact? Is this argument foolproof or something intended to entertain the reader? Let us see what befell the NEANDERTHALS.

THE NEANDERTHALS' EXTINCTION

Probably you have heard of the Neanderthals. If you haven't, still—as Australians say—*no worries*! Here is a short account of the Neanderthals.

The Neanderthals were humans who became extinct between 20,000 to 30,000 years ago. "Though there is a debate about whom these people were," the report says,"but there is no question that there are none left...."

Now the question is: "How can we avoid meeting the Neanderthals' fate?" To answer that question, we must know how they perished—beforehand. There is also a talk of genocide, enmity and constant battles between these communities,—the laws of the jungle, or the survival of the fittest. We don't know for sure. But there is also the question of technology and therefore succumbing to vagaries of weather as another possibility. These aren't my own words. It isn't my creation. And what I have presented here is just a summary. But the point is this: "there is no question that there are none left. All that remains of a thousand Neanderthals' groups that roved across Europe and central Asia, are a handful of ambiguous funeral sites, bones, tools, pieces of art, along with some DNA that modern humans inherited from them." You can read more about it at www.popsci.com/science/article2013-05/.

Now do we still question the possibility that such an ancient human community did really perish? We don't have to. Besides, to prove that the foregoing assertion is not fictitious or something that is simply imaginary, you don't have to go to Siberia or Antarctica to research on whether the extinction of the human race is a possibility. No. Just look around you—in the city where you live: start from right there. Where are the indigenous or native human communities? Where are they? Where are the animate and vegetations—the life that originally inhabited the whole stretch of the city?

THE SUKUMA SUB TRIBES

I know that whenever this question is brought before us, we tend to say they moved. Whither? I mean, to where? Probably they haven't completely evaporated into thin air. Extinction as a notion, if we are to be more objective, is far reaching. Take the Sukuma people of Tanzania, for instance. Today we say they are the most populous tribe in the country, is it not? But objectively, that assertion is questionable. The author knows from the tales from his father that not all tribes that we identify today as Sukumas were Sukumas a hundred years ago. Having been born and grown up in the colonial district of Biharamulo, the district whose inhabitants that has since pre colonial era interacted with the rest of Kahama and Shinyanga and rest of modern day Sukumaland, I know from my father that this region was inhabited by so many smaller tribes that were completely distinct from one another, and from the modern day Sukumas.

The point is this, if they parted from one another in different many ways from morphology to traditions and languages, where are these other communities today? Where are the Sumbwa? Where are the Zinza? The Himba?

Though the author doesn't love to believe they became extinct, but his sheer love doesn't have an iota of influence on the reality. Did they become extinct? Probably not! Were these tribes or communities absorbed into the mainstream Sukuma people? In all these questions, I have no way of knowing for sure. Forgetting the extinction as an alternative, and therefore, yes, they may have been integrated into the mainstream Sukuma, but is that what we want for our society or our offspring? Even if that makes everybody happy, count me out still! My concern is: where are these other tribes?

I know people whose ancestors were the Zinza or Koki but now are absorbed among the Nyambo of Karagwe and Kyerwa or Sukumas of Kahama much as are the Hinda and Hima among the typical Haya tribes, not because they don't know their background? No! They still have morphological traits with their ancestors albeit intermarriages; and they know their origin and though deep inside they crave to be "themselves", they feel "comfortable" that way—to lose identity!

THE MASAI

We can probably consider the Masai too. What about their traditional way of life? What if they don't adapt to changing technology and stick to cattle rearing for the next couple of generations? What about the future of a tribe or community that migrates to the cities and dwells outdoor under the gigantic trees or uninhabited houses plaiting the city woman folks and guarding the houses of the elites as the industry for the community?

THE HINDA DYNASTY

And when the author talks about the Masai, he does so with neither malice nor conceit. In fact I am certain he does so with deep empathy.

I know he does so with deep empathy because his is a Hinda dynasty whose kinfolk are the Humas—a people who like the Masai descended from the north and dress alike and have their way of life surrounding the cattle—besides fluidity of their traditional ancient homelands as we are about to see.

Long time ago when I was in school, I read a history book. It was about East Africa. And one of the topics in that book was *The Peopling of East Africa*. To cut the long story short, in the book a map had been drawn to illustrate the topic in question. Whereas the book showed all other tribes as we know them today, and in their present locations, among the tribes surrounding the Lake Victoria was a tribe the book identified as the Hima. The authors indicated the Hima as a tribe that extended from north or south of the river Kagera into south and north of Tanzania and Uganda respectively. As historian, or objective researcher, one will strive to prove this assertion as right or wrong. Let us attempt to do the same.

We have the same Ankole cattle in both regions. We have the same names of the villages and lakes and rivers, and clans, and traditions in both regions. This is no secret. There are has been such names as Isingiro and Mitoma both in Karagwe, Tanzania and in Uganda. There are the Siita, Koki and Hinda clans in Kagera as are in Uganda to mention but a few examples.

Here is another point. We also know what we learnt in history— the first historical sites among them the iron smelting sites. Among iron sites we cannot miss are the Engaruka in the north east of the country and Bweranyange in the north west of Tanzania. Bweranyange is in Karagwe, Tanzania, to mention but a few. Whereas everybody knows this as a fact, very few mind to know how. We can safely conclude that they, the Hindas and the Humas—coming from the north—brought down the iron technology to the south during their conquest of the territories further south.

Are such immigrations possible, real? Let us see. Don't we have the evidence of other immigrations as evidence? Don't we have the Ngoni people from the south, the Manyema from the Congo, the Arab descendants and settlements along the slave trade routes—among others as testimony of the interregional migrations? So, when did they come? The question is, was this author of *The Peopling of East Africa* right or wrong?

We can safely conclude that, coming from the north, they brought Iron Age to this neighborhood during late Stone Age. Long time, huh? Not really! It is safe to assume for instance that, because of such immigrations and introduction of the iron technology in Bushubi, a territory that was originally fell under the Karagwe kingdom before they split up, a village known as Kabaheshi was established. Kabaheshi, deriving its name from the foregoing background, connotes the *Village of the Ironsmiths*. Enough said.

Now to be precise, and going back to the possibility of extinction of the human community whether from by internal or the external forces, the history books categorize the Hima or Humas—call it anything—as originally a non-bantu community.

However that doesn't object the role of intermarriages. Yet in 2010, the government documented records indicated that mainland Tanzania was 99% blacks among which 95% were Bantu with the 1% of Asians and Europeans; period.[14]

It kept quiet about the other 4 percent. It kept quiet about the Hima, the Huma, and the Hinda for instance—and of course the other Hamitic people, the Masai besides the Nilotes—the Luos. If this people yield to its being erased from the map, however only symbolic, it is in itself extinction.

Let me repeat: however only symbolic , if this people—the non Bantu Hinda or overall the Huma, the Masai and the Luos—yield to its being erased from the map, however only psychological, it is yes psychological, but extinction nonetheless. And naturally all life or mortification i.e. extinction, begin in the mind.

Still the question recurs: where are the Himas? We fortunately, yes fortunately, have oral tradition and pre-colonial history books narrating how Speke met king Rumanyika in Karagwe for instance.

We fortunately have oral tradition and pre-colonial history books evidencing how the American Henry Morton Stanley met king Kibogora in Bushubi for instance. We can of course read about the Hinda and Hima settlement in this country many years before the white men set their boots in this country in the books *The Hinda Bakama* or even in *The Forgotten Mandate* respectively.

These records evidence the fact that they existed in Kagera since prehistoric times. Now, here is the question: Are they extinct or are they among the recently United Nations-accounted-for stateless people? This doesn't seem possible or sensible if these are among the people who actually created or developed the states in our communities long before colonial states were forged.

All said, still the question recurs: where are the Himas, the Humas, the Hindas—at least on the official level?

Still you can't get it? I mean you still can't see how extinction is possible? How does the foregoing hypothesis concern you? I know some of my readers in Karagwe or beyond will say: *"binkwatilechi,"* for I am not Hima or Huma, Hinda or Ganwa. *"Binkwatilechi," is* a Kinyambo terminology for "how does it concern me?" Well, for such indifferent people, or those who will leap and shout *Halleluiah* in profound joy, for them and their cohorts, here is their answer. First of all, it concerns you. What comes around goes around. The forces that exterminate the one community, will in the long run exterminate the whole race. Mark my words. That's the natural law. The intelligent people don't sit around and say let the genocidal tribes or sects massacre others. What we have recently experienced in Pakistan, Afghanistan, Rwanda, Kosovo, Kenya, Somalia, Nigeria, Mali or even in the *United Islamic States* is not a sport intelligent people can sit around and cheer up. This is certainly a situation on which president Museveni referred to when he said: *Enkobe'ento esheka echibira nchisya!* This is an analogy of a little monkey that makes fun of a bush fire burning down the forest—its own shelter!

THE FULL CIRCLE: A TRUE STORY FROM THE ANCIENT KINGDOM OF BUSHUBI, THE KWA AND THE HAZHABE

Is this idea about a sick nation—or healing it—a realistic one or simply idealistic and imaginary? Let's see. Let's consider a few cases we can closely relate with—cases that will illustrate importance of adaptation or rather, staying ahead of time.

Talking about the adaptation to the changing environment, or whether extinction is caused by internal forces or those from without, probably the Kwa and the Hazhabe offer a more discernible example. What will happen to the remaining bands of the scanty and far apart bands of Hazhabe people whose livelihood depends on nature in northern Tanzania? We have another one and a more vivid case. It is about the Twa.

THE DISPLACED TWA PEOPLE OF BUSHUBI/NGARA TANZANIA

In his book *What Makes People Rich and Nations Powerful*, Festo Michael Kambarangwe brings to life the forgotten stories he learnt about through oral tradition but which have recently been supported from the book "Forgotten Mandate (www.amazon.com)," a book by, E. K. Lumley, the first British district officer in Ngara, Kagera, Tanzania. E. K. Lumley indicates the existence of the Twa People in the earliest years of the 1900s. The Twa are,—well, that's a wrong verb—were, is the word. Thus many historians and writers believe that the Twa were the first humans to settle in that part of the mainland. It is they who covered most parts of ancient kingdoms of Biharamulo, Bushubi, Bugufi, Buha, Rwanda, Burundi and Karagwe among other parts of Kagera long before the Bantu and the Hamites who moved in from both the Congo and down from the north respectively. Now the question is: Where is this Twa nation today? Where has it gone to?

We can get insights into that question from the book *The Forgotten Mandate*. In the book, Lumley writes about having come into not only physical but personal contact with what was probably the last band of the Twa nation migrating from one part of modern day Ngara to another in search of fruits and game. Ngara is a district in modern day Tanzania comprising of pre-colonial kingdoms of Bushubi and Bugufi. What is astonishing is that they, the Twa, could communicate with their fellow Bantu and Hamitic neighbors in some dialect not very different from Kishubi language as it is spoken today in Bushubi, Ngara, Tanzania. To know something more about the Twa, they still inhabit Rwanda, Burundi and especially today in the eastern Congo where forests are still supportive of their natural lifestyle—but they are a people whose population is fast vanishing.

The Twa are said to be a shorter species of humans. Though this is generally true, some of the respondents don't seem to agree nonetheless. They object that the Twa were originally shorter or pigmies like their brethren of the Congo forest. At age of around 80, Mzee Buyoya, as he is popularly known, is one of the old men who lived in the area at the time when the Twa were numerous and distinct as a community in Ngara. He disputes this theory. He says they were not distinct from the mainstream Bantu. He only consents that traditionally they were potters. They molded pots from clay and sold them to their neighbors. This was their formal industry and it was an adequate industry at the time when no iron tools such as saucepans were in place. Their neighbors needed them—I mean the Bantu and later the Hamites—needed the Twa and their pots.

They didn't till the land or rear animals. What for? Mother Nature provided very bountifully and generously for them! At the time indeed fruits and roots were plenty. Animals were ubiquitous. Farming? What for? Yet slowly as the forest was besieged, if they needed food crops or milk—which from our research seemed doubtful—they exchanged them with their pots through barter system with the Bantu crop farmers or Hamitic cattle herders! Their demise began with the population growth especially among the Bantu and Hamites.

As I narrate about the communities in Ngara district, probably a hundred years ago, bring to mind the scenario of say Dar es Salaam City before the time of the Germans to date. Now back to Ngara, as the population grew, more forests were attacked! They, the Twa, were constantly put on the defensive, failing which, they kept moving and moving deeper and deeper until when they had no more space to flee to. Probably they were assimilated and merged into the main Bantu communities. Probably they moved further into the neighboring Burundi and Rwanda. We don't much know about these magnificent potters for now. But one thing is certain nonetheless: the Twa aren't anymore in the official books as one of the tribe in this country. That is to say, they are either already a nation that is extinct, or a-would-be-next extinct nation—to make a safer assertion—an assertion that should worry the Hinda or their Hima sibling, Masai and the Zaramo!

Is this farfetched? No sir! We doubt if the last national census recorded the Twa population. Forget the Twa for now. Let us go back to the Hazhabe. Let's go to northern Tanzania—the land of the Hazhabe! Where are the Hazhabe today? How many are they? Who knows? Who cares? Did the last census organizers care to count them? Well, who could? They live in the forests depending on *Mother Nature* deep in the forest chasing animals—running from humans. Did they vote in the last elections? Who represents them in the parliament? I would really like to know. Very recently Clouds FM, a local radio in Dar es Salaam, Tanzania, aired a program in which the Hazhabe petitioned a plea to protect their motherland. The Masai too. But for now forget the demise of the Zaramo, the Huma and the Masai. The Hazhabe are truly an endangered species, while the Twa people are probably already an extinct community—at least in Tanzania—love it, hate it! Finally, from the first British ruler of Bushubi to the existing descendant of the last Igwes of Bushubi, a story that only very few had learnt about through oral tradition, the forgotten stories about the peopling of Tanzania, and above all, unearthing of the existence and extinction of the Twa People—at least in Tanzania—has come to the full circle in your hearing, in your reading.

THE LAST BO PERSON TO LIVE HAS DIED!

Now the quest to have a safer conclusion about the above, brings us to one more challenge. And that challenge is to prove if really this is not imagination of this too *idealistic* author—as some reader will have already labeled him. When this challenge came to me, I recalled what CNN had reported recently. When I say recently I mean it. It is an event that has happened in our most recent times—the times we may call post-Tsunami. Here is an account as reported by CNN from New Delhi, India:

"The last member of an ancient tribe that has inhabited an Indian island chain for around 65,000 years has died, a group that campaigns for the protection of indigenous peoples has said. Boa Sr, who was around 85 years of age, died last week in the Andaman islands, about 750 miles off India's eastern coast, Survival International said in a statement. The London-based group, which works to protect indigenous peoples, said she was the last member of one of ten distinct Great Andamanese tribes, the Bo.

"The Bo are thought to have lived in the Andaman Islands for as long as 65,000 years, making them the descendants of one of the oldest human cultures on earth," it noted. With her passing at a hospital, India also lost one of its most endangered languages, also called Bo, linguists say. "She was the last speaker of (the) Bo language. It pains to see how, one by one, we are losing speakers of Great Andamanese and (their) language is getting extinct. (It is) A very fast erosion of (the) indigenous knowledge base, that we all are helplessly witnessing," read an obituary in Boa Sr's honor posted on the Web site of the Vanishing Voices of the Great Andamanese (VOGA) project. Anvita Abbi said, "Boa Sr was the only speaker of Bo and had no one to converse with in that language. Project director Anvita Abbi, a professor at New Delhi's Jawaharlal Nehru University, met with Boa as recently as last year. "She was the only member who remembered the old songs," Abbi recounted in her obituary. "Boa Sr was the only speaker of Bo and had no one to converse with in that language," Abbi told CNN. Her husband and children had already died, the linguist said.

"Other than Bo, she also knew local Andaman languages, which she would use to converse, according to Abbi. Boa Sr was believed to be the oldest of the Great Andamanese, members of ten distinct tribes. Survival International estimates there are now just 52 Great Andamanese left. There were believed to be 5,000 of them when the British colonized the archipelago in 1858. Most of those tribal communities were subsequently killed or died of diseases, says Survival International. The British also held the indigenous tribes' people captive in what was called an Andaman Home, but none of the 150 children born there survived beyond two years of age, according to the group. Boa Sr also survived the killer Indian Ocean tsunami in 2004. She recorded in Bo what she saw when the giant waves arrived. "While we were all asleep, the water rose and filled all around. We did not get up before the water rose. Water filled where we were and as the morning broke the water started to recede," reads a translation of her tsunami narrative posted on the VOGA website.

"Activists are expressing alarm over her death," This report said. "Boa's loss is a bleak reminder that we must not allow this to happen to the other tribes of the Andaman Islands," Survival director Stephen Corry said in the statement. Andaman and Nicobar Islands authorities put at least five tribes in their list of vulnerable indigenous communities. According to Corry's group, the surviving Great Andamanese depend largely on the Indian government for food and shelter and abuse of alcohol is rife," concluded the report.

Without a doubt extinction is no more speculation or idealistic. It is real!

A SUMMARY OF THE RISE AND FALL OF THE GREAT POWERS

The relative strengths of the leading nations in world affairs never remain constant, principally because of the uneven rate of growth among different societies and of the technological and organizational breakthroughs which bring a greater advantage to one society than to another. But this is just a general term. There are subtle factors behind growth. Attitude of the masses and leadership and generally the ethos of the society toward work and one another which we can term as "manpower revolution" provide real factors.

The Rise and fall of nations—in modern states situation—can yes be explained by yes its ethos and the mindset of the youth and therefore education in the country but Economic Change and Military Conflict have been at the core. In his book Economic Change and Military Conflict: from 1500 to 2000, first published in 1987, Paul Kennedy, argues that the strength of a Great Power can be properly measured only relative to other powers, and he provides a straightforward and persuasively argued thesis: Great Power ascendancy (over the long term or in specific conflicts) correlates strongly to available resources and economic durability; military overstretch and a concomitant relative decline are the consistent threat facing powers whose ambitions and security requirements are greater than their resource base can provide for (summarized on pages 438–9). When a nation experiences, in words of Kennedy, "greater difficulties in balancing her preferences for guns, butter and investments, then the decline is around the corner."[15]

Now we move on to illustrate that no matter whether the nation is Africa or America, Europe or Asia; no matter whether the people are is black, red, white or yellow, and no matter whether that country is powerful today or not, it can still collapse. Having discussed and illustrated that extinction of a nation is real, I understand someone will question the validity of using such tribes as Twa, Masai or Bo.

Let me now engage you in the analysis of the civilizations and nations that once were so powerful that ruled vast kingdoms and national states but later fell apart. In this book we are engaged in the analysis of the major causes of the fall of nations while hinting about the solution—a subject we shall concentrate with through the following book in this series—a book analyzing the ideal scholar.

We are attempting to lay down factors that prove that failure is more conceived in the inside before it walks into the outside world.

We are attempting to illustrate that there is a secret of success much as a cause or failure and that it all begins in the character of a people, its ethos, leadership and how its youth are allowed to conduct themselves.

We are attempting to analyze and illustrate that even great civilization fell when they walked away from their core values and ways of life—albeit an awareness that yes a society as well as its ethos ought to change overtime—to reinvent itself.

Beginning with a summary of the factors behind the decline of ancient Greece and ancient Roman Empire, empires that ruled the world such that everybody said they could only rule forever.

What happened to them as to cause their downfall? Here are some key factors for their downfall: Conflict and competition between city-states broke down a sense of community in Greece.

There was also constant war divided the Greek city-states into shifting alliances; it was also very costly to all the citizens. There was increasing tension and conflict between the ruling aristocracy and the poorer classes.

Greek colonies around the Mediterranean knew about Greek culture but were not necessarily loyal to Greece.

The neighboring states were increasing in power and were more unified than the city-states of Greece. Besides, different city-states had completely different forms of government and ways of life (e.g., Sparta and Athens).

Philip of Macedonia, to the north of Greece, had a strong military and a unified monarchy which gave him the power to eventually conquer the Greek city-states (338 BCE).

Eventually the Empire became a dictatorship and the people were less involved in government.

Over time, Rome was increasing in size, power, and trade. By 146 BCE Romans had conquered the Greek city-states.

Roman Empire couldn't endure too. Why? Heavy taxes were paid by the provinces to support the luxury of Rome; the conquered people began to resent this.

Rome's army became too large; the hired soldiers (mercenaries) in Roman armies were not Romans and not loyal to Rome. Inheritance of the title of Emperor was unstable; this led to power struggles, violence, and insecurity.

The Empire became too large and the borders were too long to defend. Trade was constantly disrupted because of wars; the economy suffered because goods could not be freely bought and sold. Conflict and social unrest was created by the wide gap between the rich and the poor. Slavery eroded the economy by taking work away from the plebeians.

The people became lazy because they were more interested in living the good life than not only in waging war against their enemies but to work. The spread of Christianity divided the Empire and caused many people under Roman rule to reject traditional Roman culture.

The society was weakened by its materialism and focus on luxury, especially in the ruling classes. People may have been suffering from lead poisoning because of the lead pipes for the Roman water supply. The division of the Empire into the eastern and western Empires weakened the power of Rome.

There are other factors of course but we believe that a civilization begins to give up its ghost from inside out. It first weakens from the inside before it is weakened and vanquished from the outside.

Concerning the decline of ancient great powers, Gibbon concluded that: "The warlike states of antiquity, Greece, Macedonia, and Rome, educated a race of soldiers; exercised their bodies, disciplined their courage, multiplied their forces by regular evolutions, and converted the iron which they possessed into strong and serviceable weapons.

But this superiority insensibly declined with their laws and manners; and the feeble policy of Constantine and his successors armed and instructed, for the ruin of the empire, the rude valor of the Barbarian mercenaries."[16]

THE DEMISE OF THE OTTOMAN EMPIRE

The demise of the Ottoman Empire was slow in coming but the Caliphate began waning by 1683 following a number of reasons. Among the factor for its demise include: failure to acquire significant new wealth following the end of profitable conquests and the inability of the rulers to make a clear choice between war and the more conventional types of capital formation; leadership ineffectiveness such as the leadership describing symptoms rather than causes, and weak administrative machinery such as the erosion of the sultan's authority, dissolution of the circle of equity and disruption of the social economic order. With Sultans becoming less sensitive to public opinion and the low quality Sultans of the 17th and 18th centuries, and struggle for power within the ruling family, the Ottoman Empire became less centralized, and as the central control weakened the demise of the caliphate was set into motion.

Others factors include: The autocratic, imperial system of Ottoman rule changing little over the centuries, while its Western European neighbors slowly evolved into fairly stable nation-states; inefficiencies originating from the size of the empire and thereof trying to keep the empire intact through internal and external wars which was a costly process compromising the Ottoman Empire's capacity to introduce reform—and then inflation set in. in then end, following the failure by the state to find remedy to these weaknesses, the Ottoman Empire of the seventeenth century was no longer the vital empire it had been a century before.

Following leadership ineffectiveness and slowness to change, many of the provinces became more closely linked to Europe than to Istanbul such were the railways systems that were built largely by Europeans, linking Europe to the coast, not to the capital and as a result, the Ottoman Empire shifted from being a producer of manufactured goods to being a producer of raw materials for European industry.

The Ottomans saw military expansion and fiscalism as the source of wealth,
with agriculture seen as more important than manufacture and commerce, and as such the Ottoman economy was a "war economy" where its primary revenue comprised booty from expansion instead of placing more emphasis on manufacture and industry in the wealth-power-wealth equation, moving towards modern economics comprising expanding industries and markets instead of continuing along the trajectory of territorial, traditional monopolies, conservative land holding and agriculture and hence an agrarian economy which itself had scarcity of labor and capital despite rich land. Also most of home-grown commodities were produced by slave labor undercutting domestic production,

industriousness, apprenticeship and technological transfer. Dependence on slave labor escalated her demise. Slaves aren't any motivated to work or innovate. Also later over the 19th century, a shift occurred to rural female labor which was less supported by the culture and state male-based labor.

As early as the 1470s, Greeks and Jews were the premier traders, not the Ottomans much as most of the capital for railroads came from European financiers. The net result was to give financiers and traders a considerable financial control watering down the internal superstructure. There was also considerable variation in monetary policy and practice in different parts of the empire. Although there was monetary regulation, enforcement was often lax and little effort was made to control the activities of merchants, moneychangers, and financiers.

Ottoman bureaucratic and military expenditure was so high and raised by taxation, generally from the agrarian population.

McNeil describes an Ottoman stagnation through centre-periphery relations—a moderately taxed centre with periphery provinces suffering the burden of costs. But it was more than that. Centre-periphery stagnation theory should also explain the fact that the failure was more internally rooted wherefore the rulers failing the masses as well as their trade partners.

Industrial Revolution on the part of Europe and in particular the Britain and slowness to adapt to changes on the part of the ottoman, saw the Empire that also lacked crucial supplies such as coal subsiding into its eventual collapse.

Slow adaptation to new technologies and weakness of the leadership in appeasing the traditionalists perpetuated the *man-manned* economic machinery which though was considered profitable at the time, the use of tamed animals and slaves to transport goods than modern infrastructure such as railways retarded both the innovation and transformation.

Consider that Aegean areas alone had over 10,000 camels working to supply local railroads and Ankara station had a thousand camels at a time and slaves waiting to unload goods. Slavery was a social system of the ottoman. (Slavery in the Ottoman Empire was a legal and important part of the Ottoman ...Many officials themselves owned a large number of slaves.[17]

Slaves were a... "class of human beings that has formed an integral part of Muslim society up to the present day....Under Islamic law, the slave had to be provided with shelter, clothing, food and medical care, while freeing a slave was considered an act of piety...Perhaps as MUCH of Istanbul's population as 20 percent consisted of SLAVEs...Once upon a time, there may have been as many as 3 million blacks in present-day Turkey, but today only 4,500-5000 remain in the Aegean and Mediterranean areas.")[18] Through the invention of the steam engine in Britain, water and land transport revolutionizing the conduct of trade and commerce—whereby the steam ship meant journeys—became predictable, times shrank and unimaginable weights could be carried more cheaply made the Istanbul-Venice route, a main trade artery, taking as much as eighty-one days in the past, now reduced to ten days as well as Sail ships carrying 50 to 100 tons and steamships now carrying 1,000 tons whereas comparatively ships like the RMS Titanic could carry 66,000 tons didn't make things easier or nicer for the Ottoman Caliphate much as was competition from cheap products from India and the Far East.

Taxation policy also contributed to the demise of the empire. Taxing the masses that earned a living from small family holdings and still contribute to around 40% of taxes for the empire resulted the eventual social-economic disquiet. Cultural practices also hitched transformation and helped to wreck the Ottoman Empire—practices such as in ensuring that an uncle or brother of the Sultan did not try to seize power, they locked the sultan away in a small apartment for the duration of the Sultan's reign, known as a kafes, never to see the outside world. Also Sultans could take several wives and many concubines. It was thus possible for a sultan to have many children, and in particular, many sons.

A practice of fratricide grew up, in which on the death of a sultan, one of the sons would become the new sultan, who would then be isolated from all his brothers. Although this did not always happen, many were executed and though the execution of Sultans' sons and brothers ended, imprisoning them instead remained common thus apparently leading to becoming Sultan after spending years in prison —which is not the best training before one assumes absolute power. And think about it: The entire Ottoman Empire was built around the Sultan, but he never left his palace and would only see a few trusted advisors. Unlike other states of Europe, such as Germany, where a weak ruler could be made up for by a powerful Chancellor, there was no one who could make up for a weak Sultan. While in his self-imposed exile the Sultan's Empire continued to fall apart losing its former provinces.

There was also a question of corrupt religious opposition to critical thinking; the corrupt *ulema* wanted to "protect" their position as heads of state. They discouraged creativity to keep the populace from information that might be disseminated through books other than the Koran.

Muslims had been aware of the printing press since the 15th century, but it was not until 1727-272 years after Gutenberg—that the Şeyhülislam released a fetva decreeing its compatibility with Islam. Expanding into the Muslim world through occupations and intervention, they carved up the Ottoman Empire at the start of the 20th century, leaving the Muslim world dumbfounded.

The Ottoman expansion came to an abrupt halt in the late 17th century but in 1603, the English historian Richard Knolles described the Ottomans as "the present terror of the world" and by the mid-19th century, Tsar Nicholas I of Russia described it as "the sick man of Europe."[19]

THE CRITICAL ROLE OF LEADERSHIP AND THE DEATH OF YUGOSLAVIA

Once a great nation that spread over a large stretch of Europe, a country that had a voice in the social economic affairs of its citizens and humanity across Europe and the world over, Yugoslavia suddenly collapsed and passed off after the death of Tito. Why?

Writing about the breakup of this great nation Cameron Hewitt wrote thus: A very wise Bosniak once told me, "Listen to all three sides—Muslim, Serb, and Croat. Then decide for yourself what you think." A Serb told me a similar local saying: "You have to look at the apple from all sides." That's the best advice I can offer.[20]

Structural problems and ethnic tensions: The SFR Yugoslavia was a conglomeration of eight federated entities, roughly divided along ethnic lines, including six republics—Slovenia, Croatia, Bosnia and Herzegovina, the Republic of Macedonia, Montenegro and Serbia—and two autonomous provinces within Serbia, Vojvodina and Kosovo.

Other factors include the economic collapse and the international climate after the fall of communism, party crisis bureaucracy and death of Tito and the weakening of communism. But certainly the death of Tito was a very strong factor.

On 4 May 1980, Tito died and his death was announced through state broadcasts across Yugoslavia. Although Tito was hardly a liberal thinker, his death removed what many international political observers saw as Yugoslavia's main unifying force. Following his death ethnic tension grew in Yugoslavia. 'The Yugoslav Drama', argues that Yugoslavia was set up to only ever truly function under the control of a dominant arbiter such as Tito, reliant on popularity and charisma, so the system left behind for his successors was unlikely to work without a similar overseer (S. Bianchini and G. Schopflin eds., *State Building in the Balkans: Dilemmas on the Eve of the 21st Century*, Longo Editore: 1998).[21]

His death ended with the death of Yugoslavia because he was the institution that was the only lifeline to Yugoslavia's life. "After the purges of the early 1970s, Tito surpassed himself in "negative selection."

Docility and sycophancy were almost the only criteria he used for filling state and party leadership positions. In Serbia, for example, he stocked the party leadership with such weak, colorless, and insignificant individuals that it is not surprising Slobodan Milosevic met so little opposition to his rise to power in the second half of the 1980s.

"Tito's Yugoslavia was undoubtedly not a totalitarian state of mass terror, but merely a moderately authoritarian, semi-efficient, corrupt, and somewhat farcical state, similar to many others in the world. The main guarantors of Yugoslavia's unity were the communist police and army. No force in the country could challenge them, and Tito always had complete control of both…

"To resolve its national conflicts and overcome its sorrowful history, Yugoslavia would have had to be exceptional. It needed a dynamic economy and modern political institutions. Tito's political "genius" consisted of hindering and eliminating creative and reformist leaders, either within the communist party or outside it… Tito, therefore, left nothing enduring. Neither workers' self-management, nor a foreign policy of nonalignment, nor Yugoslavia itself survived."

On May 4, 1995, the 15th anniversary of Tito's death, there were no official commemorations in any part of the former Yugoslavia. The media made few comments, almost all of which were negative and sarcastic. Up to 1990, around 14 million people had visited Tito's mausoleum. But for the anniversary only family members, representatives of the small and politically marginal League of Communists, and a few others came to his grave, which is no longer protected by the presidential guard of honor. The myth of Tito had vanished!"[22]

In the final analysis, for the innovation to take place so that an individual person, household, organization and society can reinvent itself can only be possible by going back to the basics if one should make a comeback. Yes of course there is no more land to discover today as it was at the time. There is no more lands in west to discover and conquer. But we surely can learn to remodel the existing knowhow to our advantage. Truly, we can still conquer something—we certainly can conquer ourselves if not anyone or anything else! "There is guidance for each one of us," said Ralph Waldo Emerson," and by lowly listening, we shall hear the right word." Indeed you are the co-creator of your own person, a person to shape your own destiny, a person to fix your own life as well as that of your family, community, organization and the nation as a whole. With the ensuing chapter's conclusion at the back of your mind—the conclusion that personal as well as national leadership is critical for any advancement—lest I judge lest I, myself, be judged, let the reader—and the leader—himself or herself identify with, and judge against the three leadership approaches below, approaches we have experienced in the country of late. The first leader was a politician. Addressing the elders in a district—a district badly affected by the HIV/AIDS pandemic in that country—his counsel was watered down by a very low tone with which he spoke. Whether he did so for personal political gains viz., fearing to annoy his voters, or for his indifference on the matter, the author has no way of knowing. One thing was certain though. Because of the nature of his address, these less informed—and therefore reckless elders gave him a standing ovation when he came to an end, joining him in this jovial moment of harmony, sharing the secret emotions—adult emotions—they both seemed to cherish—the culture he should be fighting in the first place, the culture of promiscuity that had plunged his people into a tragedy of profound magnitudes the disease having killed thousands leaving a hundred thousand children homeless on the street begging—or engaged in stealing and other vices such as prostitution as means to make the ends meet.

The second leader was an arrogant autocratic administrator. And I must say, right from the onset, that I don't support what this district commissioner judged as the best form of leadership.

Following a drastic and persistent fall in school performances in his district, he made a surprise visit among a number of schools only to find the teachers on the streets selling cookies during class hours—to make a living. He caned the teachers in public!

From the verdict against the third leader, I would like the reader—and the leader—to judge whether it was progressive, or not for the elders to unanimously throw out this priest from their district.

His crime?

Was it on religious grounds? Oh, no sir! Madam, in his homily that Sunday in his church, he had, with great enthusiasm, addressed his congregants that that district—a district with the highest rate of dropouts, lowest academic performance and a pitiable per capita income nationally—would not progress because of indifference on education on the part of the children and their parents, collapse of family institution and therefore high rate of divorces and cohabiting, highest rate of promiscuity and a culture of marrying one's young daughters in return for money or cattle, a large part if which is used on the drink and promiscuity, and therefore high rate of HIV and AIDS, high rate of deaths, low life span, high rate of ever expanding army of street children, high rate of crime, idleness and gossip, inaction and indifference to affluence and prosperity with the principle of "Mektoob" that is, "it is written," belief in sorcery and generally a complete absence of ideals or values in that community etc., the culture this society ought to change if it has to progress.

5. PERSONAL SELF EVALUATION

"The way of a fool is right in his own eyes, but a wise man listens to advice."—Proverbs 12:15

We have discussed the symptoms of a sick nation through the preceding chapters. Through the proceeding pages, you will be led into details of, and the remedies to the problems the sick nation faces. But let me say momentarily that reforming education system and the reproducing a new curriculum based on relevant home-grown impetus in order to build the moral fiber and self confidence among the youth is key. This is the bedrock of the successful new beginning for the nation that is at risk. Educational system should be structured in such a way that our people are pressed to think about, and do the in-depth learning as they seek to have, give, and be more.

Education must focus on making life better, longer and meaningful for—well, the majority! But I wrote this book after I had discovered, as I mentioned earlier on, that there is great disarray in the administration of many nations. But when I say there is great disarray in the administration of the nations, I mean many of us have failed to manage or lead our own individual lives. I also refer to the mismanagement of the self, the households, the organizations and human society as a whole. The disarray, from here, trickles down to almost every other areas in the society. But what is more tragic comes into play when there is disarray within the academia.

It is this group of learned men and women we should expect to identify the problems the society is facing; and not only blow the whistle—which is by itself a very important step—but give us the required leadership aside from clear cut solutions. Unfortunately, many doubt if this is happening. Do they know that one day they will be held responsible when our society gets sick on their watch? I don't know! Their hope, explanation, or culprit? Yes they have an impressive list: the government, parents and the youth! Finding alibis, pointing fingers, putting the blame on everybody else but themselves! Unfortunately, that's not what they should do or be!

THE MAJOR WEAK SPOT IN A HUMAN SOCIETY—IN RETROSPECT—WITH SIMILE TO THE TANZANIA AND THE BRITISH SOCIETY

Very recently, I attended a forum on education in Tanzania. It was a very big event that ran for two hours covered by ITV in the illustrious Nkrumah Hall—a building named after one of the highly respected sons of Africa, and first president of Ghana, Dr. Kwame Nkrumah. And mind you, this is not a kind of the middle-of-the-road or mediocre university? It is one of the few reputed universities in the whole of Africa—the University of Dar es Salaam. The agenda was to discuss what had gone wrong in the country's education system following mass failure in education in the country and what the alternative way forward was. Unfortunately I witnessed the lecturers among them high-ranking professors struggling to address the problem at hand. Well, yes, they rightly pointed out the fact that we have a problem as far as education was concerned.

Sadly, I realized that the problem couldn't be more profound because even our intellectuals themselves seemed to go on listing problems after problems without delving into real solutions. What's more, they even—what seemed like very unfortunate—emphasized lack of direction as one of major handicaps in the education system in the country! Yes the political leadership cannot ward off their accountability, but what did the academicians do to sway the decisions in the right direction? For me they seemed to point fingers to everybody else but themselves. In so doing, they were indeed, passing the buck. How saddened I must have felt! I did—as I still do—suppose that they were the responsible people when education went wrong, and accountable when the education system collapsed, not to mention when the nation lacked direction and therefore sitting on the edge of the cliff heading toward the rocks.

I expected—let me be honest with myself if not with anybody else—to gather fresh ideas from the academics. I really looked forward to constructive variety of inputs from the custodians of education and establishers of the future of the nation. But I was disappointed when very little was forthcoming in terms of alternative solutions from our scholars aside from citing healthy examples of what other countries have done better. And what's more, I expected our scholars to at least list down the areas where we have comparative if not absolute advantages relative to our peers for the discussion to be objective and productive. For even though we have problems but do we not have anything positive? Not even one?

I also looked forward to learning how we found ourselves here. How did our peers make it? This is only the beginning. What was the mind-set of the nation and her leadership both in the areas of education and politics at the time? What are the new areas of considerations today? Responding to these questions is the first step in the right direction.

Other questions should have included such questions as how did the leadership among these successful economies rally the people behind their agenda? What new ideas did they bring? How can we adapt these ideas to our environment? These are pivotal questions we should ask ourselves should we, as a nation, augment and transform into an industrious people and a modern economy. For this change to happen, a review of the content and methodology of the education we provide in our schools should have been at the forefront of the discussion.

But again, none was forthcoming—and there was nothing I could do about it. My hands were tied. I and many outsiders didn't get airtime to share their ideas. And this is another major source of concern. If the members of the same club—the same men and women who in the main share ideas—will day in and day out repeat the same answers, where do we get new ideas from? It was in fact one of the factors which promoted publication of this book. We need answers. It was why I found we needed immediate answers to respond to our problems—including the foregoing.

On the brighter side of things, I must admit that I learned there were a few things on which we had consensus. Such things include the fact that the youth hold a key place should the change be meaningful and lasting. We also had the same take on the fact that, to turn the tables around we had to enhance transformation among the youth, the leadership and the society as a whole. How, when, and who should do what—besides what exactly should be done as draft proposal—are areas whose answer spaces remained blank.

There is one more question to which I must respond, a question any keen reader is by now eager to know. And the question is this: Why did I attend this forum? I attended the forum to learn and share ideas having researched on the state of education for a couple of years until then.

I wanted to share my side of story. I also looked forward to learn from my superiors. It isn't by no means surprising that I was least gratified by what I learned.

I have to say I was indeed less heartened by both the failure to address the weaknesses in our education system and the failure to put forward the comprehensive therapy or plan. It, then, became clear to me that to draft an alternative *Way-Forward* was necessary as far as education—in its narrow definition—or broadly, the country's social economic change was concerned. In the end, to give answers to a-sick-nation problem, vitality of education and that of the economy are key and knotted—together."[23]

ARE YOU OKAY WITH YOUR SITUATION?
If it is true that the health and vitality of our country's economy and political position are linked to strengthening our educational institutions, it follows therefore that our personal economic health as individuals depends on the vitality of education. That's why to affirm whether we should make scrutiny of our economic health and redress the education itself, we must first do a little analysis about ourselves and our careers or businesses.

But then, do we need personal self evaluation? And, yes, what has it to do with education or economic system? These are questions some of my readers are asking. What about you? I mean you personally! How do you evaluate yourself? How do you evaluate your community? For if you are okay with yourself, if your community is fine with you, why then bother? Why change the system of your life when it works well with you? And if it is detrimental to your progress and your future, why keep it? This is the rationale of doing self evaluation.

Let us now examine the facts about you—yes about you the reader—together.

When you are mentally and spiritually troubled, and feel hopelessness, you are personally sick even when you are physically alright. Probably you have faced the same situation where you don't know what to do after doing almost everything possible. You have done everything necessary but yet you feel something is still nagging and there is no real progress. You inherited wealth but it is not growing or hasn't exceeded the levels where your forefathers left it and indeed it is shrinking by the day, then yours isn't a healthy future. Yours isn't a healthy life when your neighborhood is infested with poverty, beggars, and drug addicts, street children, HIV and AIDS, hopelessness and a neighborhood where environmental waste, prostitution and other forms of criminality are an industry. You have no peace of mind? Then yours isn't a healthy life. Depending on hand to mouth form of economy, can never make anyone any wealthy; you know that but you cannot do anything about it; then yours isn't a healthy life.

When to you, affluence or ease of living is a myth, yours isn't a healthy life. Yours isn't a healthy life when you have got no money, and cannot make your ends meet. If this is true about you, and you have no way out, then yours is far from longer, happy and meaningful life. You cannot say or expect to live forever young, raising strong intelligent, happy and healthy children leading to a healthy family continuity if you don't rise to the challenge. If you cannot rise to the challenge before you, if all this is true about you, then yours isn't a healthy future. If this is true about you, when your life is not in your hands, then yours isn't a healthy life. If this is true about your neighborhood, when life in your neighborhood is generally in mess, then yours isn't a healthy life.

WHO IS A HEALTHY PERSON

Thus redefining our terms, a healthy person is the one who is growing in thinking and, sustainable in his career, is delighted with what he does professionally in his or her career or vocation which is profitable and gratifying to all or majority of the parties involved.[24]

My own sentiments? Oh, no! Yes the work is mine but it is in consensus with the UN. The World Health Organization defines health as "A state of complete physical, mental, and social well-being, and not merely the absence of disease or infirmity."

And what about your business or career?

Is your organization a healthy one? Today many businesses, no matter whether large, medium or small, have been badly shaken and many have closed down. The surviving ones, remain heavily indebted and many operating below their true potential. A large number of businesses are operating at loss. Yes this is due to both external and internal factors, but when such a situation is analyzed under a high powered mental and spiritual microscope, you and I will come to terms that it is mainly due to the elephant in the room—a skeleton in the cupboard.

Yes the economic crisis made the impact quite dramatic, yet the future of our businesses and our nation depends on decisions we made yesterday but more so on what decisions we make today. Business corporations as well as nations need to re-evaluate how they work internally if the transformation should be a reality and meaningful.

Your corporation or company is sick when it is not growing relative to investment you put in. It is sick when employees don't work as hard relative to how you give them incentives. When productivity is low, let alone sustainability, but also the breakeven point is not in the horizon, your business is not healthy.

What's a healthy business then? Do you know what the key performance indicator is? A healthy business is the one that is independent, sustainable, growing, interesting, and profitable and gratifying to all parties—staff, management, owners, and the community—and what's more, it is environment-friendly etc.

What about your school and education in the country? Your school is sick when students don't pass even when they attend classes and teachers are always there. It is sick when teachers aren't motivated and are only there to wait for the month end to collect the salary and bag a small portion home while the larger part is stashed in the beer bottle through its narrow mouth. The school or college is sick when you don't have initiatives to redeem the situation and numbers in terms of passes and registration keep on falling year after year. It is also true that a seriously sick education system can be identified when its graduates pass with colorful grades but they can't do nothing concrete or when they are motivated to work or keep on learning. But in the end you have yourself to blame for the demise of your health as well as that of your business or career and the people around you.

Now back to the question: do we need whistle blowers? Does the society need them? Really? Let us see.

FERDINAND MARCOS AND A SOCIETY WEEPING FOR CHANGE

We began this discussion from the previous chapter by praising the audacity exhibited by one Benedict Emanuel. It seems to me that his was the spirit that Ferdinand Marcos exhibited when he realized that his country, The Philippines, was far too sick and at risk before he was compelled to announce his worst worries no matter what would happened to him. We, one more time, pay tribute to Benny, Ferdinand Marcos and the Filipino people for the decision they made—decisions to come out. After Marcos had declared that the country was a sick nation, and that somehow they had to take steps, he listed down as alternative remedies to the Filipino problems, the Filipinos took him from the streets and put him in the state house.

To emphasize that this is a quality that is seriously sought after, not only among emerging nations but developed ones, let me remind you that when Barack Obama realized and told his countrymen that *"America was better than this,"* almost like an emergency, with his wife Michelle and daughters Malia and Sasha, the American people took him from the senate and put him in the White House!

Now here is a question directed to you from the American voters, the good people who gave Obama the mandate to change America: If really America was far better than that, what about you, your household, business or society? Truly, we live in the times when new ideas are worth than a million dollars—and both the recent economic crisis, the mass exodus into Europe, Islamists extremism in Nigeria, Somalia, Car and Syria and Iraq have helped to put that into perspective.

On the part of Ferdinand Marcos, what had he really observed? Let's hear it from the horse's mouth as he summed up the fears I have for a nation whose people don't heed my appeal and act immediately.
"The Filipino, it seems, has lost his soul, his dignity, and his courage," declared Ferdinand Marcos, later a longer serving President Ferdinand Marcos of The Philippines. *"We have come upon a phase of our history when ideals are only a veneer for greed and power, (in public and private affairs) when devotion to duty and dedication to a public trust are to be weighted at all times against private advantages and personal gain, and when loyalties can be traded...Our government is in the iron grip of venality,"* he said, *"Its treasury is barren, its resources are wasted, its civil service is slothful and indifferent, its armed forces demoralized and its councils sterile. We are in crisis. You know that the government treasury is empty,"* observed Ferdinand Marcos.

You realize you aren't Ferdinand Marcos. I am not. We are, certainly, not Filipinos—excepting the Filipino reader of course!

Our problems aren't necessarily the same as theirs. But I hope you realize how strong his observation was. Despite all these woes, if the administration of the state, and the people don't seem to realize the mess they are in and as a result of such illusive contentment they cannot do anything about it, they are finished. And notice that what I say to the Filipino, I say it to you the immediate reader.

That's why it will be worthwhile to attempt to channel the Marcos fears toward our society if we should be objective about the real magnitude of tragedy we are facing.

Ferdinand Marcos gives us a very example and so is Obama. Of these two, it can be said by many of my readers, it is hard to relate to, then go back to the beginning of the book and meet Benedict Emanuel, an individual who is like me and you. He holds no public office in the ranks of the two others. But he has had courage to do his part. This is the true spirit this nation needs. We don't need the spirit of Konyagi, the local liquor brand which claims to be: *the spirit of the nation.* This is the true spirit we need to adopt if the nation has to rise again from its knees and assume its rightful position ordained to her by god in as far as its location, history and resources are concerned.

Truly we cannot solve the problems we face useless we honestly chat out our problems—and listen to one another. We, I mean the academia and the citizens—cannot afford to leave the future of our lives in the hands of the third party—be that donors or the self motivated president and his government. You agree no third party insurance policy ever worked for the any person, right? That's how we should conduct ourselves. That's how we should engage the government and the households. And the beginning of this change is in the coming out and chatting our problems —openly. Truly, Ferdinand Marcos couldn't be more right when he said that: "There are many things we don't want about the world. Let us not mourn them. Let is change them." For indeed, "The world suffers a lot not very much because of the violence of bad people but rather because of the silence of good people," aptly observed Napoleon Bonaparte"

As we edge to the end of the chapter you should have, by now, observed that I am directly addressing you, yes you, my immediate reader that he should take action. I am also by now addressing especially the indifferent reader especially, one who says, "I am fine, my children are in the top end schools or even abroad; and my business or position in the public office is ok." I don't know you! One thing though I can tell you with certainty. If the nation is drowning, it will drown with you. That's why you should be mindful of the fact that however much a nation is wealthy, it cannot and won't stay as healthy for long if it doesn't change its priorities—overtime. That's an analysis we are going to end this chapter with. Sadly, no nation can have right priorities without establishing national ideals—ideals that trickle down to individual persons, families, corporations and institutions; ideals and principles that set the bottom-line; ideals that create the middle ground; ideals that favor all but repress none! No nation can ever remain wealthy and strong if its people opt for quick fix, eyeing short term gains than focusing on the long-term realities. "A society will collapse," rightly admonished Karl Marx, "if it ceases to produce material wealth!"

THE DECLINE OF THE GREAT BRITAIN AS A WORLD POWER

Briefly almost anyone analyzing the rise of the Great Britain as the world superpower will simply identify agrarian and industrial revolutions as factors for her triumph. Some will mention her naval power as a factor for her triumph. But behind these apparent factors there are bona fide dynamics within a society that are behind rise of a nation. The same can be said about the decline of any nation. I mean by analyzing the failure of any nation we can identify factors behind rise or fall of nations. These are true success factors and naval power or industrial revolution is merely the necessary end-product.

But before we analyze the factors behind rise and fall of nation, and in this case, the decline of the United Kingdom as a world power, let's first clear out any doubts about our subtitle: The Decline of the United Kingdom as a World Power: is it true that the UK has declined and is no longer a world power?

The British Empire was at its height, the largest empire in history and, for over a century, was the foremost global power. By 1922 the British Empire held sway over about 458 million people, one-fifth of the world's population at the time. The empire covered more than 33,700,000 km², almost a quarter of the Earth's total land area. As a result, its political, legal, linguistic and cultural legacy is widespread. At the peak of its power, the phrase "the empire on which the sun never sets" was often used to describe the British Empire, because its expanse around the globe meant that the sun was always shining on at least one of its territories.[25]

Today Britain has lost her influence and her economic as well as social state is in jeopardy. She cannot compete with the United States, Japan, China, or even her neighbors Germany and France in terms of her economic power and influence in the world affairs. How did Britain rise to power? How did she decline to the extent that she is no longer a world power? How did she lose her influence on the earth?

Many associate the decline of the empire to the wars that she fought, two major wars that milked her resources and drained her muscle. But is it all? Why hasn't she recovered after all these years? Let us go deep into the British society to analyze what dynamics that are real factors behind her decline.

In his confidential dispatch which does not, needless to say, reach us from him and was presumably written for very limited circulation, but it is so unusually forthright and timely, as to merit publication virtually in full, written from the British Embassy in Paris on March 31, 1979, addressed to the Rt. Hon. David Owen, MP, "Britain's decline; its causes and consequences" Sir Nicholas Henderson who was then the ambassador for the Great Britain to France declared the backsliding of the UK's muscle in international affairs when he said: "We are unable to influence events in the way we want because we do not have the power or will to do so," he said adding that "our standards have slipped."

Identifying slow or low GDP growth, low productivity in what he termed as, "the essential and long-term problem of productivity;" he further cited the output per man-hour in manufacturing industry to be lower in Britain than France and Germany; lack of professionalism in British management (something that can be said to be unprecedented); bad attitude and poor priorities about which he said: "We have a different attitude towards a career in industry. In … Germany…industry has tended to attract the best people, whereas in the United Kingdom those leaving school and university seem less prepared to make a career in industry than to join a merchant bank in the City of London or one of the public services. It is partly a question of tradition and prestige but also one of finance…."

Whereas in a sick nation professionals migrate to politics, he cites for instance the French foreign minister, Mr. Francois-Poncet, who began his career in the Foreign Service and then had a spell in industry. Other factors for the decline of the UK include migration of British engineers to France or the States for better working conditions; adding that: "…so far as the management of major capital projects by government is concerned our vision appears limited and our purpose changeable, at any rate compared with France and Germany," he said.

"This," he continued, "This is particularly noticeable in transport. We started work on two large plans, the third London airport and the Channel tunnel, only to cancel both. To arrive nowadays at London Airport from a French or German airport is to be made immediately aware that our standards have slipped."

Citing another flaw, he said: "In trade-union structure, as in management, our present difficulties are rooted in the distant past…"

Both as a symptom and factor behind the weakness in the society, he cited inter-relation between the economy and foreign policy admitting that there was a decline of British power in international affairs.

Citing the failures in the international policy that led to the decline of her influence and devaluation crisis of 1967, he did not shy away from the fact that: "General de Gaulle was able to say the same year that the United Kingdom was too weak economically to be able to join the common market," adding that indeed "...we are unable to influence events in the way we want because we do not have the power or will to do so." He also added "...anyone who has followed American policy towards Europe closely over the past few years will know how much our role as Washington's European partner has declined in relation to that of Germany or France...because of... economic strength."

With an attitude and the role I can relate to what Tanzania seems to be playing in the East African community, he blamed the decline of the UK on staying behind when other move forward toward a greater cooperation rather remaining "In every respect, except distance, we in Britain are closer to our kinsmen in Australia and New Zealand on the far side of the world than we are to Europe," he quoted. Putting more flesh to the bones he said that: "Referring to the ideal of European integration, Mr. Anthony Eden said in January, 1952, "This is something which we know, in our bones, we cannot do...For Britain's story and her interests lie beyond the continent of Europe. Our thoughts move across the seas..."

At the start of the European Coal and Steel Community the Financial Times described it as a "cross between a frustrated cartel and a pipe dream," substantiating that "we held back from joining in schemes of greater European unity; ...Then when the others showed that they were determined to go ahead on their own we found that we were unable to prevent them doing so or to shape what emerged in the way we wanted. ...The recent intensification in the Paris-Bonn relationship," he continued, "owes a good deal to our economic weakness, as to our a-European diplomacy.

President Giscard is not really very interested in us at the moment and gives the impression that Anglo-French relations only feature in his mind when the annual summit comes along. It is sometimes said in London that if only we pursued our interests in Europe as ruthlessly as the French did we would have a scoring rate as high as theirs.

This is another example of how we overestimate our influence and our nuisance value: we do not count in Europe like the French; the other countries of the community know that they can get along quite well—some say better—without us as they have done for years.

"But there is another distinction which I must make in parenthesis here. French policy is certainly hard-headed now, but there is more to it than that: it is constructive about Europe (e.g. direct elections, the European Council, the Three Wise Men) which makes the ruthlessness both more effective and more acceptable to the rest of the community," he said before he admitted that:

"the facts of our decline are too well known for us to be able to persuade foreign observers that there is really little wrong with our industrial scene... we have come nowadays to be identified with malaise as closely as in the old days we were associated with success. In many public statements Britain is mentioned as a model not to follow if economic disaster is to be avoided... The French press is full of articles about Britain's plight...

"But what is amazing looking back is the way in which the British government reached so important a decision. The full British cabinet never dealt with the question.

"Neither the prime minister, nor the foreign secretary (Mr. Bevin was in hospital), nor the chancellor of the exchequer, nor the lord chancellor, were present at the ministerial meeting which took the decision against British participation in the European Coal and Steel Community (ECSC). ...

"We have indeed gone so far down market that we now tend to become subcontractors where we do not get the benefits of high added value. (The British manufacturing industry, may it be said in parenthesis, has also found itself unable to meet the demands of the hard-headed British consumers who have increasingly looked to foreign producers).

"The half-heartedness of Britain's political commitment to Europe is reflected in a similar lack of total involvement by British industrialists in meeting the requirements of the highly competitive continental market."

THE FUTURE

As said Sir Nicholas Henderson, "Even the most pessimistic account of our decline contains grounds for hope. The fact that France and the Federal Republic of Germany have managed to achieve such progress in so relatively short a time shows what can be done if there is the necessary will and leadership. Anybody who remembers the state of affairs in those countries in the decade following the war and compares it with the present day must conclude that nothing in a country's future is inevitable and that everything depends upon the national purpose. So far as we are concerned, if the fault that we are underlings lies "not in our stars but in ourselves", we are surely capable, unless our national character has undergone some profound metamorphosis, of resuming mastery of our fate. But a considerable jolt is going to be needed if a lasting attenuation of civic purpose and courage is to be averted. North Sea oil should provide the material impulse, just as coal did two centuries ago. There are human elements that favor us compared with others: our political stability and the absence of that tendency to explosion that could always afflict France.

"It would be outside the scope of this valedictory dispatch to try to chart the course that we might follow to turn around our present situation. Obviously there are no simple solutions and the difficulties are to be found as much in attitudes as in institutions. At the risk of oversimplification I should like to end with three conclusions …

"First, if we are to defend our interests in Europe there must be a change in the style of our policy towards it …We should be able to put at the service of the community the imagination, tolerance and commonsense that have formed our own national institutions…Pragmatism may be a good basis for the government of a more or less uniform country speaking a single language.…

"This may call for the sort of originality of political thought in foreign affairs ….Secondly, viewed from abroad, it looks as though the facts of our present circumstances are not universally recognized in Britain.

The British people do not give the impression that they are fully aware of how far Britain's economy has fallen behind that of our European neighbors or of the consequences of this upon living standards. Naturally people are conscious that they are better off now than 25 years ago but they may not know to what extent others in Europe have done much better or of the effects needed to reverse the trend. As Isaac Newton wrote, the important thing is "to learn not to teach". It may be our turn to learn from others, having been teachers for so long.

"In this fact-facing exercise the authorities may have a role to play so as to ensure that the public do not remain in ignorance of something that is a matter of national concern. It is impossible for anyone of my generation to forget how little the British government of the 1930s did to enlighten the British people about the rise of Nazi Germany.

"The needs today are certainly of a different kind but there does seem to be a responsibility upon government to prevent people being unaware of something that will certainly one day affect their future.

"There is also a task of explaining the community to the British public rather than making it the scapegoat for our ills.

"Finally, and as a corollary to this process of enlightenment, there would appear to be a need at the present time to do something to stimulate a sense of national purpose, of something akin to what has inspired the French and Germans over the past 25 years. No doubt the sort of patriotic language and flag waving of former times is inappropriate for us today.

"The revival of Germany has not owed anything to that kind of stimulus. But nevertheless the Germans have felt motivated by the dire need to rise from the ashes in 1945, and they have had to recover from their past politically too....and the obligation that every one of them feels to make a contribution to economic, as well as political, recovery...

"The French on the other hand have found their national revival in a more traditional appeal to patriotism. They started at the bottom of the pit but it has not only been de Gaulle who has played on the need to overcome the country's sense of defeat and national humiliation.

Giscard is no less ready to play on chauvinistic chords. In a speech that he made recently that lasted only eight minutes he used the word "France" over 23 times and the word "win" seven times... readier to make sacrifices …

"These then are the words with which I would like to end my official career, and if it is said that they go beyond the limits of an ambassador's normal responsibilities I would say that the fulfillment of these responsibilities is not possible in Western Europe in the present uncertain state of our economy and of our European policy.

"A representative abroad has a duty to draw the attention of the authorities at home to the realities of how we look, just as he has an obligation to try to persuade the government and people of the country to which he is accredited that present difficulties must be kept in perspective. The tailored reporting from Berlin in the late 1930s and the encouragement it gave to the policy of appeasement is a study in scarlet for every postwar diplomat. Viewed from the continent our standing at the present time is low. But this is not for the first time in our history, and we can recover if the facts are known and faced and if the British people (or Tanzania people for that matter) can be fired with a sense of national will such as others have found these past years. For the benefit of ourselves and of Europe (for Africa for that matter) let us then show the adaptability that has been the hallmark of our history—and do so now so that the warnings of this dispatch may before long sound no more ominous than the recorded alarms of a wartime siren."[26]

6. THE YOUTH: A LOST GENERATION

"Real knowledge is to know the extent of one's ignorance."—Confucius

As humans we have a tendency of clinging to things of the past or less meaningful habits we ought to have done away with. This, unfortunately, is the situation in which we find our education, the youth and the society as a whole.

Here's a dramatic event that happened many years ago when the author was but a young boy. I bring it here to show the analogy of what is happening and the consequences we should expect as a result. The event happened almost in the sky.

Well, did I say almost? It happened over the Ruwenzori Mountain—one of the highest dwellings of humanity. It happened at the time when the author's father worked for a mining company in Uganda. This was a little before we returned home during the standoff prior the Tanzania-Uganda war.

I can close my eyes and see the beautiful mining town of Kilembe and the hills and the ever green scenery throughout the horizon.

I can see the magnificent theatres and clubs and all facilities of a typical modern civilization that have left a big mark on me. Kilembe is a sizeable mountainous mining town high in the skies attached to the earth by the heights of the Ruwenzori. Kilembe therefore was a so very modern town with very many wealthy men and women famous locally and internationally. Among the famous people at the time, Mukwangara was tops but for quite reasons you cannot call ordinary. Source of his fame? His old and the slowest Volkswagen Beetle from which he derived the famous name he adored—Mukwangara. Mukwangara in *Luganda* vernacular means old or uselessly outdated. Driving a car whether in front or behind Mukwangara was quite something. It was fatal.

Lethal. So you had either to overtake him by all means, or else park the car by the roadside and let him vanish before you switched on your car. Why? Simple. You parked lest his old car failed and came back bumping into your face or your rear depending on the position you were in. Yet he would still as slow as a snail vanish in style!

That was standard. Individual personal friends had failed and so teams of elders of respected people beseeched him to dispose off the thing, or else park it in a garage and let it rot there where he would always go back to admire this vintage stuff when he wanted to, without having to risk killing other people in the neighborhood or getting himself killed by it. I know this is true because my father was one of these elders. But he wouldn't listen.

He swore over his dead body that he wouldn't sell the thing. It was a vintage souvenir to him. The Chinese have a saying that fits Mukwangara's opinion. They say: *The Older the Better.* For him it applied to cars. The older the car, the better the machine, maintained Mukwangara! I didn't comprehend his logic for only wine and alcoholic spirits turned best with age.

I learned that logic never applied to machines or cars! Cars and machines do tear and wear out as they age. But that wasn't sense that Mukwangara would buy into. As I grew up, I learned that he had a point. We live in a generation where our youth craving quick dollar, they don't take time to create quality stuff. That's why old is gold especially today. You can forget the car makers and venture into music and see for yourself. I will come to this with details later.

On this evening, well that was one sunny Saturday, unfortunately before the Kilembe Mines Authorities had sanctioned him against driving the thing, the day when the road was clear and the traffic had cleared for many copper mine workers were on a weekend break.

Then as the light wind hit from the high Ruwenzori heights, Mukwangara's old vintage beetle and quite a tired car sped faster past our roadside big house close to the highway down the green mountain to Kasese town at the foot of the living mountain.

People were excited. The event caused a great animation and fanfare.

Finally Mukwangara had been speeding his beetle already.

We cheered him as he sped past from the Kyanjuki hills down town. Others assumed that he was driving to a grocery or a club somewhere in town probably to grab a drink or some merchandize in the supermarket downtown. He was cheered like a real hero. And hero he was. He loved great things. One of his other greatest treasures was his dog. He had a black and white dog he adored so dearly—a dog that looked like a horse in terms of its size and magnificence. Now as he sped, no one ever projected what was going on in his mind or the tragedy that was in the making! A little less than five minutes later, he had vanished, disappeared.

Adults turned and left. I joined the rest of my peers, the children, happily resuming our *Up and Down* which was literally rugby before we switched to *Tutatokamu Maragani*. The latter is a sport in which a group of children stood in a circle, locked themselves in a hula hoop or a large ring, made of plastic, tied around their waist and jumped around spinning in a circle with no hope of getting out until presumably they fell dead singing its own name: "how shall we get out of this situation?"

The two were our favorite sports those days. Before the sun set the whole of Kilembe was in shock. Two events had ensued.

Yes, Mukwangara's old car's speed was one thing but indeed how he had survived death was a miracle that only Mary mother f Jesus could have supplicated. Belatedly, after crushing on roadside coppery rocks, he had sped cruising the fierce waters of the river Nyamwamba before he was rescued by a mining rescue team after they were tipped of the adventure by a few miners on duty high on the floating chair-lifts which were a set of electric chairs that commuted the miners across the treacherous deadly canyon-like Ruwenzori ridges.

What a spectacular show that was! A few days later I saw him with Plaster of Paris all over his body. He had had one of the most fatal accidents in the whole of Africa.

He had defended his vintage for centuries and it had fooled him for as many years back. But finally the inevitable had come to pass! His old rusting car had yielded! Breaks had failed or rather rust failed him.

To this Lincoln said, "You can cheat some people all the time but you cannot cheat all the people all the time." Emerson said "What you are," said Ralph Waldo Emerson, "What you are, stands over you the while and thunders so that I cannot hear what you say to the contrary."

The Mukwangara story is typical of what is happening in our society today. It is the same thing we see pervading our education system in the country today. Like Mukwangara's beetle, is education in the country.

And the youth and the society as a whole fall in the position of Mukwangara himself. Both the beetle and its driver and passengers will yield one day if we don't act fast and now! What is the solution?

You recognize you are now engaged in discussion of the challenges facing our society today and alternative remedies if we should rescue the youth and guarantee the future of the nation. The insurance lies in building the ideal graduates or scholars. Who then are ideal graduates?

Building ideal graduates ensures that we produce future ideal youth and citizens.

To be able to address the challenges facing the nation, we have got to address challenges facing the youth.

While we shall discuss in a great deal about the principles of success and the fact that one cannot succeed if he doesn't encompass certain qualities through the proceeding chapters, let us briefly here say that today we experience certain negative characteristics pervading the youth group which slowly spreading through every social and economic patterns of this important population group.

Look around you. Where's the next Mwalimu Julius Kambarage Nyerere? Sokoine? Where's the next Dr. Mengi? Where is the next Dr. Kimei? Dr. Mwakyembe or Magufuri? Prof Shivji? Prof. Mukandala? Where is the next Filbert Bayi?

We don't even see the replacement for the local Tx. Moshi William even five years down the line! *Where're our efforts?*

Unfortunately, some constructive insights aren't vivid to so many.

We see the world is almost at stand still. We don't see talents procured anymore as it was through the past generations.

As a nation we have crossed the 50th anniversary. How seriously have we evaluated where we are relative to where we ought to have been? Our priorities? Are they right? Have we looked outside the box for new sources of growth? These can be new ideas in education or economics whether at personal, household, corporate or national level. We can change or choose to remain as a weak and dependent society as we may be today. We can really do everything we want.

We only have to choose what we want to be—and just be. Yet we don't have enough space or options to make decisions as we please. If the youth in the country prefer leisure to labor; if the country has an aging population; if we cannot reeducate our youth or transform them; if our workforce cannot innovate or produce sufficiently because that's how they have been conditioned by the education in place; if a nation's budget is sixty percent dependent on donor funds, if the budget on education is only dismal, if we are slow to respond to new needs and ideas, do we then have a say over our future?

Are we then any free as a people? Is it any wonder therefore that David Cameron and his American counterparts impose on us conditions I cannot bear to mention without being washed with shame when they, themselves, are protecting their children against the same? What are we learning from Greece's recent contemptible rescue package? It really doesn't matter whether you are in Europe or Africa when you are poor—you have to give up your dignity as a person or society.

And how outrageous it is how our leaders are quiet about it, or especially when they cannot come out loud and clear in support of president Museveni or Mugabe who have severally stood up and out against the same? When we see a nation losing arable land on desertification; when we see a nation's cash crops losing markets by volumes sold in shrinking prices; when we see a nation's sixty percent of its natural resources depleted through mismanagement and poaching, and thereby raze ecosystem; loosing cloud cover and potential rains and thereby ruining agriculture and tourism, and therefore national income; when we see a rise in poverty and thereof youth emigrating into the cities; when we therefore see skyrocketing unemployment and social economic disorder; when we thereof see a nation further trailing into helplessness and waning individual and overall national self confidence and self esteem, however unwelcome that is, but we surely must then realize that we—as individual persons households institutions corporations and the nation as a whole—are slowly decomposing!?

Though it is a wonder that under these circumstances, if such a society still has some form of life in it, and if it still desires to stage a comeback and reclaim its own right to life, prosperity, liberty and dignity, it must do something about the foregoing circumstances.

Failure to do so, failure to rise to the challenge, is to surrender to whatever life—and David Cameron and co.—throw at you.

We all know what Uganda went through attempting to reinforce its Ugandan African cultures. We all know what Cameron attached as precondition to aid among commonwealth countries.

We all know what is going on in Libya with deposition of Gadafi.

We all know that many African countries didn't love what was going on before and during his deposition. But we all know very few African leaders dared speak out. And we know why. "Amani mache," so goes Ruhima-Runyambo saying, "Amani mache gatel'micho milunji!"

It literally means that the weak people tend to be agreeable. They are not free to say or do what they want. And that doesn't only affect the low income countries alone? No!

Sir Nicholas Henderson who was then the British ambassador to France said in that confidential valedictory he wrote to The Rt. Hon David Owen, MP in London concerning the backsliding UK's muscle in international affairs saying: "we are unable to influence events in the way we want because we do not have the power or will to do so."

But that's not the last resort. It's not desirable. It's not one of the options. It is out of question.

Do we really know that we have problems with the youth? If so, what are these problems—and to what extent are we not on the same page?

How does the youth form the core of both the problem—and solution? Part of the solution is to glimpse at what our youth do today with respect to their daily lives with respect to work and education in general.

How does the youth play as the back bone of the nation? But , do we know we are part of the problem or solution therefore?

To illustrate, call to mind such situations as those of Nigeria, Congo D.R and Tanzania, countries which generously offer conspicuous examples of natural resources wealthy nations which yet remain so dependent economically—and intellectually. What would happen if we empowered the youth—in terms of work or technical skills and character—to take charge? Nigeria is a leader in drilling mineral fuel from bowels of its rich soil. D.R. Congo, like Tanzania, is richer in diamond and gold. Tanzania is the only mining home to tanzanite—whence it derived its name.

While Nigeria enjoys the pride of being a leader as exporter of fuel, her leadership is only in crude oil, whose lucrative jobs are foreign controlled. Besides, Nigeria has to import its own gasoline and diesel from the same countries that imported her oil only this time refined and therefore more expensive.

Nigeria has had to subsidize its fuel for its local market as a result. Refining it at home would accrue with it economies of scale involved, creating employment opportunities at home, opportunities that are presently enjoyed abroad. On her part, Tanzania as it may be same for DR Congo or any other mineral rich country, is one of the country with richest gold and diamond reserves.

But she earns only a smaller proportion of its gold and diamond revenues. What happens in most crude forms of partnerships in the world today, is that the soil is hauled and exported overseas to be extracted for ore and then philanthropically the foreign investor determines what he will give back to the government. Tanzanite, a precious ore only mined in Tanzania, provides one of the very conspicuous illustrations of the change we need.

Though tanzanite is only mined in Tanzania, India and Kenya are the world leaders in exporting tanzanite to the rest of the global market. For instance in 2005, global export figures for tanzanite show that out of total annual sales figures for tanzanite gemstones amounting to $400m, Tanzania received a mere $16m.[27]

According to Eng. Paul Masanja the commissioner for minerals in the ministry of energy and minerals, for instance, India exported tanzanite worth of dollars 300 million (T.sh509 billion) in 2013, while Kenya earned100 million dollars (T.sh173 billion) from tanzanite sales the same year compared to a scanty 38 million dollars (T.sh45.5 billion) value of tanzanite exported by Tanzania—the only place in the world where tanzanite is mined—losing about 80 percent of the value of annual tanzanite sales.[28]

But with credit to President Museveni on admitting that there are places his government had gone wrong, addressing Rich Management club members in Nairobi, Kenya, recently, he indicated that though Uganda is one of the leading coffee growers and sellers, but she received only one dollar for every kilo sold losing 14 dollars by exporting it raw to the UK where it is refined by nestle and sold as instant coffee at 15 dollars.

In other words Museveni said Uganda was actually donating 14 dollars to the UK government. Countries following this model of investment will be poor and get poorer as the sun sets each day eternally until He comes He who shall judge the world. Amen.

And the real question is this: Where is that great country gone to—a country mother to Mwalimu Julius Kambarage Nyerere and other great names like Salim Ahmed Salim, Asha Rose Migiro, Anna Tibaijuka, Shaban Robert and many other great scholars and international leaders and inventors. Recall that Tanzania is the land home to Kilimanjaro, the Serengeti, Zanzibar and Ngorongoro.

This is the land home to natural beauties that pressured Dr. Leakey and Mary Leakey to come down to this the country.

Many Europeans, Americans and Asians choose to make this country their homeland after they discovered its beauty. We know many professionals and diplomats who decided to stay put long after their term of service ended. And this is nothing new. Indians and many Persians have since of old chosen to make Tanzania their home. It is the land which lured Seyyid Said, the Sultan of Oman to shift his capital city to this country in the 17th century.

Dr. Livingstone was persuaded to leave the country but he didn't accept to leave until when his health began to deteriorate. Furthermore, when the Ngoni from South Africa set foot in the country they stopped trekking further north choosing to stay and make this country their permanent home. Many years before the Ngoni trek to Tanzania, the Nilotes and Hamitic Hima from north and majority Bantu population from the Congo arrived here. All these groups fell in love with the country and settled down for good thereby ending their treks further north or south, west or east respectively. At the global level, where are the fresh R. W. Emerson's or Benjamin Carson's? Where's the next Napoleon Hill? The greatest sportsmen of the last generation, where are they?

The author has searched but cannot find today another Shakespeare, Julius Caesar, Mahatma Gandhi or Lincoln. We don't see either Karl Marx or Einstein today. Where's the new Newton?

Who can fill the shoes of Julius Kambarage Nyerere, Kwame Nkrumah, or Nelson Mandela in the continent? Tell me! Where are Muhammad Ali, Pele, Ronaldo de Lima, Zinedine Zidane, Tiger Woods and Michael Schumacher internationally as we locally don't see new Filbert Bayi, Gidemus Shahanga, Nyambui or Lunyamila and Zamoyoni Mogella in the world of sports?

Whereas we have better facilities and sources of knowledge than the golden generation of the past but surprisingly we cannot compare with the last generation one little bit! Why? Now the question is: Is this generation a lost generation? Is it a generation of weaklings? Is it because we are born differently and so lack natural talents?

I don't buy that. The real problem lies in the thought-pattern of our youth. And it is the educational policy makers and academics who have failed to accommodate the youth. If this was the case we then need to work on attitude, character and mindset. We would also need to evaluate our priorities.

Just ask yourself: Do we have solution or even an attempt in place to retrace our feet back to where we went wrong—where we lost the trail? Our society needs a *revival program*. Not a religious one though. We need academic transformation and social-economic change. We need to revise and reform ourselves as individuals and society as a whole.

Realizing that the failure is also attributed to the failure at the family level, our society needs spiritual renewal. We can then safely now say we need to overhaul the ethos of our society. We need to overhaul our social system. And this is a noble choice when it deems necessary to break and rebuild all over again.

Do you realize that sometimes the best way to build is to break? We need to break the negative mindset in our society. We need to change focus. And priorities.

We have got to change the thought pattern and transform how we learn, train and teach in our homes, schools and workplaces and identify, incentivize and recognize new ideas that lead to prosperity in the society. We need to recognize thinkers and achievers and reward them.

Did I say focus? Thought pattern? Transformation? Yes, all of that. We could do with changing all that. Look around the society and you will be astonished at the value we place on partying than we put on work. We place more attention on arts and entertainment than we value education. We spend heavily on arts and artists themselves than we spend on education and real work—learning, reading and writing of books—which seem to be of less importance among the leadership and corporate sponsorship.

We praise burial services than looking after the sick. What do you mean? You rightly ask.

The society as a whole is organized to provide proper burial ceremonies than preserving, recreating and making life better. This is nothing but a sign of resentment and hopelessness. Presently, we see a new wave of mob justice and revenge from youth in the streets especially against the wealthy people. The youth mobs today are taking things in their own hands by burning down to ashes the cars or the driver or both. Why is it recurrent? Hatred! Envy!

And if the attitude: If I cannot win, I will let everyone else lose! It is a tooth for a tooth and nail for a nail. Back of it is to surrender to the circumstances one faces. It is also due to loss of confidence in oneself on one hand, and in the system on the other in particular.

But these people are as well these drunk often when in action. Recently a mob burned down a person convicted for stealing some goods from a shop. Proof? How did it start? Somebody saw someone chasing the deceased shouting *Mwizi, Mwizi, Thief, Thief, Chori, Chori...!* Enough! One picked a shovel. Another one picked a match box. Another one filled several plastic gallons of petrol and rushed after the mob. Another ran with a machete etc.

Soon the cameras witnessed a great fire one that could be envied only by the fires of hell. How did they prove he was not innocent? A person must be considered innocent until proven guilty.

At least here lawyers discovered some useful idea! This culture has far deep problems. It causes a spirit of animals amongst us.

It causes trauma to children and builds revengeful hearts and hatred among the people in the society. Rwandan genocide or killings among the Sunni and Shiites in Arabia started that way—Arabs killing their own brethrens.

In India Muslims and non Muslims slaughter one another in masses to date. It started the same way. What a nation are we building? What is the future of a nation like this? Where has humanity gone to?

If you questioned why get concerned by the youth, you now know the majority of culprits are the youth.

What do you expect from a youth whose mindset is what Rebecca fine described as, "The dog-eat-dog, CLAW YOUR WAY TO THE TOP, ANYTHING FOR A BUCK MENTALITY SO MANY BELIEVE TO BE THE ONLY WAY TO WEALTH! ….If you are not yet where you want to be in terms of income and personal success, "the problem may not be what you are doing so much as how you are doing it. And that begins with how you think."[29]

What then should we expect of the future country home to youth with such a disposition! Have you ever considered the fact that it is not what we have at our disposal that makes us better, healthier, wealthier or freer? It isn't not the environment we are in that makes us better or lesser.

You may be astonished if I told you that I have breathed the same air and washed from the same waters Jesus breathed and bathed but I'm not anywhere near his greatness! Yes it is true! Some of you and I are breathing the same African air Jesus breathed. I have drunk and washed from River Kagera—and the Nile back in Uganda—the spring of the waters which served Jesus when was an asylum seeker here in Africa around two thousand years back.

We are engaged, you realize, in laying down the CT scan to generate cross-sectional view and, three-dimensional images of the internal structures of the body of our society as a nation and human society as a whole, an analysis we need before we know if we have a problem and if so, reach the decision on what we should do to transform the society.

You also realize that through the previous chapters we introduced to you how Benny did a great job by narrowing down the problem we have from a vague "everything is wrong," to something generally more specific.

And though he mentioned that the author had briefly explained something about the problem at hand, one thing he hadn't been informed of by the author at the time.

Though the author had sent a summary note discussing the problem as a profile for his maiden training program for schools and workplaces intending to empower the youth and the nation as a whole: households, schools, business sector, the public sector and the development partners, the author had actually set out to organize and write a training material for the program.

Call it a material or book, the author was engaged in putting down a comprehensive assessment of the problem, its symptoms, causes, effects, who are victims and what are the alternative solutions. Here notice you are privileged to be reading through that comprehensive program. With this book the author has gone to the specifics as probably Benny had demanded subconsciously. That's why we believe the ball is now entering in your court for before this book was written you probably had an alibi. Now you have no more alibis. The publication of this book exposes the reader as it shames the mediocre. As for the positive minded reader, here is my message: raise your chin, force back the gathering tears, for the genuine smile is building up within you. Victory is coming. Amen!

Here and now as your gifted eyes and good hands touch this book, recognize you are engaged in something of greater meaning to the future of your life and that of your own family. As you navigate through, look around and try to reflect on the previous chapters with attention to the diagnosis or health check of the society.

Are you happy with your life? Your job? Education? Are you happy with present prospects of the society today? The youths? Students? Employees? Are they rightly contributing to the value in the society? Do you have to supervise your employees? Many employers find the adults to be old and cold blooded while the youth seem to be shoddy, sloppy and crude and indolent in the eyes of the adults. The youth?

Yes, the youth. Do they seem to be as you would have wished? Do they know their responsibilities? Do they even reckon to have one? Do they offer you with the right role models for your young children? How do our people conduct themselves? Do they work as hard or simply sit back and complain? Corruption? Quick fix?

And what about the leadership? Is it all ok? Who is to blame? Stop it! I mean stop the blame game. Jesus asked his disciples thus; "What have you done more and better than the others?" And yes you cannot blame the leaders. No society can produce leaders dissimilar from itself. For someone to successfully lead such a nation, he must think differently—he must do and be different from the herd. What have you done about it?

Very recently, I crossed a street and a big billboard reading *The Legal Sector Reform Program welcomed* me. The words Reform and Program caught my attention. I wondered if we really have reforms in the land.

The moment triggered me to think of the as many of such programs as Public Sector Reform Program and many other government reforms. Such reforms cannot—well; I wanted to say *such reforms cannot be effective*. To be more spot-on—such reforms have never been effective or efficient. They have never delivered lasting desired impact. It can never be so unless we tackle the problems from the source. The legal sector, the public sector and the government are all formed by the people and are for the people. Reforming the methodologies or department, or even the government, is useless and a waste of funds and time and resources if we don't really reform the people themselves first.

We can do this by influencing and thereby reforming how they think. We should work on their thought pattern—and how they prioritize their preferences in life. It is only after we have reformed the mindset of the people that we can actually think of other skills or even reforming the structure and system to make them work more effectively. I must make a remark on the fact that we have some good programs as well as some good youth and some good leaders in our society. Well, we have some good reform programs too. The question remains on the commitment among the leadership and the people toward these reforms. Nothing ever grows on its own. These reforms have to be nurtured and they need a very close notice. This doesn't only require funds. But it requires something else viz. the mindset change.

As you read simply recognize that the failures and malfunctions of, or within, the systems are nothing more or less than the symptoms of the real inherent ailment we exhibit as a society. They are not the root of, or problem itself. To find the solution we must tackle the problem by the roots. If you had doubts when you first put your money into this book, probably by now you are beginning to realize that "You Got the Right One, Baby!"

7. SIGNIFICANCE OF THE YOUTH: THE YOUTH AND THE FUTURE OF THE NATION

"The future promise of any nation can be directly measured by the present prospects of its youth."
—John F. Kennedy

Whenever the topic about the youth comes to the fore, the youth tend to be on the defensive ready to protect themselves expecting to be criticized or attacked. So I know some of my readers from this age bracket will already be grumbling saying, "here now comes the old course—*The Youth of Today."* In fact I know such a topic tends to put them off right from the onset. They consider such a discussion as a blame game.

They fire back saying the author is self righteous for "even your parents referred to you in the same way. So what's a big deal?" And their verdict is partly true. The only difference is the magnitude of the potential laxity or mediocrity—which also cannot be blamed on the youth again. The today's youth face a very different situation. Technology has changed a great deal. ICT and globalization are working against convention. Environmental changes, economic crisis hand in hand with growing world's income disparity, and the rise of the axis of evil that surrounds terrorism has bequeathed our youth with a very unfortunate and tragic position.

So I will not concentrate with the blame game. Indeed here is my promise—a promise I must make to the reader right from the onset. This is a different story. Yes we will focus on the youth, but the only difference you are going to see is that, we aren't going to simply put the blame on the youth. We will as well explain why we believe the youth can do—and be—far better and greater things. We will also, in this book, attempt to describe where we as elders went wrong. And that's not all. We will attempt to offer alternative solutions—solutions that remedy the prevailing mediocrity leading to awareness amongst the youth that they can do and be far more and better as persons—mediocre or not.

Through the preceding, but especially the upcoming pages in this book or even the whole series, you are introduced to the need of developing the qualities of the ideal person—qualities we impart to our trainees—ideals that transform the mediocre children, students, employees, sportsmen, and politicians into superstars. It is then these true superstars, these ideal citizens, who turn the organizations and the nation into super brands and superpowers. In fact, as if to demonstrate how pivotal` this topic is, we dedicate the entire volume on the topic, i.e., The Ideal Scholar (or graduate) as a separate paperback.

In this chapter, therefore, we will dedicate our efforts more in laying down both the significance of , and how you can actually identify today's youth. If the youth still ask why us: then the answer is that this group is so pivotal to the future of the nation than any other population group. Yes it is a bracket where besides criminals, we find more mediocre members of the society than in any other, but it is a group consisting the largest number of scholars, or graduates, a group from which the future leaders come from, a group which therefore is the backbone of the nation.

Yet, we decided also to concentrate with the youth because, unfortunately, despite how key the youth are to the prosperity of the society, our youths lack qualities that otherwise make a person productive. They lack objectivity and good attitude—the things a person ought to gain on having graduated from schools. But since character or ideals are things you cannot buy in the open market, schools and households ought to install these virtues in our children. Yes the schools will say the students are spoilt brats: because why? Their parents didn't prepare them. And they are right. It is true. But in our present situation where the very same parents are spoilt themselves, who to turn to?

We must therefore start from the scratch. Schools should start to remodel the future generation. It is critical and viable to begin with schools because that's where we can make a great impact—an d at once—now that the situation presents nothing less than an emergency. It is in schools where we can reach many children by means of, or rather if we have the specific "*antidotal*" curriculum. It is in the schools where the children spend most of their active hours—hours in which unfortunately they learn new things—good or bad. It is in schools where it is easy to project and institute good role models.

Yes we know that as parents we must also play our part, yes we know our children are our responsibility, but for a society to build national ideals, we need a national platform.

Besides, we cannot have a nation with a variety of conflicting ideals. This can only help to create a nation without identity. Besides, we can't wait to have these ideals in place now that we recognize that these ideals—ideals or qualities we compare with the GPS that literally work as a an inbuilt compass needle that guides ships through dark voyages—don't only determine but also govern individual's success as well as the prosperity of any society.

Is it this matter an important subject worthy a lengthy discussion? I mean the youth, are they an important segment that we must be concerned? Let us go into details so that we can get hold of the right perspective.

THE SIGNIFICANCE OF THE YOUTH

In analyzing the significance of the youth, we must first come to terms with one important question: Why bother about the youth? Why not let them go to hell? Why don't we concur that: If someone messes with life, let him go ahead? If they want to hang themselves give them more ropes. After all it is his or her life, is it not? It is not yours or mine, is it?

Unfortunately it isn't so. The youth, we have observed, are pivotal to our lives. We have analyzed this before but for clarification: They are the immediate workforce; the future leaders; they make up the future families of this and any other nation. Thus if we allow the youth to crumble and decay in drugs, alcohol promiscuity and poor character in general, we will never progress but deteriorate as a nation—unless we import the people and particularly the youth from such highly populated countries like China, India or swap in some several million youths from countries with reasonably higher and better educated youth from one of the most populated African countries such as Nigeria or Egypt—in some sort of Pan African spirit! Good idea!

I am myself a great believer of globalization, migration and diversity. Yet, I still feel a little unnerved by such an arrangement. Indeed I can't help asking myself if that nature of recruitment of citizens from all over the map can create a country—the Tanzania—we desired, can it? Good God! I believe in adapting children and caring for the needy as a noble thing to do both morally and intellectually. Yet I do believe in a cohesive family. Say what you want to say, but you can never build a nation by importing people from the outside world whether that is by red card, yellow or some form and model of the Green Card.

Let's leave that to America. Not everything America does, such as some of her social order, is palatable to Africa—for instance. Some of my readers will bring to mind, besides the US, examples of Australia, New Zealand, or Israel but they are different scenarios. You can only develop a nation by developing the people and the youth especially.

The youth form a very significant population group if you have to discuss the growth agenda. Mind you this is the population segment consisting persons who are still in schools pursuing education, and the larger workforce including our scholars. If we don't act, and act now, if we don't redress the situation, we must expect nothing but calamity! And this is no joke. Just read on!

The youth form two thirds of our population. Many are either unemployable, unemployed, under employed or in wrong vocation. Notwithstanding that even those employed both private and public offices aren't any motivated to work hard, by itself the foregoing position poses potential tragedy.

The youth have lost hope on the future, turning to drugs, alcohol, ganja also known as marijuana, prostitution, robbery and other vices thus making the youth a group very prone to poor health, mediocrity and low productivity, HIV/AIDS, imprisonment, certainly pre-adult-deaths. If the trend persists, we will lose manpower in terms of deaths, uselessness, hopelessness, poverty, insecurity to many—itself a disincentive to production of material wealth—and high dependence ratio and dependent economy.

If we cannot repair this "youth machine", we are conspirators in the very ruination of our youth, and purveyors of the downfall of the nation—the nation we seek to preserve, honor and advance. If no attention is cast upon this group–and now—the situation is going to go out hand only in the near future, such that the very population bracket on which we should place our hopes, will be a cost to the public, the government and tax payers in terms of thieving, healthcare.

This is indeed a very big opportunity cost if you think of what they could produce, aside from what we could produce in secure and peaceful low-dependent-ratio situation at household level—which will be reflected in the overall national figures—and what we could do with the same investment we will be directing into the rehabs.

It is the youth who are the workforce. They are also the future leaders. It is the youth who are the future parents and thus the heads of the future families and of this nation. Imagine a nation where most couples have drug addiction or even who are HIV/AIDS infected! Yes we consider this to be a very crucial discussion because if the youth lose hope in the future, they will turn to quick fix, drugs and promiscuity. They will also resort to criminality as an industry.

What nation do we then expect to build out of hopeless drunks, HIV fearless people and a generation that pervades drug abuse? And therefore, this is the final verdict: If a nation has to advance, it has to begin with, and focus on, the youth. First things first!

IDENTIFYING TODAY'S YOUTH

Following enormity of the significance of the youth, of course having indicated above as to why they behave the way they do—albeit in the nutshell—we are now obligated to focus on the characteristics of the youth, characteristics which set them apart from the rest of the population brackets.

The reader must also be aware of why we focus on the characteristics of the youth. If we can identify what sets them apart, as a group, of course having indicated the group's significance, we are obligated to lay down what sets the youth apart—and apart not in terms of age per se, but character. We have already been initiated into why —like a doctor—we need diagnosis of the patient.

Here's the today's youth—love it, hate it!

You will identify the today's youth by their character. The modern youth is least responsible in many ways. The youth don't know they have problems in their lives—none whatsoever. Whether it is drugs, alcohol or adultery, it isn't a problem. He will chase anything that walks in a skirt. Every semi attractive woman is a potential quickie. He never thinks that he is committing adultery—married or unmarried—and marriage? What is it for? Among the youth, it isn't sin to go against Ten Commandments anymore. Adultery? It is a game! It is a way of life. He is sick. And distressed. Anything alcoholic—especially hard liquor—will see him through the darkest hours of the night after a day's hustle!

Indeed the drink is considered as a kick on their moods if they have to face their daily lives fearlessly. Drug trafficking as well as drug addiction therefore are a career and a life style. That's why an industry in drugs and weed is on the rise! To them hard work both in school or industry are a laughable idea. The less work, the better. Quick fix—or *Ujanja-Ujanja* its Swahili word —is a genius! The author has been privileged to interact with many households and to work among several organizations, and he has witnessed how mediocrity and *Ujanja-Ujanja* have crept into the core of our society—both at workplace and at home. I probably am the author now breathing who has had the misfortune of having seen too many people do too little work—and still get promoted and a lot of praises too. Truly I can't tell you how distressing it is. To have resigned from a lucrative job for good at the age when many are still looking for employment should illustrate the foregoing statement!

Remember we are engaged in the analysis of characteristics of our youth, a process which, like any medical diagnosis process, seeks to establish symptoms of the malady that has pervaded the youth if we should heal them. The youth do very little work—if any—turning to quick fix: they wrongly say that singing, modeling or even break-dancing doesn't entail many of boring years in a zoo otherwise named as a classroom. They have wrongly interpreted the fact that: "Education isn't knowledge, it is action." They say education can only be verified—and vilified too—by only what we get in life and get it quickly! Classrooms and workplaces are places they equate to zoos rather than palaces or places leading to palaces as it were in the past! They forget even Michael Jackson, despite his unique talent, spent time creating and rehearsing new songs and styles, and that he put great energy in his break-dancing to be a legendary he was!

The youth have lost hope. For them, hair dressing, modeling and Hip Hop are their vocations. Quick fix is their approach to wealth. They want to get rich but they don't want to work. Females choose hair dressing as vocation. And that is praiseworthy! They have escaped another hot career among the girls and young boys: Working as waiters and waitresses in the mushrooming bars and restaurants with part time in other areas such as serving as night shift bar maids and part-time commercial sex workers. Hip hop and modeling, studio Djs and all middle-man-ship are where their hearts are! With social and academic blindness, they don't realize that only few of them make it to the top, leaving the majority in disastrous tragedy and their successes often short-lived. Industry or farming isn't their favorite calling. They choose to do anything—legal or illegal—provided at the end of the day it fills some money in the wallets whether it is morally good or not.

They crave attention and hence modernity, and therefore, the American hip-hop, modeling, sports or some Jamaican dancehall stars are the role models for the modern youth. Ghetto boys and school dropouts are another category of their role models while dropping out of school altogether is the ideal life style—blindly rehearsing the biographies of Bill Gates and Steve Jobs—whom they identify with as fellow hustlers! You now realize that their choicest forms of career places or offices include the bars, casinos, barber shops, etc. The market place is the roadside terraces down the streets where they sell Hip Hop, Porno or X-rated music CDs, and drugs—and flesh! Many are involved in the selling or buying or both. It is a sport and an industry. To them hooliganism is almost a culture and to rebel against everything straight is like a religious duty.

Do they care anyway! They don't give a damn. They believe in getting rich anyhow and are willing and ready to die while trying! Many have poor character and lack quality and skills necessary to gain or retain the wealth they earn. Most of them put their money where their mouth or the zipper is. Most end up as a result not only in the middle, but in the tail while they should be leading.

There is also a noteworthy attitude. They like to party—and do with great enthusiasm like there is no tomorrow. The women booze, and pick fights. They engage in rampant, random, and unprotected quick sex—anything for money. The youth don't care about the family. There are rampant divorces and neglected children among them. They don't confess to their misconduct. Their souls are sick. They don't accept who they are or what happened in their past. They aren't ashamed of the persons they have become. A failed youth doesn't know that he is desperate and in a mess. He doesn't hate those days but instead he is proud of his deeds!

Though on the surface they seem arrogant and think they are above the average citizens, and are not born to work but spend, they are weak inside. They eat chips and that is all for they aspire to be soft—like a pillow. After all they say they don't have to strain with education or work to get money. They live to attain what they desire regardless of how they acquire what they desire—and this is their setback.

Indeed they have lost hope both in schooling—and in themselves. They are no longer individuals who have an identity and personality to call theirs. As a result they conform and play the game, they do the agreeable things.

They are unadventurous and give much respect to opinions of others. They spend larger proportion of their active life in barber shops or in the "camps" daydreaming. They consider the more advanced countries such as the US or even South Africa as heaven. They do everything in their power to get there. They proclaim that they had better been born dogs in America than be humans here at home. We see rampant self neglect among youth. That's not all. The modern youth prefer leisure and pleasure as career and lifestyle. They hate to think or read books. Briefly they have surrendered to deprivation. They are not persons they were born to be.

That is one picture of the youth especially those in the contemporary category. The second picture is that from the mainstream masses. They have accepted paucity. They have accepted to be second but still second far runner ups. They have yielded to be the runs of the mill. They see no other vent for escape but to do some menial work and earn a daily bread if they are lucky to be hired on the day wage work after lining up for hours to sell the only merchandise they can offer which is the body, and then go home to their shacks and once again begin mingling with all kinds of insects infesting the house, insects which are already eagerly waiting for him or her for his scarce blood, blood dirtied by low quality local liquor or diseases.

Wealth, health, happiness, freedom, choice and plenty aren't in his arm's reach. They are vocabulary to him. He lives for today—did I say today? Wrong! Hour is the word. He or she lives on hourly basis. Sadly, this is his life—a life without long term goals. And as such, without long term goals, without education and constant self advancement at the center of the strategy, any prospects for triumph will be as short as his abandoned pair of school shorts or as tall as her skirts when actually the possibility to acquire anything one desires is as high as the heights of the Kilimanjaro!

As I write, right now I am in what you can call a Public Square. There are services ranging from relaxation, refreshments, meals, music and alcohol. After I arrived here I could not but look at the youth. Some of them I know. I have just parted with them after paying them some money for the work they had done. They don't want school.

They want money. Now as I took my place for a drink, I couldn't help but hold my breath waiting for the buzzing detonated bomb to explode any moment. They are partying like there is no tomorrow. Looking at them I realize transformation that will enhance a *Back to the Classroom Movement* and attention to the right kind of education will do us no end of good.

Either way, we must transform the youth and empower them in order that they can participate in the material production and thus earn a fair share of their own lives. But this requires self-sacrifice on the part of the adults and us who are in power whether at household, school, workplace and national levels. Besides, calmness and safety are among the most important factors for economic development. This environment creates an environment where cooperation thrives and thus people are able to learn from one another and work and gather together.

Contention, insecurity, and spending time and resources on reconciliation or reconstruction instead of production are situations on the opposite lane which attract poverty, not prosperity.

Our youth have stopped reading anything educational besides entertainment news and sports. They seem to listen or talk to no one but probably to the invisible 2Pac or 50 Cent, the great prophets of their new religion they call Hip Hop. Their annual calendars cerebrate the birthdays of these prophets and the messiah in the name of Bob Marley.

They can only buy and share amusing hideous tabloids we have in plenty. Internet and entertainment channels like DSTV are their classrooms, pastime and industry.

This isn't anything near blessing for any parents and the nation when the youths, the energetic people, the workforce we look up to for survival, spend a useful whole day or even little resources they have trying to impress others in terms of clothes, fashion, or spending hours in front of the mirror, forgetting to impress the most important persons in their lives—themselves, their families and God.

What about time or punctuality? They care no more about time. They don't wear wrist watches. What are they for?

They are not employed by anyone and they don't seek to be employed anyway. Instead they have arts and music to fall back on.

So they don't care, with or without getting employed.

Instead they wear a listless number of clutters of ubiquitous bangles of football brands such as Chelsea Football Club, Barcelona, Real Madrid, Liverpool, Manchester United or Manchester City, Milan, Bayern and Arsenal—or even the cool brands of Adidas, Nike, Armani, Fubu, etc.

They will as well add more wristlets and bracelets of various other sorts—excepting of wrist watches of course. And they have good reasons to do so. And the reason is not because the Chinese phones they keep so much busy have time "apps," though? No! Time is itself un-updated. They hate time.

They have nothing to do with it. They are time wasters. And they pride in it that they even proudly sing that they spend mornings and nights in bars and clubs. They seem to believe time is youth-unfriendly. And besides, they work round the clock—doing what they do best—idling!

You will also identify them by their religion—*The Bad Boy Religion.* Indeed, in their inclination for quick fix as an approach to money, and unable to stop at nothing evil to make money in the 50 Cent model of Get Rich or Die Trying, you will also recognize them by their names. As such, they adopt names, nasty names that illustrate their faith in the *Bad Boy Religion*. Their names including Dudu Baya (a deadly beast*),* Gangwe Mob (a notorious mob*);* Mr. Simple (literally I don't dream of bigger things*),* Zero Brain (*There's nothing in the head and I'm proud of it), Muzungu Kichaa literally denoting An Insane White Man*; or one who is out of his mind; Mchizi Mox (the Crazy guy) and Crazy G both standing for insanity or lunacy etc., etc., all say a lot about the direction the new generation is taking the nation.

Surprisingly, they aren't ashamed to compose songs—songs they sing proclaiming to make money—no matter how they get it. What is rather so amusing is that their vulgar language has taken over the media houses and the advertising houses and has ultimately pervaded the general public and the household. Vulgar language is now common in the naming of our products and services. It is as well common in our conversation today.
Such ads and products as *Chizika* i.e. lose your mind, or friends who call each other *Kichaa Wangu* (i.e. a person who is out of his mind) is not anything less than troubling. It is disquieting. We are sowing a seed of perversion. We are creating wrong role models.

And in so doing, unawares, we are promoting thieving, prostitution, armed robbery, shoplifting, drugs, embezzlement of public funds etc—so to speak. We are creating a nation where people entrusted with the public coffers split the funds amongst themselves and we do not only let them walk free, but praise them for work well-done. We hail them as cool guys!

We create a country home to people who don't care whether the stolen public monies leave the hospitals without medicines, health insurance without doctors, schools without books or libraries and labs, water taps without flowing water, banks inaccessible by the masses, shops without affordable goods and services, courts of laws without justice, cars without roads or comfort and as a result homes without families, and generally a nation on its knees where the people slave in their own country.

Now who are they? I mean who are the people within this group we call youth. Where do we find them? Well is the question important any way? It is. Because if we identify them, when we find the right prescription, that's when we can foretell the magnitude of investment required. Besides, if this group consisted of only the street and ghetto boys, a group of dropouts and some cantankerous hooligans with bad temper, folks with bad upbringing springing from single parent families; or those on the streets, or even those with lower levels of education, we would have very little or no reasons to worry about. But that isn't the case here. This generation we call the youth transcends age, education position at work, family background and wealth.

Nevertheless even if they were from single mother families or street children, in as long as the phenomenon is pervading the society today, we are not safer. The street children, cohabiting parents, single mother's phenomenon and generally the collapse of the family institution alongside HIV and AIDS are together so common that we aren't any safer anymore. We aren't any safer anymore even if we had to deal with only this group. But that's not the case again. So who are they? Really? So who are these people? Where do we find them?

They are a group of youth migrating to the cities. They are a group of the youth born in the city. They are youth who drop out of school. Sadly they include the students in all levels of education. They spend longer time on internets—for educational information? Never! Students even at University spend more time on internet in cafes or on their mobile phones not for educational purpose but in the main, watching Hip Hop, Dance Hall or preferably XXX rated pornography.

This I have witnessed myself. Several times without number I have witnessed students at the universities —of all schools—watching porno during prep time! And this is no fiction. God is my witness. And you can join in with the recent event where in India members of parliament were caught watching and exchanging porno on their iPads during the session!

Our youth also can also be identified by the activities they are engaged with. They spend most of their useful time exchanging love messages and images from Instangram or Twitter or fueling rumor on the Facebook! You will see them—men and women—in the growing mushrooms of clubs clubbing. They are also in the barber shops "neating" themselves—and others—up. They also occupy the gyms shaping their bodies for some standard waistlines, developing six packs or broad-shouldered and sturdy biceps. You will see them on the beach tanning their skins to command more attention and higher prices in the market place. You will meet them across the streets or the highway selling blue movie CDs but covered under some martial arts or decent gospel music CDs!

Again this is not a syndrome unique to Tanzanian, India or only the Third World. Nay! Gavriel Solomon and David Perkins in their work: *Learning in Wonderland: What Do Computers Really Offer Education?* Indicate same-same concern among American or rather western society. *Their concern is this: Having students connected to e-mail does not automatically have value. Students can employ it to gossip rather than engage in reflective discourse.*[30]

You will identify them by their hair styles: dreads or some funny kinky "Kool cutz." You will also identify them with their dress code. Indeed you can distinguish them from how they dress. A modern youth dress in a unique way! They prefer jeans and t-shirts. They have even taken great trouble to compose songs praising jeans and t-shirts as a cool form of dress. The tops hang midway in their bosoms exposing their underpants. They prefer to hang some earphones on their ringed earlobes. Men wear heavy rings and hang huge metal chains brushing the soil as they swagger passing by. They swagger and punch the air as they walk. Men display boxers. This adds flavor to their cuts and outfits they purchase in the ubiquitous men's wear shops.

They dress on t-shirts displaying foreign artists or top Premier League footballers. On their heads they hang crooked caps imitating anyone whether it is 50 Cent or anyone among a sea of hip hop stars or any other middle-of-the-road foreign artist. For them that is life. For initiated adults, such life is filled with emptiness and nothingness. It is an empty life. Theirs are lives overshadowed by mysticism and illusion. Not a real thing. To them there is no genuine hope for and sustainability of the bright future.

Ladies dress horribly erotically. They display tattoos of serpents and scorpions on the exposed valleys or ridges of the breasts of the modern female youth. These girls (and boys) bleach their skins to become white but they end up becoming really white in their brains.

They display their breasts and the deliberately display the hills and valleys on the chests. Medals pierced through the tongues and their blossoms. The rings hang through the navel. Their bosoms or the breast are tattooed with their favored star icon—the Scorpion. They call it a lucky star. They believe by doing so, they evoke the magic there is in the successful and elegant Leonardo Di Caprio, a Scorpio at large, himself Born on November 11. They believe he is successful because of his star. They forget the real fault. And the fault, according to Shakespeare in Julius Caesar: "The fault, dear Brutus, is not in our stars; but in ourselves, that we are underlings!"

Medals and tattoos are pierced through in their bodies such as in the chest, the tongue and the bosom. By now you must have begun realizing that even to ponder about the lives of these youths is a regrettably mournful experience! Indeed if you are a parent, but are not strong enough, strong at heart, you can cry—and cry aloud and without shame—like a newborn infant!

I was conducting training for the youth when one of them from DRC admitted that we are losing track. He said one day at the college, which was of all places, the University of Dar es Salaam, he found himself in the presence of a girl whose chest was in total nudity and the pair of her breast literally hanging midair when he volunteered to help out. "Hey," he called out almost murmuring! The girl turned. Pointing his index finger to her chest he said "you forgot to cover your chest!"

Now see her reaction! She shook her head with great compassion with contempt for the backward person, a person who had actually volunteered to cover her naked breasts! Shaking her head, as if to ask where do you come from and then with great self assurance, she told him "it wasn't accident. It was modern fashion!"

Fashion at the university! If that is true among high learning institutions, what about the streets of Manzese, Kibera or Kawempe? I've seen girls whose deliberately outstripped sidelines of their breasts and a valley in between tattooed with a winding open-mouthed rattle snake! Think about it!

Only a couple of years on, this same pair of breasts will be breast-feeding, nursing the infant! What kind of an infant will she be?

As we have indicated, the leading role models for our modern youth are American artists. Our youth know not that even the same artists aren't themselves ideal Americans! They, our youth, are influenced by the west, rejecting themselves, their culture and their society; and thus hanging nowhere like balloons.

That's why they speak American slang, and turn to music. American models are their inspiration. They have lost passion for, and personae of, their own culture and thus hanging nowhere like balloons hanging in the mid air belonging nowhere.

Notice however that when we talk of styles we don't mean everyone with the same styles belongs to these youths. No.

The difference is that the modern youth doesn't necessarily do what he wants. They either do so to imitate American hip-hop stars or they just do it to rebel the system for reasons unknown even to themselves. You will still identify them by pride they crave to display but indeed the low self esteem that envelopes them. We can also tolerate Di Caprio's charm.

But what I can't explain is why a serpent on a good pair of breasts! The question is this: What future prospects are there for a nation of this mentality? You—the reader—tell me (you can find my email is at the bottom of the book)!

But is it a problem for a person or group of people to choose their own path or life styles? Is it meddling on other people's affairs to question what your neighbor does or does not do?

Let us see.

What happens to one of us affects us all. The recent Ebola pandemic and religious conflicts like those waged by Boko Haram or ISIS, albeit regional, or even insecurity and poverty thereof in North Africa and Middle East have helped to put this matter into perspective.

And the biggest problem is in the questioning itself. It is a big problem in that we don't know if it is a problem. No society ever developed if she had no ethos or guiding philosophy of her own.

That's why as I have indicated earlier on, the author has dedicated a whole separate volume on the same agenda.

Let's take another example. When for first time they realized the problem we are now discussing, in the United States, they recognized it as one, I mean as a problem, and as such worked so hard to avert it. Probably you should recognize that if a nation projects and therefore lets its youth choose wrong role models is disastrous, we must create and promote our own role models.

Otherwise we remain blind followers. And we know what befalls blind followers. They end up falling in the deep dark ditches—fallen, gone—forever Fallen, fallen is Babylon the great as chants the Revelation of John.
I believe some of my readers will question my passion for style and fashion—or even modernity—believing the author wants to cling to the ancient stone age. No, sir! I refuse your accusations, madam! To put the records right, I am not opposed to style, fashion or even personal freedoms and innovation whatsoever as far as dressing or personal identity is concerned. I don't hate smartness or elegance at all.

Concerning style, fashion or modernity—call it anything—it is distasteful to see the youth, the most energetic and dynamic group, the source of innovation and the workforce of the nation spending invaluable two-thirds of their day—topping it up with every little resources they have at their disposal—trying to impress others in terms of how they dress or fashion themselves, and spending many hours in front of the mirror forgetting to impress the important persons in their own lives—themselves and God. I don't hate globalization. I hate the illusion it has brought to our society. Globalization doesn't advocate self hate. Hating everything about you—or whatever is local—and uphold everything foreign is not only distasteful, it also fatal. No society can develop when it focuses only on beauty and the earthly pleasures of the body. You and I—especially the government and the corporate—"have a responsibility to improve society.... The acquisition of sound in-depth knowledge is clearly one of the most important factors that these individuals should feel a responsibility to stress. To do otherwise," aptly wrote Ben Carson in Think Big, "To do otherwise, is not only selfish and irresponsible, but also unwise ...Because I feel strongly about this, I want to go on record with as strong statement: If we would spend on education half the amount we currently lavish on sports and entertainment, we could provide complete and free education for all students in this country. The dividends that we would ultimately reap would be phenomenal. America (or Tanzania, for that matter) would quickly rise to prominence as an intellectual nation. Once again, we would be the nation that the rest of the world yearns to imitate in terms of creativity and economic prosperity."

Paul Apostle wrote thus: "For those who live according to the flesh set their minds on the things of the flesh; but those who live according to the spirit set their minds on the things of the spirit." He didn't end there. Apostle Paul proceeded warning that: "To set the mind on flesh is death (it is suicide), but to set your mind to the spirit is life and peace! For the mind that is set on flesh is hostile to God, it doesn't submit to God's law and indeed it cannot; and those who are in flesh cannot please God (or themselves)."

The reader recalls I didn't write this book to make a good impression on every one who picks this book in his hands. I rather wrote it to forewarn you against what you are getting yourself into. As for the society, considering the significance of the youth, if you as a family or nation cannot do anything to reverse the situation, to heal the youth, you are not only already a sick but a lifeless society—if you know what I mean.

Recall the youth are future leaders. Yes the leader of the future. Now think of a kind of leader from among such a group of people? Also think of it this way. If this country is say Iran, a country with 75 percent of the youth population and therefore 60 or 75 percent of the voters. Imagine the kind of the president, the leadership and the policy makers they will choose for us if the youth are of the category we have discussed!

There is also another tragedy. Since credibility and good character is only upheld by few individuals and families, something amiss among most families, it is certain the leaders and policy makers will come from few families that have ideals and uphold good character, this trend will slowly turn the nation into a monarchy. And that's not all. It will turn into a monarchy ruled by a fool! Yes, a fool, no matter whether he is considered as a genius in that shattered island. He is not a genius but a fool because in a blind society, a one eyed man is a king! This is a tragedy to a nation.

Youth empowerment is pivotal to national development. To come to term with the foregoing assertion, notice that for development to be real, a nation must have plans in place.

Yet it takes time and goodwill of the majority for the lasting change to be real and fruits to materialize. That's why the youth present a group of key stakeholders in any growth agenda. But there is another reason. It takes time to change ideals or bring about change. Today it is only the adults who are willing to, and engaged in, change.

I fear that by the time the plans are mature and ready for implementation, these people are already tired, retired or gone forever—swept away—dust to dust. Then the youth will occupy the offices of duty—prepared or not. This we cannot escape. If a nation has to progress therefore, it has to begin with transforming the youth. The youth must be part of both the preparation plans and implementation of future programs. Indeed nothing can be far from the truth that the youth are the backbone of the nation. Indeed, in my view, a country whose youth aren't progressing, is a nation that is certainly progressing backwards. In words of John F. Kennedy: "The future promise of any nation can be directly measured by the present prospects of its youth."

ARE THE EDUCATORS, THE PARENTS, THE SCHOOL OWNERS, BUSINESS SECTOR AND THE GOVERNMENT BLAMELESS?

Having analyzed the weaknesses among the youth, the question is this: is everybody else blameless? We all share the blame. The educators (teachers and writers) contribute to this failure. We don't seem to concern ourselves with the events now happening in the society. We don't seem to spend enough time thinking and preparing first ourselves to meet the change, or to provide leadership to the youth. For teachers, for instance, everything is business as usual. Rarely do they spend adequate time in the classes, let to serve as mentors and counselors to the youth under their charge. In the main, this is due to the fact that most are not in their choicest vocations.

The rest of us make mistakes of wrongly assuming that the teachers aren't highly motivated because of low pay. But pay and pay alone cannot—and will never—make anyone concentrate with what he is doing. What happens is this: the teachers pass the buck to the headmaster, saying to themselves, "after all I'm not the owner of the school!" And most aren't! You cannot blame them—and they say: "Of course someday I'll leave this God-forsaken-career," if they ever leave! Why? Because of this same habit of lack of ambition and indecision, they—after a short while (at least it is believed)—become less acceptable in other vocations. It is same thing in other professions, you recognize this.

The teachers too have lost hope. They conform. They surrender and accept the bad spot in which they are. They don't persevere to change situation around them—let alone the children. There's rampant self neglect in the education sector. They have accepted cheap ways and forms of life and career as fit and deserving for them. Thus the middle is their possible location while they should be leading.

Finally, having come to the end of this chapter, I hope the reader is now well equipped to not only ably evaluate whether there is a decline in the moral standards in our society or not, but also to draw out solutions. Yes we know that in this country—and generation—are youth who have taken advantage of the recent progress in education and information technology.

Yes we know there are youth who have managed to achieve unprecedented results in terms of personal development as well as wealth creation with the help of the modern technology, ICT and globalization —accomplishments which no doubt no one would have dreamt of during the past generation. The question is this: while we blame ICT and globalization, why some young men can still take advantage of the same while the majority succumb? This scrutiny prompted me to conclude that we need a different kind of education. This scrutiny prompted me to conclude that we need a different substance—and we need new approaches in the way we manage our homes, schools or classrooms, businesses and the nation as a whole, or else we lag behind and find ourselves circumvented by both the knowledge base and our competitors!

What we have done therefore, in this chapter, is to analyze some of the major weaknesses most likely to have an effect on this generation. That's why I have asked whether we were blameless in as far as the decline of the moral standards among the youth was concerned. In the long run we all suffer when the nation turns into a labor reserve or dumping place for the overused wastes from our trading partners and neighbors as its citizens become squatters and slaves in their own country.

As we edge to the end, let also the school owners, the parents, the business sector (yes, the business sector too is accountable for the sector will otherwise go on hiring mediocre employees and sell its products or services to such a hopeless market) and the government censor themselves as to whether they are blameless. And here is the challenge: rather than pointing fingers and playing blame games, ask yourselves: what have I—until now—done more or better than the others?

The question is not about who is wrong and who is right. The concern of now is this: if this is true even in the very least of its extent, wouldn't you agree that we desperately need to transform the mindset among students and the youth as a whole before even we think of scaling up our technological or any other resource base? If this is true then that we need to transform the mindset of the youth and students even at the university isn't it logical then that we have got to transform our education curricula and overhaul the whole social cultural and psycho economic system?

8. ENTERTAINMENTATION OF THE NATION AND THE FATE OF THE NATION

"It is no measure of good health to be well-adjusted to a profoundly sick society." —*Jiddu Krishnamurti*

I began writing this chapter only four years back. I wrote it for a number of reasons. One, I wrote it following the recent shocking scandalous academic performances in our schools. I also wrote it because of the pressing paradigm shift—a shift from quick fix that pervades our society: our homes, schools and workplaces especially among the youth. Now bring to mind the fact that the youth are the decisive population group if that society has to have sustainable growth.

Yet when there is collapse of education it's the youth who are mainly affected. And when the youth fail the whole nation's future is in jeopardy. We have discussed the backsliding levels on education and the morals among the youth. A couple of years ago, I began working on this project empty-handed. I literally began from the scratch.

Then year by year, little by little, my little file on the chapter kept swelling as the education performances, on one hand, and character among our youth on the other, continued declining.

As I write today in 2014, I'm even looking for a better term to replace *archaic* words or statements I used then. What is happening in schools and among youth in the workplaces or in the streets is no longer a shock to me anymore! No.

And the reason why there is such unprecedented decline, is not mainly because we lack facilities and resources. No. Behind this decline, is the mindset—the factor which determines our preferences and the decisions we make—of our society in general, and the youth in particular.

To illustrate the foregoing statement, let's compare the analysis of preferences among the people in DRC, Kenya and Tanzania based on a research on preferences or top of mind awareness or a craving the people want to associate with conducted by Ogilvy Africa.

Based on observation of people involved in each market, when assessed by category, four of the five top preferences in DRC, based on the top of mind awareness and a craving the people want to associate with, put soap, detergents, and toothpaste at the head.

Thus, DR Congo's leading preference was skewed toward the outward personality—something that is closely related to the nation's love of music. Kenya's leading preference went to the mobile telecom brands or in general the communication industry.

Analyzed from the fact that the corporate segment made up about 80 percent of the telecom business revenue, Kenyans could be said to be a people who were business minded. Uganda's preferences were closer to those of Kenya. Now let's censor Tanzania.

In Tanzania, the category of entertainment and, specifically, DSTV, an entertainment provider, was by far the leading preference of the nation. Another radio station in the country revealed that this country was leading in a number of news papers across the whole of East and Central Africa—to put them in one group!

Was it because this country is a reading nation? Was it because of other reasons? Culture? The radio inquired from its listeners. What shocked me was that out of all these papers, 84, almost 80 percent were tabloids! Tabloid is a type of popular newspaper with small pages which has many pictures and short simple reports mainly entertainment, gossip, humor and scandals about film and sports celebrities and famous personalities like politicians.

We must remark that though this may not be a true picture of the whole nation, or the true nation's mindset, the analysis can surely give the leads as to why we are where are.[31]

FURTHER SHOCKING REVELATIONS

The secondary schools national exams for 2010, revealed that 50% of Form Four students had failed! Two years later the record hit a new national mark, where the students who failed rose to 64%.

The seating MP for one of the constituencies (Kigoma North) reported that failure in his constituency had hit an-all-time high i.e., 98%.

Think about it. In a hundred students who completed secondary schools in 2012, ninety eight failed. They scored zero!

This isn't fun. It's a terrifying revelation. It is indeed more than that. It is a national tragedy.

Probably it affected only the backward regions? Nay! This decline doesn't only affect the peripheries such as Kigoma or Mtwara.

According to a research by Uwezo, a local NGO, almost eight out of ten students in a sample of 42,000 primary school students in 38 different districts, could not read—not only English a foreign language, and yes the medium of instructions in secondary schools, but also Kiswahili—the mother tongue, the national language.

The capabilities of same-same students in numeracy, was only about 30% on average in all these districts.[32] Indeed as posited Henry Giroux, *Public education is in dire state of crisis...It is not an isolated crisis solely affecting a certain aspect of our society...*[33]

Let's re-examine the facts. 50% of Form IV students did fail in 2010 national exams. The number of disqualified candidates doubled in 2012 from the previous year. In the year 2012, a number of forgeries and fake certificates and thus dismissed or disqualified candidates has more than doubled as compared to the past years.[34]

Recently a group of male students in the country went to greater heights. They joined hands and raped a female teacher. From another school?

They didn't know her? Nay! She was one of their teachers. They knew her. She taught them in the classroom for the past couple of years. It was deliberate. This news—however exaggerated it may seem—is not in any way amusing! It never will be! It is scandalous.

Again whether our curriculum allows students to score A's in classrooms while they are unproductive and disoriented both at work or life in general, the education they get is not only simply useless but tragic. For indeed knowledge isn't our problem. We have so many academicians in every other field. We also have the stock of information almost everywhere especially today with ICT.

Our problem is not knowledge per se. It is indifference. It is inaction. The Cuban motto for education puts the foregoing statement in perspective: *Estudio y Tlabajo:* Education and Work.

And you don't have to go to Cuba to gain knowledge of this verity.

That small country in the Caribbean, because of the same motto, built for us schools that still stand amongst us. You can only go to Kilosa among other schools, and see for yourself. It is not the US, Canada or EU but Cuba—a very small and besieged country in the Caribbean a country ravaged by the trade embargo—which with the same spirit, has sent more doctors to the West African Ebola-ravaged countries of Liberia, Sierra Leona and Guinea than all other countries put together. This—mindset—is an area on which we need to focus our lenses. When I think about it very closely, I am convinced that the problem is even bigger than that.

Our youth have boycotted work. They have no desire or intention to work especially in the farm or take a factory work. Many among those educated in the college wrongly assume that knowledge is the power. It isn't. And never will it be, unless it is used to produce something original and tangible—something that others can eat, drink or wear. People need something that can make them be or feel better.

That's where a good music or art or a book comes in—aside from needs that nourish the body. You recognize as well that the ongoing economic downturn validates the foregoing statement. The economic crisis was a result of closing an eye on what we have just said. Please take time to ponder about this statement!

As we analyze the situation on the ground, as long as we don't find measures to mitigate the foregoing assessment of things, the recent low performance in schools, poor attitude among the youth and escalation of boycotts among higher education students and in general the silent boycott against schools and decent life and choosing instead therefore quick fix, we are led to believe that the situation is slowly but steadily getting out of hand. With the tenacious quick fix—the quick fix anchored by the system we have in place, and the failure to respond, loop us into a more complicated mess.

The traditional teaching methodologies and the examination system all support the very handicap we see today. And this isn't only about schools. At family level we have almost relinquished upbringing of our children to—well, I wanted to say the government. No I don't know who! That is what we see reflecting back to us—from the way we teach and examine students in our schools.

Talking about quick fix, our students don't care about education itself but exams—how to win, to pass. That's all. They forget memorizing doesn't represent learning! Scoring alphas and betas cannot make one rich or prosperous.

Mere knowledge doesn't justify that one is educated. Indeed the author is tempted to suggest that the highly classed students are the ones who should be at the bottom of the class in the ideal environment in the prevailing system. And the logic is plain!

Those who perform at the top may otherwise be students who know how to manipulate the situation. The author knows in his class students who performed at the top because of superb skills in manipulating teachers and lecturers.

Some of these so called best performers were rather the cunning male and female students who knew how to stash bits and pieces of premeditated answers' sheets within their body parts, in clothe hems of their clothes or under their desks. They could also be people who knew how to mob up together and share the answer sheets.

I have interviewed a top student specializing in ICT in one of the top colleges in the country and over the second or third long neck of— was it Serengeti? Or Kilimanjaro lager?

That's when he admitted that he never even wasted his time studying hard. He said he knew how to play with the lecturers. He cultivated good relationships with them. Several times he offered to serve in their private projects—and never demanded high pay.

Then he would simply be led to know which questions will come from which topic. That's when he would start studying. And this seems a fair play on the part of the lecturer. This student didn't have adequate time to prepare himself for exams dedicating his time on the lecturer's private money-making machinery.

But what about presentations—verbal physical presentations where a student has to defend his observations? To this he admitted that his advantage lay in his gift in spoken English language.

His fluency in English made people want to hear him more and more such that they never got themselves concerned with substance.

He confided to the author that he never went to a presentation without a pint of liquor deep in his brain slowly as he went to work. That gave him confidence to face the challenge. Alcohol was a kick to him. I didn't know whether this is in itself not a sign of low or a complete lack of self-confidence. *"Again* with my connections with the lecturers, I have a way of helping my colleagues in my study group..." *he said.* "As a result of my connections, even when I am not at the college (as we spoke) they are working on our group work. My course work is steadily big enough. That's how I have always come out top," this modern youth boasted over the third beer as he wrung his hands savoring how smart he was over the glass of the glass of the crazy golden liquid he gulped down, and a smile formed and blossomed on his face self-assured of his tricks in anticipation of the bright future. I have seen miracles! And surprisingly, his is not unique.

The account reminds me of a gentleman who sat next to me in a restaurant one morning at Kilwa Road Restaurant Kurasini, Dar es Salaam, Tanzania. This restaurant is located only a stone throw from the Tumaini University laws department. On this morning I had just dropped by to have my breakfast when I found myself in a conversation with this guy next to me. I had watched him as he gulped down his meager breakfast before he ordered a bottle of Konyagi. Konyagi is a local strong liquor brand. With maddening love, he kissed the bottle and closed his eyes as the hard liquor negotiated its path down his unfortunate esophagus. He kissed his dear bottle one more time and then opened up.

He told me he was downing the hot stuff so hurriedly and informed me he had to do so for he was getting late for the morning lecture! Christ church! So he was a student! I learned very quickly that he did laws at the Tumaini University—of all universities. Mind you this is a church institution. Why? I mean why liquor this hour? I couldn't imagine why he had to take such a drink before his lectures. My question was answered without any probing. He wasn't ashamed of it. Without liquor he didn't grasp anything whatsoever was taught in the lecture rooms.

All these observations bring us to the conclusion that the poor performances in schools— and at workplaces— resonate, in the main, from the attitude of students and not mainly the because of lack of facilities. Wouldn't you agree that *Dewey was right when he criticized those who sought to liberate the child from adult authority and social controls?* "[35] It is probably in the same spirit that the United States enacted what they called *America 2000* as a need to formulate and institute national standard first in education but also and probably more importantly in the social economic turf.

It is probably with reference to the rising number and trend of the drug abuse in our schools and generally among the youth the seventh goal of the *America 2000* stated thus: "by the year *2000* , every school in the United States will be free of drugs violence and unauthorized presence of firearms and alcohol and will offer a disciplined environment conducive to learning." Do we have anything in parallel?

If we don't respond appropriately, we will be leading the nation into catastrophe. We cannot fight a war with tools we don't have. We have got to start from where we are. It is through education that we initiate into youth the ability to master nature and themselves which is self management and management of people and environment around themselves.
Besides; the students and youth agenda- envelopes the families or households the corporations and the entire society since indeed the youth form the most important group if we have to appropriately address development or growth agenda. The youth are the Tanzania of tomorrow. They are the future minds and mind—shapers of tomorrow.

How connected is this to the youth or vocation we choose and the nation we intend to build? Though we encourage diversity, but the industrial scale in which our youth today turn to music, arts, modeling and any other quick fix than academics or industry casts a shadow of doubt on our prospects. We understand that in some more advanced countries these are indeed model vocations and academics, yet with an economy that is still anchored on the back bone of the hand hoe, our choices must be different. We need more people and ideas in agriculture and in our factories.

We need more resources and time in the farm and industry. When arts, beauty contests and modeling or even music turns out to be a national vocation, is never a healthy destiny to a nation like ours. And we are partly to blame.

What are we doing in order to give our children an upper hand over the television, and internet? The parents in the past generations were so tyrannical and whatever the parents said went. Today it is very different.

With liberalism, personal freedoms are so much observed. What have we done about it? Thirdly, today the students and their parents want results—immediate results. That's why they ask why they should invest in education when they only get out old and doomed, less active and back on the street, jobless?

We have failed to create employment or environment for self employment. Also and probably the biggest fault ingrained in our education is the failure to create employment. But since a big number of graduates are needed in factories and farms, what can they do when there's nowhere to absorb them?

The educated person is in trouble. He needs a certain kind of work that is mentally engaging but he can only end up being a menial worker.

I fled from work because I'd worked enough to know I needed change. The youth are boycotting this situation. Instinctively or through observation, the youth boycott classes.

And they need a chance—and they need answers. That's what I'm saying. Looking back I realize I was brave enough to get myself out of this rat race.

We the parents, the corporate , the government and media are also blame for the shift of preference toward quick fix and entertainment.

You realize, don't you, that if we present artists as wealthy role models—and often they are—the students tend to study very little throwing all cautions to the wind, for after all that's where there is big dough—aside from the fact that music or modeling doesn't entail many years of studying. And sadly it is turning out to be a culture of our society.

Is this unfounded? Oh, no!

Attaching a certain thing or idea to even an unrelated stimulus generates the same effect in the long run especially if the conditioning is done among young learners.

Such conditioning is more effective during childhood. In fact James Watson based on the method that Pavlov[36] had demonstrated for animals once boasted thus:

"Give me a dozen healthy infants, well informed, and my own specified world to bring them up and I will guarantee to take anyone at random and train him to be any type of specialist I might select—a doctor, lawyer, artist...and yes into a beggarman and a thief regardless of his talents...abilities vocations and the race.'[37]

Open your eyes. We are amidst models, arts and a hip-hop generation. Astonishingly (music or art in general) is becoming the national vocation! A country that is on vacation can never heal in the long run. We are slowly but steadily building a Hollywood nation! It is mediocrity. It is not a Hollywood-Hollywood stuff, if you know what I mean. And though it may please few, many or even the whole nation, but I don't like it one bit. Recently a young man was expelled from a radio where he was deejaying because he snored on air off his golden liquid dinner during his show. How did someone know something was wrong?

Before the program was over, he began and went on snoring as if the radio was in the business of demonstrating how people can snore best. It is no comic story. It happened at the time when I was listening to the same program. It is not a question of personal freedoms or globalization or liberalism or modernity. No! It is mediocrity. In this case, I am prepared to stand alone. It encourages me that in some cases one man forms the majority.

Thomas Jefferson was right. *"One man with courage is a majority."* Economist myself, I am astounded by some of our economists who evaluate Hollywood based on what it contributes the gross domestic income. Wrong! A nation cannot grow without the people who conduct themselves in a certain way; or without science, technology, industry, agriculture and efforts to build the middle-class.

The middle class and, especially, the upper class consists of people who behave in a certain way—as we shall see soon. For the society to behave in a certain way, the leadership or the elders of the people must formulate a national philosophy that reinforces first the paradigm shift, and then leads the nation in a certain direction.

In that society—a society that is likely to progress—they enact laws that promote work ethics. In that society they praise and pamper hardworking people as they arrest idling and quick fix. We are going to see what the US did in response to backsliding youth before we close this discussion.

Paul Apostle did the same. In order to build a progressive nation he summoned the elders thus:

"We beseech you, brethren to respect those who labor among you…and admonish you …to esteem them very highly in love because of their work," wrote Paul Apostle.

For us we do things differently and expect results. This is a definition of insanity according to Albert Einstein bridged by the author. The scriptures say: *They left that what they ought to have done, and they did that which they ought not to have done, there is no truth in them.*

As for us there is no wisdom in us: We praise that which we ought to have despised, and despised that which we ought to have praised. By the foregoing statement I don't mean to say we rid the society with the idlers and their cohorts. No sir!

Paul Apostle wrote to those who are hard working thus: *"Be of peace with them. And we exhort you, brethren, admonish the idlers, encourage the faithless, help the weak, be patient with them all."* But to what extent, that's where I am curious!

We have got to help the students appreciate the fact that life is all about choices and sacrifices; a choice between academics or other crafts and professions on one hand, and quick fix on the other. A country that is on vacation can never heal. No nation ever progressed when every youth turned to music and art.

Much as I am opposed to it, I know there are talented serious musicians among these youth. For these we ask you to help them. We are concerned with those who do know what they should be doing in the first place. These we need to help to identify their chosen innate calling or vocations. We must help to demonstrate that there life elsewhere if one works hard.

We must let them learn that, even in art, modeling, music or sports, or even when for vocation you choose priesthood, politics or "house-wifing" or even "house-husbanding", the difference between those who succeed, and those permanently stationed at the bottom is something we acquire yes, through the classrooms, but essentially due to our character and attitude. It is not talent and talent alone that determines achievement.

Academic records don't represent character, intelligence or personality. That is why we ought to instruct our youth in the ways of self-discipline, "balanced living" and why and how to have harmony first with oneself, but as well with the others, harmony with your career, family, social activities, and the world at large.

So this book isn't meant to teach biology, history, commerce or traditional economics. There're lots of such books. Materials for such fields are ubiquitous but haven't solved the core problems of the society one bit as we shall discuss through the proceeding chapters presenting and illustrating what youth say about, and demanding from education. Notice also that this program does not even labor or intend to ensure that students score an Alpha in that subject or a beta.

For that would be meaningless if the study itself was irrelevant and irresponsive when it comes to addressing challenges facing the society and problems students and the youth face. The youth demand answers. Every form of education is of no value unless it helps you to find who you are and what you want to have and be in life, and how to get there. These ideas, these values, form the core of what we can call meaningful education.

Meaningful education is one that will addresses individual person's problems, problems addressing the family institution, solves workplace problems such as low productivity, and the problem the environment is facing. The education we seek, which this book offers, is an education about you! This is the knowledge—the education —now highly sought after especially when it is relevant and homegrown.

No one wishes to be an emissary of doom—a messenger of bad tidings—the author included. Yet the catastrophe we face calls for someone with vision, someone with courage, a person who—in words of Stephen Covey—can stand up and climb a tall tree and after scanning the way ahead, shouts back at the top of his voice to the men on the ground below; and says (hey), *"Wrong Jungle!"*

It shames me to know that we haven't engaged ourselves enough in identifying and tackling the problems facing our society head-on. It is shame we have thrown all cautions to the wind to the extent that we no longer know how to get the society back on its feet. Doing a mistake is not a mistake. Repeating it is.

Why is this discussion important? Why now? As a country, transforming our education system has been long time in coming! Indeed the foregoing statement cannot be overstated. With simile to Tanzania, you recognize we needed transformation long ago—and indeed immediately after our independence of the flag in 1961. We would have done with a complete shift from colonial education agenda that produced modest workforce to facilitate in colonial economy as clerks—not thinkers nor experts—to one that empowers the local people and builds capacity to think rightly—and do the most needful. It is irrational to think we can progress under the present situation. Trying to move on without addressing this inherent and devastating problem is not only unwise, it is indeed absurdly fatal. Thinking otherwise is an understatement of the facts!

9. WHAT SHOULD WE TRANSFORM: THE YOUTH OR EDUCATION?

"If we don't change direction soon, we'll end up where we're going."
—*Prof. Irwin Corey*

Through this chapter, we will be discussing the fate of our education in the country—and the world at large—in the eye of the youth. It is by no means a less important matter considering the question of democracy. They youth have the right to listenership. They are not represented in the national assembly or parliament. Those few who are elected don't represent the typical majority youth interests besides the fact that the youth question the level of democracy in such national organs—organs they see as machinery of the ruling elites as the recent national and political parties' elections helped to reveal. It is also important to know what their concerns are.

Is it important? Yes, given the group's critical role in taking the nation forward—or backward along the growth path. And you will be soon be shocked not only by the fact they raise but also by the fact that they have strong allies on their side—allies we will introduce soon. For the youth it is like they are always told what to do waiting for the unseen future during which time they can be eligible to voice their concerns. That's what has always created—and perpetuated—a club of the rulers on one hand, and that of the rebels on the other. But the question is this: why education?

Why should we be now engaging ourselves in this discussion about education? It all comes from priorities subject to the scarcity of resources as recommend the principles of economics. The point is this, we have so much to do. Our country has so many problems.

Every ministry and almost every department; from that of defense, to that health, agriculture, labor, that of gender and the genuine rights of the deprived women and children—albeit a curious platform for cantankerous activists, etc., has problems due to budget deficiency. What should we attend first? Where should we invest our scarce resources? Resources? Yes, resources if we are at all left with any!

On discussing the legacy of Mwalimu Nyerere, a re-known scholar and lecturer at the University of Dar es Salaam, Dr. Ayub Rioba, said in a television panel discussion recently, that, yes Mwalimu identified the three major national challenges: poverty, diseases and ignorance, but if we fight ignorance, we will have fought all the other enemies: disease and poverty. Therefore to concentrate our few resources and efforts fighting against ignorance, on education is paramount! In 1997, President Clinton indicated in his state of the union address that education would be a primary focus of his second term.[38] That is why the battle lines for us as individual persons, households, organizations and the nation as whole should be drawn around education. That's why this chapter, and major part of the remaining book in this series, will focus on education.

What you are going to read in this chapter therefore, is originally an adaptation of the statement made by an anonymous person—or persons—claiming to be representing the views of a larger group of youth describing themselves as *The Anti-School*. The document found its way in the hands of the author by sheer coincidence. It arrived by email after the sender had been inspired to do so following the lecture the author had made regarding the needed change of direction in our education. What will surprise the reader is that, though it represents the views of the majority of our youth today, the youth we have labeled as misfits, you will be astounded to find that actually the anti-school sentiment has the support of the highly distinguished individuals, among them notable academics from a number of famed colleges and universities around the world. Though the author doesn't agree with every word they say, I am sure the reader will find it to be an eye-opener in the discussion this book is focusing on.

Let's hear it from the horse's mouth. Here's what they say about education:

The school has lost its track. In fact don't take your child to school. Don't, until when those responsible have made major overhaul both in the education they teach there, and school system itself. If they don't, you will be wasting your resources, and the time—and the rights—of your child. And here is why:
I don't remember what I learned in school. If I were to take high school exams today, my grades would be poorer (and it is a fact). How many of us remember what they "learned" at school? We can only remember genuine skills like reading, writing, and a few other skills that are genuinely meaningful to our lives. We can as well readily remember spot-on information such as how the sun rises from the east and sets in the west, counting one to ten, reading and writing such important information as our names or even—yes, magnetic poles, etc.

To say that most of the things we learn in classrooms are less interesting and useless is an understatement! (In fact I wanted to say it is a crime, having studied laws, I didn't want to bring up matters I cannot substantiate—legally, I mean!)

What we learn is often not applicable to our daily social as well as business or economic lives. No wonder we tend to forget most of this crap—and forget it very quickly. They are clutter to a young learning mind, sowing seeds of discouragement against learning. Remember a child learns better by encouragement and cannot learn when in a state of discouragement. He also learns better when he recognizes the education he receives is useful to its recipient. The student therefore ought to be taught how to manage himself and his day to day life, such as how to make and manage money, how to run domestic appliances he needs at home or fixing such appliances etc.

And this is not baseless, nor is it work of an emotional imbecile. If anyone had this imagination, then let him think again! For rather it is rooted from famous schools of thought—the Greek concept of Paideia, and the second is what is known as the University of Chicago School. In short, education ought to have been placing the emphasis on the needs of the learner and the approach to education ought to have been means to ends.[39] The Anti-School theories lack no support. According to Bobbitt, one of the founders of the University of Chicago school, schools ought to engage in activities that that enhance abilities ranging from *"the ability to care for (one's) teeth...eyes...nose, and throat;...to keep home appliances in good working conditions..."*[40]

The point I am trying to make is this: Our brains are made to store only useful information. There's no space for useless garbage in our precious memory banks. I hate schools (so the Anti-School think-tank say—not the author). Why? (Let's hear it from the horse's mouth) They have very little to offer (and at what cost!). They don't give individual students an opportunity to choose what they would like to do, or learn; or mind to ask if they care for it anyway!
When one chooses to study economics at the university, one chose to study economics—not statistics, quantitative methods or econometrics—and why? Why should it be compulsory for me to pay for, and study something on which I've no interest at heart at all? I've decided it is going to have no connection whatsoever with my economic life, so why push me? Well, I know to some of those reading this epistle, this might sound ludicrously ridiculous and silly.

Why? They will say: *How can you study economics without statistics or econometrics? Impossible*, they will say. And to this argument some will laugh: *Ha, ha, ha—believing* they are interconnected.

Look here. The point is this: If I could, I would study everything. But it's not practicable, feasible or accomplishable. (Why?) All things teach us something. But, sadly, we have no choice. We have got to choose—life is all about making choices—rational choices.

And this question of targeted or discriminate learning is so critical if learners should learn with enthusiasm and gain meaningful education. Learning things that really matter to us, things that are o significant to our own lives, and developing skills that can be put to immediate use is something innate and spontaneous to us as humans. We see this all the time among the children. The children want to know and understand everything around them. They question everything.

They learn to spell to the letter and speak languages without us teaching them. It doesn't matter how complex that language is, the children still master it. Effortlessly the children can grasp and are able to speak several languages at a pace that shames adults who are stocked in a contemporary classroom filled with computers and modern high-tech gadgets such as talking machines to help him learn faster. The infants learn to sing, laugh and dance without formal schooling. We would never propose—at least not yet—that we put our infants in school so that they could learn to speak properly. And if we did, we would probably turn this nation into a nation of inarticulate tongue-tied people, and then the schools would demand more funding so that they could do the job properly.

Children are constantly seeking opportunities to learn. But sadly we take this precious love and sense of natural learning and subject it in an environment where it is smothered, choked, suffocated, stifled—and finally it is butchered before it is laid in its eternal grave through life!

Unfortunately, we are so conditioned to associate schools with learning. As a result when schools fail, students fail too. The foregoing statement illustrates the current situation. Sadly, when our children fail, we demand more schooling and better facilities. Thus the government puts more money into education, more same-same teachers, and more same-same environment, more same-same cheating, more same methodologies etc. It is only plentiful of same-same things—things we do not desire or need because they have actually already failed—indeed things which have brought us here. You and I are the witnesses.

You and I have seen people cheat during exams. I have seen people cheat at work. They cheat and cheat until when they begin cheating themselves. If you didn't know why people cheat in the holy matrimony, now you know, no?

You and I have experienced or read about people who cheat God—of all cheating! Forgetting about misconduct in the government, deceit is rampant in churches as well as in mosques for the same reason. Deceit was conceived in the minds of all those who went through our education—male or female. Our education has implanted in its victims the wrong notion of greatness that has already arrived, or on the way and about to doc. It never arrives or docs though. Our education had sown in the minds of our *men of education* the hunger to get without working. It has therefore castrated its victims of their ability to reinvent their lives besides formal employment—a lifestyle that domesticates you for life. It is no wonder—and the foregoing explains why—the least schooled are more self-employed and more self-reliant and fuller members of our society.

No wonder students are disillusioned. They don't give a damn about degree papers. Indeed with doctored academic results and ubiquitous fake graduates, who does? What students want today is, for instance, to know English language, get a good job—and raise a good family. That's why we don't encourage you to take your kids to school. Trust me it's a waste of time and resources. Look at yourself! Indeed if you try to evaluate what you have achieved over the years, you will—without shame—confess to yourself that you didn't get a fair the return on your investment. What your kids want therefore is the least amount of schooling and the most of learning—and more learning is possible outside schools, in the streets, on the ground.

Again, we no longer have a say over the choice of the vocations we will take on graduation.

Education, and worse more, the current vocations are but an old-fashioned form of a routine or lifestyle—call it anything. The employment available to majority of us can only be hand to mouth. This is not what went to school to get. It is a bloodsucking financial system aside from the fact that it doesn't not only favor us as individuals, but also it does allow us to have a say over the choice of the life style we want. It is a form of life subjected upon us—a life of abject poverty. We have ourselves and our families to feed, haven't we? Yet many of us cannot manage to have, let alone run our own families.

Count and see! So schools, or using a better word, classrooms, are no longer places where one can learn important skills or get any meaningful training. They are money making outfits. Out of their end—a goal of making money—we are right to question if they deserve to be called schools.

Schools are no longer social goods. They are a business establishment. They sell a variety of education they advertise as good for everyone only to get the uninformed parents paying the schools fees. What's the difference? They teach A, B, C D, etc as others teach how to drive a car or cook—and they all get paid. Like any other business, schools today crave to sell their products for super profit. They pay expensively for advertisements to hook customers just like how other forms of business do. They sell some form of education or profits motive just like those who are selling timber, bricks, or potatoes. Have you questioned yourself why law firms don't advertise their businesses until as of today—for we don't what tomorrow will bring? Law as education ought to have been, is considered a social good a necessary social service. I also assume that by advertising we can lure the society into the wrong decisions pertaining to such services.

Have you ever troubled yourself to question why schools are walled all through and not an open-air environment? Why they carry sticks and cane our children? Why the best disciplinarian is promoted to the discipline master and eventually headmaster or headmistress?

Why no parliaments in schools? Students would turn and flee from the school! Or why when anti-school innocent citizens otherwise known as students boycott classes the government deploys armed battalions of armed forced? To keep the streets clean and of course to stand with the schools tax payers!

As conventional business diversifies its product portfolio, the school has embarked on creating so many combinations even when they are unrelated. We know many mushrooming colleges for watered down courses which don't help the students by the owner to extract money from the masses. Just look around you. They command with an iron hand: Study economics, econometrics, statistics, quantitative methods etc. And all you can do is to say *Yes Sir! Yes Headmistress!*

Why do we have to pay so much for, and spend much time on something that we don't need or deserve? And here's the problem. The labor market, in particular, or the society in general, considers school certificates to be equivalent, or synonymous, to education. Unfortunately!

Yes it is wrong but sadly many people still believe certificates represent skills! It is wrong! It is off beam! And sadly no one of our academics or social and political leaders here at home has dared to rise to the challenge and address the matter.

Whether they shut up on personal grounds, ignorance or indifference, I have no way of knowing. But I bet no one can keep quiet on such a grievous mistake unless he has no good intentions at heart—or is uninformed!

With this education system we are crafted to serve the other people's interests, and impress the people we don't even know, or care about. We also are forced to do this because of the crooked nature of our present day's labor market. McLaren was right when he stated that, *"Schooling is generally perverse in that it strives through its curriculum...to hide from students and the general public the gaps in our society, the contradictions of our stances and our intolerance of difference. (Ours is not an) empowering education, but a perverse form of prohibition in which desire as human agency is not permitted to explore its own constitutive possibilities. Students are treated as objects of consumption as they are simultaneously taught the value of becoming consuming objects,"*[41] *in an environment where, "Students are denied access to forming their own destinies (Ornstein and Hunkins p.50)."*

Here we present another lame duck: the human resource personnel. The human resource personnel have not risen from their drowsy past. And as a result they have not helped the CEO or MD, and the business owners to change this attitude. They have failed to help the CEO and the MD to be able to identify and help to advance the ideal employee of today. They have failed to identify what is the ideal education or training.

The hr manager or director has failed to take the leadership role he ought to have taken. As a result we who are in schools are forced to cram formulae and old fashioned outdated theories—theories that are valueless and therefore have no meaning not only to our lives, but to the employer. Need we say that that is another job description and a position that should have been long struck from the organigram?

And here is one of the failures of the HR. What is shocking is that we as graduates and job candidates, we get judged based on the time we have wasted memorizing weaker substance of lesser models!

Schools are no more sources of skills or education. Every time someone mentions the word "learn", sadly people instantly think of "memorize", then, formulae, principles and theories.

Just look at all that memory-enhancers, mind-maps, the enormous focus on the past papers among the teachers and students, and cheating of every variety, sizes and shapes, secretly orchestrated by the official school machinery. Teachers even encourage students to help one another during exams. They cheat and they pass without credibility. (Honest teachers have confessed this as something common practice in our schools today).

Cheating is premeditated. It is motivated by the intrinsic capitalist motive: the profit motive. The performances then are used to attract fresh students and retain continuing ones.

We began cheating others until when we have now advanced in cheating that we no longer cheat one another, but we teach ourselves. This cannot go unchecked for long if the nation has to rise up and stand on its feet once again.

Lies? Fiction? Entertainment? No sir!

If we could assemble all headmasters, school owners, school managers, invigilators, teachers and students and asked them if the foregoing assertion is true or not, for failing to deny or accept the fact that the majority are indeed purveyors of the system that enables students to pass in order to attract parents to enroll their children in such schools, many would cover their faces with the palms of their hands in deep shame! Is this *Schoolophobia* justifiable? Let us see.

If you or I visited the same schools we went to over years, we would undoubtedly find the same environment, the same classes and same desks we left there long ago—only now a little more watered down.

We would find almost the same textbooks and educational materials; we would find that the methodologies, tasks, practices, statutes and guidelines unchanged since we were but infants. We would probably find the same teacher wearing the same dress he wore years back.

Indeed, after visiting more than 1000…schools, Goodlad concluded that most students are not engaged in problem solving tasks, but passive rote-tasks and they are rarely asked to initiate anything…or create their own products.

In short, real learning rarely takes place in schools."[42] In words of David Orr: "Campus architecture is crystallized pedagogy that often reinforces passivity, monologue, domination, and artificiality. My point is simply that students are being taught in various and subtle ways beyond the content of courses."[43]

Henry Giroux and Peter McLaren went even further in expressing contempt for the very society within which schools exist...referred to students as prisoners, to teachers as prison guards or dupes of the system, and to schools as essentially prisons where students are locked up intellectually, and emotionally thus restricting their free expression and democratic actions. Schools are considered to be highly discriminatory places that sort and track students for various jobs that extend class differences in society.

Schools participate in perpetuating the social logic of production and consumption, which benefits the few and marginalizes the many...there is nothing positive in it about teachers or the school processes; it deals instead with how teachers and schools turn off students. ...Teachers enforcing rigid rules and students focusing on right answers; learning to be stupid; and learn not to learn... (and *as a result students) adopt strategies...to please their teachers. The successful students become cunning strategists in a game of beating the system—figuring out how to outsmart the teacher, how to get the answer out of the teacher, or how to fake the answer.* (Their ideas like *P*aul Goodman's thesis is that) our society is sick and full of spurious and false values that have produced sick schools...schools have little to do with education; (*instead*) they provide jobs for millions of people and a market for text book companies, building contractors, and graduates of schools or of education. In the early grades, schools provide *"a babysitting service" for the parents and keep kids off the streets. In the middle and senior years, "they are the arm of the police" providing corps and concentration camps paid for in the budget under the heading of "Board of Education." From kindergarten to college schools teach youth to adjust to a sick society and provide and universal trap in which democracy begins to look like regimentation. (Goodman's solution) is to do away with compulsory education... (referred to as) miseducation and to try to drastically cut back formal schooling because the present extended tutelage is against nature and arrests growth...if schools were eliminated education could be open to all and could become a genuine instrument of human liberation: learners would no longer have an obligatory curriculum imposed upon them*; they would be liberate from institutional and capitalistic indoctrination.

There would no longer *be discrimination and a class society based on possession of a mere certificate.*[44]

Although it may seem a little weird, the Anti-School movement is at the page with most progressive theories and positions agree upon as watered down traditional standard school practices. These include*:* "(1) the authoritarian teacher; *(*2) excessive reliance on textbook methods; *(3)* memorization of factual data and technique by drill; (4) static aims and materials that reject the notion of a changing world; *(*5) use of fear or corporal punishment as a form of discipline; and (6) attempts to isolate education from individual experiences and social reality." The schools further did *control students not for their own good, but for the good of the adults.*[45]

Besides, schools are *unconcerned about higher planes of understanding, enhancement of the mind, or self knowledge.*[46] This , probably is in line with what Charles Silberman wrote about.

The Anti-School advocates what he, Charles Silberman, called*: Humanizing American Schools* because schools were "*repressive, and they teach students docility and conformity. He believed that schools must be reformed*... "[47]

Ivan Illich… went beyond his contemporaries in his *Plans for Remaking Schools*. He argued for a new society that required the prior deschooling of society.[48]

Schools and schooling ought to help us learn to master ourselves and nature. They were created to help us learn with ease, be prosperous and freer. Schools ought to have no purpose beyond fostering that kind of purpose. Unfortunately, the schools we have today do not foster learning.

The prevailing education system has also failed to address self reliance and sustainability of personal effort for instance income generation. This is one of the major handicaps among the educated. To a real man of education, getting hired for a monthly salary is neither the end, nor rationalization, of being educated when he actually remains a slave to the same employers—most of whom—the employers—are less educated.

Occupying a high office, owning big buildings or a couple of a 4x4 cars, or even possession of a private chopper or a jet plane isn't, and will never be, the SI unit for a success.

A little analysis of the most of the American hip-hop stars has helped to put the foregoing statement in perspective. On the other hand, being a pauper, or in general, failure to be prosperous is not, should not, cannot, and will never be accepted—or tolerated—as a gold standard or lifestyle for a man of education. Because of its significance, we will revert to this statement with more input.

Education, as it is today, destroys morality altogether. If you want to prove this claim, closely watch the men of education—professors, professionals, politicians, clergymen—you name it. It all stems from how teaching environment is organized in our today's classrooms besides the frustration the educated man goes through immediately after he stumbles upon truth about his demise and unfounded hopes. Count and see the shocking number of alcoholic medics and addicted business managers who live on borrowed from bottled bravery.

Well—that's one side of the same picture. We have crossed fifty years of the same education in our classes. Some countries have the same education for over twenty centuries— centuries such as Greece. For a doubter, to prove the foregoing statements, only one has to count in order to see a number of matrimonies that are shambolic and children abandoned by their parents—learned parents and politicians. And by destroying morality, education has razed humanity. Again count and see a number of youth from the schooling families and countries that join the club of the sybarites and lifeists in the night clubs and whorehouses for physical pleasures not to talk about those who join Islamists and Jihadists to kill and annihilate life. This is not a happy ending parents hoped for when they chose to invest in their children's education—in the first place.

In words of David Orr, "This is not a happy world that any number of feckless advertisers and politicians describe. We have built a world of sybaritic wealth for a few and Calcuttan poverty for a growing underclass. At its worst it is a world of crack on the streets, insensate violence, anomie, and the most desperate kind of poverty.

The fact is that we live in a disintegrating culture. In the words of Ron Miller, editor of Holistic Review: "Our culture does not nourish that which is best or noblest in the human spirit. It does not cultivate vision, imagination, or aesthetic or spiritual sensitivity. It does not encourage gentleness, generosity, caring, or compassion. Increasingly in the late 20th Century, the economic-technocratic-statist worldview has become a monstrous destroyer of what loves and life-affirming in the human soul."

And what can we say?

Indeed because it is our men of education who literally govern our society, it follows therefore that it is safe to say that our educated men and women—politicians, public servants, business leaders, clergymen and academics—in words of David Orr: "have done what no invading army could do: they destroyed (the readers as well as the authors city) an American city[49] ... other costs, those of unemployment, crime, higher divorce rates, alcoholism, child abuse, lost savings, and wrecked lives. In this instance what was taught in the business schools and economics departments did not include the value of good communities or the human costs of a narrow destructive economic rationality that valued efficiency and economic abstractions above people and community."[50]

In harmony with the foregoing argument, David Orr wrote that: "In the confusion of data with knowledge is a deeper mistake that learning will make us better people. But learning, as Loren Eiseley once said, is endless and "In itself, it will never make us ethical." Ultimately, it may be the knowledge of the good that is most threatened by all of our other advances. All things considered, it is possible that we are becoming more ignorant of the things we must know to live well and sustainably on the Earth." This is what David Orr called sane means, mad ends. "What went wrong with contemporary culture and with education?" he asks. The insight can be found in Christopher Marlowe's Faust[51], a character who trades his soul for knowledge and power. But if you can have knowledge and power in your possession without life what is knowledge or power for?

Truly the misery the human society has endured in the face of the unchecked love for our classrooms is imponderable. I know parents who have spared no penny to take their children to better schools— boarding schools or even abroad —unawares that sadly that's where the seed of downfall and the massacre of the self and education itself is sown since the education they get there is irrelevant and in so doing they end up, as believed Freire, "facilitating self-depreciation."

Indeed in words of Sutton: "persistent ethnic and class divisions are reproduced though schooling somehow and...the institution of schooling, does not appear to be leveling the playing field between the social have and have-nots."[52] But the foregoing statement shouldn't deceive the haves to imagine that they are better off or safer for that matter. They are not better off or safer one bit. In fact in total we are all worse off! No one wins and all of us vanquished, Yakub Gowon was right!

What they, the youth therefore, see with the respect to schools is not cynicism. It is also surprising that it is almost a universal fact—albeit with different magnitudes—love it, hate it.

There are still more shocking revelations about education—and schools. Schools lag behind the rapidly changing world trends and technology. Schools rarely give due attention to the immediate needs of the society and therefore long-term failure is by no means unguaranteed! And this is not this humble author's—Kambarangwe's—insinuation.

It may shock you to recognize a person who accused schools to the extreme than I can go. "School failed me," said Albert Einstein, "and I failed the school. It bored me. The teachers behaved like feldwebel (sergeants).

"I wanted to learn what I wanted to know, but they wanted me to learn for the exam.

'What I hated most was the competitive system there and especially sports. Because of this wasn't worth anything and several times they suggested that I leave…

"I felt that my thirst for school was being strangled by the teachers who the grades were their only measurement.

"How can a teacher understand youth with such a system? From the age of 12, I began to suspect authority and distrust teachers."

Would you still doubt if I suggested that it is time to try out something different, something new? "Schools failed first, parents were second, and then students followed in their steps," concluded the Anti-School.

The society originally demanded schools to foster understanding and learning for our children. We wanted schools to teach them skills that they can use to solve practical problems of our society—which are bountiful!

A primary or grade school child should be able to learn practical skills and be able to solve problems at the family level like fix a flat tire, rectify electrical problems, manage home finances, relate more and better with people and environment around us etc—and develop integrity and positive character—the things that affect our lives so significantly.

But as I write this I even find it irrelevant because in the first place we are so aptly trained to be poor and not to think of prosperity and possibilities and thus as poor as we are, ability to solve day to day life challenges such as to repair a flat tire, electric or any other home appliances and management of home finances are things we shouldn't be bringing into the mix, no? These skills themselves seem irrelevant for the masses who attend these schools know nothing about. Can you now see how fatal and enormous the problem has grown?

Our curriculum should help my child learn first basic domestic skills, do some cleanliness, help with domestic chores etc., and become a responsible person who adds value and make life better for himself and people and environment around him starting with his family, his coworkers and his neighborhood. When Mwalimu Nyerere said "they are traitor's," he was right.

And it seems to me his idea transcends one single context.

They are traitors those who fail to transform our education. These children will cry out to us for having failed to transform their lives by transforming education. Our children are people who won't be able to give back to themselves their families and the society.

This is how we sow the seed of animosity in our youth. If they fail to learn such basic skills and character as children, suddenly life becomes more complex until, like any institution, they begin to think more about themselves and forget the purpose for which they were called in the first place and as a result, they fail in their higher calling for which they were ordained.

Truly there is great deal of disarray in our schools and education system as a whole. And it all stems from the endemic weaknesses such as lack of priorities, corrupt minds among those in power and their cohorts seeking effortless dough. It is no wonder those who go through the same system become victims of the same system. That is to say, our elites also have inherited the same syndrome. The recent political and financial scandals in the country can't have helped to put the foregoing into perspective.

Thus our students lack good role models among not only the politicians but also the professors and schools administrators. "Students hear about global responsibility while being educated in institutions that often invest ... in the most irresponsible things.

The lessons being taught are those of hypocrisy and ultimately despair. Students learn, without anyone ever saying it, that they are helpless to overcome the frightening gap between ideals and reality.

What is desperately needed is the faculty—and administrators—that builds and represents role models in terms of integrity, care, thoughtfulness, and institutions that are capable of embodying ideals wholly and completely in all of their operations."[53]

The bottom line is that we should be able through education to address staggering unemployment, rampant crime, crumbling family institution, alcoholism, child abuse, senseless consumerism, and generally wretchedness and hopelessness and giving up on life among youth.

Ours should be an education that helps the students to understand the real problems our society is facing. And that is not all. Our students do not only need the ability to come up with solutions to our problems, but as well the ability to participate in the real process of actually finding and solving the problems our society is facing today—and tomorrow. In the end, we come to a realization that as wrote Ornstein and Hunkins: Youth don't need half answers anymore such as education is good for your life. Rather they want complete answers. They want to know how exactly—and when.

They are not outside the education machinery itself. They are within and for life. They seek to appropriate it and bring it to bear. Learners must acquire abilities to produce or generate and consume or put knowledge to use, or generally education. Ornstein and Hunkins suggest rightly that it is the task of the students to take advantage of education and to make it their own, to personalize it.[54]

Having come this far, I am certain that it comes as no surprise to the reader, now, that—according to anti school—schools are on the whole preoccupied with their finances, personnel, buildings, and so forth, and not the students themselves or even more particularly assisting students to learn and master themselves as well as the environment around them—and taming both themselves and nature—for human development. We can say as long as the number of schools as institutions is on the rise, learning decreases! Imponderable, is it?

Education was not meant to be another form of an industry or business. It was what is it is and that is education.

And that explains why it was and still has to principally be provided by the government as the custodian of the interests of members of that nation. Notice however that I am referring to the government of the people, for the people, by the people. It is no wonder therefore the solution of more schools or more schooling to the school problem cannot not work anymore.

Yet what is more shocking is the fact that the situation gets worse by the day because of the rapidity with globalization and ICT extend their siege on us—notwithstanding the good things they may offer.

You the reader may join the author in recalling a few years back when we had a few establishments in terms of schools such as Cambridge, Harvard, Oxford, or even locally Ihungo, Kahororo, University of Dar es Salaam, Tabora Boys, Rugambwa School and a few others which were truly what you could call establishments. today we see ubiquitous schools everywhere with nothing new in terms of original or even true innovative schooling but instead a great deal of invention in the naming of the schools or rather branding. Branding doesn't anymore guarantee the value to the end user or therefore to its market.[55]

We believe in order to repair and redress the problems within education system and make it compatible with the needs of its consumers and now as it is, when it is faced with a down turn we need dialogue first and secondly listening to what consumers of education have to say. We aren't in contention with academics initiating proposals, conducting researches, gathering data and reviewing them. We instead strongly believe they should engage the public. They should *"...make contact with the parents and other lay people...obtain feedback from learners and evaluate programs (and communicate back)."*[56]

This is probably one factor that should have been at the head of the list of the factors behind the downfall of our education and society as a whole. And in this there is a need to go back to the beginning of education.

At the time, education or learning process wasn't a prejudiced process as it is today. There was nothing that was predetermined as wrong or right as it is in the eyes of the infant. But decisions were reached after one had explored two different situations— impartially. That's how they chose to eat one kind of food and forbid another.

That's how a child stops touching fire and goes on suckling the tits of its mother—as plain as it may seem to the reader.

The point is this: you can't really reprogram schools to make them produce more learning when as it is now, the prevailing schooling system has reached its peak. The only remedy lies in reinventing education or learning, and how we educate and learn as we shall discuss going forward. Please read our other title *How Universities under Develop You!*

We see the youth demanding definite achievable goals in schooling. We realize that they demand specialized knowledge and not general knowledge. We realize they demand a significant cut in time spent in schooling considering the pace and rapidity of change in trends; and the success factors and growth drivers and generally, the processes governing results or *The Governing Dynamics—aside from the decline of the average life span—among the majority.*

The today's youth deserve and demand guidance to self-training. After all we ought to address the fact that even after many and long years of learning, immediately after school, and schools of whatever level, most are left as *orphans* academically—orphaned by the system that is supposed to look after their interests in the first place.

With no job and on the streets the majority of graduates are desperate and without hope. As for the privileged few, they end in jobs or occupations that are less than what you could call decent jobs! Indeed most of such jobs are the ones that help to diminish one's own self-esteem turning them into modern slaves. Theirs are forms of life that don't put one's life in one's hands. The author is a witness of this personal tragedy.[57]

Following the mishaps we have stated, our schooled youth, then slave for the rest of their lives to make the ends meet for themselves and the children or else…well, starve or even die prematurely!

There is also another tragedy that the youth face. Many fall into a category of even retiring before they even had a privilege of proving their worth or gain returns from their investments in education through working. It is not different from the prelude to the Arab Spring.

After failing to secure a job whatsoever, a graduate in Tunis had no more options left for him. He chose to buy a few merchandize with little monies he managed to secure; and as a vendor of last resort, he packed his merchandize on the streets in the city. It didn't take long before his entire mobile shop was literally railroaded by the city authorities in the name of keeping the city clean. What followed was unprecedented.

He did the necessary. He committed suicide. Not a normal one though! It was peculiar. He set himself alight burning himself down to ashes. Ashes to ashes he returned to his Maker in style. And that was only a little beyond his teens. the reader can revert to the event with more details in this very book but suffices to say here that the event triggered the pandemonium that led to mass protest leading to political Tsunami in the Arab world and a change of regimes in many western countries from The States to France and Greece and almost any other country that hold elections since then.

The statement you have just read denotes that this is the best age for the thinking men who want to enter politics. They only have to have a plan and act with urgency and comprehensiveness, if the people should bid them enter as they tread toward the State House or any public office.

If you are one of such people with ambitions into politics or public offices, read the part on creativity both in this series and in the book: *What Makes People Rich and Nations Powerful. What I say to the reader with ambitions for politics, I say the same to the one with ambition in business and every other calling or vocation.*

Caution should be made among the educators and policy makers therefore. Students are not the passive consumers of some generic educational products anymore. They are free persons desirous of learning. They are mysterious and whatever they do is in response to exploring the mysteries of the world. Hence empathizing with them will ignite whenever transformation we crave whenever it matures—with or without better conditions.

What can we conclude from the Anti-School public statement? Briefly students don't fancy the kind of education we have in place today. It is not advantageous to them. Besides, they consider it as superimposed upon them. Therefore they cannot engage themselves in searching for such an education anymore. They sabotage it. And they delightedly do so through boycotts or dropping out altogether.

Observe therefore that in preparing our youth to be ideal graduates or scholars, and therefore naturally ideal citizens and good leaders, we are even doing a far more important duty to our nation and the people today than ever before.

Today many students don't find it delightful or necessary to make it through the conventional and traditional classroom sequence from kindergarten up the University Heights.

As leaders or adults and responsible parents we cannot let them go through life as orphans. They need us as much as we need them. Probably we need to embrace change and transform our thought patterns, as many scholars have begun reckoning this dire need. Among them in Tanzania is the outstanding Professor Nkunya.

Addressing the East African initiative on education and youth recently in Arusha, a good Professor emphasized the need to meet this challenge head-on. Ours is an education or curriculum that weeps for rescue. It starves for the new ideas. It craves infusion of alternative thought in its fabric, in order to meet the changing educational and social economic terrain.

One of such needs is to critically start building character and right attitude among students and the youth in general as is summed up in this work through the proceeding chapters.

Worst of all in this new era of ICT, globalization, economic downturn and East African Community at hand, if we don't embrace change and the needs of now, if we don't respond timely and appropriately, we are otherwise building the future slaves—slaves in their own land!

And this is the worst form of humiliation a sane learned and patriotic citizen can himself endure or receive as tidings that this is the only possible future for his or her nation and offspring—and receive it with great joy. Nay! Truly, ours are no more better prospects.

Finally don't be deceived by how the youth today seem to be quite impressive on the outside. Deep at the centre of their hearts they suffer.

This by itself is a sign of emptiness ad nothingness deep inside. That they are arrogant is a sign that they are indeed engulfed by worry, anxiety, fear or its extreme state—indifference.

These are signs of futility and hopelessness, frustration and despair. Such persons are home to bad emotions and wicked negative inspirations of fear, jealousy hared, revenge, greed, superstition, anger and quick fix. They have no positive inspirations of love desire, faith, hope, familiness, enthusiasm, self esteem, honesty and candor. But that's not all. They don't seem to realize that by behaving that way, they welcome miseries since such attitudes drive away the positive inspirations for prosperity.

What is important is that, if this was something exhibited by an individual or groups of youth I a certain region we wouldn't mind much. But with the national footprint, this prevalence is a disaster. It is a tragedy! Solution? Well, let's see! Coercion? No! That will not work.

The government can deploy the armed regiments and the infamous Field Force Unit but that battle cannot be won by machine guns or artilleries, not even the drones by airborne attacks.

The students can rebel and join the oppressed guerrilla fighters in the vast bushes we have in plenty but that won't work too.

They are like a man with a tooth pick fighting against someone with a loaded Kalashnikov. That battle can only be won through transformation of the mind and behavior change by winning the youth—to your way of thinking.

It can only be won by a program that helps to win back the confidence of the youth. It can be won by engaging the youth in the educational programs and curriculum development in which both curriculum and development are defined from the youth's point of view as well as the general society.

This is probably what Freire called the *"Pedagogy of The oppressed"* describing how people can move from different stages to ultimately be able to take action and overcome oppression.

To effect major change, at what Freire calls the "critical transforming stage," people must become active participants in changing their own status through social action that aims at changing the larger social order...dialogue between students and adults who are sensitive to change. The curriculum is to focus on community, national, and world problems—and is to be based on a core or interdisciplinary approach.[58]

Until when that happens, the prosperous and peaceful Tanzania remains to be speculative!

10. LOW GRADUATE SELF EMPLOYMENT—THE DARK SCAR IN OUR TRADITIONAL COLLEGE EDUCATION

"Observe due measure, for right timing is in all things the most important factor." —Hesiod

Through the preceding chapter, we analyzed the various weaknesses in our education system—albeit weaknesses in the eye of the extreme view on education. We both are the witnesses that though the view is extreme, it offers an alternative view point. And the case is this: The problems we see in our education and society today, don't solely spring up from the deficiencies among the students—the youth themselves. That is why we need a broadminded analysis. That is the primary handicap on those who want to transform education fixing their eyes on only that angle. The school, or the society as a whole, has to rethink itself out, and find ways and means to change when it deems necessary. And this rethink should be *ad infinitum*—which means it should be done constantly or rather incessantly! As such, it is not true or fair to take it: *"for granted that there is nothing wrong in the schools (and that) it was the student (and not the school) that needed to be changed."*[59]

Now we will move on to illustrate one of the areas in which the anti-school sentiment is valid. Through the following pages, you will find an astounding story. It is not necessarily a good one, mind you, nonetheless an important one! It is a true one, nonetheless. I know it is, because I, the author, has experienced this situation on the first person account. Here is something more that can be said about it: It did help my decision to change the course of my life.

I'm writing it here hoping it will help you meet the genius who is within you as it happened to me almost eight years ago! We have indicated that to a man of education, getting employed is neither the end, nor rationalization of his being educated. But to be prosperous or especially successful and free, according to one's definition (within limits of course) , is an essential indicator—which nonetheless men of education have successfully managed to achieve so awkwardly.

Our graduates are slowly coming to terms with this handicap. Anyone who questions the foregoing claim may find rationale in the ever increasing wave of readership—or popularity and influence—of such books as Poor Daddy Rich Daddy by Robert Kiosaki, Think Big by Ben Carson, Think and Grow Rich by Napoleon Hill, Science of Getting Rich by Wattles D. Wallace, you were born rich by Bob Proctor, and What Makes People Rich and Nations powerful by this author—among the titles in the inspirational genre— besides various initiatives promoting alternative lifestyles and ways of learning evidence this claim. That's why that the traditional schooling is no longer valued anymore is no longer a secret.

And these aren't the claims of a cynic or an average author. Both Illich and Freire contented the larger system is oppressive and in need of a major overhaul. A.s. Neill wrote from experience of running his own school Summerhill in Suffolk England thus: "...*we set out to make a school in which we should allow children to be themselves. In order to do this, we had to renounce all discipline, all direction, all suggestion...all is required was what we had—a complete belief in the child as a good not an evil being. For almost forty years this belief in the goodness of the child has never wavered; it rather has become a final faith...The child is innately wise and realistic. If left to himself without adult suggestions of any kind, he will develop on his own. Those who will become scholars will be scholars and those who are only suited to sweep the streets will sweep the streets. Those who will study will study, and those who prefer not to study will not— regardless of how teachers teach or what they say. If a child wants to go to class, great; if not, so what?*[60] Probably that is on the extreme. I believe students should be given choices within limitations again of course. Rights of course come with responsibilities.

The suggestions we present in this chapter aren't mere words of a frustrated graduate. There is meaning in the *Anti-School* approach, at least to some extent, since some of their arguments are in sync with not only great authors, but the ones who have themselves extensive and in depth knowledge in the matters of curriculum development. In their great book, Allan C. Ornstein and Francis P. Hunkins, concluding a subtopic on curriculum development, said: "*Perhaps all those involved should think of curriculum, the result of curriculum development, as an open system. By accepting this, teachers and students would celebrate the challenges, realizing that these are needed to disrupt their knowledge system, in order for learning ... and ... personal transformation to occur. Curriculum as an open system is a journey for all involved, a journey to be experienced with zest, not a destination to be arrived at and then stored and hoarded.*"[61]

Is there any explanation that vindicates the youth to believe and behave the way they do?? Let us examine the facts. With the fact that our today's youth who form two third of our population are what you could call a digital generation, and they are therefore faster, we need to respond to their claims immediately before it is too late. The youth want too quick results. They want to get rich and successful in their chosen areas sooner than later. And what's more, they know it is possible.

As we will rationalize concerning the attitude on getting rich or succeeding in any of their chosen vocations below, notice however that the pro school argument should be that despite examples of such successful people among them dropouts who have had incredible significant accomplishments, with righty education they would accomplish far more.

The argument should be that though one is today a local businessman or celebrity, but that he would probably be an international businessman as we speak. the argument among th pro school should emphasize, for instance, the fact that I've met many people who believed that they would make it—with or without education—people who t regretted and realized that to make the ends meet without education (I mean any kind of specialized training in one's chosen field) was as hard as finding a broken needle in an enormous haystack in the field.

The pro education should rationalize how the only possible occupation for a day dreamer as only back breaking wage labor—something that is totally unworthy when compared with one's talents. The pro education should refer to such true experiences like the author's.

A few years ago, I met a person I knew very closely since my boyhood. I met him in Shinyanga. He was at work. But what a work! It was a backbreaking chore of washing clothes when I first met him. Not with the machine though? No! He washed with his hands. The next time I visited him he had a bundle of male and female clothes before him—still washing. He was not an insane lunatic. No. Nor was it his hobby. His own? I mean the clothes. No sir!

Other people's cloths! It was his occupation. He had dropped out of school choosing to engage in the cross border black market that thrived at the time. This is no fiction. It is real. He is real. His name is Safari—one of the smart guys during our youth hood. He was so smart a boy that the author was driven to envy him several times without number. The pro school should also address the fact that getting money is one thing, and retaining and generating it is another.

We will discuss through this series how millionaires who almost owned the world died as paupers. Making money can be easy. But keeping it different. You cannot therefore become wealthy in approaches similar to pulling a rabbit out of a hat. To prove this we don't have to go far off. Right here on the country we have a number of artists who got money but only in the course of a couple of years became paupers.

They, the youth and the children, crave results—big ones and—now. Poor guys! You notice I have said crave. Not want or desire. It is something they need beyond the normal desire. The pace of change is so fast that they cannot wait for long to finish school or go for the advanced degree or some post graduate courses to be able to earn money enough to fit in the system.

They are faced with ICT and globalization. The IPAD culture, social networking and dreaming big, demand spending to remain in the picture. The today's youth also are faced with the problem associated with the mergers. Today vertical as well lateral combinations are the order of the day. And with high-tech and automation, mergers squeeze the ever dwindling employment potential to the limits. And above all there is a new monster and she is already in the bedroom: The shrinking economy and generally the unbending economic crisis.

That's why we truly need to guide our youths. The trouble is if left alone, the culture of *Get Rich or Die Trying* if left un-tackled will mislead the youth than guide the nation to prosperity we need and deserve. This is the right mindset—the right response.

Let us now examine what vindicates their claim to quick big success.

HOW THE ATTITUDE OF THE YOUTH IS VINDICATED

The youth have conspicuous examples of young successful businessmen of our times. We can talk of inventors such as Zuckerberg whom everybody knows being the founder of facebook, why not? But we also know a number of internationals who have made it in politics or sports in their youthful years. David Cameron led the labor party before he successfully led it to victory and himself as prime minister at the age that vindicates to anyone that anything is possible. The Brazilian football star, Neymar, among others, is already a millionaire at the age when many are still in school.

Here at home individuals Joseph Kusaga, the Clouds Group CEO and Managing Director, Ruge Mutahaba, Leonard Chacha, January Makamba, Zitto Kabwe, Halima Mdee, John Mnyika—among others—besides some local artists who don't necessarily possess even modest education, let alone having an advanced degree in their possession have helped to influence the paradigm shift.

This impressive list helps to inspire others outside the traditional prosperity ladder. You cannot blame them, can you! How can you! One more time think about Zuckerberg—the facebook founder—who at 25 and now turning 28 is worthy 5 billion dollars!

That's why the youth feel very little love for the traditional linear breed of education. Did I say Linear? Well yes. Linear. Let us see how Cambridge Advanced Learner's Dictionary defines it. *Linear measurement is relating to length, rather than area or volume.* You see. It isn't anything to do with cumulative or rather bulging or radiating form of education but simply crossing a number of years or series.

It is something involving a series of events or thoughts in which one thought or event follows another one directly. What is not written here is that once engaged in the linear form of learning or education, one seldom goes back in his own tracks to pick up the inputs from where he began. any linear process never reconciles itself with the other lives or rather it never reconciles itself to the other realities of life even when they are just in the vicinity, provided they are on its east or west, south or north.

What is important to this kind of the process is that it is on its track obediently following its predetermined track in the north direction even when it may be a road that leads to nowhere.

The great writers of the great dictionary added something so spot-on that I would like to share it with you. This is what the men in guard of the old don't want to put in practice let alone hear about it.

The Dictionary says to break the linear thought pattern you need "… mental exercises…designed to break linear thinking habits and encourage the innovation that is needed for innovation.

"Our youth need to know what does really drive our lives as the society but more so and particularly what drives their lives.

Recognizing that the youth have high hopes and that the sky is their limit, now take your time and think about the poor youth. They don't need your house anymore. Your car is outdated. Your phone is an old and obsolete gadget your son or daughter is not *gonna* feel proud to inherit. Your thought pattern or mindset and pulse are so limited.

The youth aim higher. They aim to cross over to the other side of the ocean. They see it. They experience their friends flying in and out from Guangzhou, New York and London. They see their peers travelling to SA on a business trip.

They demand a lot. That's the troubling problem—a troubling problem to the old generation. But the most striking one is the fact that they deserve better things. They deserve freedom of movement but more so the freedom of thought and freedom to choose. After all we have got the resources to deliver and achieve this challenge. I mean we as individuals and the society as a whole have got this ability if the environment is right.

That ability is innate. It is deep in us, beckoning, ever eagerly waiting to be put to use! Cathy Williams couldn't be more right when she said: "There is nothing worse than a fine brain stagnating out of lack of use!"[62]

THE FRUSTRATED SCHOOLED MANAGER AND A SUCCESSFUL EARLY SCHOOL DROP OUT

What is now being presented to you, is a true story. It is a story that presented itself to the author in no dramatic way whatsoever! As you are about to establish, it was an event that led to series of events, events that were themselves simple and plain in nature.

Yes it was only a simple and queer event to attract attention, but it led to a dramatic shift in my life—as you are about to see! And about this story, I know it is a true story because the person I refer to with the pronoun "I," is me, yeah me, the author.

I was serving as promotions and sponsorships manager at Celtel in 2006 when we ran a promotion that triggered a shift in my mind against formal employment and its upward career growth ladder.

Celtel was a Pan African telecom company that had over fifteen operations in the whole of Africa headed from Amsterdam at the time. I resigned and moved on before this company was taken over by Zain and now Airtel.

It should be brought to the attention of the reader that my capacity at the time, led to my extensive countrywide travels. Now though I traveled the country over, it was during my trip to Mbeya City—a city in the south of the country—that led to the unveiling of the whole revelation.

My maiden trip to the southern highlands began with little fanfare. And I traveled by road. I preferred to drive because I wanted to have an eyeful of the region, especially the renowned Kitonga Mountains. I took the driver of course. However, it wasn't long before I regretted my decision to travel by road. I was overwhelmed by the winding ever rising narrow tarmac track as we cycloned into the sky over the southern highlands.

I was breathless the rest of my trip fearing we would not make it to Mbeya in one piece. You are going to read more about the Kitonga Mountain in this series, but it suffices to say here that you catch a glimpse of dramatic view of the things you would not have believed to be possible. One of the things you wouldn't consider as possibilities is to come back in one piece, scanning a few kilometers deep at the foot of the Kitonga and looking at the number of car wreckages.

To be honest, I hated my job too. In my capacity, and because this was a national promotion, it was my obligation to oversee the event of presenting the said prizes to the regional winners—prizes we presented physically. Now the prizes included the grand prizes—the building materials enough to finish and furnish the whole house. To facilitate the distribution and logistics, we commissioned third party company, one dealing in building materials, to oversee the logistics and delivery of the materials wherever the venue was for that was a national promotion.

That's how I first met him. I met him the next morning at the Sokoine stadium. For anonymity I will call this guy by his only first name viz. Paul.

Now here is another coincidence. The motto of that promotion—as is of the intention of this writing and its twin training program—was: *Making Life Better*!

Having arrived safely a night before, I woke up very early in the morning to check on the program beginning with the venue—which was the Sokoine Stadium, a football stadium in the City—and the logistics.

The program was on schedule and analyzing all about me, I concluded that I had nothing to worry about. I was wrong!

The prizes handover went well though. But that's not an important part of the story, except for one thing: the event facilitated my meeting with Paul. He, Paul, was the guy in charge of the logistics. From our first meeting, he seemed to be a genuine person, one you could trust. But he was also so simple that you could expect anything dramatic from him. That's how life can be tricky.

Now here is who Paul was in contrast to me. Whereas I worked for a big pan African organization where I held a high managerial position, poor Paul worked for a privately owned building materials and logistic company in the position of the sales clerk. Mark the contrast! Naturally he was not highly schooled and received no fringe benefits I was entitled to. Frankly I felt a little bossy and I pitied him during our first meeting. I bought him dinner and footed a bill for his few drinks to console his heart's excruciating pain over his unfortunate circumstances. Why not? If you were in my position yourself, you would do the same. No matter how evil men have become, the true compassionate human ego created in us still lingers.

The narrative we are now relating is the after-party one-on-one meeting in which we chose to have a few drinks together somewhere in the city to cerebrate the success of the event, and of course getting to know one another better. And we didn't do so for the love of a drink or ritual in the cold southern highlands. It was important to do so, since we would be working together for the next couple of weeks.

From our conversation, I learned that whereas I'd just graduated and ever since had served with the world class organizations for the past eight years, Paul had dropped out—one way or another—just after secondary school. But behind all his apparent misfortune, he began learning how to manage the business over the years when I pursued my academics and the years after my graduation when I worked as an arm chair officer in different companies.

The differences between the two of us were now very clear to me and far removed from one another—only that the tables had turned upside down. That's how history has proved to be very theatrical—like circus. When we first met, he was the underdog—at least in my imagination. Yes he was an underdog also to the person drunk of the illusion of the degree papers. But he was not. In fact it wasn't too long that I wisely, nonetheless thunderstruck, I assumed my rightful position, the underdog from the *underworld*, as he assumed his—the lecturing role.

He lectured to me how he came to own a house in the city, a house which now sheltered his family whereas I still had to cope as a tenant sharing a roof with a bunch of noisy singles and couples I didn't care about or love to be with. A simple description of the persons we shared a house will describe how our lives were on two different extremes—albeit unbelievable tricky relationship.

One of my fellow *inmates* was a drunk who owned two women; another was a single boy whose room saw different women every other day while another was a young woman who slept the whole day and dressing strangely disappeared in the dark of the night as soon as the sun set. There were others who didn't care about anything but peeking on anyone who was around for any clues to furnish the gossip they loved to fuel. That was one of the differences that sharply set us apart. The second was equally humiliating. Though Paul worked as a sales clerk for a private company you couldn't call big business, for the past five years, he had been owning and managing his own company or business—a skill he had learnt by doing. And you already know it. His was a business in building materials.

The third difference that set us apart was that whereas I spent hours in bars trying to manage my idle free hours before I went to bed back home, he had no such thing as free time. He spent his evenings at his hardware shop.

Again, because my schooled wife worked in the government, on her return home she needed a good rest, his served as the manager and accountant of their business a few meters away from their residential house he came home to relieve her after his office hours. Because of the nature of her job, my wife arrived home late in the evening after having woken early in the morning, wasting four hours a day commuting to her office as she only waited for the month end salary as her opposite number did quite the opposite. The other difference was that I was coincidentally on the borderline of quitting from such kind of job, for self employment, whereas at the time he was already a guru! His hardware shop had just conceived and had brought forth another house he leased, and another shop whereas I was barely finishing furnishing my house—quite a modest house. Accordingly, a few months later, I mean after our first meeting, I resigned, and was jobless struggling on my own new feet like an infant who learned to walk despite my many year of having been instructed in the ways of business and economics at the university. It is during the same time that we met again. I was driving my hand-me-down three doors Suzuki Vitara procured through strenuous bank facility my employer had generously afforded me, while Paul was driving a five door 4x4 land cruiser—his employer's? Oh no! It was his toy.

And as the Americans say the most successful person is the one who owns many toys! That was not all. Whereas I was just starting a business in building materials which didn't work anyway—and I'm not ashamed to admit it—he told me his had grown enough to give birth to yet another one, which now had created an opening for his brother. I was jobless trying to make my company stand on its own feet, and he was hiring graduates like me to serve him.

The last time we met, I'd just gone out to a club in Mbezi with my wife for a little recreation. Now because I was out of job, I ordered a few drinks and bites. I had to do so and do it very carefully like how Greece is now rationing her moneys after the failed bail out, for I was learning to cope with austerity despite my many years of working as a top manager.

He and his wife on the other hand, didn't seem to care for the money. They really seemed to be in a partying mood. Probably he had had another big kill! I was so ashamed of myself this time—I must admit. Honestly! I hated my education and felt really disgraced. And of all humiliation to a man fit to be my own driver or messenger at Celtel or Tanzania Breweries or Carlsberg where I served as a sales, marketing and brand manager, he was now many times ahead of me.

I was top in the classroom and especially numeracy both of which sent this guy packing and dropping out of school. But now imagine a dumb student in the class, poor in numeracy and commerce; now training me how to do business and how to add up the assets and minimize the liabilities, downsizing the overheads, taking advantage of economies of scale—and in the process—reaping off the margins!

He was also teaching me a lesson on how to take a good care of your spouse! I was ashamed of myself. I pitied my parents and the dreams of my parents—dreams on my education. I didn't want to think of my children's future—or of my marriage! I felt contempt for my teachers and lectures at the university. I couldn't find the word that described the feeling I had for politicians and the policy makers—and still I do.

LAST WORD

We have, through this chapter, been presented with the vindication of the youth who are not fond of school or education any more. Should we blame them anymore—anyway?

Besides, since you didn't witness—on the firsthand account—what I tell you, and therefore you cannot be in my shoes to feel exactly as I felt that day and days after, and therefore likely to be least convinced, think about it this way, if this is true even one little bit, and if you were in my shoes, would you be proud of yourself in this position? Wouldn't you also agree with me that the position we fall in as individuals and society isn't anything near blessing , yes?

Again you will probably have begun to realize how privileged you must now be with the publication of this book, no?

Now as I edge to the end of this chapter, I must remark that I mournfully began this chapter with nothing close to gloom—gloom that was accompanied by contempt and humiliation on my part but now realize that that was indeed a blessing—blessing in disguise nonetheless. Truly my fortunate encounter with Paul helped me in so many ways. Before I met him, I counted myself as someone more powerful than those beneath me academically. It was dead wrong.

But in all these blessings, one that should be at the head of the tree, is that whereas for all the years I had counted my adversaries—and indeed I had had quite an impressive list—after meeting this guy, I realized I was wrong. I had overlooked my troubles and had failed to locate my one and only one greatest enemy, and certainly one who had caused miseries and troubles I encountered my whole life than the rest of mine enemies combined. He is the one principal enemy and the most malicious of all. Surprisingly, his name didn't appear in the list. I didn't think he could be. Do you know who he is?

Did you ever notice you could be facing the same calamity I was facing? I was introduced to my enemy thanks to Paul. That enemy was—well, it is still the same enemy and adversary I have to tame and be cautious with. You want to know that enemy, yes? That enemy is the one you and I walk around with. If you didn't know yours and mine, forget about mine. Go work on yours for I will now introduce mine to you. Well—if you want, you can find his name at the front and back covers!

Ever since then, I have learned my lessons. Though I am not advocating ignorance or illiteracy, which doesn't describe Paul anyway—I have learned from him the importance of dropping out.

You cannot progress if you don't drop out one way or another. You cannot get something without letting go of one thing or another—be it beer, cigarette or girl friends. It also applies to career or vocation, heaven or hell. It is pure economic theory of choice making—forgoing one thing to get another. Paul had dropped out of school to be successful—in his own way. I dropped from work. So what's a big deal? He had goals and knew what he wanted. From the beginning and we go to the university or apply for a job without a streamlined goal or plan of action. We don't want to believe such success on his part or failure on the part of graduates and executives is a coincidence. No success or failure of such magnitudes is coincidental! No!

It is wrong priorities, wrong ambitions and misunderstanding what modernity means. It doesn't mean to be hired by someone—and especially big multinationals. It doesn't mean to work for life. It doesn't mean to do everything everybody else is doing—person or country.

Now since our youth are so much concerned with modernity, we must analyze if it is a bad thing. It is not. Yes we need modernization. But what is it? What does it mean? It is technology. It is constant evolution and keeping pace with changes. But modernization on its own is not good when it sets its focus on the outside world. Modernization must be of the people, by the people, for the people. Vladimir *Putin* helped to put the question of modernity into the right perspective when he answered: "Yes we need modernization , but to attain sustainability, we need (yes*)* foreign capital investment... (but even so, we need*)*   innovation (here*)*   at home!"

Empowerment of our people and especially the youth is pivotal to the growth agenda or national development. But with the extent of the mess we already are in, we need new ideas, new homegrown inputs, if we should reverse the situation. No true and lasting change shall come from outside. No true and lasting change shall come from outside. Yes we need foreign capital, technology, and skilled manpower. Yes we cannot manage on our own for now. But no growth agenda can rise from a short term perspective based on imported ideas, plans or manpower.

Any natural and thus lasting growth should be organic, and must come from the people themselves. Think about it. How can you build innovative workforce and grassroots growth path when the psychology behind your model is that of the ancients who expected the angels to descend down to earth from high heaven and do some miracles and then immediately ascend back from whence they had come?

Experiences from our recent privileges on cancelation of national debts on one hand, and lessons from China or Botswana prove otherwise—among others. Mineral or fuel rich countries of Africa or Asia have not gained any progress from descending white angels.

On the contrary, the human angels of today instead of smelting gold and diamond into wealth for the local people, they ascended back to whence they had come from with not only gold and diamond or gas and oil! They ascended back with local self confidence and self esteem, thus leaving behind not only waste materials such as underground useless holes and heaps of underground soils and overused polluted rivers and contaminated air alone, but also waste intellect, overused polluted minds and contaminated hearts and souls of our people. We can only progress through grassroots strategy, strategy that leads to advancement and evolution of our people's own initiatives and homegrown ideas.

For advantageous modernization, yes our society needs foreign capital investment both tangible and intangible, for the impact to be sustainable. The society has as well to reinvent itself beginning with the homegrown impetus addressing the mindset of first the youth, but also the self-righteousness of our academics and finally the will of the leadership at all levels from the household, schools, workplaces and among religious and government circles. This is the modernization we need. This is the innovation our society weeps for. These are things that can transform the society from one that is at the receiving end, to one that is at the control of her own destiny, one that can even influence the destiny of humanity.

As for the reader who began this chapter with apprehension, let me say that the *Anti-School* has some validity. The reason why it has not attracted much attention is due to their *failure to draw out a consistent and comprehensive proposition* establishing a set of principles and the description of the process that would lead to the desired end. And this handicap is conceived in the failure to look at the good side of your opponent. You—yes, you the reader—could be doing the same mistake even right now as you read this line! Finally, a statement must be made concerning this book—and chapter.

I must state that I wrote this book with the reader in mind—a reader who may be in the position I was in at the time (and that reader who is a little mediocre. I also have news for the top student or employee or even that businessman who is very successful!

You can do more!

But I must also go over the fact that I didn't write this book to impress anyone, much as I didn't write it to pick on someone! I wrote it to inspire the reader. I wrote it to inspire the reader to find meaning in whatever he does in life. That's why I wrote this book and chapter. I wrote it to help you make out whether you are in the right course—or not. I wrote it, that ultimately, if you are not, you may turn and flee! I wrote it to assure you that you can accomplish this goal today, or after ten years—that depend on you—really.

For after all, it is your life that is under the microscope—not the author's! I wrote this chapter to assure you that no matter how long it may take, change has finally come! I wrote it because I knew the day is coming when this nation and the human society as a whole would need a book like this one. I wrote it because I knew a day had come when this book was going to be opened and read amongst our schools. But above all, aside from the fact that you don't need one at the expense of another,[63]

I also wrote this chapter, this book, to pronounce—in words of Mark McCormack that: "I don't have an innate prejudice against intellect or intelligence (and graduate degrees for that matter)," he said, "but," continued Mark McCormack, "they (intelligence or graduate degrees) are not substitutes for common sense, people sense and 'street smartness'!"[64]

11. WHO IS TO BLAME?

"Every man can make mistakes but only the idiot persists in his error!"
—Cicero

Having reviewed where our society—or any other nation—goes wrong, the question pops up: Who is to Blame? Well, did I Say who is to blame? Oh, dear me!

Well, forget it. I don't involve myself in that. Forget I wrote that sentence—in the first place. I recant it—however shorter that sentence is. I am even ashamed of myself for just thinking about it. Let us seek solutions—together.

That's the right course. That's pragmatism, materialism. Okay?

Let me instead recall a piece of a tale from one Abunuasi.

A TALE OF ABUNUASI
One day Abunuasi took off and went out to fetch firewood. That was necessary those days in Arabia when there were no gas cookers or power. Luckily he found a tree with dry branches.

It was only a few meters from the highway. Being himself a materialist, he grabbed the opportunity. Hastily, he ascended the tall tree. Sitting on the far side of the branch of a tree he began chopping it off from the main tree trunk.

If you can clearly make the mental picture of his position, he was now hanging in the midair on a branch that he was cutting loose from the stem of the main tree. He was in fact cutting down, detaching a piece of a tree that connected him with the main tree.

People came and went on their ways passing by never minding what he was doing—minding their own business. Whether they did so fearing to meddle into other people's affairs or not, I have no way of knowing. What I know though is that almost everybody didn't care what was going on. But not all of the Arabs were unmindful of other people's needs. When one of the passers-by saw what he was doing, seeing how strange that was, came closer and warned him that unless he shifted from that position and sat on the trunk of main tree and cut the branch from that other side, in that position he was in, he was going to fall off with the branch he was chopping off.

He should have known that he would fall off of course unless he absurdly imagined the law of gravitation wasn't at work at the time and space he was in and that therefore he would float in the air! Abunuasi didn't heed his advice. The man having warned him, took off and went on with his own business. Abunuasi went to work with great enthusiasm. Chopping the branch on which he sat, suddenly he fell off flat on the ground.

Now the question is this: Was it a prophecy? No sir! Do we know why Abunuasi didn't heed the advice? Nope! Whether he was dumb, or some ancient genius who craved to prove everything on firsthand account, I have no way of knowing. What I know though is that little than a few minutes just after the prediction was made, the branch gave way, and with it he fell off lying breathless at the foot of the tree on the ground underneath. Recovering from the shock, still sound and safe, he pondered at the *prophecy*.

He couldn't but consider the passerby to be a modern day prophet. He couldn't wait to be reunited with a divine man—a seer. Running as fast as he could with all energy he could muster, he caught up with the *seer,* and catching his breath, panting, he wanted to know how he, the *seer*, knew what the future had in store for other men—literally begging. Because he regarded this stranger so religiously, he begged him—literally on his knees—to know when and how would his death pull in so he could set his affairs in order and welcome the old man death with as much grace as he could muster!

You cannot blame Abunuasi, can you? He had just witnessed his prediction actually come to pass! This man wasn't a seer though. He wasn't. He was only a sensible man. He was only no less than a strong believer in the nature's law. To Abunuasi, he was a prophet. If you think about it, that isn't different from how religions of the world sprang to life.

Think of it! His demise—I mean the fact that he would fall off—wasn't a prediction one bit. Really. He wasn't a prophet. He was a realist. What he said was only logical. That he would fall, wasn't a prophecy. It was common sense. Logic. Science. The consequence of hanging in the air chopping off the part of a tree that held together the branch he sat on and the main tree was more than knowably foreseeable and equally ruinously catastrophic. That he would fall was as simple as I can bet my life on the fact that there shall be night tonight, excepting of the extreme curved parts of the earth in the North or South Pole of course—if you have a spark of some geography. What you sow, the same shall you reap. Period!

THE CRISIS OF EDUCATION IN TANZANIA: SHOULD WE FIRE THE MINISTER OF EDUCATION, DR. SHUKURU KAWAMBWA? Very recently, and persistently, I have heard people reacting to the examinations results, results in which for instance over fifty percent of students in our secondary schools failed, pointing fingers shouting: "The Minister for Education, (Dr. Shukuru Kawambwa) Should Go." Some of these voices come from very senior people. That's why really I was shocked and therefore dragged into the debate. That's when I found that some of these people were in it for political gains—and personal interests. Not all of them, though. Others were naïve and you cannot blame their naivety on them.

Notice that I have no personal connections whatsoever with the minister—genetic, political or business! After all, when this book gets out the term of the government he serves might already be expired! So I have no favors for the minister on one hand or malice whatsoever toward his adversaries on the other. And I say this "with malice toward none, with charity for all!"[65] The foregoing assertion doesn't, however, nullify a good gesture of goodwill on Dr. Kawambwa's own part if he chose to tender his own resignation if he recognized that he had failed the job—or the appointing authority.

For all the people grumbling for his resignation here is their answer: That's not the solution. It never will be. He, the minister, is not the problem—and the problem is not even the appointing authority for the appointee remains one of the best the society could offer. The solution therefore lies in tackling the core problems we have in our society. Whether we all accept Big Results Now as lasting solution or not—Big Results Now, being the most recent attempt to revamp developmental and educational issues by the government—doesn't matter at all. But that's an attempt—and we should be praising such attempts, than if the government held back and went on with business as usual.

Having come this far, it is safer now to rationalize together. Do you realize that our problem is bigger than is resignation of the minister? For reasonable results, the response should at least be in the same magnitude of the problem we want to solve. That solution therefore is a simplistic one. Do you realize that the minister for education is not the minister for youth? Do you realize that Kawambwa is not to blame for our performances in sports? Dr. Kawambwa is not the minister for health services, is he? He is not the minister for industry or factory works, for that matter! He is not in charge over every other household in the country. I have mentioned these other areas to try to open the reader's eyes a little wider. I have explored other areas to illustrate that we have problems with our youth and their mindset on education and life as a whole in this era of ICT than we seem to appreciate.

And what about drugs and the elephants tusks that are ferried across our borders? Dr. Kawambwa is only the minister of one ministry. He is not the prime minister either. Even so, he is not a cherub! He is just a human being like you and me!

We have consistently performed so pathetically in sports. We have been thrashed by our neighboring national teams in football competitions such as losing to Uganda 3 nil in several games both at home and away for several years now despite personal involvement of the president himself. Despite the hand of the Brazilian super coach Maximo, our performances never soared to the roof. And what about Maximo? We petitioned for his ouster because we wanted quick results when he believed in organic growth—and he was a stern disciplinarian!

Did you consider that we have performed so disappointingly in the Olympics for over the last generation even when we share borders, genetics and heredity with the generation of ubiquitous gold medalists in Kenya, Uganda and Ethiopia (for we too have Nilotic, Hamitic and Cushite communities in the country albeit a small population as compared to Bantu)?

In the health sector—to mention but only a few examples—the nation was stunned when we heard how our top medical doctors almost amputating a leg of a patient who actually was admitted for the chronic problem in the head; and on the overturn, they operated the head of the wrong patient. One of this unfortunate pair didn't love it or survive it. He died a little later as another had to be referred to India to reverse the situation. How ashamed I am to have to write about this sad event!

Emmanuel Mgaya, 19, and Emmanuel Didas, 20, checked into the Muhimbili National Hospital on the same day in the same ward, each with planned a surgical procedure—Didas to repair a knee damaged in a motorcycle accident and Mgaya to remove a brain tumor. Because of their shared first name, however, hospital staff mixed up the two patients and ending up operating on Mgaya's healthy knee and removing a non-existent tumor from Didas' brain.

Didas was left partially paralyzed from the unnecessary brain operation, and Mgaya received the brain operation he needed two weeks later but died soon after surgery. Mgaya's family declined to sue the hospital……The surgeons involved with the mix-up were suspended, and the staff was ordered to give written explanations.[66]

Such actions aren't actions of poor or absence of medical or surgical expertise. They are rather a function of our culture. They are results of our character, attitude. I, the author, has had to arrive at this conclusion unhurriedly. We have had to consider many factors. Among these factors, recently, in another operation, a doctor sewed back the abdomen after a successful surgery on the patient.

That's not a problem. The problem was that he had left a couple of those fancy tinniest surgical scissors beautifully and impeccably stored in the patient's abdomen!

The outcome? That's obvious. He didn't recover. His journey to the kingdom come was prompted against his will.

The point I am trying to make is this: technical success on its own is void. You recognize that despite the successful surgery, the poor patient's condition moved from good to bad and bad to worse; and worse to worst. And when I say character, I don't point fingers to the professionals alone. Let us attempt to analyze what others said.

What did the authorities together with the parents and relatives of the deceased do? Some of them along with my readers will say it was written. It was his fate and destiny that he should die by scissor.

No. I refuse to accept that claptrap. And I have reasons to believe so, because such negligence continued to happen time and time again. And that's not all. In one of these faults, one of the informed and concerned relative questioned the doctors about the persistent pain in the abdomen of his relative a couple of days after the successful surgery.

What were the reasons from the nurses? It was normal that patients would endure some pains of some sort a couple of more days after the operation. The relatives didn't give in. They petitioned their concerns to the administration. That's how this time the patient reclaimed her life. She would have died hadn't it been for the persistence on the part of the family members who insisted that she should be rechecked.

Then when a fresh medical examination under high powered modern machines—which aren't lacking—scanned the patient's abdomen, what they saw defied human imagination! They traced down a set of alien objects in the deep parts of the abdomen. You bet it. The second surgery saved the life of a poor fellow. What is it that was missing? Order. Discipline. Passion.

Here is a very important remark for the reader. Does the description that I have given above fit exactly as the events were happening on the ground in the surgery rooms, or at the airport, or in class, or in the National Team's, or in Yanga's, Simba's or Azam Football Club's dressing rooms?

Well, I cannot be in two places at the same time. And so far as I am concerned, whether the facts are as exact as they occurred or not, doesn't bother me at all. It doesn't deter an iota my cause or the course or the lessons thereof. There is this myth most elites assert as law that no research, no right to speak. I refuse to accept it as conclusive. I hate it because it is used to defend wrongdoing and incompetence—or even personal interests.

I agree intentional targeting of others is wrong though to prove whether one's assertions are personal or not is hard to gauge—even though I am not a lawyer and I don't intend to be one in the foreseeable future—but these are the things we must address.

Do I know everything about such professions or holy matters? Having no arrogant intentions of proving myself, or my smartness, over anyone in such areas that have left even the brave and intelligent drawing back, let me, quoting Donald Rumsfeld, only say: "I am more concepty!"

Besides, I feel blameless based on what I consider to be good intentions. Didn't Umar bin al-Khattab, according to the hadith—in as far as justice to such an act of whistle blowing is concerned—quote the holy prophet as saying: "Actions are (judged) by motives (niyyah)?"

Really, when we are guided by good niyyah, or intentions, we shouldn't worry an iota.

We shouldn't therefore attempt to hide such scandalous mess, allowing it to be kept under the carpet, or in the cupboards—in our homes, schools, workplaces, in the government or even in our churches, synagogues and mosques in the nation.

All the same, you cannot hide a carcass for long for soon the stench will surely expose you. (And for national interests—what are those? And how are they weighted against what?)

Besides, I cannot see how one can be fairly judged under questionable laws or norms we are challenging. Besides, what I say is valid because the author doesn't stay on the moon. He sees and hears and evaluates what's going on both at the top, at the bottom and in the space in between.

To analyze why we should not shut up against misdeeds assume someone steals the public funds. If he does so, we will not have roads or the services the government ought to provide to the citizens—with or without eyewitnesses.

Faced with this dilemma, the best thing to do is to accept that we have problems to ourselves, as are with our governing laws and norms.

"In keeping silent about evil," rightly observed Alexander Solzehnitsyn, "in burying it so deep within us that no sign of it appears on the surface, we are implanting it, and it will rise up a thousand-fold in the future. When we neither punish nor reproach evildoers . . . we are ripping the foundations of justice from beneath new generations."

That's why we hail the constitutional reform efforts. I hope our good neighbors in Kenya, Rwanda, Uganda know this better.

The German history drips with manifestation of the foregoing verity. The rise and fall of dictators and the recent jihadist insurgency vindicates the fear I have.

Do we have any justification? Well—do we need any vindication? The author doesn't live on the moon. He has personally witnessed incompetence and negligence in the medical system much as he has seen it in the social and political arena. He, the author, is the victim of the recklessness within the medical system. The author lost a son under the same circumstances. This is not something I write with emotions or based on uninformed sentiments. I look for no personal financial or political gains, nor do I seek revenge or compensation. I write this remark, "With malice toward none, with charity for all."

The author included the following comments because that's how he has grown out to conduct himself during any medical transaction involving himself or his family member after losing a son on his first day on earth—something I considered not as medical flaw but management incompetency. That happened at TMJ in Dar es Salaam, Tanzania, in 2006.

In the article titled When Surgeons Cut the Wrong Body Part—reporting the sad event we have already reported above— *by Tara Parker-Pope,*[67] on December 20, 2007 4:19 am, a person going by only one name of Jasson wrote something we have adapted thus: "Although many cases go unnoticed, but these statistics are enough to give worries. It doesn't click in my mind ….in Tanzania…operating one's head instead of a knee! I am not a radiologist but I can imagine if the bones of the patella and skull look the same. Are these human mistakes as most people put them! I am not trying to blame the surgeons but all medical practitioners that are involved in the operating events, should feel responsible. I still stand to be corrected, but my comment here is that if all the standard procedures are clearly observed before operation, and that the involved individuals have their minds set for the activity, then these mistakes stand to be minimized."

Following the same event, on February 5, 2009 10:07 pm, a person who only introduced oneself as Tacs333 wrote: "Grow up people! It's your body! Have a say of what goes on. Be informed. Why should it be guess work for all concerned? As a person, do we not all make mistakes? Help yourself if at all possible. Yes, medical people are supposed to know what is going on! But we are not perfect—are you? Help us help you. Be informed, and concerned for your loved ones. Most are ready to complain and condemn but do not want to be responsible! Why? Is it easier to blame someone else? I have been on both sides of the fence, and I prefer knowing what is and what isn't!" concluded Tacs333.

"I think a patient should recognize that they have the ability to prevent this," said Dr. Angood. "Each time they talk to the surgeon or people involved in the procedure, they should verify that it's the right leg or the left arm. As they move into the procedure area, the patient and patient's family shouldn't hesitate to ask, and re-ask, the nurses and the providers, 'Are you sure we're doing the correct side?'"

Having given you my word that I speak: *"With malice toward none, with charity for all,"* it gives the author the privilege to advance his line of thought.

LAZINESSITIS: THE CULTURE OF INACTION AND LACK OF AMBITION

Rooted from our history of slave trade, colonialism and socialism, our people's lack of initiative or ambition is not news nor is it sin. But what is sinister is that it has been ringing through our ears but as it echoed time and time again, we chose to christen the facts we don't love so much as *Rumors*. We said it was *Hearsay*. And indeed we love the rumor. An intelligent opportunist investor in Mwanza City, Tanzania opened a club and named it *RUMORS*—a place where rumor mongers and lovers of beer and ambiance would meet—and he made a fortune!

But we also are witness of the slogan *Watufunga lakini chenga twawala*. This is generally the culture of our people. We say: *It is ok. There is no problem*. I say it is not okay. I say there is a big problem. Gone are the days when in the village we planted trees and cleaned the road to please the visiting ministers or the president. Losing the game to a foreign team and saying it is okay consoling ourselves that we had the best footwork is not helping us in anyway.

That's misinformation and total lack of priorities—or wits altogether. It is nothing but lack of ambition and personal-leadership. I write this chapter with the two unfortunate groups in my mind. I write it with the thought of the demise of the majority of uninformed poor, and of our nonvoting fellow citizens (the animals) whose suffering is beyond bearable levels.

The minerals and drugs are ferried outside our borders. The trees are cut mercilessly as animals are evacuated from the country by massive numbers and we seem to say it's no problem.

Recently a big row evolved between the authorities and the media over seven hundred breathing animals that were ferried outside the country besides rhinoceros and elephants' horns. Yes, no one can now give an exact account or audit of the numbers of elephants killed or of tusks and breathing beasts ferried outside the country. Yes, most of these are foreign owned businesses.

Yes, it is by the hand of the foreigners but no foreigner can successfully seize and pack a massive animal in a chatter plane and then fly over our borders without a hand of a local person. Not even a massive Nigerian or a Sumo Japanese or Chinaman can lift a baggage of drugs or minerals respectively across the airport without a hand of local machinery.

Recently minister Mwakyembe described how a team of senior officers at the airport facilitated the process of lifting drugs in our airports. He even actually held them accountable dismissing them. We need such leadership as Dr. Mwakyembe's. Yet dismissing someone and hiring his replica with same intentions of getting rich or die trying is not helpful. It isn't either far off from a quick fix. Is it not adequate or a truly a lasting solution. This is a culture Dale Carnegie called inaction. But it is more than that. It is lazinessitis—a new disease that pervades our society today.

So what is lazinessitis therefore? It is the malady where the infected patients lose appetite to work hard. They lose ambition or motivation or inspiration to do anything. They have no reason to do so. They have surrendered. This is a malady of quick fix at industrial scale—a strange desire to reap without sowing. It is mob psychology. It is first degree of laziness—laziness to work—and think. When I look at this malady in our society, I get inclined to believe in superstition—I want to believe the Germans spread some potion across the country that the Brits would not get anything out of us.

But I should also remark that this is not a problem only confined within our borders. I am referring to the human society—yes with simile to the Tanzanian society. Through my previous books we indicated how fake degrees are everywhere from the States or Kenya and India. Laziness and indifference are now global only that they may be at industrial scale in one country, and at scanty in another. We must therefore heal the society and especially the younger generation against quick fix. And this is no simple task.

Quick fix has pervaded our society. Lazinessitis is a fondness. In short there is rampant inaction, anarchy and senselessness or mindlessness.

THE MINISTER IS NOT THE PROBLEM

No one, I repeat, no one—through time and space—has ever solved a problem once and for all without first understanding what really his problem was. Having known what it is, he will then want to know where did this problem spring from, or how it started, before he can think of any growth. That goes for us. The seed of our problems was sown long ago beginning with the time we came into contact with the outside world. It is because of the nature of our contact that we fell under slavery and colonialism—the two major human tragedies throughout recorded history—save of course the tragedy humanity suffered during the times of the biblical Noah. If there is anyone who questions the claim that our troubles began with the time we came into contact with the outside world, he has only to revisit how one chief Mangungo of Msovero was conned into signing the bogus treaty with the German notorious liar, Karl Peters, thereby placing the whole of Tanzania—from Kilimanjaro in the north down to the southern highlands to Bushubi—even the author's forefathers' ancestral kingdom.

The seed of problems our society is facing today, was sown during slavery and later through colonialism. Then this seed sprang into the mindset of the Tanzanian, down into his household, before it blossomed in schools. That's how finally it matured up into the end product which was then packaged in the factory line beginning with liberalization, globalization and information technology before it was placed in the hands of our today's youths. But as far as the real problem is concerned, we bear the responsibility in that we didn't do anything about it until today fifty three years down the line. The point I am trying to make is this: until as of now, we have offered no other options or safeguards against the education that perpetuates the same tragedy. If we had alternative options or even safeguards, our youth would face liberalization of cultures globalization and ICT with restraint, discipline, moderation and command. If we did so, the burden of the blame our already weakened shoulders bear would be lessened so much that the author wouldn't have to write this book.

For the self-righteous grouch out there who will say: it isn't me, pointing his index finger the other side saying: it is the government, the truth is this: all this is happening under our watch whether in our homes, in our neighborhoods or classrooms, in workplaces, in the parliament or in the government. Let us pick a few examples on how the whole picture has changed. Mwalimu Nyerere, knowing too well that our people were not ready for a fully fledged modernization, tried so hard to delay liberalization—whether economic or cultural. And that's not all. He even rejected vehemently to open the mining and the rest of the natural resources to the outside developed world. Instead he embarked on education and building the mindset of the Tanzania people, preparing them to take charge of their own country and of their destinies. He knew more diamond or gold was mined more in the head than in the soil. We are going to see through this series and in particular a volume on the ideal scholar that it is neither the physical muscle nor the financial capital that makes one nation rich and another poor. It is all in the mind.

Today, what we see is that, in contrast, we have declared open season to everything. And the results are in open. Do you want to question this assertion that we are back trailing? I have already hinted about how we have been thrashed by the country we liberated from shackles of poor mindset and devastation under General Amin. In fact with the poor performance in sports and football in particular, the then sitting president Mwinyi swore over his head that he would never again attend a football match after he was shamed as the guest of honor and president witnessing his nation being humbled at home.

In his words he said: we have become the head of a madman—a head to which every barber has an access—thereof coining a term *Kichwa Cha Mwendawazimu*! The international sales figures of coffee and especially tanzanite have helped to illustrate the foregoing statement in its true perspective. Does coffee cross the border to Uganda or Kenya into Tanzania—or vice versa—making us or them big coffee growers—at least in the books? Whereas tanzanite is only mined in Tanzania and Tanzania alone, and hence its name, Tanzania is the far third exporter while India and Kenya are the world's leading *producers* of tanzanite.

You cannot proudly let the investor choose what to declare as revenue or give back as tax unless you are a half wit. That is another way of analyzing a nation with no ideals, another way to identify a sick nation. Truly, the reader can no longer question the wisdom wrapped in the words of the proverbs (25:28): "He who hath no rule over his own spirit is like a city that is broken down, and without walls...." Such a city is what in Dar es Salaam we call "Shamba la Bibi"—a no-man's-land!

The author went to school during Mwalimu's era to testify what is being presented to the reader. The author experienced personally how education was meant to reach all Tanzanian children—all, rich or poor. The author saw how schools and teachers were proudly Tanzanian; and books were plenty and accessible to all. What's more, these books were written by local Tanzanians and hence were relevant to, had our problems at heart.

He, the author, on joining secondary school, journeyed off into the far free education schools on the government warrant and, besides the advantage of detribalization, he gained from education, call it traditions or cultures of the other tribes, wherever he went.

The author experienced how patriotism and hard work and a sense of responsibility were nurtured through activities and songs we chanted at school beginning with patriotic songs such as T*azama Ramani, Tanzania Tanzania, Mapinduzi ungali mtoto mdogo nimepewa nikulinde mpaka kufa* (literally meaning I will protect the nation and its ethos until death) —albeit the latter being a party song but it made little difference at the time because we were mono party state etc., etc.

We were made proud of reading and writing. That's why in those days very few cases of fraud were possible. We had, in this country, a very high rate of literacy during the first administration. We had strong family institution. Tanzania qualified for the African Cup of Nations. We won gold and silvers in the Olympics.

We were respected to the extent our countryman Salim Ahmed Salim serving as the president of the UN General Assembly was considered for the United Nations Secretary General only to be vetoed fifteen times by the US.

He went on to serve as the Organization of African Union Secretary General for a very long time. You know his name. Salim Ahmed Salim it is. His countrywoman Dr. Asha Rose Migiro followed in his footsteps to serve as the UN Deputy Secretary General—among others.

That's why much as we blame the education at the time we came into contact with Karl Peters and his cohorts, we want to go on record stating that the Mangungos of today are degree holders and PhDs., the same men and women who are supposed to be in guard of our democracy and the future of the nation.

Well—enough said, no?

By now I can see jubilant readers out there. I can see the smiles on the faces of the youth. Nonetheless because of what I say about the adults, they shouldn't be celebrating. They, too, have their share of the burden to shoulder, for they are the copilots of the ship on which our society is sailing today.

The youth are the immediate trend setters and role models to their young brothers and sisters. The path the youth follow is naturally the trail their juniors will follow if we offer no other option.

So if the youth are indolent, to expect the nation to have the bright future is not only unrealistic but it is indeed unreasonable. Indeed it makes us contemptible.

We therefore all bear responsibility—collective responsibility—you realize.

The *You-Are-Wrong-And-Resign-Approach* by itself will do nothing positive apart from creating jobs for a greater number of people not because of long term decent job creation but because of the turnover—a huge turnover following a very slim shelf life of the job.
We have only recently witnessed a number of enormous cabinet reshuffles following mismanagement and poor performances as one would call it. We hail minister Kagasheki for his resignation. A few others were dropped and never complained in public—at least we are convinced Minister Philip Murugo, the then deputy minister for education took his dismissal with a charitable grace, following his unfortunate international tongue-tied speech in which he misspelled Zimbabwe for Zanzibar as one of the states that united to form the United Republic of Tanzania. But one minister didn't shut up. Responding to the parliamentary committee on the decision to drop all the ministers who were considered to have underperformed, the minister for livestock, Dr. Mathayo didn't accept he had underperformed. He was never allocated with adequate budget. He didn't have adequate resources to hire or run the ministry to the required level. It was for that reason he believed to ask him to resign was unfair.

Now my point is the same. The new minister, where will he or she get resources to turn the ministry around? Resignation is never the solution. We have deeper problems that cannot be simply cured by the cabinet reshuffle. We are all witnesses of the most dramatic resignation of Premier Edward Lowassa. Did I call it dramatic? Yes it was. In his final words resigning as premier he used almost the same word. *Nimesemwa Sana:* which is to say: *You have talked so much about me*. Did all the ills and corruption end with his resignation? Did his resignation ward off mismanagement? To what extent? All these are truly debatable but I doubt if resignation is the remedy to such deep-rooted national hitches. We are naturally corrupt. We are born selfish. And our education is already trembling from fear of being butchered. If we can't face these facts, our battle is a lost war already.

THE TIME IS NOW: A NEW DAWN HAS COME

We come to the end of this chapter trusting that you, the reader, with your good judgment, will not lose sight that through the preceding chapters we have placed sufficient reasons before you to realize whether your life, career, or business calls for transformation.

We are certain the foregoing analysis will help the reader to find more ground, more reasons, to do so. You now therefore recognize that the ball is now in your court—and all eyes are on you. You realize the time is now. I trust you cannot miss the fact that a new dawn has come; and that there's never been a better time for transformation. Schools have failed. Youth don't want to work anymore.

At work people don't work and because of low productivity and a complete lack of personal initiative, our neighbors are filling the spaces both in the public and private sectors; as our true leaders are demanding change. Parents are complaining. The future is uncertain. The nation widely weeps in agony. Her suffering is unbearable. Her independence is a hoax in her captivity into a beggar and dependent economy. She hungers to be self-sufficient and a prosperous free nation. That was her hope and dream when she fought for and won her independence. But these are dreams shattered. They are shattered by all of us—we who are also beneficiaries of the change she is weeping for. We are therefore the men and women responsible for her comeback—much as we have been responsible for her downfall. And we know—that with the publication of this book—it is possible if everyone plays his part!

But I know there are some of my readers who will say: *this is an exaggerated lamentation of the melancholic doomsayer. The nation is okay and we are doing fine*. Well, I don't know who exactly this person is. And I don't know if he knows I don't talk about a small group of people who benefit from the demise of the nation; but the nation in its totality. I would like to tell this someone that with the recent documented observations as far as our economy and the state of the nation thereof, we recognize that the dream this nation had—a dream to be self-sufficient and a prosperous free nation—is kaput.

Indeed aside from economic indices, the recent examination failures cannot be bleaker! The overall trend of not only the school performances, but also the performances in the other fields of the society: industry, sports, the family institution etc., in the country are on the cliff—heading for the rocks. But the fact is that this hasn't started today—mind you! So where has the people been hiding? Do we still blame the current minister of education? Should we? Let us rationalize together.

Employers began—no, were through—questioning credibility of graduate employees for long now. Such examples include the editorial of the Guardian of June 5, 2008, titled "Education System Overhaul Overdue," which showed that ATE, Association of Tanzania Employers, had declared that most graduates performed poorly at work. (That is they are under qualified). While many find our graduates as under qualified, we on the contrary find graduate employees overqualified for day-to-day mainstream roles at workplaces—which is what a flock of employees are for! You don't expect a manufacturing or a mining company to only hire top executives and managers, do you?

Again, as private researchers and concerned citizens—and parents too—we have found a significant number of graduates from any prestigious universities in the country, or those educated abroad in Australia, SA, China, Japan, the UK, or even the USA who fit in neither category nor the explanations above.

That is, they are not simply over or under qualified but, in fairness, they are "ill-qualified! What this suggests is that, their qualifications are not in sync with actual needs on the ground. And this suggests that what we teach in schools today is far from being relevant to the needs of today; their qualifications—and therefore our curriculum—don't match with the needs of the employer—and their own needs—on the ground.[68]

The IMF, the International Monetary Fund, Magazine of February-March 2012 helped us realize that this is not new or unique to us in Tanzania though. That's why the report recommends what India has done.

Following the same trend, Indian industry—or the nation thereof—didn't try to cover up the fact that it had the problems, in the name of loyalty to the country. On the contrary, in the name of patriotism they tabled the matter. That's how they uncovered the problem.

That's how they faced it head on. And their problem was this: the traditional education produced fresh grads that weren't attuned to the needs of the industry—in term of both the work skills and winning character.

That is how they embarked on creating in-house schools and training programs at work to formally reeducate or reorient the fresh grads as well as old employees—as the ministry of education obviously learns from the lessons on the ground to internalize such programs into national curriculum.

Recently we heard that the Form Six students in the nation have done wonders in the national examinations. Scoring an alpha or a beta in an exam where too much overemphasis is placed on wrong or irrelevant notions or models is less meaningful than if they scored a gamma in a curriculum that is relevant and comprehensive.

Should we point fingers to the incumbent leadership? No! Never. With the kind of attitude we demonstrate, with the level of laisser-faire and quick ix we seem to love, without leadership anarchy would kill us alive. So thank God at least we have the superstructure—albeit one of some curious variety.

Is this a new crisis? We recognize this isn't a new crisis. Never! It was hatched long before independence. Our level of performance in education or in sports is a legacy of both slavery and of colonial education whose emphases were not to revolutionize the thinking among local people. Slavery implanted into the mind of a Tanzanian that he was beneath humans.

Colonial education emphasized basic skills with the intention of creating a group of clerical support workforce! Ujamaa didn't do much to promote industry, competitiveness, punctuality and desire for prosperity.

Because we have not repaired the situation, today, observations reveal that the overall trend of the schools performance in the country is pathetic—to say the least. We have for long been looked at as a laughing stock.

And these aren't my words. Minister Dr. Harrison Mwakyembe has warned about our representatives in international bodies who have decided to assume the role of the good boys and girls by keeping silence during the sessions.[69]

Whether they keep their mouths shut for purely academic, communication skills or interpersonal skills, I have no way of knowing. But behind it is incompetence of some kind—incompetence "that conceives timidity and low self-confidence.

Addressing a number of Tanzanian students studying in German, Ambassador Karume also cautioned about timidity among our people. He stated that a frightful people, people who do nothing fearing to make mistakes cannot innovate or progress. He called this state the fear of the unknown—the fear that has plagued development in our society.[70]

With the publication of this book, with this gesture, this is indeed the moment the nation has been waiting for—a moment we ought to respond to our challenges with class and dignity.

You realize there is so much at stake. New solutions are needed. We are the losers—and the beneficiaries. Our children too, are, even the more potential losers. And we have no other option. We either rise to the challenge or perish.

Is anyone blameless? Schools? Employers? Trainers? Parents? Policy makers? We aren't! But gone are the days of pointing fingers and passing on the buck. May be Mr. Molo Mwafulilwa the second master at Lutengano High School provides an exemplary responsible attitude.

During the author's maiden introductory session at the school to introduce the training program we offer, a program from which this book was conceived, a program aiming at changing the attitude among our students and the nation as a whole; a program that emphasizes that our attitude and character—the reason why we are where we are—described how one day he was disheartened to see one of his students from the past few years cleaning sewage in the neighborhood of the school down in Tukuyu, Mbeya, Tanzania.

And talking about the right attitude, when one of his secretaries blundered, Barack Obama said: "the buck stops with me!" Responding about the hard decisions he made as president including the war on terror, George W. Bush said: "I always felt it was important to tackle the issues today and not to try to pass them on to future presidents and future generations!"

Dale Carnegie wrote so nicely in his book *How to Stop Worrying and Star Living* that, "I used to blame my troubles on other people; but as I grow older—and wiser I hope—I have realized that I myself, in the last analysis, am to blame for almost all my misfortunes." Lots of people have discovered that as they mature up. King David repented so solemnly saying, "I have erred so terribly…I have conducted myself so foolishly!"[71] And Napoleon? Did he ever admit to make mistakes? Let's see! "No one," said Napoleon at St. Helene, "No one but myself can be blamed for my fall. I have been my own greatest enemy—the cause of my disastrous fate." [72]

So, is our cause a realistic undertaking therefore? Is not there a sign of hope that we are finally holding a discussion about our problems head on? Aren't we addressing the challenges in uplifting performances in the classrooms as well as at workplaces? Aren't we really addressing our social and economic challenges? Let us face it. Admitting that we have problems to ourselves is the first step toward the right direction. That's the only best way of solving our problems once and for all. Truly, there is so much at stake and the time is no longer our best ally. Therefore if we want a big and timely impact, we must discuss our problems with utmost soberness.

We cannot expect to solve the problems we face by looking at only the best there is, or—even the very worst we do so well—by hiding our heads in the sand fearing to face the truth about ourselves. We can neither solve our problems by trying to ignore we have problems—in the first place. Neither can perfume hide for long how stinking your dirty pig is; nor can running from your own problems; nor investing in the feel-good-air and cheating yourself that all is okay; nor through use of colorful paintings whether physical or emotional can really heal your misfortunes. Indeed "if merely 'feeling good' could decide" aptly observed Professor William James of Harvard, "If merely 'feeling good' could decide, drunkenness would be the supremely valid human experiences." But it can never be so. So perish the thought. "As a cure for worrying," said Ralph Waldo Emerson, "As a cure for worrying, work is better than whiskey."

12. THE FEAR OF UNKNOWN: THE REASON WHY WE HAVE FAILED TO MOVE FORWARD

"Our lives begin to end the day we become silent about things that matter (to our lives.)" —*Dr. Martin Luther King Jr.*

We have, through the foregoing chapters, discussed the weaknesses in our society. Whether that has been a courageous act, or just an exercise of civil and human rights as enshrined both in our constitution and the UN charter of human rights on the author's part, is not important. The important thing is this: The reader must also not lose sight that being a responsible citizen, father, and head of the family, the author rightfully assumes the role of the leader in providing much-needed leadership for his own person, his family, and his community, if not the society as a whole.

But it is also important to state that—which is another important thing—no society has ever developed without doing a detailed health check, or an impartial analysis of its health. (And I say this hoping that the phrase the health of the nation is not a vocabulary anymore). It is important to remark that in this analysis, we have in the main covered the youth and education. Education is probably the biggest change agent. That is to say, if we have to transform our society, we must make a thorough analysis of how healthy is our education, an analysis that is focused on seeking new ideas to meet the ever changing environment.

We can, at this point in time, conclude that the weaknesses in our education therefore, project the weaknesses we have in our society—weaknesses springing from education: the curriculum, the content, the structure and in general the education system as a whole. Surprisingly, our education, the curriculum, reflects the weaknesses in our society. But because one emanates from another, the society and thereof, its leadership reflect the state of the health of education in a society. The point I am trying to make is this: if we have to transform the society, education must be at the forefront. And that's not all. It should be homegrown. In the final analysis, if a person or nation doesn't adapt to the changing world, no matter how top he or his nation is today, it will not be far too long before in words of Boyd Bode; one *"would be circumvented and left behind."*

The forging chapters, you must have noticed, bulge with nothing new to many of us for indeed many of us know our problems but rarely do we come out and talk about our problems. Why? Generally speaking, we tend to keep quiet about our problems due to our history. It is our history that has built the culture of keeping quiet about our problems even when we already know the truth and the costs we already bear. If we go into histories of our nations, many of our countries are some kind of united kingdoms, kingdoms in which tyrannical kings ruled with an iron hand. Kingdoms were like personal estates of certain families. That's why therefore the monarchy did what was good only in his own eyes. That is why the kings were brutal. That's why the kings were not popular. They were not, I am not going to shy away from this fact that they were unpopular even in Bushubi, Biharamulo and Karagwe where the author's forefathers ruled until the early days of the independent United Republic of Tanzania.

They didn't have reasons to watch their personal conduct. After all they were not voted for. Besides, the kings were the judges and disposers of all affairs. The sentiment against the traditional rulers is still prevalent among the communities where the ruler and the ruling class had the strong grip over the ethos and affairs of the traditional society. Kagera region in Tanzania and southern Ugandan communities provide a very good example—of course if we close our eyes on the excess tribal conflicts among our neighbors of Rwanda and Burundi.

They didn't have reasons to watch over their personal conduct. After all they were not voted for. Besides, the kings were the judges and disposers of all affairs. The sentiment against the traditional rulers is still prevalent among the communities where the ruler and the ruling class had the strong grip over the ethos and affairs of the traditional society. Kagera region in Tanzania and southern Ugandan communities provide a very good example—of course if we close our eyes on the excess tribal conflicts among our neighbors of Rwanda and Burundi.

The reader will not lose sight that, despite her all unspeakable definitions of freedom—whereas most of our countries pamper our presidents as if they were emperors—in America a seating president is not above the law, and he therefore can be impeached. The Water Gate Scandal in which president Nixon was forced out of office for misconduct and use of office for personal political gains helped to put the foregoing assertion into perspective. Bill Clinton had his share of the other side of democracy as president when he survived impeachment from the Monica Lewinsky saga—thanks partly to Hillary Clinton's exemplary leadership and standing by his side. That is different from most of our countries where seating presidents have immunity against charges.

THE MAGNA CARTA

When a person disagreed with the monarchy, a situation similar to what is common among most of our young democracies today, he had nowhere to turn to. This situation grew so much as to sow a seed of unjustified fear, a fear also we will classify as the fear of the unknown. Indeed the citizens were called subjects, subjects to the monarchy.

In modern day's democracies, the president is not the employer but the employee of the people. And as such, he can be fired anytime. To say the least, naturally this triggered constant fear among the people. This is the first basis from which our politicians became so powerful and haughty, on one hand, and intensification of the fear of the unknown on the other.

The Magna Carta document was drawn up in 1215 when King John of England was forced to agree to limitations on his power and therefore granting freedom of speech and deeds to the people by the monarchy based on the principle that: "No free man shall be arrested, or imprisoned, or deprived of his property, or outlawed, or exiled or in any way destroyed, nor shall we go against him or send against him, unless by legal judgment of his peers, or by the law of the land."

The Magna Carta was also a document the king was forced sign to acknowledge that no one, not even a king, was above the law. This became the fundamental principal of English justice, the basis of the United States Constitution (the rights to "life, liberty and the pursuit of happiness") , the inspiration for the French constitution The Declaration of the Rights of Man and of the Citizen (French: Déclaration des droits de l'homme et du citoyen), passed by France's National Constituent Assembly in August 1789, is a fundamental document of the French Revolution and in the history of human and civil rights. The Declaration was directly influenced by Thomas Jefferson, working with General Lafayette, who introduced it. Influenced also by the doctrine of "natural right", the rights of man are held to be universal: valid at all times and in every place, pertaining to human nature itself. It became the basis for a nation of free individuals protected equally by law forming the basis for most modern democracies.[73]

Secondly, because of our low levels of education, we are ignorant of our personal rights. And ignorance is the best habitat for the fear of unknown.

That's why ignorant people are the most fearful of all. That's why autocratic leaders love to keep the people ignorant.

Indeed the budget allocated on education can help to tell you the intentions of the leadership in this matter. Poverty also is another serious cause of the fear of unknown. A poor person is not sure of his next day. He is least assured of what will happen to him when tragedy hits. That's why he is weak at heart. A good example of his low self-confidence is his bargaining power. It is very low. He is ready to take any job at very meager pay uncertain of whether he will be able to put food on the table.

That's how the employed men are enslaved by their employers fearing to break away and lose their source of survival. For them the employer and not their brain is the umbilical cord to life. It can be clearly illustrated how the poor and the least educated are the highly affected victims of the fear of the unknown from their strong belief in sorcery and superstition.

However, the fear of the unknown soared during slavery and colonialism—the two major evils human had to contend with. Under slavery, a slave was reduced to the level of a tool or machine or even any beast the slave master owned and put to use as he wished.

Colonialism wasn't very different from slavery except that rather than transporting the slaves to overseas, they were tamed at home and used as tools to serve the colonial master. These two systems, robbed the slave and the colonial subject of his self-esteem and self-confidence as a person, thereby eroding all the remaining sense of dignity and humanity in him. These two systems worked so rigorously to emphasize the inferiority of the subject and at times manipulated the holy books to justify how cursed were the subjects—the most popular being the curse of Ham and Canaan (Genesis 9:24-27) who are alleged to be the ancestors of for instance the black slaves.

In such verses, the slave master and the colonial master justified their rule and oppression as ordained from the maker when it is written cursed be ham and Canaan, slave to his brothers. What they didn't observe is their brother's part. If they were brothers, they had same genetics and same same intelligence. This they didn't teach. Indeed they even didn't teach us to read and write. When we knew to read and write they hid the bible or taught it in the only authorized foreign language—Latin or any other foreign language. And in this piece of history, there is a sign to all worthy Africans and all the oppressed of the world.

Because of all this history, our people have developed fear which is often unjustified—the fear of the unknown. When a person reaches the extreme of this fear, he faces the most severe of fear in that even when he doesn't have to fear or when he finds that there is nothing to fear about, he even fears the most fearing that probably something even worse was at hand. How can he have no reason to fear? He reasoned! In addressing the fear of the unknown, I have made my tale so long. I have done so to encourage people to speak up when it needs must be.

To speak up when it needs must be, to cultivate self-esteem or self-confidence by the way of encouraging people to seek education in all its forms, to inspire people to work hard and become wealthy and self-reliant: and on the other hand, to encourage the other party to listen to the others in that we are interdependent and that in the end our good can and is always only possible and best when we live in harmony with the others around us—the richer vs. the poor, the upper vs. lower class, the educated vs. uneducated, the white vs. the black, the employer and the employee, the ruler and the ruled, the captain vs. the crew and the passengers etc.,—is the burden of this chapter.

CASE STUDY: THE SPACE SHUTTLE CHALLENGER DISASTER

Working as an engineer for Morton Thiokol, the manufacturer of the solid rocket boosters (SRBs) for the Space Shuttle program, Boisjoly wrote a memo in July 1985 to his superiors concerning the faulty design of the solid rocket boosters that, if left unaddressed, could lead to a catastrophic event during launch of a Space Shuttle. Such a catastrophic event did occur less than a year later resulting in the Space Shuttle *Challenger* disaster that resulted in loss of lives of all crew members, putting to halt the space expeditions besides halting the manufacture and supply of the solid rocket boosters and ultimately the employment of a number of people both at NASA and Morton Thiokol. This memo followed his investigation of a solid rocket booster (SRB) from a shuttle flight in January 1985.

During his investigation, he discovered that the first of a system of two O-rings had failed completely, and that some damage had been caused to the second O-ring. The O-rings were two rubber rings that formed a seal between two sections of the SRBs...intended to seal the joint, while allowing for the inevitable movement between the sections under flight conditions. …. The system never functioned as designed. The rings were supposed to sit in a groove and seal the joint between the sections of the booster. It was found, however, that flight dynamics caused the joints in the SRBs to flex during launch, opening a gap through which rocket exhaust could escape. As the joints flexed, the rings would come out of their grooves and move to a new position in the joint, a process called extrusion. The extruded ring would form a seal in this new position, but during the time it took for the ring to shift, the joint was unsealed and hot gases could escape, a process called blow-by. These hot gases would cause damage to the rings until the seal was achieved.

Boisjoly's investigation showed that...cold weather made the rubber hard and less flexible, meaning that extrusion took more time and more blow-by took place. He determined that if the O-rings were damaged enough they could fail. If the second O-ring had failed, Boisjoly realized, the results would almost certainly have been catastrophic with the complete loss of the shuttle and crew seemingly the only outcome.

His investigation found that the first O-ring failed because the low temperatures on the night before the flight had compromised the flexibility of the O-ring, reducing its ability to form a seal.

The temperature at launch had been only 10 °C (50 °F), the coldest on record.....Boisjoly sent a memo describing the problem to his managers, but was apparently ignored. Following several further memos, a task force was set up—including Boisjoly—to investigate the matter, but after a month Boisjoly realized that the task force had no power, no resources and no management support. In late 1985 Boisjoly advised his managers that if the problem was not fixed, there was a distinct chance that a shuttle mission would end in disaster.

No action was taken.

Following the announcement that the *Challenger* mission was confirmed for January 28, 1986, Boisjoly and his colleagues tried to stop the flight. Temperatures were due to be down to −1 °C (30 °F) overnight.

Boisjoly felt that this would severely compromise the safety of the O-ring, and potentially lose the flight.

The matter was discussed with Morton Thiokol managers, who agreed that the issue was serious enough to recommend delaying the flight.

They arranged a telephone conference with NASA management and gave their findings. However, after a while, the Morton Thiokol managers asked for a few minutes off the phone to discuss their final position again.

Despite the efforts of Boisjoly and others in this off-line briefing, the Morton Thiokol managers decided to advise NASA that their data was inconclusive. NASA asked if there were objections. Hearing none, the decision to fly the ill-fated STS-51L *Challenger* mission was made. Boisjoly's concerns proved correct, despite his prayers that he had been wrong. In the first moments after ignition, the O-rings failed completely and were burned away, resulting in the black puff of smoke visible on films of the launch.

An aluminum oxide seal plugged the hole at the last second, preventing the loss of the orbiter at liftoff. At 58 seconds after launch, buffeted by high-altitude winds, the oxide seal gave way. Hot gases streamed out of the joint in a visible blowtorch-like plume that burned into the external hydrogen tank. At about 73 seconds, the adjacent SRB strut gave way and the vehicle quickly disintegrated. Boisjoly was relieved when the flight lifted off, as his investigations had predicted that the SRB would explode during the initial take-off.

However, seventy-three seconds later, he witnessed the shuttle disaster on television. After President Ronald Reagan ordered a presidential commission to review the disaster, Boisjoly was one of the witnesses called. He gave accounts of how and why he felt the O-rings had failed. After the commission gave its findings, Boisjoly found himself shunned by colleagues and managers and he resigned from the company.

For his honesty and integrity leading up to and directly following the shuttle disaster, Boisjoly was awarded the Award for Scientific Freedom and Responsibility by the American Association for the Advancement of Science in 1988.[74]

THE TITANIC

In April 1898, an "unsinkable" Titanic, was crossing the Atlantic Ocean travelling from America to England, with 3,000 people on board. While many people found the expedition a luxurious voyage with immense value for money, one Mrs. Marshall didn't concur.

Screaming, she grabbed her husband's arm—Jack was his name—shouting; "It's going to sink, that ship is going to sink. Save them! Save them!" Did anyone listen? Nope! None! Did anyone do something about it?

They all did nothing! Nada! No one listened to the noble warning only that they regarded this seer's warning as "hysterical ravings of a woman who had gone mad." Trying to cross the ocean in record time, the titanic struck an iceberg near midnight and—yes the inevitable happened! She sank! Finally!

Result? Most of those on board perished. Why? The Titanic did sink because—just like The Space Shuttle Challenger disaster—safety precautions had not been observed thoroughly. Lives were claimed simply because there was inadequate supply of lifeboats.

Only 13 people survived. Fingers point to the British Government's Board of Trade which allowed Titanic to sail with insufficient lifeboats. Captain Smith however bears a big blame. First he played down iceberg warnings. Secondly he hadn't made sure the vessel had enough life boats.

And thirdly he allowed the lifeboats to be lowered at the nadir that is the worst moment, or the moment of least hope and least achievement: the wrong time. Furthermore, he was also accused of being one of the first to leave the ship.

Besides, company signals were different from distress signals complicating emergency matters. The first lifeboat to leave the Titanic had only 12 people in it when it could hold 70 grown men. Now as you read and ponder about these events, sad events that nonetheless are intended to call the reader's attention to heeding advice from the others, an effort to encourage our people to listen to one another, I know it is easy for you to say this is a farfetched example.

And you may be right because these two happened a million years ago and a million miles away?—well no! It is true they happened many miles away from the authors residence in Dar es Salaam Tanzania but it is only a hundred years now since the Titanic sank and it is only less than four decades since the Challenger broke off!

You are right nonetheless. You need something you can easily connect with, something you can closely relate to through the author if you have to buy into the whole thing. Perfect! The failure to pay attention or heed warning happened right here at home only recently—and the author is a witness of the precedents he will now lay down for the reader.

THE MV BUKOBA

I was in my room at the tower block reading my notes preparing myself for the university exams in 1996, when I heard the unheard-of news. It was breaking news on Radio One, news that shocked me out of my mind! I couldn't believe it. No! It was impossible. It was impossible. No. I'd personally sailed severally by it.

It was inexplicable. I couldn't believe it. Impossible—I said! It cannot be! That beautiful ship couldn't sink despite these reports that the Lake Victoria passenger ship 'M V Bukoba' capsized on May 21,1996 with over a 1000 passengers' on board—albeit conflicting figures—just 30 minutes before reaching Mwanza port. Only 53 people survived.

President Mkapa declared three days of national mourning. Governments and individuals all over the world sent their condolences![75]
How did it happen? Here are the facts! According to its standard tonnage capacity, the boat would have no more than 430 passengers according to Wikipedia[76] with medium tonnage of the cargo not more than 850 tons at its fully operational capacity at the time of its manufacture about twenty years back in 1979. But because of the same unfounded belief, people didn't care. They wanted to travel and they had to. And I cannot blame them. To be honest, I don't believe I wouldn't board the boat myself. I didn't believe myself in the sinking of boats. It had never happened before. How could it be so now?

Impossible! recalling also the hype that accompanied the time to do so, I mean the time to board the ship, I can't see I could have responded differently, honestly, if I was told it could sink. In fact I recall I once sailed the same boat when it was almost submerged and the water kept filing the boat as the crew kept emptying the water back into the lake. But did anyone give a helping hand out of the real sense of how that was the matter of life and death? No, sir! People went on feasting , as probably the wealthy immoral people didn't notice a thing as they went on consummating the love of their loved beers and opportune lovers in their secret cubicles. Luckily we arrived safely in Mwanza that day. So how could I ever imagine that a boat could sink? Impossible!

Now it also happened that among those voyaging by the boat, was a big number of the people who couldn't miss their businesses or even the wedding reception the other side of the shore. And therefore the partying moods hang in the air. Huge numbers of passengers was not therefore unexpected.

So when the few decent officials stopped selling the tickets admitting people on board, passengers didn't understand the fact that the boat was overcrowded, nor did these enthusiasts heed the warning that the boat was fully packed. No one cared to know that the tickets were sold off. The corrupt officials accepted the money and admitted more people on board through the corners so that the boat was overcrowded more than three times its standard capacity.

The matter became even worse because those who didn't get the tickets wouldn't listen. Never had a boat capsized in the Victoria. They had no reason to think about such an option. The boat was naturally so slow that somehow some of the stiff naked fools did swim and boarded a boat a few meters in the waters.

Albeit voyaging as slow as a snail, the boat crossed over to another port of Kemondo Bay, 23 miles away before it set sail to its final distant destination in Mwanza city. You couldn't blame them. How can it have happened now? Impossible!

That was not all. A great number of people were left at Bukoba port. So these who couldn't swim, took private express transport by road over to a nearby port, Kemondo Bay, only 23 kilometers away, where it would pick some more cargo and few people with genuine tickets. The boat arrived after taking longer time than it would ordinarily.

The reason was obvious. It was overloaded. The captain didn't care. Many more passengers eager to travel paid more bribes. The officials couldn't reject the bloody money. They competed for the free money. It was an open season.

The more passengers maneuvered and boarded the boat as the captain and crew stashed more money in their heap pockets for the ambiance once they anchored at the other shore. It was not long after the boat set sail from Kemondo bay, though, that it soon began to tilt on one of its sides. The crew struggled with the management of the cargo and the people were moved to another side as the boat continued sailing.

The tragedy was not over for though the crew began casting away the cargo into the waters, finally, slowly, a beautiful ship MV. Bukoba gave way and began subsiding, before it completely failed and capsized 56 kilometers from Mwanza city—its final destination. And yes you bet it right. Only 53 of people survived.

Did people learn from it? Nope. Not the government or the crew or the people learned their lessons from this sad event. Despite angry speeches and sentimental vows on both the governments to bring the perpetrators to justice in order to make sure nothing like it ever happened again—never in this country again—it took only a few more national events to dissuade the masses with the hype from the news media and we forgot about the tragedy!

MV SPICE ISLANDER

That we don't heed lessons is how the MV Spice Islander capsized in Zanzibar en route to Pemba only years after the MV Bukoba tragedy. According to witnesses who were interviewed by the local radio stations, MV Spice Islander capsized drowning with three thousand people on board—a number estimated to be six times more than its standard.

The most curious thing is that while people had no space to sit on, and that there was not even a space to stand on, more passengers boarded the ship as the authorities watched. Imagine! The standard four hundred people boat admitted in over six times its standard passengers besides the cargo! What would happen?

According to the witnesses, before it set sail, it tilted and the official captain rejected to captain the ship claiming misconduct and overcrowding. What happened? His superiors vowed to discipline him and strip him of his captaincy—or even fire him! How could he be such rude not to follow the orders? That was insubordination—they claimed! A reserve captain was summoned and for whatever promises, he took over.

Whether he was competent or whether he was not drunk, we have no way of knowing for the government's commission of inquiry is yet to put the finding in open. All we know and we can say without hesitation is that no sane captain would take that risk—whether he was promised a raise in his salary or even the ownership of the whole island of Zanzibar and its spices! It wasn't long enough after the ship pulled the anchor back in order to set sail, right at the port of Zanzibar , when the boat began sinking tilting sideways. That's when the people began shouting saying *Get Us Out. Get Us Out! Get Us Out! You Are Killing Us!*

This strange captain wasn't a complete drunk nincompoop! He listened and heeded his passengers' voices when he anchored again to let the frightened souls get away.

Finally, thirteen people decided to leave the boat before fifty more scrambled in. As the boat set sail again and this time there was no going back.

Then the ship titled the more. The more waters entered the ship and it tilted more and suddenly began subsiding before it capsized. Until as we talk about it, no major finding s or feedback from the commission set to investigate what happened. Despite international aid and support in the marine technology and internationally accredited divers who came to help us save lives, until as of now years after the tragedy had hit, have accounted for the lives of the deceased—and no high powered machines could save the lives or property.

Are those who make such silly mistakes only the ordinary or average people? No madam! Even kings and presidents fail to heed advice or listen to the things that matter most to their own lives.

THE SARKOZY SLIP UP

When Francois Hollande chose *Le Changement: C'est Maintenent* (change is now) as his campaign slogan, Sarkozy, the then seating French president, like many seating presidents, blinded by the routine lavishness, took his opponent for granted. Instead of watching his own steps, as well as challenger's, to be able to notice if he was on track or that actually he was losing touch with the French people, he was completely unaware and probably indifferent about what was going on in France.

That's why instead of bringing into the country probably the most famous East-Germany-born female serving as first female German chancellor in the name of Angela Markel to spice his candidacy, he should have known his problems were at home. He, President Sarkozy, didn't know how the average citizen in the countryside in Southern France or even someone in the suburbs of Paris suffered from the ongoing economic downturn. People were demanding changes, but because, like most men in power, Sarkozy didn't connect with the ordinary Frenchman. He didn't even notice that they had problems.

Consider Sarkozy's reelection campaign. The first thing he did as president was to have his salary more than doubled. And he had reason to do so. He had his life lifestyle to grapple with—his newly begotten Italian girlfriend Kara Bruni and of course known for his bling-bling dress code—a lifestyle that didn't make matters easier for him.

On the other hand, the average Frenchman had lost every drop of hope. The economy grew very slowly. The ordinary citizen had no job. The salary didn't even rise to match the rising prices of the necessities of life, goods and services, because of low disposable incomes.

Then the economic crisis hit. The markets collapsed. The wine factory nearby closed down. His farm or wine products didn't sell anymore. His neighbor had been laid off from the same wine factory—someone from whom he could get support. Recession had the factories shut down. The ordinary French man who depended on a wage labor for his subsistence had nowhere to go.

One month elapsed. And another followed. He still had no job. Where did he get money to feed his family? Then there is another person in Paris. His house rent grace period elapsed. The house rent was due. He lived in a modestly decent apartment.

Now that he had no job he had no house rent, no food and no money. The socialist Frenchie landlord had vowed to throw him out if didn't afford the rent the next couple of weeks. He contemplated to go to the street. But he had family to look after. He had a few options. Leave the town and go deep into the rural French villages where francs didn't count much and life was easier. He could also run away from his wife and children and struggle on his own. That would make life easier. But Paris wasn't easy. Some among such people in the end surrendered and gave up on life and tightening a rope on one's neck, he breathes his last giving his ghost back to his Maker. What about his family? What about the neighborhoods? And their votes?

I must remark that such failures are homemade. At their root was the poorly managed economy. Yet there is, as well, the mindset of French people themselves. This is where he had to center. To solve his re-election crisis, Sarkozy had to visit, go home to, these problems.

Yes there was the global crisis but as president he had first to seek domestic solutions. He didn't. You can't blame him. He spent most of his time abroad. He was detached from the French people he was supposed to be connecting with in the first place. He had lost both the common sense and then the common touch.

It is certainly, following this urgency for change, Sarkozy was shocked out of his mind when he lost the first round, before Mr. Hollande was elected president after the runoff.

My point here is this: Realizing his own handicap, appealing for reelection in the runoff, Sarkozy told the French people that *I've heard you!* That was so belated. He had lost the first round! It was too late. Even though the French people are considered to be so romantic, neither did Markel's magic, nor Kara Bruni's charm suffice to turn the ordinary Frenchmen on. It was too late! The horse had already jumped out of the stable. This time they wanted something more—something that touched their lives. Sarkozy had failed long before the run off.

THE CHAPTER'S LAST WORD

Fritjof Capra was right. "The reasons for calling for change vary," aptly said Fritjof Capra: "The reasons for calling for change vary, but the sense of urgency for change, is shared!" We have through the foregoing chapters tried to illustrate that our society calls for transformation. We have demonstrated that it is possible and to your own benefit—if you listen and heed counsel. Yet indeed, in my experience, "men go to too far greater lengths (trying) to avoid what they fear than (trying) to obtain what they desire," rightly observed Dan Brown.

We don't have to defend where we have gone wrong. We have rather to rise to the challenge. But whether we accept our weaknesses, hide our faces in the sand fearing to face our problems, or even attempting to run away in the interim, is not my problem. What my problem is, is our failure not to learn from both our actions and our inactions.

Liberians have a saying that fits our situation very well. "A donkey can travel whatever distance, but she cannot come back home a horse." You are the sufferers and beneficiaries of the decision you make today and in the future.

But who am I addressing? I am addressing you—yes you the reader. May be you are a student or graduate at work. You are probably a teacher or lecturer in a school or college. You could also be a parent. You could also be a government official with influence somehow to make it happen. You could also be a school owner or a training manager or her boss; you could also be, the MD or CEO himself or herself. You could be a government official or politician with influence to make this change realistic. Don't simply sit there and wait for somebody else to implement this change. Start on your own now. Implement it in your Family, School or organization. Adapt it in your workplace training programs.

If you do so, not very long when it is due time, you will be dumbfounded at how tremendously lucky you have been to have been introduced to this program. Only commit to mind that the change begins with only one person: YOU! And that's nothing new. In history it has always been so. It was one person who invented, fought for or implemented changes we see today: Abraham Lincoln, Nelson Mandela, Julius Kambarage Nyerere, Rosa Parks, Columbus, or Julius Kambarangwe and a many other names, names that can fill this and a few other pages, names of the people who decided to make hard decisions, decision that meant life or death, but decisions that would lift up the lives of the rest of their family members and fellow citizens.

Indeed City Group was right: "One bold idea can transform a company, an industry or an entire nation. One man or woman, one person can make it happen—and indeed that person could be—and should be YOU! [77]" (Besides, your work will not go unnoticed. In supporting this program, not far too long from now when, adapting words of Napoleon Hill in his magnificent book Think and Grow Rich, *"the world will discover and reward you"* for your services—the services of high order to humanity—and to yourself and your family!)

Finally, having been led through these pages, I suppose, you certainly now recognize the significance of admitting truth about ourselves, if we have to change and prosper, or ultimately, if we have to bury our heads in the sand and decay. We can never change our circumstances or prosper when we are always burying our heads in the sand fearing to face the challenges we as individuals are—or the society is—wrestling with. "He is my dearest friend," said the Holy Prophet (SAW), "He is my dearest friend who points out my drawbacks to me and gives me a gift by doing so."

At this point in time, every person has got to ask himself, as every society has to ask itself the following question: How does my life and the decisions I make pertaining to my family, school, business or the country relate with the Challenger Space Shuttle disaster? How does it relate with the capsizing of the MV Bukoba, or the Spice Islander? How does it relate with the Titanic? What lessons do we learn from Sarkozy? If you did a little self-scanning you would find that you are indeed a human titanic only a few meters before you hit the iceberg!

When André Labuschaigne was installed new MD at PEP, a mass retailer in SA, he observed and addressed the situation very close to the one we are facing as a nation today.

PEP was operating under the old paradigm, the old South African apartheid system. It was a company that therefore naturally was made to cater for the white South Africans. Most of its services and shopping malls certainly displayed the "Blacks and Dogs Not Allowed" banner. Employees worked as slaves and were treated so. They were believed to have no any input except manual labor.

Products so produced were branded and priced to suit the traditional market. But things had changed. A free south Africa, a rainbow nation meant that blacks were now a new power to reckon with. They were majority and the new redistribution of income and power meant more opportunities to the black South Africans much as the new zeal and self-esteem and craving for personal dignity. So really everything had to change to embrace the sweeping changes that were happening in the new South Africa.

Products so produced were branded to match with the new South Arica employees were empowered and their inputs treasured and rewarded. The company began working as a team of partners and people with mutual respect toward common goals. Like magic he transformed the company that was giving up the ghost to once more a thriving company and lively neighborhood and society as a whole.

What special magic did he use? What were the secrets behind this sweeping change? He didn't need the body parts of the albino, or some magic potion as some of us in East Africa would. It was honesty. He didn't keep quiet about, or hide his face in the sand fearing to tackle the legacy of apartheid his company was facing. He immediately addressed the situation and reformed the company taking it to heights that were considered impossible among the old school.

The transformation he engineered brought changes and growth that defied human imagination. Recalling his assessment of the situation at the time, the assessment that fits very well with our society today, I find that truly, "Our society today, is like the Titanic! Only our Titanic is only already leaking, on its way to an iceberg; an iceberg we thought was 100 kilometers away but now realize it is only 20 kilometers away. The sea is stormy and we have too many passengers on board. We need to dissemble the ship, stay afloat, change direction; reassemble and build speed boats, weather away the storm and sail to a safer place...It can be done! But it will take superhuman efforts. We need the passion of the people to do it. But I know we can do it, because... Ordinary people—people like you and me—can do extraordinary things!"[78]

13. GOING BACK TO THE BASICS: THE PRINCIPLED UNIVERSE AND THE RAW LAW OF NATURE

"Order is heaven's number one law." —Alexander Pope

INTRODUCTION

Through the preceding chapters, you were presented with an analysis of a sick nation. We have seen how beginning with the wearing away of ethos of the human society, the youth in a nation, choose quick fix as their model approach to success. We have seen how some of our people—young and adults—have become so successful in the process, and as a result, they have deceived themselves—and others—into sanctifying quick fix as the best way to success and prosperity—and therefore a nation's way of life or philosophy. This is dangerous and it should be arrested if a nation has to stand on its feet once again.

If we let 50 Cent and his philosophy of get rich or die trying, hand in hand with the apparent accomplishments to such men youth and adults, accomplishments achieved by whatever means possible: drugs, prostitution, embezzlement, theft, conning and trickery, gambling, etc., we become purveyors of the same philosophy, a philosophy in which there is no proper channels or processes in which success or prosperity can be acquired. The reader can indeed scan around himself and appreciate the fact that the positions of power in all levels among our workplaces and in our families are acquired using quick fix and trickery.

We have seen many men and women tricking men and women into walking down the aisle only to regret much later after the "I-do" word has escaped the mouth, followed by a ring, the two of which go on to imprison one into a matrimonial cell he or she didn't foresee coming or needed. We know of secretaries who trick their bosses into a relationship and ultimate marriage. We know of many housemaids who trick their bosses into marriage. (You will probably recall from the book What Makes People Rich and Nations Powerful how even Frida maneuvered her way into marrying the author's own father—albeit a short-lived marriage). And the author coming from a big polygamous family is a witness of how even in our families, children and their mothers use the same approach to win favors from the patriarch, an approach that dates back during the biblical times since Cain.

Cain killed his brother Abel, to warrant his position as the heir of Eden. Jacob who with the assistance of his mother tricked his father old Issack into the first born's birthrights; how the Jacob bothers who sold into slavery their brother Joseph; how Tamar tricked Judah his father in law into a sexual act that brought forth Perez, Judah's heir; how Ruth with the help of Naomi her mother in law tricked Boaz into marrying her and bore him Obed his heir, father of Jesse father of David, king of Israel; how Bathsheba tricked king David into installing his son Solomon king over Israel after him; and the analysis can go further down to how Mary Magdalene won her special place among the disciples by unmatched trick using her long beautiful hair to clean the feet of the Lord, or how Judas made his way into the possession of position and wealth as minister of finance and later acquisition of 30 pieces of silver by betraying Jesus.

Again, whether coincidence, or not, the author has no way of knowing—yet in spite of unprecedented exemplary deeds, deeds that set leaders apart from the others but in history but even some of the greatest leaders of our religions went to greater heights, taking a lot of trouble to claim rights to leadership. Count and see. What is so saddening is the fact that today the positions of power among the academic institutions, the government and even in the churches, mosques and synagogues are also acquired by quick fix and trickery. We also know at one point or another, religions claimed the rights to sell the rights to heaven and made a fortune out of it, or religious leaders ordering their congregants to kill their political or business opponents on the promise of claiming a place in heaven.

We have witnessed students male and females using whatever means possible to entice their examiners into first classes and scholarships aside from fake degrees both in the country and aboard. Any doubter can easily analyze for himself how we have recently witnessed Indian parents climbing high examination tower blocks to pass on answers to their children; how the incumbent leaders falsify constitutions to stay in power in Congo or Burundi—among other countries the; how the clergymen auction to their parishioners the title deeds for earthly estates and a place in the afterlife, churches which blossom amidst our community; or others incite their adherents to set themselves alight and kill those who don't believe the same way they do promising them a place in the gracious heaven, and in the process cleansing the opposition and creating empires for themselves—thank God history is not on their side and the world is changing and turning a deaf ear and a blind eye to such leaders.

What is depressing is that once these individuals get into power using quick fix or trickery, a culture that is so contagious, the same people go on to run their families, academics, organizations, churches and nations using same tricks: quick fix and trickery. The downfall of education, rise of atheism, the economic crisis that remains prevalent today, and generally moral decline together illustrate the contagious nature of the culture we seem to tolerate.

As we acknowledge Goodluck Jonathan for conceding and even congratulating and peacefully handing over power to his rival, the Nigerian newly elected President Muhammadu Buhari's vow—and we salute him—to crack down on such quick fix is an illustration that this practice is common and prevalent.

What worries me out of my wits and as such compelling me to blow a whistle about it is the fact that it is in the human nature of the beast to love quick fix. And it doesn't end there. Because of how sweet it is to have quick accession to power and wealth using short cuts, this culture has become relentlessly contagious. Because of its contagion, this culture has adversely affected good character in our society.

In fact good character such as hard work, discipline and industry are no longer praiseworthy. In fact it is astonishingly surprising how good character demonized today as contemptible! Work hard and give your faithful service and loyalty to your country and position and retire with modest wealth, and you are a laughing stock! The ideal retired public servant must be swimming in dollar bills. He must have stakes in all major businesses in an outside the country.

It is for these reasons that we had to write and incorporate this chapter in this book. To say the least, the quest to crack down on this growing hideous culture—demonstrating the fact that the Universe, or *Mother Nature*, is highly principled, and therefore that success, long term success or wealth, (I repeat, long term success or wealth) is possible only when one follows and lives a certain way of life—is the burden of this chapter.

THERE IS A CERTAIN WAY TO SUCCESS

Following the downfall of persons who were once tops, the dynasties that once ruled, institutions and organization that led in their line of expertise and business, churches and denominations of all religions that are losing out in terms of their credibility as true religions or denominations no matter how many wrongly guided people they may recruit today, the rise of atheism and unprecedented freedoms in the free America, the failing states and nations that are now slumberously stretched out in ICU, side by side with the crumbling of civilization in the face of globalization and ICT and specifically the recent social and economic crisis, we are forced to come to a conclusion that these failures rise from the fact that somehow somewhere we have crossed the lines and have gone overboard. Yes, we encourage innovation but we believe in self-possession fearing to walk away from our true selves senselessly throwing away all cautions—like senseless animals!

Ultimately we come to a sad realization that somehow somewhere true principles of success and lasting prosperity have been overlooked. It is because of this saddening verity that it is in the interest of the reader as an individual person and of his family, the interests of the institutions and organizations, in the national interests, and those of humanity as a whole, that we return to the basics, unleashing new ideas, beefing up of fresh alternatives.

And the starting point is this: "Everything," yes, everything, a very good word for Ornstein and Hunkins to begin this analysis with, that academicians in the field of curriculum call *Realism*, something we call materialism, reality—and yes everything, "is derived from nature and is subject to its laws. Human behavior," they continued emphasizing this beautiful idea that, "Human behavior is rational when it conforms to the laws of nature and when it is governed by physical and social laws."[79]

As beautiful as it is, we will for now leave it at that as we move to what they have called social laws—laws which govern business and every worldly lasting success, the latter which can be said to govern the religious success. And the conclusion above is right. Indeed it is from how we conduct ourselves here on earth that we can claim a stake in the hereafter. This will be cushioned by Wallace D. Wattle from his must say wonderful book Science of Getting Rich as introductory lines in this magnificent book Science of Getting Rich, lines from a chapter he titled: There Is A Science of Getting Rich.

"There is a science of getting rich," he began, "and it is an exact science, like algebra or arithmetic. There are certain laws which govern the process of acquiring riches, and once these laws are learned and obeyed by anyone, that person will get rich with mathematical certainty.

The ownership of money and property comes as a result of doing things in a certain way, and those who do things in this certain way whether on purpose or accidentally get rich, while those who do not do things in this certain way no matter how hard they work or how able they are remain poor. It is a natural law that like causes always produce like effects, and, therefore, any man or woman who learns to do things in this certain way will infallibly get rich..."

By the time we finish this analysis, we shall have concluded that really: nothing springs up from the earth and function automatically! Having introduced the idea that there is a certain way of doing things successfully, the idea which is itself embedded in the very domain—the fact that in the domain of intellect everything is derived from nature and is subject to its laws—and therefore that human behavior, is rational when and only when it conforms to the laws of nature and when it is governed by physical, and social laws, the latter of which are governed by the former, we now move to illustrate how the foregoing statement is the beginning of every wisdom under the sun. Parallel to the foregoing, the proverbs counsels thus: "The fear of the LORD is the beginning of knowledge; Fools despise wisdom and instruction."

THE PRINCIPLED UNIVERSE

The universe is principled. This is the ideal which is shared by almost every civilized people and every credible religion of the earth. Here now follow the facts, facts that are nonetheless imponderable, but facts that illustrate that you are heading for a downfall if you are not in tune with this law. And to put an emphasis on this law: no matter whether things seem to be going well with you, if you are singing or playing the wrong notes, it follows therefore that you, shall for sure, fail—in the end.

The universe is invincible. And she is stiff naked. You follow its laws and win—or don't and fail. You have read many times how persistence is key to success. Yes it is but only when it is tune with the laws of nature. We are likely to misunderstand this canon when we see people succeeding using methods we didn't comprehend. Failure to comprehend a principle doesn't disown it with its credibility. So really no matter no matter how many times you try, you will fail in the end because the principles of the universe are rigid. Its laws are raw, and somewhat seemingly *unrefined*—and unbending. It is just as natural and unchanged as from when it was first installed by the Maker himself (or herself)!

Having learnt that the earth is principled and unbending, it follows therefore that its justice is such that it will throw itself on your feet if you go by its laws and regulations. Yet it will vehemently stand up against you, to whip and thwart every other of your plans otherwise well-thought about if you try to go against its laws. The nature is a just umpire. But much as this umpire can be just he has his other side—a bad side. He is an unyielding and conservative.
You have no choice. There's no either or situation here! You either follow the law and thrive or rebel and deteriorate! The choice lies with you!

We are going to attempt to show you that the universe since its making follows a certain natural law and its justice is such that it will throw itself on your feet if you go by its laws and regulations. Yet it will vehemently stand up against you, to whip and thwart every other of your plans otherwise well-thought about if you try to go against its laws. The nature is a just but unyielding and conservative umpire. You have no choice. There's no either or situation here! You either follow the law and thrive or rebel and deteriorate! The choice lies with you!

You cannot fight against the universe, or change its principles. You can only play along. That's what we have learned from the case study of Pep. André Labuschaigne knew there was law governing success. That's how he transformed his company. His successes came about because he knew no quick fix approaches ever brought results, lasting results the company and society needed—and deserved. He made the difference because he went back to the basics.

And think about it! If we believe there's right and wrong, which is innate to us as humans, then we believe there's a certain way, or the right living. Incidentally, there'd be no right or wrong if there's no law. The universe or nature has a specific way in which it works. It is no guess work—r trial and error business. Its laws are no longer liberally refined to meet situations. Its behavior isn't situational.

Besides, look at it this way: the world is a million years old. That is an age enough to have established laws even if it began without one. Even if it began without one single law, after a million years of trials and errors and guess work, it should have established some laws. To illustrate this assertion, put yourself in the shoes of the Maker. Remember when you were growing up; how you made friends and indulged so much in their needs. Remember how you almost submitted to every need of our friends be it an act of kindness or money loans. Not anymore; am I right? Some began not reciprocating.

Others began playing games with you letting you down and tainting your loyalty. Some even took you for granted and didn't repay back. What did you do? You began streamlining our working relationships with them. Today you have set principles by which you work with friends and strangers. Even if he began without such restrictions, even if God began as the greatest liberal, that's not the kind of thing the Maker could fail to learn—and do himself, no?

You realize that this is a very important analysis if I had to rationalize with my reader why he should behave and live in a certain way; if he should succeed in life! You realize that this is a very important analysis if the reader had to be persuaded to change his thought pattern, and ultimately, the way he leads his life. You realize that this is a very important analysis because we all tend to believe otherwise when enough reasons and proofs have been placed before our laps. You are not different. I know you!

You want reasons and proofs. You want to know why you have got to change and lead your life in a certain way, why not every route leads to success, why quick fix and trickery cannot work in the long run. As such, I made this analysis to illustrate to those of us who think they can sit down or go on their knees and lo! Suddenly they are rich, healthy, peaceful, and happy just like that. If you were one of people with such ideas, think again!

Indeed this is a secret only known to very few people who no more less than deliberately they chose to keep this secret hidden from the rest of the majority. It is indeed a major reason why very few families actually thrive and by virtue of their virtues, find themselves controlling and therefore ruling the world beginning with ruling their own souls and thereof their destinies thereby forcing other people and nature, to serve them. As for the ignorant majority, theirs is a destiny of serving those few initiated in this law for the rest of their lives. We don't want the latter to happen to you!

HOW DID THE AUTHOR FIRST GET INTRODUCED TO THIS SECRET?

How do I know this secret? You ask how I was first introduced o this secret myself. The author found himself coming across this secret because of the advantage he has had. His own father's family tree envelops a long history of recorded ruling dynasty long before the white men set their boots on the African soil south of Egypt.

Beginning with probably the most foreseeable Bunyoro Kitala down to Ruhinda's trekking south to Karagwe, and then Biharamulo and Bushubi in Tanzania, he learned how this clan had maintained the sense of belonging and how it managed to rally people behind its own agenda—to influence and win people to its way of thinking. The author also gained from the invaluable enlightenment his forbearers gained from engaging with a great diversity of people and cultures as they trekked down. They learned and brought down knowledge, skills and spirit from the more advanced neighborhoods of the prehistoric Egypt; passed down from generation to generation for more than twenty generations through oral tradition, part of which is now recorded or documented history, you will agree this is invaluable reserve of knowledge.

Besides, a keen reader and inquisitive researcher, the author's father having gone through the colonial seminary education where he literally did nothing in the ways of cramming the scriptures but to study and fuse together theology, natural science, history, philosophy and traditional education in one vast form of knowledge that many considered him as an encyclopedia—albeit a very different one (in that it was a walking encyclopedia and it cherished the traditional education).

His mother was another source of education—this very education we're discussing right now. She was a stern disciplinarian who set rules and saw to it that they were followed. She didn't only do that. She would also add with a twinkle in her eye that you should follow certain rules unless you want to become like the rest of the boys with abhorable habits doing pitiable works in the streets. The author was also born in, and raised in a family of more than fifty people put together, a family of men and women of imagination. I must say my brothers and sisters have been my prime teachers. consider also my father's large family, a family of several step mothers(and some of his father's in laws) from different backgrounds, and half brothers and sisters and servants he had to learn from, contend and consent with all teaching him lessons unthought-of.

It must also be reported that the author was born and grew up amidst intelligent siblings—and yes some of them were extremely intelligent some of whom were actually considered to be genii. It is these siblings, his brothers and sisters—who taught him how to read and write and who guided him toward some pursuit of excellence apart from having set high standards for him. Therefore alongside his own education—albeit a modest university education—and an education from his interaction with different persons from different backgrounds from primary education to the university and military national service, all accorded him an advantage that not many have had the privilege of having. This is just in part. But briefly, from these two major sources, the author was inspired to examine and establish facts and factors that are unchanging and that determine success.

I have not only read extensively, I have not only researched extensively, I have not only done extensive observations; but far more remarkably, I have comprehensively meditated upon all these situations to be able to connect the dots and synthesize the almost solid facts. Let me say that from all these sources, it was made known to the author that nature or the universe follows a certain unbending pattern. And it follows therefore that the people who swim accordingly tend to succeed in whatever they do. The opposite is true to those who try to oppose the pattern or work against it. Proof and passing down this secret to especially to the unfortunate majority who never had the advantage of coming across the secret of success, to unveil this secret so that in the end the reader—and the nation in general—can go back to the basics, is indeed the burden of this chapter.

THE DENTAL FORMULAE

The world is indeed principled—and works according to its own ways. Have you ever considered the dental formula? How are teeth arranged in all animals? Isn't a certain kind of arrangement in our teeth such that incisors, the sharp teeth are placed at the front of the mouth to cut food when you bite into it? Aren't the canine teeth four pointed teeth in the mouths of most animals placed at the sides to chop the harder kinds of food? Aren't premolars and molars the large teeth at the back of the mouth in humans and some other animals used for crushing and chewing food? Aren't there the 32 total of the teeth in the normal human mouth?

Now consider the whole human or even animal's mouth. It consists of these sharp teeth. Yet they are surrounded by vulnerable sensitive flesh like the tongue. Theirs is a hard work and rough work of chewing down hard things we call food. Look at how the dangerous are the teeth and how the sensitive is the tongue, and yet they live in complete harmony roaming about freely in such a dangerous environment? Don't they rarely do collide or grind one another but instead work in complete theatrical but symmetrical harmony? Why? How? Law. Unfailing Principle.

THE TECTONIC PLATES, THE VOLCANOES AND THE TSUNAMI

While in the ignorant societies people used to worship and give offering among trees and mountains where natural hazards such as volcanoes appeared, it wasn't the gods that summoned the attention of the community. It was rather the natural science, not the gods, at work. Every circumstance you face, every event you see happening here on the face of the earth, everything that happens to you or another person is never a once off event. It is instead just a series of events. They are all part of one single major process broken down in series.

Surprisingly, every process you see, happens to be in or follow a certain pattern or trend. Everything that happens here on the face of the earth, the earth quakes, the floods, the drought, the bounty or scarcity, every tornado, flooding—you name it—is an outcome of some processes that preceded it whether underneath or on the face of the earth!

First of all, let's very briefly consider the volcanic eruptions, and thereupon, the flowing of lava, the Tsunami or any flooding of the seas. Aside from the melting of glaciers, both of these events are results of the adjustment of tectonic plates underneath the face of the earth. The earth is formed by strata of layers called plates. These plates shelter the earth's surface from heat that abides deep in its core. Whenever the plate movement among these plates happens at uneven rate caused by imbalance on the face of the earth or underneath, then a space is formed somewhere between these plates. This crack or an opening then under the same law of gravity and free movement lets the molten or fluid lava flow through towards the vent and finally to the surface of the earth.

That's why lava flows regularly around the Oldonyo Lengai Mountain and not on the hills of Rulenge back in Bushubi, or why not in your hometown. Whenever these plates play in their regular movements or adjustments, at a certain rate, the two plates may collide literally blocking or obstructing the free flow of both the movements of the tectonic plates and oceanic waters underneath, and thus respectively a hole can be formed in the plates deep down the core of the earth resulting in a volcanic eruption, or the overflowing of the seas we experience on our shores high above. That's how Tsunami washed the Asian coast claiming numerous lives with it. That's why it happens regularly in Malaysia and west coast of USA or Japan, and not in Zanzibar. The account is custom made to suit a lay reader as well as a learned person in the ways of the geographical studies realizing that teaching lessons in geography or even geology isn't the intent of the book now in your hands.

THE COSMOS

"The author (that author being Napoleon Hill, I must add that the immediate author shares the same belief) is not a believer in, nor an advocate of 'miracles', for the reason that he has enough knowledge of Nature to understand that Nature never deviates from her established laws…This much the author does know—that there is a power, or a first cause, or an intelligence, which…causes water to flow downhill in response to the law of gravity, follows night with a day, and winter with summer, each maintaining in proper place and relationship to the other."[80]

I, the immediate author, am convinced that Albert Einstein was right. "I am convinced," said Einstein,"I am convinced that He (God) does not play dice." The planets and stars bigger than our earth hang in the space but they don't fall on us. And they run in their own same-same orbits year after year without colliding against one another. *"*He created the havens and the earth in true (proportions*) ," so it is written in the holy Koran Surat AZ-*Zumar verse 39:5*,* "He makes the night overlap the day and the day overlap the night. He has subjected the sun and the moon to (his law*): each one* follows a course for a time appointed.[81]"

THE PATTERN OF THE HUMAN LIFE

This, the pattern of the human life, is indeed the area of our concern. A child is born and will grow up and pass out. No escape. There's no turning your back on death! There's no either or. It is a one way traffic. In our day to day lives, the sun rises from the east, and falls in the west, come rain, come shine—year after year. Night fallows the day. The rain season follows the dry season. With the heat from the sun, the sea water evaporates. Then the rain is formed. The rain then falls on the mountains and flows through rivers filling back the lakes flowing back to the sea. That's why the sea is never full. And that's that! That's the universe! That's the principled universe.

THE COUNTING CONTEST

In worldly terms, let's contemplate about the game I have called the *Counting Contest*. Here's how it is done. The two people contest for a prize. A big one! To win that prize, one has to arrive first at the number twenty which is the final destination. The game is no random or a gambling rambling scramble! The contestants are given equal chances and choices to win the prize as is fundamental principle of success in life! We are all given, well; the majority of us are given a pair of feet, a pair of eyes, and a pair of lungs and kidneys. We are given a pair of ventricles and auricles on both the west and east side of the heart. When a person's heart or lungs are malfunctioning it is often because he spoiled them with cigarettes, hard liquor or fats. When a person cannot see well, it is mainly and primarily because he or she, or someone else like one's parents, or the country's health care system was dysfunctional and therefore didn't take a good care of his or her eyes etc.

Back to the sport! The two contestants compete by counting numbers beginning with one. Contestants take turn to count, one after another. The rule of the game is that a contestant cannot count three numbers consecutively. You can only count one number or two numbers at a time after which your opponent takes turn to choose and count one or two consecutive numbers simultaneously until when a seemingly lucky contestant arrives first at the number twenty and he is therefore the apparent the winner. One more condition remains though.

To affirm he is really a winner, he has to win at least twice in a row. Why? The contest is never won once because you have to prove that you did not win by chance. Thus you must win twice or thrice in a row. You cannot win by chance. Practically, chance cannot guarantee your victory in life. Let us look at the working of this game very closely. In this game, a person who knows exactly which are key numbers, should pick the same to win, and if so, he or she goes on to win in the end. It is no trial and error kind of contest. These numbers are the secret winning numbers. Enough with theories.

Now what's the secret? What are these numbers? Take time and ponder about this secret before you read on! This is very important for you to grasp the eternal sense of raw law principle of success!

To make life easier for you, the secret prime or decisive number is number 17! Notice however that like all successes, you cannot and will not arrive at this number without a specific, particular, definite, explicit, detailed, precise exact route which is what the winner follows! This is a set of specific and particular numbers. If you ponder about this mind boggling fact, you will realize that quick fix as a path to prosperity is not only erroneous or misleading as an approach, but indeed it is a waste of time and resources. It is self-defeating!

Recall how practically this game works!

Contenders choose either to start counting or come second. Now let's say contender A starts the counting. And remember to win the contender must hit number twenty first. Contenders cannot count more than two numbers at a time. He can only count only one number or two in a row. Enough with the rules. Let's try it practically.

Here we go!

Contender A (counts): One.
Contender B: two.
Contender A: Three.
Contender B: Four, five.
Contender A: Six, seven.
Contender B: Eight, nine.
Contender A: Ten, eleven.
Contender B: Twelve.
Contender A: Thirteen, fourteen.
Contender B: Sixteen.
Contender A: Seventeen.
Contender B: Eighteen
Contender A: Nineteen, twenty!

As you can see Contender A wins. Immediately after he hit 17 and stuck with it, he was on his way to victory unless he was insane and nincompoop to just count nineteen and stop there allowing his contender to mention the number twenty. That's why often an initiated contender will simply stop after his opponent hits seventeen and sticks there. However to confirm his victory so as to win the prize the game has to start all over again. Let's now change to another pattern as below:

Contender A: One, two.
Contender B: Three.

Contender A: Four.
Contender B: Five, six.
Contender A: Seven, eight.
Contender B: Nine, Ten.
Contender A: Eleven, twelve.
Contender B: Thirteen.
Contender A: Fourteen.
Contender B: Fifteen.
Contender A: Sixteen, seventeen.
Contender B: Eighteen.
Contender A: Nineteen, twenty!

By losing the second contest, contender A would not win and his earlier victory would be annulled. It would be void. He had to win for the two or three consecutive wins. By winning twice in a row, contender A is a genuine winner.

Why is it important that he had to win twice in a row? We need a working formula. Not a game of chance. We don't buy in trial and error approaches. We need a principle that will work through and win the test of time. If he lost the second time, the title would still be open and the prize unclaimed. In my classes when illustrating this game, I have in fact let some of my contestants win the first round but choose to win the next time not only to claim my money back but to prove I can win if I want to. I do so to prove there is a certain specific path one has to follow to win. As you watch the game closely, now watch the winning route. At this point in time, you have probably recognized that number 17 is the requisite, or rather an indispensable number, if you have to arrive first at the finish line, which is Number Twenty.

Observe the numbers closely as we begin focusing our attention on the contest. Here are the numbers:
1, 2, 3, 4, 5, 6 ,7 ,8, 9, 10, 11, 12, 13, 14, 15, 16, 17, 18 ,19, 20.

Here they go again…

Contender A: One.
Contender B: Two
Contender A: Three, four.
Contender B: Five, six.
Contender A: Seven, eight.
Contender B: Nine, ten.

Contender A: Eleven.
Contender B: Twelve.
Contender A: Thirteen, fourteen.
Contender B: Sixteen.
Contender A: Seventeen.
Contender B: Eighteen, Nineteen.
Contender A: Twenty!

Now contender A is a sure winner, for he has proved beyond doubt that the route he followed is a specific and certain one.

You must have yourself stumbled upon the secret that number Seventeen is an ace of the game. That is to say you cannot competitively arrive at twenty without first hitting number Seventeen! That's why when the winning contender landed at number 16 had to round the bend with number 17 to win. He didn't do that and lost the game away. That is my first point. The second point is that for you to arrive at the number, you must have specific route making sure you keep your feet on the track—keeping the train on rail. This track or rail is a set of specific numbers. You realize that this isn't different from child upbringing, don't you? You cannot heal a spoilt child when it is too late. Indeed this is no different from attempting to mend a broken mirror! It is futile, and you know that! From this analogy, we learn that the environment to win or acquire victory is set in place from the earlier stages. A child is prepared to meet the challenges of the future during this specific period of his life. That's during the counting process.

Let's take a step further. You have probably noticed that you have to strike number 2, 5, 8, 11, and 14 if you have to strike 17 and eventually win. If you are the first to land on these numbers, you are on the right track. You realize that you have not yet triumphed whether you begin the counting process or even when you arrive at such a winning moment unawares, or by chance. You cannot win unless you know what you are doing and are focused along the way much as when the winning the moments or numbers come calling. Now you realize that if you hit number Fourteen it is guaranteed that you'll hit Seventeen. Number 17 then in turn determines who wins in the end. To keep your feet on the ground you must either take control of, or over, these numbers by force of arms or treaties. In the world today those in power—in business, politics or academics—do so by all means necessary even by keeping this secret hidden from the masses.

The foregoing explanation describes the process toward victory or success in pursuit of any goal you may choose in your life. This can be choice of vocation or a certain specific station in life or your ultimate number one or a lifetime goal. This is the only way you can keep the train on the rail. Observe the numbers one more time before we move to another mysterious number: 1, 2, 3, 4, 5, 6 ,7 ,8, 9, 10, 11, 12, 13, 14, 15, 16, 17, 18 ,19, 20.

PK NUMBER: THE MYSTICAL SECRETS OF NUMBER 3
The dynamics of victory, in this game, are governed by a certain number. And that number is 3. The first number and second most important numbers in the series add up to 3. The first important number plus the governing number viz. Number 3 give you the second important number 5. Yet it has to add up, I mean the Number 5, to the same magic Number 3, to give the next important number 8 down to number 17 which when adds up to the same Number 3, the number that govern the winning dynamics, to give you number 20, the final winner or score line.

Now the conclusion that Number 3 holds a special place in the hidden mathematical contest above, may seem so dim to many. Its explanation may even seem imponderable even to the genius. But more remarkable is how this number 3 features in our lives. Such is how it features in many sayings of the wise. Let us observe only a few examples here.

Buddha said: Three things cannot be long hidden: the sun, the moon, and the truth. A. P. J. Abdul Kalam said: If a country is to be corruption free and become a nation of beautiful minds, I strongly feel there are three key societal members who can make a difference. They are the father, the mother and the teacher. Confucius said: By three methods we may learn wisdom: First, by reflection, which is noblest; Second, by imitation, which is easiest; and third by experience, which is the bitterest. Robert Frost said: In three words I can sum up everything I've learned about life: *It Goes On*.

Joseph Addison Said: Three grand essentials to happiness in this life are something to do, something to love, and something to hope for. Laurence J. Peter said: If two wrongs don't make a right, try three. William Wordsworth said: Life is divided into three terms—that which was, which is, and which will be. Let us learn from the past to profit by the present, and from the present, to live better in the future. Bear Grylls said: Survival can be summed up in three words: *Never Give Up*. That's the heart of it really. Just keep trying. Thomas A. Edison said: The three great essentials to achieve anything worthwhile are: Hard work, Stick-to-itiveness, and Common sense. Lao Tse said: I have just three things to teach: simplicity, patience, compassion. These three are your greatest treasures.

Christopher Morley said: There are three ingredients in the good life: learning, earning and yearning. Confucius Said: Wisdom, compassion, and courage are the three universally recognized moral qualities of men. Garrison Keillor said: Thank you, dear God, for this good life and forgive us if we do not love it enough. Thank you for the rain. And for the chance to wake up in three hours and go fishing: I thank you for that now, because I won't feel so thankful then. H. Jackson Brown, Jr. said: Never forget the three powerful resources you always have available to you: love, prayer, and forgiveness. Mark Twain said: It is by the goodness of God that in our country we have those three unspeakably precious things: freedom of speech, freedom of conscience, and the prudence never to practice either of them.

Ray Bradbury said: I spent three days a week for 10 years educating myself in the public library, and it's better than college. People should educate themselves—you can get a complete education for no money. At the end of 10 years, I had read every book in the library and I'd written a thousand stories. Stephen Covey said: There are three constants in life....change, choice and principles. Denis Diderot Said: There are three principal means of acquiring knowledge.... observation of nature, reflection, and experimentation. Observation collects facts; reflection combines them; experimentation verifies the result of that combination.

Chris Rock said: There are only three things women need in life: food, water, and compliments. Lou Holtz Said: I follow three rules: Do the right thing, do the best you can, and always show people you care. Steve Jobs said: An iPod, a phone, an internet mobile communicator... these are NOT three separate devices! And we are calling it iPhone! Today Apple is going to reinvent the phone. And here it is." And that's not all.

Before his soul began ascending through the hanging staircase towards the hanging gardens of the eternity his, I mean Steve Jobs' last words were the same words he repeated three times: "Oh wow! Oh wow! Oh wow!" Plato said: Human behavior flows from three main sources: desire, emotion, and knowledge.

Are you already bored by this number 3? Yes that's what I want. I want you to recognize how it is endless—how probably it is not by coincidence that it is so.

Israelmore Ayivor said again that: "I can see only three planets in the entire universe, namely Heaven, Earth and Me! Heaven shines its glory on Earth and the rays keep falling on Me! I have a call!"

Isabella Poretsis said: "Knowing the truth. Feeling the truth. And acting on the truth. Are three very separate entities." Jeffrey Fry realized that: "Great leadership involves three things. The ability to realize when you are wrong, willingness to learn from it, and an eagerness to change course if necessary." Vera Nazarian said: "Love is made up of three unconditional properties in equal measure: Acceptance, Understanding, Appreciation. Remove any one of the three and the triangle falls apart. Which, by the way, is something highly inadvisable! Think about it—do you really want to live in a world of only two dimensions? So, for the love of a triangle, please keep love whole."

John Keats said: in *Bright Star: Love Letters and Poems of John Keats to Fanny Brawne*: "I almost wish we were butterflies and liv'd but three summer days—three such days with you I could fill with more delight than fifty common years could ever contain(Quoted from *The Great Hand Book of Quotes*)." Israelmore Ayivor said: "Thoughts are roots; Words are leaves; Actions are fruits! Every success tree has all working normally!" Brian O'Nolan, writing under the pseudonym Flann O'Brien said in *At Swim-Two-Birds*: "Well-known, alas, is the case of the poor German who was very fond of three and who made each aspect of his life a thing of triads. He went home one evening and drank three cups of tea with three lumps of sugar in each cup, cut his jugular with a razor three times and scrawled with a dying hand on a picture of his wife good-bye, good-bye, good-bye."

Enough! I mean enough with what others say or imagine. What about you? Let us now focus our lenses to you—yes, you the immediate reader—and all that surround you. Most houses have three bed rooms. The traditional kitchen had three stones that held the cooking pot.

You probably have already observed that however rich you may be, the standard is three meals a day. It doesn't simply happen as an accident or coincidence. Our medical doctors prescribe drugs in-take three times a day: morning, afternoon and after dinner. A child (you were) is born after a sojourn of 3 days by three months or nine moons in her mother's womb. Chicken eggs are hatched after seven sets of three days equivalent to 21 days.

The body structure amongst most insects and animals are set in place in three segments i.e. the head, the abdomen and the rear part or tail. Your body is no different. And what about your fingers? Are they not in three segments?

A man's life is never complete without passing through three major events, excepting of course the Roman Catholic priests, monks, and nuns. These events are birth, marriage and death. Moreover, human life goes through three stages: childhood, adulthood and old age. A man's death is internationally mourned in three days.

And it doesn't end there. A year is a set of four threes i.e. 3 months in four equal parts or twelve months. The sun shines in the set of four 3s i.e. 12 hours. The dark sets in after a day and stay for a set of three hours that cover four laps. A day is a set of six 3's i.e. six sets of three hours equal to 24 hours. An hour is a set of twenty 3s. A second is a set of twenty 3s. The year is set of four 3's.

The Greenwich Time zones are sets of a hundred and twenty 3's. The one hour lap or time zone is a set of five 3s; i.e. fifteen degrees. Like how the sex of the children switch over from male to female after three children, the longer year, which is a set of 122 sets of three days, returns after three years of shorter years.

Take football for a change. With this in mind, the football teams tend to build their teams following almost the same pattern with three major departments among them the defenders and goalie in the rear, the midfielders and finally the striking force. Most successful football teams are built around three key important players or combination in the forefront.

The winning Liverpool Football Club had MacMannaman and Robbie Fowler and Stan Collymore. The great world football champions Brazil had first Bebeto, Marzinho and Romario[82] while the second victorious team had a wonder trio of Ronaldo de Lima, Rivaldo and Ronaldinho. But they had Pele, Didi and Garincha in 1958 and 1962 trio of Pele, Tostao and Jairzinho. The mighty Real Madrid had Robarto Carlos, Ronaldo de Lima and Zidane.

The invincible 1999 Manchester United team was built around the same pattern of major three players' combination of David Beckham, Andy Cole, and Dwight York.

Most of winners of the Fifa world footballer awards wear number nine shirt which is a square root of number 3. Asamoah Gyan wore the Number Three shirt when he rose to be the African world cup scorer ever when he scored against Portugal in 2104.

Joke? Well, call it anything but the third most populous country remains the world's richest country. Again, which among their children do you think rose to the international prominence in the family of Emilia and Karol Wojtyla Sr. back in the Socialist Poland? In fact that same name remains the most adored man of the past and present century. Take your time. Think about who this person could be. Ready? You are right. It was their third born child you now recognize as Pope Saint John Paul II.

When a player scores three goals known as hat trick, he takes into his possession the round football the twenty one other players had equal chances of hitting or having it in their possession on the day. Not any other number of goals. Not four or even five. Score four or five goals no more prizes. Trace it in your family. Trace it in every other competitive game and see. Try to examine Rugby or Racing or American Football or Baseball. The principle is the same. It also applies to business much as it is in the family or household unit. Trace.

While production isn't of any lesser importance but corporations seem to put more emphasis on top three operational departments, namely; HR, Finance and Marketing—as we have three departments in the family unit—the father, mother and children.

Finally, let me say I don't believe in black or white magic. But going back to the counting contest. You may not believe in this entire thing. But what about such ubiquity? Why for instance would Gyan cling to a shirt that is often for defenders while as captain and superstar, it was in his powers to take any number? You must have not heard that he has even been associated with magic, yes? Number 3 shirt could be one of his magic. Notice also that in any contest only the top three are considered winners.

Many music bands put to use only three female dancers even when they have a pool of dancers in the background. Boney M, Julio Iglesias, Bob Marley, Lucky Dube etc. As such Bob Marley even identified his backup singers by "I Threes," who were Rita Marley, Judy Mowatt and Marcia Griffiths.

In the hospitality industry the high ranking hotels begin with a three star status. When a noncommissioned officer in the military is awarded with three bars, he is recognized as a primary commandant of the others named the Sergeant. Notice also that after this rank there's no more V's are added to the rank of the Staff Sergeant.

A three star military officer viz. the Captain is officially the first chief top rank. A three Star General is considered the first supreme position in the military settings.

When we began lessons on essay writing, we were told it must be in three sections: introduction, body and conclusion, a canon that not only minister Murugo used in his famous speech on the formation of the United Republic of Tanzania, but also authors and the reader have through time held so dear to us even in our adulthood. Standard measurements also abide by this number. A set or a dozen is a set of threes. A meter is made up of three feet. You have probably heard of the great misfortune, a faint-hearted gold miner's story. He failed three feet from gold. The most famous page of The Sun, the magazine with the greatest readership in the UK is page three—which has been for 44 years a sales switch. Indeed most editors place most important news on page three.

In public service or even among private corporate executives most deputies third in the ranking tend to step into the top position crossing over their immediate bosses. It happened in Russia a couple of years ago when Vladimir Putin stepped down as President and Medvedev, the third deputy Prime Minister took over. Not the prime minister himself or his number two. In athletics before the splinters compete, the umpire counts three to start a race.

However much I may attempt to evidence the above conclusion, it may remain to be considered as sham to some of my readers nonetheless. But very soon you will be shocked to find that indeed the whole thing is so breathtaking. It works in our day to day lives as it was also at work during creation much as it is experienced today in the pattern of the child birth.

Have you ever scanned the pattern of the coming of babies as we made a mention about it before? If the first three children born to a couple are males or females, after the three children of the same sex are born, the number four child switch to the opposite sex. Just look around you and I can testify to this. After she had had her third baby girl, I told Monica, that her next baby would be a son. A couple of years later Ananias was born.

Now here is the question: How did I know? It wasn't only that. The author's boyhood-self told his sister Angelina that because she had had three sons, the next baby would be a baby girl. Three years later Angela was born as prophesied. And that's long ago when I was but a teenager. This is a true account and my sisters Monica and Angelina are witnesses.

What is astonishing is that in some cases it doesn't matter whether the baby is naturally the third born or by virtue of the children now living, for this mysterious number to come in with its mysteries.

Notice also that however mindboggling this seems to be, I didn't suggest this extra ordinary idea based on guess work. It was based on serious observation. My mother had had the children in the same pattern. My big brother Clement had had three sons before my niece was born. He himself is junior to his three living sisters. We have to illustrate this matter further seeing how it has left many questions unanswered. The author is himself one of the three brothers after whom Angelina was born. My big brother Julius has a son as his first born and three daughters after him. Fortune has three sons and the fourth will be a girl if they go that far.

During the patriarchal biblical era, they didn't count the females and indeed they rarely documented about them. That's why the bible simply mentions her in the book of Genesis, saying only that sometime later Leah conceived and had a daughter she named Dinah.

She is just mentioned by chance in explaining how Jude inherited the firstborn's birthrights. No one knows for sure about her birth. But we can tell from the pattern of things that for sure Dinah, Jacob's daughter was actually born after Levi. The sex of the fourth born baby has a tendency to change from either male to female and vice versa. That is to say Jacob begot Reuben, then Simeon and then Levi before Dinah—his only daughter—was born. It was after Dinah that Judah was born. Why? How do we know?

Of course it is the laws of nature. Husband and wife pay due attention to one another during their first phase of their marriage. It is natural. The sequence of love-making is regular. Here then comes the analysis of the relationship between the lifespan of the male versus female chromosomes; i.e. Y and X, and the relative swimming prowess of each. The male chromosome is ordinarily so fast. But it has its drawbacks. Its lifespan is so short.

It follows therefore that, because of the law of average, it is very likely that the Y chromosome i.e., the sperm that produces males, will fertilize the egg when it is released. On the other hand, if the frequency of sexual intercourse is so much irregular and far apart—which is natural during the second phase of the marriage i.e. after the first three to four up to five years of marriage during which the third baby is born—the fast swimmer but short-lived male chromosome will expire before the egg arrives.

Now the slow runner but long living X chromosome from the male, i.e., the sperm that produces females, will still be there breathing—alive and kicking—waiting! So when the ovulation takes place, the fixed X that is released, then combines with the X from the male partner to form the XX combination, and the baby girl will follow after the ninth moon. Simple! This explains the ubiquity of male children during the first phase of marriage—other factors held constant. The author is the third born. His senior siblings were boys forty years ago. His younger sister—the fourth born is named Angelina.

Still doubting? Jacob had only two children to Rachel—his second and most favorite wife. And what do men with great frequency with their most favorite wives? Can you guess if these kids were males of females? You are right. They were Joseph and Benjamin. We are certain based on this explanation and the law of average that if Rachel had had another child—a child born after the sequence we described above—he would be a he-baby. That's all we know about him.

But we don't know what his name would be.
No one—not even this author—knows whether ole Jacob would name him one of the names of his forefathers such as Isaac or Ibrahim or even something completely new and fresh such as Kambarangwe, Festo, or Michael, Drogba, Lincoln, Julius, Madiba or even Usain Bolt. We don't know for sure.

There is one more thing we know nonetheless. For those seeking baby boys, or baby girls, you already know where to start: pamper your wife! Indulge into her happiness and desires; coddle her; treat her, spoil her if you want a baby boy—and as economists say—the reverse is true!

But for now that we are concerned with the ubiquity of the *KP Number*, and the ubiquity of 3, we can all recall when we were young in schools. Our teachers said: on your marks, get ready, go. Three counts! And what about the doctor's prescription of drugs? Are they not prescribed three times a day, morning afternoon and after dinner? Three! Three! Three!

NTIMBA KATARIKWENDWA AND THE MAGIC NUMBER
The discussion about the influence or authority of the Number 3 above, reminds me of one Ntimba Katarikwendwa. We met back in the late-seventies after dad had retired and settled into the village. Because compared with Ntimba we were younger and novices to the ways of the village life, he became an instrumental friend and patron playing the role of a big brother to us—my brothers and me.

He was not learned. In fact he never set his eyes on the inside of a classroom in his entire life. But surprisingly, he was a true believer of the principled universe. He believed there was a certain pattern of life that attracted success or failure. This is how I proved his belief in the principled universe even though I didn't care about it then.

Young as were, we went about a number of farms in the village hunting for fruits. *Obunana* or a species of smaller banana that is eaten when ripe and paw paws were our darling fruits. I noticed those days that some pawpaw trees can be too tall and thin such that you cannot climb them up. Yet as old and tall a tree becomes, the more it produced the most delicious fruits. So there remained only one alternative. That was reaping the fruit by a stone—I mean by hitting it with a throw. Now with regularity of almost an authority, Ntimba never missed out. With frequent regularity he hit the target at the first stone throw. Now here is the cream of the whole story. Whenever his first throw missed he would try for the second and the third time. And that's all. When the third throw missed, he resigned, threw the stones away and moved away to another tree even when its fruits were second rated.

He then frequently taught us saying, "Hey, let's move it! Let's go to another tree!" "Why? We asked. "Ekawaida yi chipapali na mabare asatu!" he rationalized in his (non-Kihima) Kinyambo dialect. That is the principle is three stones, and so if you miss for the third time, you will never hit the pawpaw even if you spend the rest of your life throwing a stone! Whether that's true, I've no way of knowing for I never persisted that far. We believed him and took literally whatever he said almost religiously. He was a typical village boy while we were new in the village. We didn't know much about the life in the rural village. We learned from him that you don't have to waste your valuable time when all odds prove you cannot succeed. We learned from him that there were principles for success—and I have only recently learned that probably he attached this secret to a certain number.

THE MAGIC NUMBER WITH SPIRITUALITY
Not Ntimba's emphasis is final. And you may be right for he was a traditionalist and a spiritist for a typical conservative catholic for instance to believe in. Yes you cannot take his conclusions as final and you may be right because he was an unlearned son of one of our neighbors back in village, Kifuye, Kyerwa, Tanzania. But what about this ubiquity?

But again, can I explain the mathematics in the game or how it so happens that a certain number governs certain events? No! I can't.

But my failure to explain it further doesn't water down the relevance or compliance to the principle. The ubiquity with which the number 3 appears truly cannot simply be coincidental. It indeed has been in operation even since the days of the first creation.

The Torah recognizes God of Israel as God of three supreme forefathers Ibrahim, Isaac and Jacob. It was Adam's third born Seth from whom the world came forth. Who was anointed to serve in the house of the lord in the whole of Israel? Think about it. Not Rueben the first born or Joseph who was Jacobs's favorite son.

Probably if Jacob had mandate over such matters he would have chosen Joseph in that favorite position. It was none other but Levi. Even though he was not the most favored son in the house of Jacob's but being third born he was anointed to serve in the house of God of Israel down to the modern day Israel. God created the earth in three days. He then finished his work in the next three more days.

The number 3 also features when God asked Noah to build the mysterious Ark.
The dimensions laid down by God Himself—the length of 3x 100 cubits by the height of 3 x 10 cubits, and the volume of 3 x 150,000 cubits respectively—obediently corresponded with this mysterious Number 3. besides, something that is almost ignore is that the lord ordered Noah to build not a normal one floor boat but a sailing three-storey building structure a.k.a, The Ark (Genesis 6:15-16). Why? When King David had erred, the word of the Lord came to the prophet Gad…as saying: thus says the lord, three things I offer you , choose one of them, that I may do it to you. Shall three years of famine come to you in your land? Or shall you flee for three months before your foes while they pursue you? Or shall there be three days pestilence in your land? (2 Samuel 24:12-13)" Why?

Though the Christian Church believes in monotheism but it is also based on the Holy Trinity. This is a belief in God in His three selves—literally. The contemporary human governments everywhere in the world have adapted the trinity concept into tripartite form of government—a government built on the three major pillars of government namely: the executive, judiciary and the parliament something the ancient derived from the same logic?

Jesus began his real work at 30, worked so hard for three years and ascended back from whence he had come at 33.

The only planet with life, according to our knowledge until as I write, earth, is third from the sun. Adam's third born Seth was the most blessed and probably one considered to have fathered the modern day humanity and civilization.

According to the Hadith, of the teachings of the Prophet Muhammad, the Mohammedans are allowed to knock the door to enter a house only three times. Abu Sa'id said: Then he (Abu Musa) came to us and said: Do you remember Allah's Messenger having said this: "Permission is for three times."

According to the Koran Surat Al-Imran verse 3:41, when Zacharias was informed by the angel Gabriel that he shall have a son, he said: "O my Lord! Give me a Sign!" to which the answer was: "Thy Sign shall be that thou shalt speak to no man for three days but with signals. Then celebrate the praises of thy Lord again and again, and glorify Him in the evening and in the morning." When Jesus needed a recess, he took with him only three disciples with him: Peter, Jacob and John as he climbed high on the mountain of olives.

Is it now surprising any more that Apostle Peter denied Jesus three times and he didn't mind until when the cock had crowed three times again? Why did Jesus choose this same number when he told Simon Peter that he would deny him three and only three times?

Why did he ask Simon Peter three times: "Simon son of John do you love me than the others?" Jonah was in the stomach of the fish for 3 days. Jesus resurrected on the third day. Why? Why? Why? Truly, the author has no way of knowing why Three. But it is probably for this reason that Tobin Wilson said: "I think in threes."

Frankly, if the idea that one number out of a thousand million others holds such a special position in human lives can still be regarded with indifference, then what about the ubiquity and the extent it pervades social human life, transcending into sports, politics and the military, crossing over to almost every major religion?

Truly this astounding ubiquity cannot simply go unnoticed! Probably an argumentative and inquisitive learner, or reader, will question validity of this analysis realizing that not every time this number is at work: that we see using two, not three, eyes; that we work using two, not three, hands; that we hear using two, not three, ears; that we walk using two not three legs hanging on the two, not three, feet;

that we smell using two, not three, nose outer openings; that metabolism undertakes cleanup of our bodies using two, not three, kidneys; that the heart pumps blood using detachable in two not three parts, left and right or upper and lower sections; that we reproduce using two, and not three, reproductive organs!

Yet though we see, hear, smell, walk, work, etc. etc., using two, not three, body parts, you should not miss the fact that yes these functions put to use two, and not three, body parts, but there is one more entity behind all these functions—you know what that is? Yes you do! The brain is the third entity behind all these functions—which is itself divided in three major functional parts. You must also not forget that though we reproduce using two and not three reproductive organs but behind all this mystery, there is a third ENTITY. You know what THAT is? Yes you are right! It is God—God whom (you can please skip the remaining part of the line if you are a religious fanatic) Catholics and the rest of the Christians denominations, though monotheists, they identify Him in His Holy Trinity!

Probably the following statement holds more water for a reader who is uninitiated in this area of study. This work, I mean the revelations we present in this book, also serve to inspire further studies in this fresh ground. That's why the author chose to excavate deep into the matter for more valuable information building on revelations we are going to further through the proceeding pages.

Suffice to say here that John Green couldn't be more right. For indeed, "It is harder to believe in coincidence but it is harder to believe in anything else." Yet we cannot go on leading this life so blindly, unguided. But we cannot also go on ignoring such a very ubiquitous coincidence. We cannot go on guessing what the future might bring. We need to prove the path we should follow—a path that will lead us to the desired destination.

And this is not baseless. In the science discipline, the first thesis or original idea cannot be accepted as a scientific law unless it is established to be an unfailing principle. Thus the first idea or assumption is called hypothesis which is defined by dictionary.cambridge.org as an idea or explanation for something that is based on known facts but has not yet been proved. With relevant proof it becomes a principle defined as a basic idea or rule that explains or controls how something happens or works: such as Archimedes principle. An idea becomes law only after it is proved to work under different scenarios. Such scientific laws include law of flotation and law of gravitational force.

Notice however that as I write, in the world today, there're such many laws that are in operation which we either already know about, or not, but even if we know about their existence we cannot explain how they operate. But again, failing to explain something or fundamentals behind a certain sequence, doesn't reverse the fact that it apparently governs other events, or has influence over the pattern of our lives. That is how the PHI outcropped. But before we discuss the PHI, let me say that finally because of its ubiquity, this number was christened. When I first introduced the idea to one of my colleagues in Mbezi-Luis, Dar es Salaam, Tanzania, he suggested that this number being itself princely, and because it has been consolidated and introduced to the international audience by this author, it be named a *Kambarangwe Princely Number*, or simply popular as a *KP Number*. And so be it!

THE PHI

One of the astounding standards of the universe is the PHI. To explain it clearly let us first clarify a closely related phenomenon namely Fibonacci sequence. And by the way, this author has not once again crafted the PHI to tantalize you. This is one of the most astounding facts which has received due attention from many writers including the most remarkable recent work by Dan Brown.[83]

THE FIBONACCI SEQUENCE

The Fibonacci sequence is a famous progression of numbers. It is famous not only because the sum of each adjacent terms equals the next term, but also the quotient of adjacent terms possess an astonishing property of approaching the PHI. What is a PHI then? Well, we will come to that only a little later. First let us give a little more attention to the Fibonacci sequence.

Fibonacci sequence includes numbers in the following series: 1, 1,2,3,5,8,13, and 21 etc., and the series goes on to the nth digit all the way as loyal as ever. The sequence is formed by addition of the first two adjacent terms in the sequence, which then forms the next number. The total is then added to the following adjacent in the series to get the next number, and the next, and the next in an endless series.

Enough of sermon! Now take 1 and 1 in the series above and add them together. What do you get? 2?

Correct! Now then take 1 and 2 and add them up. What is the answer? 3? Good boy! Correct again! Go on now taking 2 and 3 and add them up. You get 5? Good girl! You can go on as far as a thousand numbers but that's not necessary! It is a waste of your useful time. They—the ratios between each two adjacent numbers—all adhere to the same principle and cling to a certain ratio—literally with molar teeth—which is a number very close to 1.6. Now what is remarkably startling is that the sum you get which is 1.6 is an approximated figure of a mystical number known as PHI.

Now why is the discussion about PHI important? It is for many reasons. One and chiefly because it forms ratios which adhere to ratios in your body parts—if you are normal—and majority of us are! Thus the human body is literally made of building blocks whose proportional ratios always sum up to PHI. Let us somehow emulate the biblical *Thomas!* Let us object to take things literally.

Let us seek some proofs. And you don't need too many implements to do so! You only need the tape measure and then your body! Then measure the distance from the tip of your head to the floor and then measure the distance from your belly button to the floor. The ratio is? A PHI? Yes sir! A PHI! Then take the distance from your shoulders to the finger tips, and the distance from elbow to finger tips. What's the ratio? PHI again! Take now the distance from the tip of your head to the position on your belly where your folded hands touch, and divide that by the distance between the tip of your shoulders, and where your folded hands touch. What do you get?

Again, take the distance between the tip of your head and the tip of your shoulder and divide it by the distance between the tips of your head to the tip of your chin. What is the ratio? Now take the distance from the tip of your chin, to the tip of the base of the opening of your nose, and divide it by the distance between the tip of the nose and the inner tip of your lower mouth. What is the ration again?

Or take the distance between the irises, which is vertically equal to the deepest part in the valley of your nose to the tip of your chin. What is the ration here? Measure again from the extreme corner of your eye that part toward the ear piece to the middle of the eye which is the iris and the distance between the corners of your eye to the middle point of your nose. What do you get? PHI! PHI! PHI! Endlessly! You can in fact try it with as many other parts of your body as you can and you will be astonished to find that all the time the ratios adheres to the same number—the PHI!

Furthermore, PHI is also vivid in ratios between sexes among numerous species. If you study the ratios between females and males in a honeybee community you will be dumbfounded to find that the population of female bees and male bees in any beehive in the world corresponds to the ratio PHI, the scientists say. That is females and males are in ratio approaching 1.6.

The nautilus with its concentric ark spiral does adhere to PHI. That is the ratios between its spirals diameters to the next, adheres to ratio 1.6. Sunflowers grow in opposing spirals. Can you make up the ratio of each rotation's diameter to the next spiral? Spiral pinecone petals' leaf arrangement in plants' stalks, what is their ratio? PHI, PHI, PHI!

If you look around yourself, you will find that almost every form of life shows astonishing obedience to a certain common proportion which converges to a PHI. The unparalleled sensation of Mozart or Beethoven's music: why was it so inimitable and one of its kind?

Beethoven or Mozart musical compositions—with for instance the first movement of Beethoven's 5th can be further divided into smaller parts that also exhibit the golden ratio or Mozart's composing by putting two-measure melodic fragments together in any order—all adhere to PHI. The corresponding dimensions of the instrument, the symphony, with which they played music, adhered to PHI.[84]

PHI is also in all architectural works of all great architects from Michelangelo to Da Vinci. The architecture among ancient Greeks, the pyramids, etc. were structured in adherence to the PHI.

Take the successes of the Toyota Company and brand or the secret why the Taj Mahal is considered one of the wonders of the world. The Toyota logos corresponding distances from one side left or right to another or top to bottom like the Taj Mahal its dimensions adhere to the PHI! If you closely observe only a few of examples we have given above you will realize that in every aspect of nature or in art, anatomy, music, architecture, industry, etc. all everywhere there is PHI! PHI! PHI! PHI! PHI! to the nth degree!
Now can such ubiquity truly be simply coincidental? Nah! Nah! Nah! Indeed PHI gives mystical mathematics. Its ratios seem to irrefutably play a fundamental building block in nature. Close observation depict that humans, plants and animals possess dimensional properties that adhere to PHI ratio.

"The astounding conclusion is that this number's ubiquity exceeds a mere coincidence," wrote Dan Brown. "That is why the ancient assumed that this number was pre-ordained by the creator. That is why they herald the number as a divine proportion."[85]

THE PATTERN OF LIFE AND HIDEN PRINCIPLES

The author was further astonished by the extent the pattern of life follow a certain specific order. The biblical Joseph based his prediction and interpretations of dreams on a certain specific order. And mind you this hasn't started today! In Egypt during the days when Joseph served in Pharaoh's premier, he predicted the period of bounty spreading across seven years period and then drought and hunger had to happen for another same-same seven years. This author's dad believed there was a certain order for the coming of troubles and of bliss—that they followed a certain number 7. "Such is how rains come and go…and arrival of spring on the earth coming back to produce its bounty…" concluded Dan Brown!

The reader will be interested to know number 7, is another number that appears so strongly as distinctive. For instance, it is said the life of man shall be 70 years only. A week has 7 days. Jesus ordered his followers to forgive 7 times 77. God rested on the 7th day,`` etc. That is to say whereas we may be today certain of one some of the laws, it doesn't mean no more laws in operation even as we speak. Nah! I only intend to say there is a certain principle whether we know it or not. Again, not because we have concentrated with number 3 and 1.6 that is not to say other numbers don't have areas where they are ordained. No. We simply don't know. But our lack of knowledge shouldn't limit our imagination. It shouldn't dissuade us from observing the facts.

Fortune tellers, tarot readers and cards all seem to correspond to a certain order. Such is how it has been concluded by Dr. Rhine and his associates at the Duke University as reported through the editorial of the New York Times that, "various percipients were asked to name as many cards in a special pack as they could without looking at them and without other sensory access to them. About a score of men and women were discovered who could regularly name so many of the cards correctly that there was not one chance in many millions of their having done their feats by luck or accident."[86]

In his book What Makes People Rich and Nations Powerful, this author described how through his own intuition could tell whether a lost item such a phone or money was not lost after all even after hours and weeks of searching and having missed it. He, described how he could have premonition on disasters or tidings of great joy even before they happened.

But the greatest of all these evidences, is a dramatic event in which Fortunatus, the author's own brother could "influence" and receive a call from a distant friend or associate without having used the known five sensory organs or means. This is no fiction. You can read more about it in the book What Makes People Rich and Nations Powerful.

It shouldn't surprise you, therefore, to notice that just like in Dr. Rhine's experiment, it worked just as well at distances of several hundred miles as they did in the same room. "Last but not least," says Napoleon Hill, "man, with all his boasted culture and education, understands little or nothing of the intangible force (the greatest of all the intangibles) of thought...there are from 10,000,000,000 to 14,000,000,000 nerve cells in the human cerebral cortex...arranged in definite patterns.

These arrangements are not haphazard. They are orderly...It is inconceivable how that such a network on intricate machinery should be in existence for the sole purpose of carrying on the functions incidental to growth and maintenance of the physical body. Is it not likely that the same system , which gives billions of brain cells the media for communication one with another, provides, also the means of communication with other intangible forces?"[87]

That is not all. The author has observed that man, with all his boasted culture and education, understands little or nothing of the intangible force that allows not only his own family to determine there is a baby coming even without official announcement, or coming into contact with the person expecting a baby, but also the ability to tell whether the coming baby is a boy or a girl.

MANTIS: THE MESSENGER OF NEW LIFE FROM GOD

Have you ever observed closely about yourself and scanned your whole environment before the coming of babies? If you are keen enough, you will recognize it once a female member of your family is pregnant and a new baby is expected in the family.

How? He, The Maker, Himself caring so much about the new life, sends down a messenger in your house and those of the family members to bring tidings of great joy of the new life, and that a new child is on the way. You probably know this insect they named mantis or praying mantis.

When he or she materializes in your house and tarries, recognize that the God of new life has sent down his or her messenger. Be prepared. You will see the messenger on the floor, or sometimes on the wall or even in the sitting room, on the verandah or the cupboard walls, etc. once he sees him or her, the author recognizes at once that one of the female family members is expecting a child. And indeed the messenger is highly protected. His life is attached to that of the new baby in its mother's womb. How? I don't know! I am a mere mortal. But the facts are true. I can only give the report of the little I have gathered. That's all. And now concerning the mantis making his or her appearance when necessary, it is astounding how really it doesn't matter if the author is at home or away. When it happens, that he is away or at home and the mantis come visiting, he normally calls his family members and they certainly confirm having seen the same insect.

What is even more tantalizing is that you can easily recognize if the baby will be a boy or girl without high powered Ultrasound machines but by simply looking at the color and the physique of the insect on the wall. My mother went a step further. She disclosed to the author that she knows someone in the family expects a baby whenever a unique scar in her body—an atypical scar, of course.

Now concerning you my readers and the rest of the world, whether they see the messenger to recognize him or her or not, or whether you see him or her and recognize the implication or not is one thing, and reality another. What is certain is the fixity of the law.

Now can we prove all these facts? It is tantalizing how we cannot explain these facts but nevertheless we cannot disregard their consistency. A snake is at once, brought to a halt from its tracks only once a woman holds both her breasts tightly together. Is this hearsay?

African magic? Never! The author has proved it himself more than twice. The first time it was in the village when he was walking alongside his mother in Karagwe now known as Kyerwa in Tanzania. As we walked, suddenly a snake rose from shrubs and crossed toward us.

But I suddenly couldn't believe what I saw! I couldn't! The snake stopped in its tracks and to my surprise, he or she even seemed to be struggling to make himself scarce. But when I turned to see my mother's reaction, I saw that the snake was on halt right in front of my mother. That's when I realized what she had done.

Mother was holding her chest. She asked me to collect a stick and hit him or her. I hit it fearing that it would attack but he or she didn't. He or she was under a very powerful spell that left it completely numb and powerless and motionless. Is the author's mother a special one? Of course she is! But it is also something that is ordained to women in the bible.

Let us see what the Lord God says concerning the powers women have over the serpent. This is from the book of Genesis 3:14 after the serpent had made the woman sin against God: "I will put enmity between you and the woman…"

Could this be more than just antagonism? It seems to me that God wanted to strip the snake with her powers of the woman. It seems to me that God wanted the woman to have in her powers the ability to tame a serpent.

Now the question is this—in response to the powers women have over the snake—are other women able to access the same powers? Yes, sir! And let me talk to you madam whether you are black or white. You have the same powers.

So, next time don't run away from the snake, or your problems. Just use your assets! If you can with the same assets thwart a more physically strong and more sophisticated and educated human male person why not tame a mere cursed and unschooled illiterate livestock?

Let me illustrate that all women learned and unlearned have powers within their magical bodies to tame even the most cunning serpent, let alone an average man. Not long ago with his wife in his farm house when the author was petrified to find a snake on the verandah peering at them as she snaked into the house.

The author immediately instructed his wife in the ways of halting snakes. His wife held her chest as instructed, and the snake could not move an inch. It was at stand still. It tried in vain until when I the author of this testimony walked outside—hurriedly? Oh, no!

There was no need for that! The author even had the luxury of trying a catwalk! My wife was a little hysterical while I even so confidently, walked with a swag. I was certain the snake would not disobey the natural law. Then I returned with a stick and at my will, and with no sense of urgency, I scanned her, the cunning serpent choosing where to hit, and hit her on the head. It was finito! Finished! Surely this explains there is so much we don't know yet. You can read some more about this tale in the book *What Makes People Rich and Nations Powerful*.

To the uninitiated readers this may seem to be a miracle or nonsense—either way. It is not. It is not even something ordained to only to my family. Indeed one of my neighbors admitted he witnessed it himself and for first time he didn't believe it was not witchcraft when he saw one his neighbors paralyze and hit a snake in the same fashion. In fact if you are a woman you can control the movement of the serpent in such a way that it can run in a certain fanciful whimsical and rhythmic pattern only by holding your breasts together and letting them free before holding them together again. I am informed that a man can do the same by holding his balls! There is no more bush around here and so there are no more snakes for me to try it. I plan to go to the snakes' park in Arusha and experiment it though. You try it. If you do you will certainly prove that such mysteries are not mysticism but verity. And what I tell you is no lie but truth and reality. If you do so, you will then again never question the fact that there's a secret formula in all aspects of life—whether we know it or not.

THERE IS NO COINCIDENCE

You recognize that we are analyzing how the pattern of life is not a random course of events anymore, but a kind causation. For instance have you ever noted that the third born tends to be regulated in nature? Why? Is it by chance? Nah! He is so because of his station in a family. It is by learning from his or her elder siblings. The truth is the young children adore their senior siblings. That's why one will pick one good trait or bad from one and another from the other brother or sister and having the privilege of learning from both of them. Again of course his parents tend to have learned their lessons on how better to look after the children.

Have you ever seen the relationship between the drivers and the baby girls? Most drivers—especially the long distance driver—tends to reproduce baby girls. In a sample of five family units very close to the author, a 100% adhere to, and offer the proof of the principled universe—that there is no coincidence. Here is an astounding revelation.

Two among these drivers have seven baby girls—a number bigger than the preplanned number of children in attempt to get a baby boy. It was futile as if to establish Ntimba's genius! It is futile unless the basics changed.

To comprehend the fact that there's no coincidence, and that the occurrences follow a certain code, standard or principle, notice that the female chromosome has longer life span than that of the male chromosome—as we mentioned earlier on.

Besides, when a driver husband is home, yes they would make love but because of his work and random travel schedule the routine he cannot control being the run of the mill in the organization, he would leave his wife with yes, both female X and a male Y chromosomes. But the male Y will pass away in a couple of days while the female X will survive time and space and live on to fertilize his wife's egg when it comes!

By the law of average a couple whose frequency or regularity of sexual contact is erratic inconsistent, irregular and uncertain will therefore reproduce baby girls than boys. No pointing fingers or medication is needed or necessary. The birth of the baby boy or girl can only best be managed by the change in the lifestyle and the pattern or frequency of marital or conjugal communion.

There are people around the author who believe that diarrhea is a sign of the coming of the teeth. That is to say, before the infant grows the teeth, it must be attacked by diarrhea. Yes diarrhea precedes the coming of the teeth, but there is no divine ordination in this one. Many know this fact but only a handful of people know why it so happens with frequent regularity! The point is this: even though almost every other infant is likely to catch diarrhea before it grows the teeth, it is not a sign of the coming of the teeth. It is not even a sign from the East.

But it's not an accident. The universe is principled. It is principled that it so stubbornly clings to its laws—literally with its molar teeth. Whatever happens is not by chance. It happens because of the *law of causation*. Let me illustrate further.

PATRICIA AND THE MYTH OF RELATIONSHIP BETWEEN TEETH AND DIARHEA

Patricia was young when I began writing the manuscript of the book you are now reading.

I had put down everything to concentrate with the manuscript. So I stationed myself at home day and night for many months for that was a very big manuscript. This gave me opportunity to observe the changes she underwent so closely. It wasn't a difficult thing to do, because she was stationed in her bed permanently. During all this time, she had never been troubled by diarrhea. Then she turned five months old. At this point in time, four things happened simultaneously—and almost instantaneously.

One, she began crawling. Her bed chamber was no longer like a zoo it used to be. Children hate to be caged in zoos. They, the infants I mean, crave to be free—like the adults. As she crawled, for first time in her independent life, she began picking up things—and they all had one destination—her mouth. Following in the steps of the previous events—the ability to crawl and the experience of picking up things, finally, diarrhea hit! And then almost suddenly, predictably, the two twin lower teeth materialized! When I saw the teeth I was astonished by the rapidity of her growth. The local people, my neighbors, said we knew the teeth were on the way. Why? Because diarrhea had persisted! But as the diarrhea persisted, I said I was taking her to see the doctor. They, my neighbors, had said no need. It was the teeth. It will stop immediately after the teeth are out. It didn't. It couldn't. It persisted even more than before.

Now the question is this: was it by some sacred divine law that diarrhea must precede the growth and emergence of the teeth? No sir! Her ability to crawl meant that she could for first time pick up some things. And as an infant, the most powerful sensory organ is the tongue. Thus for her everything she touches will go to the predictable destination—the mouth! It is therefore predictable that some filth and bacteria thereof will naturally infect her with diarrhea.

THE RAINFALLS

Let's consider the coming and going of the rainfalls. If you are inquisitive only a little you will notice that here in Dar es Salaam, Tanzania, we experience rainfalls during Christmas days—almost as a law. This has prompted many naïve followers of the Christian faith to wrongly believe it is so to signal the might of the Messiah; the latter assertion, of which I don't object of course. For them it is meant to mark the Messiah's birthday! It isn't true! Don't believe it! Don't buy into it! God has His ways and a thousand of them if He has to prove his might. If God wills to do so he can do so through more obvious and elaborate ways.

It is neither Jesus who showers us with some form of the heavenly drink, nor a result of the cracking of divine Champaign bottles before the angels sing *Happy Birth to You Lord Jesus*. It is due to the shift if the doldrums. At this particular time of the year, due to the earth rotation, the sun is over head in the south of Dar es Salaam, Tanzania. Geographically, Dar es Salaam is adjacent the long shore of the Sea of Dar es Salaam you call the Indian Ocean. Now, with the long stretch of the ocean alongside the overhead sun rainfalls must be formed. The sun then hits and heats up the sea water massive evaporation must take place. The dry land chills and the clouds then cool down at night cooling the moisture forming dews high up in the clouds. The dews then solidify to farm rain drops which after saturation point they cannot hold them anymore. That's when the rain falls on the face of the earth. It's a reason why by the dates 23rd down 27th of December, every year, these parts of East Africa receive Christmas rainfalls!

Never be deceived! God has many ways to establish Himself and His might. God proved His might before Pharaoh when he turned the staff that Prophet Moses held into a snake. But that was not all. The Egyptian magicians managed somehow to conjure up some snakes from their own sticks and ropes. Pharaoh laughed at the man of God so heartily and despised his signs. God couldn't let that happen on His watch. He can never do so. Soon enough Pharaoh was dumfounded to witness the snake that came out of the staff that the Prophet held swallowing all the little snakes his magicians had perfected. I can recount a long list of how God can manifest himself. He showered the land with manna from high heavens to feed Israel. He deceived and vanquished Pharaoh when Israel passed through the Red Sea.

When Jesus released the ghost the curtain of the temple sliced itself and was asunder in twain from the roof to the floor of the temple. The mighty Bar Jesus deceived people with witchcraft flying high in air denouncing the teaching of the apostles in Rome during the first year of Our Lord. Apostle Paul knelt down on his knees and prayed before the deceitful man fell to the ground *Phuuuph*, busting into pieces right before the audience of naïve Italians who believed in him. David defeated the giant goliath. Daniel survived the lion in its own den. Shadrack, Meshack and Abednego survived the inferno. If you would still say those are historical and biblical tales of an old weak and unknowledgeable bunch of old folks, alright! You have a point. Not everyone believes in the Christian faith. I will now recount how God cannot be deceived, something that happened in my presence.

Here's a true event that I personally witnessed. It happened in Katera, Karagwe, now Kyerwa district, when persistent drought besieged the land. The barren clouds and the drought brought forth hunger and devastation among the people. On this day the mass was on going. And I was there—in the chapel. I saw the wind and a dark cloud forming in the high heavens over the hills of Kafuro a few miles from the village chapel. From the church where I was, I could see the dark cloud. Now the Evangelist, (note that this is a true story and I was there but for anonymity I will only introduce him as the Catechist) couldn't miss the opportunity. With this gesture from high heavens, he rose to the occasion.

Taking the advantage of the situation, he decided to rationalize his religion and his personal divine might. He suddenly began speaking in the "tongues." I was impressed. But there was no pigeon hanging on the top of his head and no fire was forthcoming. In a sudden shift of events, he had become very emotional like someone under the spell of the strongest ancient spirits. He prayed endlessly diverting from traditional catholic style to the creative prayers of his own calling upon his Gods. I didn't know if he called the Gods to save the people from the tragic drought or to spare him from shame. "This is your turn Lord. Let this congregation know that you are the only God. Let the people know your might and that of me your loyal servant in Jesus name..." and we replied "Amen!"

The evangelist persisted calling and praying to his God! Despite the endless series of long litany of creative prayers, not even a single rain drop was forthcoming. Not one. Seconds turned into minutes, minutes into hours. But there was no rain. Not one! I peered outside through the window. The clouds were barren. The nimbus cloud, the dark-grey cloud which often produces rain waved goodbye.

Half the cloud on the promising east turned into cirrus, a type of light feathery cloud that is seen high in the sky. When the dark threatening clouds on the west gave way to cumulus, a type of tall white cloud with a wide flat base and rounded shape, I gave up. I caught the glimpse of the Catechist anxiously examining the clouds. Any remaining iota of hope that the Catechist had hung on had finally disappeared, gone forever. He closed his and prayed intensely. But it was useless. There was no rain and no showers. Nothing. There was nothing. Nada!

Soon the darkness turned to light. The scorching rays of the afternoon sun peered through heaven in a smile as if to mock the Catechist. The sun was so scorching if to punish the rest of us who had hoped God was so that cheap.

The heavy clouds and the winds soon turned and fled to the bordering Rwandan and Ugandan hills just a few kilometers away! The sky was clear once again. The sun rays swept the whole village chapel. The man of God was astonished. No! That's not it. He was shocked. He had deceived God. God deceived him in turn. But no! God punished him! I have never seen the longest mass. Later that hour, he closed the mass in style and drew the cloth away and fled. I have never seen the longest religious mass! And that's not all. An astounding fact is he wasn't the same person a few months later when I left the village on joining the boarding school at Kahororo Secondary School. Later that semester he was saved after he was found hanging by the rope attempting to commit suicide by the rope. His wife had caught him in an act!

HIV/AIDS AND THE RAW LAW OF NATURE

Does the *Raw Law* of nature apply to all the social aspects? Certainly! The principles of the universe envelop all circles of life—and of death! House work, social and commercial prostitution, *Bar-Maiding* as some forms of industry, HIV/AIDS or even wealth tend to blossom among certain communities. In my own country, HIV/AIDS is ubiquitous in certain specific regions or amongst some tribes. It is not coincidental that Bukoba, Mbeya, Makete etc., all exhibit strong HIV /AIDS prevalence. Why? It isn't by miracle or chance. In Mbeya it is due to transit goods transnational business and long distance truck drivers who station there on their way to deliver goods to the land locked central African states such as Zambia, Malawi, and Zimbabwe or even the eastern part of D.R Congo. The long distance drivers—humans as they are—tend to establish long term marital relations among these regions when they are loading or crossing the borders.

That the extents of the HIV pandemic are different among different communities is not just coincidental or the work of the Gods. Indeed the difference is due to the fact that we have different cultures and traditions in Kagera or Dar es Salaam in Tanzania, and how each community perceives promiscuity and prostitution. The author is a witness of how in some communities in the regions sexual relationship is praiseworthy while it is considered taboo in others. You can notice this by how elders or traditional songs in these communities dissuade against or promote prostitution. Take Kagera region for instance.

Yes, the proximity with such towns as Mtukula and the thriving cross-border business in Rukunyu in Uganda, areas that were more or less like the No-Man's land and therefore no rules or regulations during the Amin era and later under Obote and the vacuum that followed for a long time before president Museveni took over, together with misinformation *in* Uganda helped to fuel cultural promiscuity and HIV and AIDS in the region and its neighborhood. These areas that commanded business in the region during the early days of AIDS had a profound effect on long term culture of promiscuity and HIV/AIDS but culture and traditions among the local communities had more impact than any other influences.

Also recognize that both groups viz. the businessmen and the truck drivers happened to be well-off compared with the neighborhood. As day follows night, women and money tended to flow and flock toward these areas. Fort, the author's brother, was right: *"Mkono mtupu haulambwi na mwanamke."* Indeed an empty hand attracts no woman. Quick fix and desire for quick money have infected the major population. Furthermore notice that when people indulge in the same form of vice for a very long time, it ceases to be one. It is no longer a haunting thing but instead the right thing to do. Soon it becomes a culture. And thus the population in these regions and religions tend to naturalize and sanctify promiscuity whether revered as some form of sport or industry. In the end, it becomes a pattern of life! You just have to hear the songs they sing in a certain community and you will judge the potential prevalence of HIV and AIDS.

The author has also observed that extreme cold weather could also fuel drinking and promiscuity. With this saddening verity, such areas as Mbeya or Makete are likely to have high rates of both vices. But it is also mindset at work since we believe a man is not a lowly beast without self-control. But let me say the truth and put the devil to shame! Just like how HIV pandemic could be stronger among the Luos for their culture of prohibiting circumcision, it is so in other tribes along the shores of Lake Victoria because of their tradition of praising prostitution, boasting of promiscuity through songs both in private and in public—praising both the act and expertise of the love affairs. Yet I know people in any of these areas who don't drink or buy or sell their bodies—no matter whether others do so for money or heat. Nothing is accidental. Signing the anti-gay bill into law president Museveni was right when he suggested that if the society is lenient about any good or bad culture , that culture thrives in that community. No wonder America is the leader in the gay industry. It is the law of causation at work. Yet in the end we all pay the price. For, "In the long run," said Epictetus "everyman will pay the penalty of his misdeeds."

ECONOMIC DOWN TURN

At this point in time, you must have noticed that the economic crisis was not a plain or an innocent coincidence. It is rather a result of how the world economy was managed at the time. Many economists and businessmen did indulge in middle-man-ship. Gambling and speculations afforded many with riches. But as a result, the system created the situation where nations had more nominal value of the wealth than the actual material production on the ground, in the factories and farms. That is why it was called a bubble—all bubbles must bust at some point in time! There was no actual production in factories and farms. There was no real production and as a result there was no real wealth. "Nothing as widespread as a global economic crisis can be just a coincidence," observed Napoleon Hill. "Behind the depression, there was a cause—nothing ever happens without a cause!" And what was the cause: "To reap without sowing." Indeed, "nearly everybody was engaged in trying to get without giving…" Read it for yourself in Napoleon Hill's glorious book Think and Grow Rich. Karl Marx was right. "A society will collapse," he said, "A society will collapse if it ceases to produce material wealth."

And as prophesied Prophet Karl Marx, Amen, and so be it, the economies and organizations collapsed with the bust of the bubble we had built in the workplaces. The author bet on the collapse of the education sector, the economy and the organizations along with it way back in 2006 when he resigned and wrote his book How Universities Under Develop You!

As I can bet my life on the fact that there shall be night tonight, excepting of the true North Pole and South Pole of course, what you sow the same shall you reap.

THE WAVE OF STREET CHILDREN AND WASTES IN DAR ES SALAAM OR PERFORMANCES OF KILIMANJARO REGION IN ACADEMICS OR INDUSTRY IS NOT A TWIST OF FATE

We have come this far thus to conclude that the escalating wave of street children in one community and not another isn't simply coincidental. The performances of Kilimanjaro region, for instance, in academics or in industry, or even how people from the northern region hold senior positions in politics, the church and at workplaces isn't a coincidence.

The social as well as economic quandary in our society today is—as has always been—an outcrop of falling morals and collapse of family institution—and generally a reflection o our curriculum. (Please read more about this regional analysis in professor Maliyamkono's book The Promise).

Good performance, or failure, has never been, it is never, and never will it be a mere coincidence. It will never happen by chance or accident. At this point in time, we have come to a position where we must recognize that failure of students in exams or their character today, is not simply a coincidence: it is a result of many factors. Poor economic performance of the country or corporations, low productivity in the country's workplaces, the increasing wave of foreign experts and dominance of Kenyans and Indians in the business sector in Tanzania which almost employs foreigners in top jobs availing only ordinary positions to the local people who slave in their own country, is not a coincidence, and cannot end, unless we do something really big.

WHY KILIMANJARO IS AT THE TOP

From the foregoing discussion, let us do a little analysis—both historical and current social organization in Kilimanjaro—factor from we can learn why one community progresses as another digresses.

Historically, Kilimanjaro has had deep roots in modern education culture probably longer than any other region following the earliest settlements of the missionaries in the region. These missionaries built schools and infrastructure that have propelled the people in the region in areas of education and industry. There is also a question of moral values. With the colonial establishment—educational facilities, seminaries and church infrastructures: the people in this region gained education and moral values that are advantageous in a modern society. The region is along the border with certainly the more prosperous Kenya, a country with a colonial settler economy helped to promote the values of industriousness and burning desire to succeed—to be top.

As a result the individual persons and households in the regions have specific goals—and make no mistake, they have goals for their children they tend to closely monitor in their desire to have them accomplish something big in life.

They no wonder become top in the class or in businesses or even in politics and in the church unlike the folks from the coastal region. Why? What's the difference? Let's try to scan both of these regions and briefly analyze the facts. To do that we go back to historical reasons again.

We, humans, tend to be influenced by the people in our neighborhood or communities that are relatively more advanced. We are also a product of our colonial masters. All of us! Whereas the north regions were influenced by the European German and British missionaries, countries that were most advanced than any at the time, the people in the Coastal region found themselves under the Arab rule for a very long time. The culture and traditions of the Arabs doesn't seem to encourage the pursuit of education or hard work. It was obvious. Unlike the European colonialists who sought people who would work in offices and probably run machines, the Arabs certainly didn't have to educate the Africans. They didn't have to promote technology, moral values or better living or social standards. We both know that they, the Arabs, traded in slaves, ivory and rhinoceros horns. You don't need to educate a slave, an ivory or rhinoceros horn you are going to sell or have as a mere hand to pull the cart or carry you, the master, on his shoulders.

Truly there was no need for educating slaves or elephants or even rhinos they considered as mere products or merchandize in their business. And you cannot blame those ancient Arabs. Besides, as I write, in the Middle East most communities don't adequately encourage education not only for the females, male folks don't find why they should work hard with oil rich bowels under their feet. The Arab countries have fuel and dollars and therefore they can fire and hire and pay any expertise they need. No wonder they don't simply discourage education—in general terms. And we say so knowing a number of countries and families engaged in education of their communities. But the Arabs have another greater setback., following their prohibiting access to education or workplaces to over half the population—the female folks—the people who actually manage the children, the future of the nation is in jeopardy.

With the foregoing revelation in the domain of our discussion, with the influence of the Arab slave masters, it is not surprising that the people from the north—Kilimanjaro and Arusha regions—are significantly advanced academically and industriously when compared with the folks of the coastal regions and those from areas along the slave trade routes such as Tabora and Kigoma—the latter of which was not developed at all but left untouched and undeveloped as a reserve labor region.

You can even analyze the differences by assessing such regions as Dodoma and Singida, the regions with very low influence of the Europeans missionaries or even through the comparisons between different pockets within the same regions where the missionaries settled Vis a Vis where traditional societies had more influence. The foregoing statement emphasizes the responsiveness of the people to the changing terrain.

In the final analysis, the culture of letting go or surrendering to circumstances you don't like only because whatever happens to you is fate and subject to the *Kismet* or *Karma* can never shower blessings of prosperity and bounty to anyone—Arab, European or African. The low degree of industriousness and perseverance among individuals and communities that believe in the *Mektoob Philosophy* where it is believed that everything is preordained or literally, *It is written,* is an attitude that is not going to be advantageous when it comes to accumulating wealth. The attitude to resign and surrender failing to persevere as an attitude has never been, it cannot be and will never shower anyone or his or her region or community with any blessings. Individuals and communities that progress behave in a certain way. That is to say they have the attitude that is friendly with education, work and wealth.

It is therefore no wonder that Professor Maliyamkono in his great book The Promise indicates that the Northern Tanzania region or specifically Kilimanjaro leads by far in registering students in classes across all levels. I'm a witness that even at the University; the most top performers come from this region, students who go on for further studies and advanced degrees. With affluence and wealthy economy, the region has another advantage or its youth. Students who are from the self-sustained and focused families don't have to rush into formal employment on graduation or to work during college years to support themselves or their families back home. Hence during school, they focus on one prime goal: education and more education.

On graduation many proceed to the master's degree and beyond because they don't have pressure to find a job. Besides their huge network has set higher goals for those who achieve higher marks as another half go into family business. No wonder they lead in academic positions such as the lecturers and researchers. They also hold the top positions in the government and in major leading organizations such as the Bank of Tanzania, all or most major top banking institutions, telecoms, the Revenue Authority and the rest of top corporations.

A big number of ministers and the prime ministers have since independence come from the northern region especially Kilimanjaro and Arusha (including Manyara).

Say what you want to say but this is never a coincidence. Is it favor? I would like also to believe that it not even favoritism. Well, the biggest favor, or favor from the Mother Nature of course was that they were where they are when the foreigners first set foot on the African soil. Those in the north became who they are today because they were here they were at the time. The communities in the coastal region are what they are because they were here they were—generally speaking. But favoritism cannot last or guarantee prosperity for long. The conditions favoring success or growth change over time. Success factors and growth drivers change with time. Truly these variations matter so significantly. But our attitudes, the behavior or thought pattern, disposition and mindset; what makes a difference is how we tune ourselves to match with the changing terrain, namely the success factors and growth drivers.

Having analyzed the factors why one region may or may not develop relative to another, here is another question to answer in as far as the strategy to lift up the levels of education and economy in the disadvantaged countries or districts is concerned. Does the rationing of the positions in education, employment or government serve the long term goals of equitable opportunities to all?

Yes rationing of positions in public services or private sector and schools may certainly help in the rationing of national wealth, yet it brings with it the danger of compromising productivity, competitiveness, and excellence among our people and quality of the products and services they produce. Indeed it is questionable if social harmony and national prosperity can be fetched when a credible candidate is barred from contesting for any position or the opportunity to advance or contribute to the agenda that serve personal, group or public or national interests only because he comes from a certain region.

With no political agenda then or now, and therefore nursing no grudges whatsoever, I, the author, can now proceed to illustrate the futility of indiscriminate rationing of positions and powers. In as far as the question of regional rationing of positions is concerned, the author was inspired by Premier Judge Joseph Sinde Warioba's response when he contested for president in 1985 when Mwalimu Nyerere retired.

Hailing from Mara region, and therefore from Nyamuswa village, a walking distance from Butiama thus the same locality with the outgoing president, Julius Nyerere, Warioba said he didn't consider locality as a condition for credibility. Rather, the latter i.e. credibility—in terms of education, abilities and character. And as premier and vice president, Warioba had both—experience and character. He lost!

Would the politics of the provinces provide an answer? I am not a politician to dwell on that one. But if asked, my answer, would be *NEVER*. I am not certain it can work under our present situation where the nation is slowly getting divided by the day based on tribal and sectarian grounds.

DONALD RUMSFELD'S TESTIMONY: THERE ARE KNOWN UNKNOWNS

Truly we are now living in the borderline between the old and a new era. Thinking about how this seems so close, I believe this is the end of an era. We are now entering, inching very steadily, in an era where we will depart from dependence on the knowledge we could verify by physical means, we are entering an era where we will begin to draw from the knowledge we know of, albeit whose working we know not. We are entering an era where we will begin to draw from the knowledge we know of, albeit whose modus operandi, or methods of operation, we cannot define or illustrate.

As such, decisions are being made today, decisions considered empirically accurate even when in words of Napoleon Hill, "man has not the capacity to understand the intangible force of gravity which keeps this little earth suspended in the midair," he said, "and keeps man from falling from it, much less to control that force…Nor is this by any means the end of man's ignorance in connection with things unseen and intangible… Last but not least," continued Napoleon Hill, "man, with all his boasted culture and education, understands little or nothing of the intangible force (the greatest of all the intangibles) of thought." Really there are things we cannot validate as to how they happen or work. Can we manage to offer proof that is beyond any reasonable doubt for all the facts we have evidenced in this chapter? We have tried to, but whether we satisfied the reader by ten or fifty percent, it doesn't matter—at all. Really! I have narrated how I have witnessed a snake getting stopped in its tracks to complete stand still by a woman who does nothing but simply holding her breasts together. But can I describe how it works? I can't—and I don't care much about it.

Read further about this tantalizing verity in the book *What Makes People Rich and Nations Powerful*. In the same book, the author adapted a story from a British man, William Edgett Smith, in his book *Nyerere of Tanzania* which went thus: "I will tell you another testimony by someone you must have heard of! Here is the story: "When I was about ten years old, my father sent me one day to accompany his first wife—one of my step mothers to another village, eight or ten miles away where one of her relatives had died. As we were about to leave this village to return home, she was given a goat by her relatives (as a present). Well, since I was a boy it was my function to lead a goat by the rope. But the goat refused to budge.

"As I was struggling with it, one of her relatives said, "Don't worry, I will make it easy for you." He took some hair from the goat's head and he mixed them with some roots. He then fed them to the goat. "The goat will follow you now!" Did the African science work? Did the goat obey? The story concludes thus: "…and the goat followed me all the way home. Yes, it was then very tame. It followed me like a dog."[88] You must have heard the name of this person. His name is Mwalimu Julius Kambarage Nyerere."

One of such incredible experiences—which I will tell you on the first hand testimony—is the fact that there are humans whose body parts are like a loose electric wire. I heard it first when I arrived in Maswa, Shinyanga in Tanzania. When it was first made known to me that a human body can generate electricity like a loose electric wire, I reacted as you do now. So I don't blame you one bit. I said: *Nonsense. That's impossible. I did sciences in my secondary school enough to know laws of electricity. Bullshit.*

Then I visited the district another day for it fell under the region I managed at the time when I offered my services in the sales department at Tanzania Breweries. It wasn't difficult to bring this up or find her, for she worked for our top distributor in the district. This was back in 2001. I was then introduced to a nice looking lady. She served as an assistant in the beer ware house of our distributor but she also served drinks in the evenings. Following my persistent resistance that evening, I personally was introduced to her. I told her what I had heard and I was frank. I didn't mince my words. I told them point-blank that I didn't believe in that nonsense. I said it was impossible. She didn't argue with me. She just stretched her unclenched fist as in the normal shake of the hand. When our hand touched, oh, my Gods! I just retrieved my hand! A high electric transmission had flown from her body sending high powered electric shock to second party—and I was that second party.

I, Festo Michael Kambarangwe, the author, testify that this is true and I have not been told by somebody else but I am the witness, and the whole of Maswa town witness with me! Indeed, if well tapped, by the estimations of what I had experienced relative to domestic electric shocks I have had, I trust that with the intensity of the electric power she generated, this lady can electrify a couple of compounds and a set of factories in the district!

Long time ago I heard a story I would like to retell here. You recognize I wasn't there when this incident ensued, and so what I present is my own version of the event meant only for learning purposes. A professor was teaching his class about reasoning when the question of the existence of God propped up. The professor denounced religions and God. He said you cannot believe in God because you cannot empirically verify his existence. A young man in this class didn't agree with his professor. He argued that reasoning or verifying existence or inexistence of things empirically such as by physically touching them was faulty.

This young man asked this senior professor something like this: "Do you believe in reasoning and empirical verification as the only way to verify things and no other way?" The top man said yes. "Now if that is the only way, then," said this young man now addressing the class, "then it is safe and rational to say that the professor here has no brains. He has no brains unless he verifies his possession of brains and we touch it. Otherwise he is neither any more worth than a robot because he has no brain as long as we cannot touch it, nor is he qualified to teach us." He paused as the professor was in total shock.

"We were not there when he graduated, and no one of us has seen or touched his brain, or his certificates. So," he continued, "So the man standing before us has no brain and he isn't worth an iota as a professor, and should not be teaching us even as I speak!" said the young student, concluding that reasoning was not a better way of analyzing everything, that there are real things you cannot prove or disprove. You must have heard his name, I mean this young man's name. It is Albert Einstein—a physicist, inventor and Nobel Prize winner.

Indeed the absence of evidence is not evidence of absence of one. Certainly Rumsfeld could have been no more right. The former US Secretary of Defense, Donald Rumsfeld, cornered on Iraq's sudden disappearance of *Weapons of Mass Destruction,* weapons whose presence had justified the invasion of Iraq (however credible that reason is by itself) , he rightly said:

"There're known knowns. These are things we know that we know. There are known unknown. That is to say there are things we know we don't know. But there are also unknown unknowns. These are the things we don't know we don't know!"

Warning! Before we go on, I would like to warn the skeptic—to give him a word of caution. I understand by casual look of things you may judge Rumsfeld as a nincompoop—and many do. But beware. Besides his great CV, his is a great wisdom. With reference to the chapter we are now concluding, a chapter written to emphasize that there is a reason for everything, and that there are things behind everything, whether we can prove them or not. Such is the state of our nation beginning with our education and the youth. We can fail to prove every reason we present here, but the ubiquity with which these things we don't yet comprehend, should bring the skeptic back to his senses.

Indeed, "The author is not a believer in, nor an advocate of "miracles," for the reason that he has enough knowledge of Nature to understand that nature never deviates from her established laws. Some of her laws are incomprehensible that they produce what appear to be "miracles." The sixth sense comes as near to being a miracle as anything I have ever experienced, and it appears so, only because I do not understand the method by which this principle is operated."[89] That's the universal verity. Nonetheless, "The great depression," wrote Napoleon Hill, the author who lived and experienced the situation our generation has experienced through the recent financial crisis, "brought the world to the borderline of understanding the forces which are intangible and unseen. Through the ages…, man has depended too much upon his physical senses, and has limited his knowledge to the physical things, which he could see, touch, weigh and measure," he declared thus: "We are now entering the most marvelous of all ages—an age which will teach us something of the intangible forces of the world about us …[90]" Indeed Wayne Dyer couldn't have said it better. "The highest form of ignorance is to reject something you know nothing about."[91]

When I was at Kahororo Secondary School, we used to sing the song taught to us by the wonderful Goan nun, Sister Rosita (May her soul rest in peace), the Canossian Sister from the Bakhita House downtown Bukoba. The song's lyrics went like this: "I believe there is the sun, even when it isn't shining. I believe in God, even when I've never seen Him." And yes I, the author, believe in God, even when I have not yet seen Him, or shaken hands with Him!

14. GOVERNING DYNAMICS: HUMAN ECONOMIC FACTOR

"They (who) seek to establish systems of government based on the regimentation of all humans...by a handful of individual rulers... (and) call this a new order. It is not new and it is not order." —*Franklin D. Roosevelt*

Through the preceding chapter, we presented the reader with the cause and effect analysis. In the analysis, we have rationalized that nothing happens by accident. It follows therefore that someone's triumph or downfall isn't a matter of accident or chance. The magnitude of someone's triumph or downfall therefore is a mathematical function of how that someone has been observant of the laws of nature—no matter whether he observed them consciously or unconsciously.

It was written that those who do so consciously should know they have fixed their feet in the right rails much as to call those who do so unconsciously to the attention of the nature's law. We wrote this chapter and book that we risk no element of chance. The ensuing chapter is written to corroborate the fact that an element of leadership—both personal as well as the national—cannot go unnoticed even if it all goes down to the obedience to the principled universe. No! It cannot. It cannot be undermined because to progress, we have to face up to the major setbacks that pervade our own persons as well as the society—and face them squarely.

But since we live in no isolated islands, and since we, humans, are social animals, and therefore that what one does, affects another, it takes a leader to align the society in such a way that those who ought to progress, should progress, and those who ought not, shouldn't be obstacles to others, if they are beyond repair.

That's why the ability to face up to our weaknesses is an important element if a society has to progress.

But since not all individuals can do so willingly, if that society's goal to progress has to be foolproof, the society has to identify its general weaknesses—notwithstanding the fact that these weaknesses don't really apply the same way to all individuals in the same society, and therefore never conclusive as rational to brush everybody with the same-same brush—the society has to face its weaknesses squarely. This is why this element calls for a certain kind of leadership—a leadership that can rally people behind certain goals and dispositions!

THE GROWTH VARIABLES AT WORK
In the couple of years after I had graduated from the university as a major in economics, I discovered most of what we were taught in economics, were far removed from being useful to us. The traditional economic theory never engaged itself with the part of us that really matter most. Our professors taught us the kind of economics that seldom had any concern with the human body, intellect and soul or spirit. I, thereupon, realized that both macro and microeconomics can seldom meet anyone's needs—in the long run.

Despite the best theories in international economics, or even theories of comparative advantage, realities lead to absolute advantage to few individuals, families, organizations and nations that have had the head start in the areas that encase inner riches such as self awareness and self love; attention to one's body in line with the belief that your body is the temple of God; the enrichment of the mind or intellect, and nourishment of the soul or spirit. These are the things modern day economics doesn't concern itself with. Truly, "unless we further break microeconomics into its tiniest forms," aptly observed Kambarangwe in his book: *What Makes People Rich and Nations Powerful*, "forms that touch people's lives as individuals, and teach them how to transform their lives."

Take Japan for instance. "The only difference between Japan and Australia is that they have better management of their human (resource, human development). Japan is a country with fewer physical resources (even tiny and fragmented infertile lands); it only has its people. And yet, they are outperforming us,"[92] said Australian Dr. John O Miller.... It is not the macroeconomic policies that economically differentiate the two or three countries for that matter, but people—leadership, creativity, culture, hard work, right priorities, and concern for the future, etc. The aggregate experiences of Japan, Switzerland, Uganda or even Botswana, even singular individual experiences in my own country and family prove the critical role of people in development rather than of resources, minerals, ocean, vast arable land, and forests."[93]

For a nation to develop, or submerge, into a sick nation state not resources or location that matters. It is attitude. It is the ethos in that society. Before we engage the reader into the analysis behind the secret of success; in order to be able to swallow the bitter pill we are about to necessarily learn, a lesson the author couldn't escape from, or hide his face in deep sand fearing to face the bitter truth, let us consider a few examples—general examples nonetheless.

North America provides us with a very good exemplar that can help us put the analysis into context. Truly, it can be said that that continent is endowed with unvarying opportunities, beginning with the natural resources and vast land, water and mineral resources. If yes it is the human resources that counts, the whole region was inhabited by both the Native Americans and the white man aside from the blacks who were sailed into the land. Yet the southern part of America, viz. the United States, is a lot wealthier than her northern neighbor, Canada.

So really what's the secret behind this contrast? If the two started at the same level when Columbus and the white man sailed to, and settled, in the new lands, what explanation is behind this trajectory—the trajectory that leads to dearth on one part and prosperity on the other? Take Nigeria. Northern Nigeria for instance bewails the highest levels of development in the southern parts of the country, and therefore echoes of grave lamentations demanding national wealth redistribution are heard across the nation accounting the for instance the coastal maritime wealth and the harbor which connects the country with the most powerful economies of the Europe and the rest of the world as the source of wealth, good education and employment opportunities in the area. This isn't necessarily true. No. it is not. It cannot be. Take the coastal communities in the East African community as an exemplar.

The East African communities along the coast demand the redistribution of the national wealth and therefore special favors in political appointments, education and employment on account that that's the only way the nation can help them to catch up with their mainland counterparts, claiming that the mainland is abundantly endowed with natural resources and privileged in terms of education and employment.

In order to appreciate genuine factors behind dearth, dispossession and wretchedness in one society as opposed to prosperity in another; in order therefore to be able to really explain why one nation is poor and another wealthy; and in order to be able to identify the areas on which to focus our

-attention, efforts and resources let us consider the hypothetical situation which was originally extrapolated by Dr. Gabagambi in *Raia Mwema*—a Kiswahili newspaper of December 17-23, 2008 under the title I can paraphrase as: "Agriculture and the Fate of Our Economy: Part three." Dr. Dominic Gabagambi was at the time a senior lecturer at Sokoine University in East Africa. Adapted from his extrapolation, take two countries, one with rich natural resources from the sub-Saharan Africa, and then take another country with poor natural endowments such as Switzerland or Japan. Then in this hypothesis, these two countries sign a contract to swap their people between each other leaving everything behind but human mind.

For the sake of this analysis, we shall forget for now the fact that we in Africa have had a historical and scientific or technological gap emanating from slavery and colonialism—the gap that yes works against us—but one that shouldn't any more be sung with great enthusiasm, or used as an alibi. (Besides, why did the Europeans colonize us in the first place? Why did the Arabs—of all the people—enslave and castrate the black people? Talking about technological as well economic muscle and not moral standards, and not anyhow justifying the wrong concept of the curse of Canaan whose descendants are Arabs anyway, why didn't our forefathers colonize the Europeans or enslave the Arabs—save for castrating anyone?)

Now what do you think would happen in a span of only ten years down the line? The new Swiss nation state or Japan on the African soil would make the most of the abundant natural resources in this country (vast arable land, minerals, evergreen forests, livestock, tourist attractions, ocean and extensive coastline, and many lakes and rivers, the people etc.), discover unthought-of opportunities, and harness them, such that only after a few years, this new Japan or Switzerland would displace the today's most populous and resourceful superpowers of China and The States as the pinnacle nation, whereas its counterpart would declare the open season and squander the wealth in Switzerland or Japan partying through the night seven days a week all year round as few elites would rip off the public funds until when the banks went bankrupt beyond the Greek standards. The elite would not sleep.

They would scramble for, and partition of the public squares and community facilities and gardens for private gains; the buildings, the roads and all physical infrastructures would be broken down, the rivers and air polluted, as the WCs, sewage system and the water pipes clogged.

Then this whole shame would climax not long enough before this partying nation in Switzerland or Japan found excuse to beg for financial support from the Swiss Government or Japan back in its old homeland.

Surely it would need to refurbish its roads, rebuild infrastructure, feed its people and run the traditionally mammoth of the government citing palpable reasons like cold weather, lack of natural resources, hilly and rocky mountainous countryside, drought, flood or even the larger population etc.

THE PRINCIPLED UNIVERSE AND ECONOMICS
Having thus demonstrated—though the previous chapter—that there's no such a thing as coincidence, economics of individual persons, households, corporations and nations cannot escape the hand of the raw law of nature. Indeed, when I reflect on the past forty years of my life, I cannot but come to a conclusion that the universe is so principled that it seems to me it is ready to cling to its own fixed order with supreme defiance and stiff-nakedness.

When the world comes to understand this great truth, when we in Africa and the rest of developing world come to this realization, we will finally stop complaining or pointing fingers. When we come to this realization we will understand that all people are the same, that they only appear to be different. The true dividing lines for mankind are not borders, color or language, but simply ignorance—and it's polar opposite. And this fine line lies between ignorance and understanding of, and submission to the natural law, and submission to the letter. We are now proud that you are now going to begin acting knowing that as wrote Bob Proctor in his wonderful book You Were Born Rich: *"Everything you are seeking is seeking you in return. Therefore, everything you want is already yours. So you don't have to get anything; it is simply a matter of becoming more aware of what you already possess."*

In harmony with the foregoing statements, the bible says that: "Behold all are yours." The only precondition is this: to take in possession what is already yours, you must lead a life of a certain way. This is nothing more than to submit to the natural law of the universe. Do not ever waste your time attempting to change the universe. Change your own person; learn how best to swim according to the flow. And that's easy for you. The universe is a constant factor. Its laws are unambiguous. It is a one way traffic. With the universe, there's no either-or situation. Instead, the book What Makes People Rich and Nation Powerful argues that, economics should explain why America remains the pinnacle nation; why China is now threatening the world powers; etc. Our education should teach us what went wrong with the Great Britain, Greece, Rome, or the Ottoman Empire?

These are the facts and lines which can help heal a crippled economy, or breathe new life into a sick dying nation. Such transformation can only be addressed through restructuring and reinvention of the education curriculum and the whole educational system in the country. It can only be effected comprehensively beginning with the households, the schools and workplaces—public and private sectors. Let us face it! No man or nation can develop without attention to the human factors. Indeed people and countries that progress do so, not because of favorable climate, natural resources, or luck! It is something within men, something about thought-pattern, the mindset. And it is a result of persistence and determination—the urge to win—to succeed and overcome, no matter how hard it may seem.

And notice that this is not lamentation. It is my agenda, my concern and my explanation. It is my contribution to economics (—or rather an educational and economic manifesto). It is the renewal of education and of economics—the economics of the twenty-first century. This is the only way we can accomplish the good intentions of the study of economics. This is human economics. It is the author's economics, the *Kambarangwe Economics*; Festo Michael's Economics, "Michael-economics," or rather *"Michonomics!"*

What then is *"Michonomics?"* While Kinetics is a science of movement, body movement, physical movement from one point to another, Michonomics is a human science, science of how individual persons—men and women—human communities, and, indeed, how nations can, and ought to progress. It is a study of internal movement; a movement within the intellect space.[94]

Now this movement is what in this book we call Governing Dynamics: the forces within you, the reader, forces that can transform you—and thereupon your life, the organization and people around you. These are forces that not only produce but govern movement toward your potential growth. They indeed are the governing dynamics.

To achieve this stage where internal movement within you generate and set into process the activation of innovative growth drivers and success factors or generally called ideals or governing variables, to respond to the terrain we find ourselves in following our history and geography or even the environment that has evolved with globalization, ICT, the rapidity of pace of change and economic crisis, we have developed—and teach—how to put them to use.

Truly the situation at hand calls for drawing a new set of growth equations. Did I say new? Oui! In order to grow, or restore your health as a person, family, institution, organization or the nation as a whole, new insights are necessary today.

We face different situations today. We experience fast changing trends, our youth exhibit a different mindset or thought pattern in as far as the approach to prosperity, wealth, health and happiness is concerned; changing tastes and the catastrophic rapidity of pace of change following ICT and globalization; growing corruption and religious sentiments, environmental changes and especially priorities of the majority which is a group of young and dynamic people, all of which are not taken into account when we developed the curriculum or the syllabus we have today.

That is why the instructions we give in our schools and training we have in place at workplaces today don't seem to attend to the new needs of our society! "We cannot solve the problems by using the same kind of thinking we used when we created them," aptly said Albert Einstein.

THERE IS A SCIENCE OF GETTING RICH

Now as we approach the end of this chapter and book, and in order to recap, let us bring in science, an idea we introduced through the previous chapters. We began this chapter by emphasizing that we should go back to the basics. Why? We emphasized that the universe is principled, and that there is a formula for everything. To illustrate this fact, let us invite Wallace D. Wattles, whose work in his magnificent book *The Science of Getting Rich* summarizes so wonderfully the idea we are putting across—the idea that there is a formula for everything, even getting rich. In other words, success is not a game of chance.

Now join me in welcoming Mr. Wattles, who will speak for himself right away without salutations. "There is a science of getting rich," he began, "and it is an exact science, like algebra or arithmetic. There are certain laws which govern the process of acquiring riches, and once these laws are learned and obeyed by anyone, that person will get rich with mathematical certainty.

The ownership of money and property comes as a result of doing things in a certain way, and those who do things in this certain way whether on purpose or accidentally get rich, while those who do not do things in this certain way no matter how hard they work or how able they are remain poor. It is natural law that like causes always produce like effects, and, therefore, any man or woman who learns to do things in this certain way will infallibly get rich.

"That the above statement is true is shown by the following facts: Getting rich is not a matter of environment, for if it were, all the people in certain neighborhoods would become wealthy. The people of one city would all be rich, while those of other towns would all be poor, or all the inhabitants of one state would roll in wealth, while those of an adjoining state would be in poverty. But everywhere we see rich and poor living side by side, in the same environment, and often engaged in the same vocations.

"When two people are in the same locality and in the same business, and one gets rich while the other remains poor, it shows that getting rich is not primarily a matter of environment. Some environments may be more favorable than others, but when two people in the same business are in the same neighborhood and one gets rich while the other fails, it indicates that getting rich is the result of doing things in a certain way.

And further, the ability to do things in this certain way is not due solely to the possession of talent, for many people who have great talent remain poor, while others who have very little talent get rich. Studying the people who have gotten rich, we find that they are an average lot in all respects, having no greater talents and abilities than other people have. It is evident that they do not get rich because they possess talents and abilities that others do not have, but because they happen to do things in a certain way.

"Getting rich (or getting anything significantly noteworthy in life) is not the result of saving, or thrift. Many very penurious people are poor, while free spenders often get rich. Nor is getting rich due to doing things which others fail to do, for two people in the same business often do almost exactly the same things, and one gets rich while the other remains poor or becomes bankrupt. From all these things, we must come to the conclusion that getting rich is the result of doing things in a certain way. If getting rich is the result of doing things in a certain way, and if like causes always produce like effects, then any man or woman who can do things in that way can become rich, and the whole matter is brought within the domain of exact science."

NOTHING SPRINGS UP FROM THE EARTH AND FUNCTION AUTOMATICALLY

"Steam ships," brilliantly wrote Napoleon Hill in his amazing book, Think and Grow Rich, "Steam ships and railroads do not spring up from the earth and function automatically. They come in response to the call of civilization, through the labor and ingenuity and organizing ability of men who have imagination, faith, enthusiasm, decision, persistence…motivated by the desire to build, construct, achieve, render useful service, earn profit and accumulate riches. And because they render service without which they would be no civilization, they (such men) put themselves in the way of great riches.…

"Millions of men and women throughout the nation are still engaged in this pastime of trying to get without giving. Some of them," continued Napoleon Hill, "Some of them …demand shorter hours and more pay! Others do not take trouble to work at all…the idea…was demonstrated in new York city, where violent complaint was registered with the Poster master, by a group of "relief beneficiaries," because the postmen awakened them at 7.30 A.M. to deliver government relief checks. They demanded that the time of delivery be set at 10.00 A.M. O'clock.

"If you are one of those believe that riches can be accumulated by the mere act of men who organize themselves into groups and demand more pay for less service," he warned, "…you may rest securely on your belief, with certain knowledge that no one will disturb you, because this is a free country where every man may think as he pleases, where one can live with but little effort, where many may live well without doing any work whatsoever.

"However," he underscored, "you should know the full truth concerning this freedom of which so many people boast, and so few understand. As great as it is, as far as it reaches, as many privileges as it provides, it does not, and cannot bring riches without effort. There is but one dependable method of accumulating, and legally holding riches, and that is by rendering useful service. No system has ever been created by which men can legally acquire riches through mere force of numbers, or without giving in return an equivalent of one form or another. There is a principle known as the law of economics! This is more than a theory. It is a law no man can beat."

Truly there is no good or bad. Good or bad is in you—in your mind! Whatever is given to you, can be transformed or metamorphosed into good or bad asset or liability. It is only in the mind. Since we are concerned with the individual being the center of transformation— transformation which is impossible without mindset change at individual level before the society can embark on a paradigm shift, let's consider a question of mindset. Let me illustrate the foregoing verity.

When I was at TBL, I worked with a person I will, for anonymity, introduce as Heri. He was personally close to me enough to know some of my secrets. That's why he was the first person to know when I took the risk to resign from my job—a job considered a privilege at the time—and take another job in the city. At the time I worked in the upcountry. And I had reasons to do so as I will describe through this series. At first he said I was nuts to even think about it. How can you even imagine leaving Tanzania Breweries? (Well, I went on to leave even the bigger companies than TBL). Now we were distanced from each other for a few years. When we met few years later, he had been sacked, and was jobless. Why? Bad luck? Oh, no! He had survived a car crush. But that doesn't say it all.

He was found unconscious, drunk, behind the wheel with a naked hooker, stripped bare to the bone, beside him. He was dragged unconscious from the beer car cabin by police patrol in the heart of that cold windy November night. And that's not all again. This accident was his eighth in the row. And I can't blame him. If you imagined that I blame him, you are wrong. I don't. For that is a beer culture. It is why I resigned from this company—in the first place.

I left because there was too much drinking there. At the time when we met I was national brand manager with a top company in the city. He was jobless then. Now when we met, which is my message, he told me: "Michael, unajua wewe una bahati sana?" That's to say: Michael, do you know that you are a very lucky guy? Was I? Really? I don't think so! Really! I don't think so! It is all about how you conduct yourself. It is how you relate with yourself—and others. It is the decision to live in a certain way. It is not about talent or luck. A certain way is something to do more with character than with work skills or one's talents and gifts.[95]

To illustrate, I studied at Ihungo High School. The school is built on a hilly terrain. If you looked at it many years back before the school was built, it was almost impossible to even think you can build a bungalow there, let alone the whole school. Nearby my house there is a very bad terrain—one like that of Ihungo. A few years ago someone bought the land and like

Ihungo, he did landscaping and today with beautiful terraces and gardens, people who visit Luxury Hotel tend to say, if they are not careful, that this man is a very lucky guy. It isn't true. I saw the land before he changed it. I saw it when he was transforming it.

Take individuals like Maria Mutola, Caster Semenya, or even Serena Williams. Though they say the beauty is in the eyes of the beholder, but when you look at these "lucky" girls, frankly, you will struggle to find any trace of conventional woman's beauty. But they, these individual girls, as young girls didn't focus their lenses on their handicaps as conventional average women would. They disregarded that side of their personality and concentrated on their physical strength. Today they are the wealthiest and most loved and admired girls as sports champions in athletics and tennis worldwide instead. Take T.D. Jakes or even Myles Munroe. Quite frankly, you cannot call either of these two gentlemen any handsome. No! They are not—and may I add by all standards. Yet growing up, they recognized that the beauty is inside. That's why they didn't sit there and weep the whole day in desperation fearing that no beautiful girl would accept their hand in marriage being that unsightly. They worked hard on their great talents upstairs instead.

And today? They are the most revered, highly successful and wealthiest happiest preachers each with one most beautiful woman that Leonardo di Caprio would be jealous of. Take scientists also. Most scientists aren't any handsome. But they are among the most impactful persons on earth.

With simile to Maria Mutola, Caster Semenya, Serena Williams, T.D Jakes and Myles Munroe, Mahathir Mohammed, former Malaysian prime minister writing about the wealth of nations, the wealth that we abundantly have in our possession but seldom put to use, said that:[96] *"We know that the wealth of a country depends on the ability and skills to translate the resources into products and services,"* aptly *said former genius Malaysian premier, " the wealth of a country depends on the ability and skills to translate the resources into products and services that can be marketed. The very rich oil producing countries had oil throughout the centuries of their existence. But," he continued, "But they only became rich when this oil was piped from the bowels of the earth and sold...Gold in the ground and wealth under our feet does not make us rich. But producing and selling it will. This is elementary'"* he concluded. *This is really elementary, is it not?*

For one more time, let us consider America's success story. This great nation was an unknown country only a few years before she was discovered by Christopher Columbus and co. Think about it! He didn't know where he was heading for. He didn't know when he would find a place to land if all the engines went mute. He didn't know if he would ever find a land anywhere anytime soon. But he had faith in his hunch. He hoped that probably he would finally make a full circle back to Europe. Then he discovered America—the America we know today. (I say so because it is believed the Norwegians and Icelanders had had the contact with some parts of North America before him.) That's just part one of the whole episode.

Then a few volunteers decided to try new life over in the new land. They knew not if the conditions were favorable. But they had confidence in themselves. They knew they were the creators of their conditions—and deciders of their destinies. They knew there were no houses in America. They knew there was no single tarmac road or banks or schools for their children. When they landed, they only had a set of tents for their housing. They had to create everything from the scratch. They had no resources—physical resources. They had no money nor did they need it. No one needed it. Not the Comanche Red Indians or their brethren would sell them anything for new useless coins with useless crown. They had no roads. And they had no flowing water. They were grossly poor materially—poor than any one of the African or poor South East Asian countries—but they were extremely wealthy in hope and faith in themselves and their resolve.

They had not collected anything from back home. But they had gathered great lessons from back home. And for instance the Irish had anger from exploitation back home. They had the Irish desire for prosperity and personal liberties. They were fed up with discrimination on the streets of London. The academicians, thinkers and anyone who had had strained relationships with the crown, those who believed they could do far more and better if they were free from the crown, individual who rejected to be protégés, and stooges domesticated by the monarchy—a person who ruled no matter whether he was intelligent or dumb but because he was the first born to the deceased king or queen—rose to the occasion.

That's why they strived very slowly to build the constitution that would bring about lasting prosperity holding those truths to be sacred and undeniable; "that all men are created equal, that they are endowed by their Creator with certain unalienable Rights, that among these are Life, Liberty and the pursuit of Happiness," for all enshrined in the constitution;[97] a constitution that recognizes rightly as observed George W. Bush that: "Nearly all Americans have ancestors who braved the oceans—liberty loving risk-takers—in search of an ideal; the largest voluntary migration in recorded history... immigration is not just a link to America's past. It is a bridge to America's future."

They then built a constitution that made the terrain almost level for anyone who craved prosperity and was ready to work hard in pursuit of his dreams. It was a kind of constitution that emancipated a person handing one's life to one; a constitution that sought "to form a more perfect union, establish justice, insure domestic tranquility, provide for the common defense, promote the general welfare and secure blessings of liberty to ourselves and our posterity..." It was the constitution that would enhance equality and freedom; the constitution that wouldn't help them not to conquer but to rescue—save for keeping blacks as slaves—which they corrected under Lincoln.

They explored the rivers, lakes and the ocean. They explored the air. They conducted tests for each kind of seeds for each piece of land. In all exploration they knew not if they would come out in one piece let alone victorious. But they were guided by purpose, desire or obsession to conquer and to prosper. That's what made her defy British colonialism. They built their new land and built factories there. They hired and developed skills based on experiences back home. They didn't export crops to Britain anymore. That's the difference with Haiti. That's the difference we see between America and Europe. That's what sets the two apart.

They had persistence, hope and faith. They also, from experience, knew they depended on one another. They cultivated interdependence and a more democratic leadership. They established their national language. They established new forms of education, experimenting one replacing it with another until when they built one standard education system. But probably the most important of all these priceless efforts, they developed and built what we can now call "American ideals," among them hard work. Everything was brand new—it was pure innovation etc. That's what made America the pinnacle nation we see today. We can learn from them.

"From the Civil War to the first half of the 20th century, the United States' economy benefited from high agricultural production, plentiful raw materials, technological advancements and financial inflows. During this time the U.S. did not have to contend with foreign dangers. From 1860 to 1914, U.S. exports increase sevenfold and result in huge trading surpluses."[98] This was shortly before she, the United States, went to war. Then the roaring twenties and series of wars set in—conditions that are certainly not in harmony with the growth of any person or nation, in the long run. Not Somalia state or its modern day pirates or ancient such people and states succeeded to remain at the top since the days of John Silver. Could the United States be declining? Time will tell!

THE PROMISED LAND
Every change, truly, starts with one person. True and lasting change begins with you—the immediate reader! And this chapter was written that you may reclaim your life and have your destiny back in your own hands. I know you can reclaim your life and become top once more, because that's what you were born to be. And this is not Kambarangwe's law. It is God's—a decree by God himself. The book of Genesis says that: "so God created man in his own image, in the image of God he created him; male and female he created. And God blessed them. And God said to them, "Be fruitful and multiply and fill the earth and subdue it, and have dominion over (it)…"[99] As we come to the end of this chapter, we hope you realize you have no more alibis as to why you should fail. By this I mean you can achieve anything—literally anything you set out to achieve. You can do so because you now know the essential and unfailing principle for success: do away with quick fix and return to the basics—the basic and unfailing laws of nature. You don't need to look to the far skies anymore. Indeed Alva Romans was right when in the following poem of his he sung thus:

"No more shall I look to the far skies; for my Father's loving aid;
Since here upon earth His treasure lies, and here is His kingdom laid.

No more through the mist of things unknown, I'll search for the Promised Land; for time is the footstool of His throne, and I am within His hand.

The wealth that is more than finest gold is here, if I shall but ask; and wisdom unguessed, and power untold are here for every task.

The gates of heaven are before my eyes; their key is within my hand;
No more shall I look to the far skies; for here (right where you are now) is the Promised Land!"

15. A GLIMMER OF HOPE: NARROWING THE BASICS DOWN TO SPECIFICS

"Tanzania Yenye Neema Yawezekana (Kiswahili for:
A dream for a prosperous Tanzania is not a dream, it is real)."[100]
—Dr. Jakaya Kikwete

As we edge to the end of this book, let me say that one of the major symptoms of the sick society is the blame game. Because as such it is so rampant and notorious, people are very sensitive about it and it is therefore exercised and counter exercised with great enthusiasm.

That's why I must remark that when we talk about our own poor performances and weaknesses as a society, we are not pointing fingers but a fact-finding mission. That's why we shouldn't hide our heads in the sand every time our attention is called upon our weaknesses in our own persons, our businesses or even in the society as a whole.

We should accept it as an opportunity to have, do—and be—more and better. Indeed to know what is behind our demise, as it seems to encroach us now, is part of the solution. That's why this chapter has been written—to narrow down what we should do in our present situation.

Therefore, now that we have the facts about our problems as individuals and society, it is half the problem solved—half the battle won. Information or research findings that we have laid before the reader, and the nation as a whole, should indeed help to reform the reader's person as well as his family, neighborhood, schools, the workplace, and the nation as a whole. So, really, isn't any attempt that endeavors to identify major concerns encroaching attempts to progress as individuals and society as a whole a praiseworthy effort?

Here is the second most important point I would like to make. Nothing comes in a bottle will ever heal the malady of any sick nation. The malady of a nation can never be healed by a check book either. And here is why. The problem that such a country faces is not physical or tangible in nature. It is mental, psychic, spiritual.

Its antidote must come from a powerful intangible force—forces that engage with the intangible human self, i.e., the mind and the spirit. That's why such a sweeping malady can only be healed—and thereupon restore a society to health—by prescribing a package of an education of a certain kind or nature.

In analyzing the problem at hand, we have come to realize that there is another setback that will come from some of us who will not cooperate, thinking they are safe. If we only mind our own self-conduct and leave our children and youth to stray saying everyone will pedal his own canoe, responsible with his own life, we deceive ourselves. We are also wrong if we think we will be safe if our families are okay when in the outside the nation pervades with abhorable habits and culture.

We cannot keep hiding our children all the time. They will somehow interact with the outside world and in doing so, "contract" the abhorable habits we so much loathe. With this realization, it is much wise to heal the society even when our families, or even our businesses are okay. And the foregoing assertions aren't mere speculations. That's why it calls for collective responsibility.

Let me illustrate.

You know why the children of the wealthy turn to drugs and misconduct? It is because their parents believe that having provided them with "everything," their children are okay! They forget this "everything," package is only in the physical world, for their physical needs. What they miss—and which is critical to their growth as responsible individuals—is love and attention from their parents. And as such, they get it from the bad-boys in the neighborhood. It is they who teach them the bad conduct. That's why God punishes those who pay no attention to raising their children in a certain way.

The point I am trying to make is this: you and I aren't only responsible for our own children, but also for those of the others. Assuming we are in the shoes of the national figurehead father or mother, let's recall how Prophet Eli, himself a noble man and a keen observant of God's laws. Though he was good in his own personal conduct before God, because he overlooked to regulate his perverse sons, God punished both Eli and his sons. Read the book of Kings.

LESSONS FROM THE AMERICAN EDUCATORS AND LEADERS

When we said that having the information or research findings, like these, is like half a battle won, it wasn't mere speculation. It was a diligent pursuit of the same goal that helped reform education and social economic shape in, and of, the United States at the time when the great nation was on the brink of total collapse. And this is the difference that made the US a different nation we see today. The slow retrogression we see in that great nation can also and only be retraced in the same domain of analysis.

The point I am trying to make is this: whereas mediocre people will shy away from their problems, hiding their heads deep in the sand every time their personal weaknesses as well as institutional handicaps are brought to their attention, when the United States realized she was amidst such a tragedy during the dawn of the twentieth century, they openly deliberated and exposed their weaknesses, and worked so diligently to combat the situation. That's what is probably amiss today!
And the foregoing statement isn't mere speculation.

To illustrate: During the last century, beginning in the first quarter of the century, the American youth rebelled against education. They rebelled against almost every other conventional ways of life. During this time, many young people decided they no longer needed to follow the conservative traditions of their parents and grandparents. This is known as THE AGE OF JAZZ. It was a period known until as I write as THE ROARING 1920s. THE ROARING 1920s was the time when young female folks for instance, boycotted traditional values of the time and began clubbing and drinking in public; they began dressing and dancing erotically—and probably the turning point when entertainment and pornography became an industry.

Considering a society that was almost puritanical—a society where self-control and hard work were important and that pleasure was wrong or unnecessary—such was a shift at an industrial scale—a scale that was to convey the same magnitude of impact, following especially the fact that the love for leisure against labor was natural to the human beast in us, like weeds are to a farm in any tropical rainforest. Anyone who has studied, history, economics, sociology, geography, public administration, criminal law or even theology will no doubt be of the same mind with the foregoing assertion!

And the foregoing analysis isn't Kambarangwe's invention. Read the following extract from The Voice America "The Making of Nation" program, and see if it is not exactly what is being wrongly replicated here at home instead of learning from it.

The roaring twenties "were a time of economic progress for most Americans. Many companies grew larger during the 1920s, creating many new jobs. Wages for most Americans increased. Many people began to have enough money to buy new kinds of products.

"The strong economy also created the right environment for many important changes in the day-to-day social life of the American people. The 1920s are remembered now as an exciting time that historians call the "roaring twenties."The 1920s brought a feeling of freedom and independence to millions of Americans, especially young Americans. Young soldiers returned from the world war with new ideas. They had seen a different world in Europe. They had faced death and learned to enjoy the pleasures that each day offered.

"Many of these young soldiers were not willing to quietly accept the old traditions of their families and villages when they returned home. Instead, they wanted to try new ways of living. Many young Americans, both men and women, began to challenge some of the traditions of their parents and grandparents. For example, some young women began to experiment with new kinds of clothes. They no longer wore dresses that hid the shape of their bodies. Instead, they wore thinner dresses that uncovered part of their legs.

"Many young women began to smoke cigarettes, too. Cigarette production in the United States more than doubled in the ten years between 1918 and 1928.

"Many women also began to drink alcohol with men in public for the first time. And they listened together to a popular new kind of music: jazz.

"Young people danced the Fox Trot, the Charleston, and other new dances. They held one another tightly on the dance floor; instead of dancing far apart. It was a revolution in social values, at least among some Americans. People openly discussed subjects that their parents and grandparents had kept private.

"There were popular books and shows about unmarried mothers and about homosexuality. The growing film industry made films about all-night parties between unmarried men and women. And people discussed the new ideas about sex formed by Sigmund Freud and other new thinkers.

"An important force behind these changes was the growing independence of American women. In 1920, the nation passed the 19th Amendment to the constitution, which gave women the right to vote.

"Of equal importance, many women took jobs during the war and continued working after the troops returned home. Also, new machines freed many of them from spending long hours of work in the home washing clothes, preparing food, and doing other jobs. Education was another important force behind the social changes of the 1920s ...

"Two inventions also helped cause the social changes. They were the automobile and the radio. The automobile gave millions of Americans the freedom to travel easily to new places. And the radio brought new ideas and experiences into their own homes.

"Probably the most important force behind social change was the continuing economic growth of the 1920s. Many people had extra money to spend on things other than food, housing, and other basic needs. They could experiment with new products and different ways of living. Of course, not all Americans were wearing strange new "flapper" clothes or dancing until early in the morning. Millions of Americans in small towns or rural areas continued to live simple, quiet lives. Life was still hard for many people including blacks, foreigners, and other minority groups.

"The many newspaper stories about independent women reporters and doctors also did not represent the real life of the average American woman. Women could vote. But three of every four women still worked at home. Most of the women working outside their homes were from minority groups or foreign countries.

"The films and radio stories about exciting parties and social events were just a dream for millions of Americans. But the dreams were strong. And many Americans —rich and poor — followed with great interest each new game, dance, and custom. The wide interest in this kind of popular culture was unusually strong during the 1920s. People became extremely interested in exciting court trials, disasters, film actors, and other subjects.

"For example, millions of Americans followed the sad story of Floyd Collins, a young man who became trapped while exploring underground. Newsmen reported to the nation as rescue teams searched to find him. Even the "New York Times" newspaper printed a large story on its front page when rescuers finally discovered the man's dead body.

"Another event that caught public attention was a murder trial in the eastern state of New Jersey in 1926.

"Newsmen wrote five million words about this case of a minister found dead with a woman member of his church. Again, the case itself was of little importance from a world news point of view. But it was exciting. And Americans were tired of reading about serious political issues after the bloody world war. The 1920s also were a golden period for sports.

"People across the country bought newspapers to read of the latest golf victory by champion Bobby Jones."Big Bill" Tilden became the most famous player in tennis. And millions of Americans listened to the boxing match in 1926 between Jack Dempsey and Gene Tunney. In fact, five Americans reportedly became so excited while listening to the fight that they died of heart attacks.

"However, the greatest single sports hero of the period was the baseball player, Babe Ruth. Ruth was a large man who could hit a baseball farther than any other human being. He became as famous for his wild enjoyment of life as for his excellent playing on the baseball field. Babe Ruth loved to drink, to be with women…"[101]

What followed in the footsteps of the AGE OF JAZZ? I will try to relate it in brief but it is no sweet news to a nation!

With pervasive low labor to leisure ratio[102] hand in hand with quick fix—something considered today as an intelligent way of making money—we are heading for a great surprise. If a nation banks on the monies made in—let alone pornography—the entertainment industry, or even in hospitality and tourism for instance, for its growth, while core economic functions are dysfunctional, that nation is heading for a trouble of unimaginable magnitudes. To say the least, that's how the great depression followed in the footsteps of the roaring twenties—THE AGE OF JAZZ. Before the great depression, or even the very recent economic crisis, the United States, the pinnacle nation of which it is said that when America sneezes, the world catches cold, the nation was engaged in rampant and unchecked quick fix.

Let's attempt, in a nutshell, to analyze the recent economic crisis! Through investing time and resources, for instance, in false non natural value creation, the nation appeared to have become wealthier. But indeed it was a bubble, an economic boom on the papers, a boom resulting not from real value from the farms or factories but resulting from trading and middle-man-ship. There was no actual growth in industry, or in productive science or technology.

Yes a number of innovations were made in classes or factories, but indeed very few people worked in real terms. The value of money and time invested in the economy was inflated in the quick dollar making ventures, and as such it turned out to be a disincentive to real work. It wasn't long enough before the gap between the rich and the poor escalated. And then what?

Finally the tragedy in the form of a bubble hit. The people were no longer motivated to work anymore, and though the productivity and revenue on the paper looked bigger, but reverse was true. Finally the climax of the crash had been perfected.

The growth they realized was only a bubble. And like all bubbles, it was only to be blown up by the wind beginning with the crash of the stock market. With the crash of the stock market, followed loss of jobs, homes and hopes for the future. That was, in short, what was behind the great depression, as well as the explanation for the recent—and yes—the ongoing economic crisis!

We who live in this generation everywhere on the face of this beautiful planet, have experienced something very close in nature and similar in fashion to the foregoing situation and explanation, and are still struggling to see ourselves out of it.

And when I say "we" I mean all of us. Not even the Unites States, Japan or Greece or the whole EU is any safer. China too. Her economy is no longer growing at a two digit figure anymore.

The US needed Franklin Roosevelt's new deal to bring the hope back. Probably we are being presented with some variety of a *New Deal* in here, no?

THE US NATIONAL TASK FORCE REPORTS EXPOSES THE AMERICAN SOCIETY
INTRODUCTION

While we are now going to dwell on the educational reforms of 1980s in America, it is worthwhile to make two remarks here. The first is that the great depression which resulted from the anarchy in America during THE AGE OF JAZZ, began to heal when the nation went back to the basics, and building, on one hand and promoting national ideals.

Secondly, with simile to the United States, Tanzania was plunged in grand anarchy in the late 1880s when the Arusha declaration—a declaration of the restoration of humanity and the formation of national ideals—and as such the people turned to inconceivable quick fix as the nation state collapsed succumbing to the few wealthy elites and their families, a situation whose legacy is still eating into the nation's fiber.

What did president Mkapa do? Benjamin Mkapa did an exemplary work—albeit with emphasis on education and industry—by regulating quick fix and anarchy. He checked the leisure ratio by creating conditions that favored those who worked in real terms as he discouraged mission town and all forms of quick fix. Anyone who wanted money, a new house or a car had to work—and work hard. Any who didn't, clearly chose to starve and depreciate in deep paucity. To be brief, the Mkapa government returned to the basics: promoted work ethics, discipline on personal character and spending, discouraged quick fix and promoted back to the classroom movement of some variety, and indeed back to the basics—in a nutshell. The reader is advised to revisit the book What Makes People Rich and Nations powerful on the successes of the Mkapa government in this area.
 Since we have emphasized that the antidote to our problem is in education, let us now learn from how America managed to mitigate and avert the imminent collapse similar after the roaring twenties—and once again rising as a pinnacle nation—a nation whose muscle we all witness today in the eye of the educational reforms of the 1980s.

THE AMERICAN EDUCATIONAL REFORMS OF THE 1980s

Following the national task force reports on education in the mid-1980s in the United States, national attention turned to the need for educational excellence and higher academic standards for all students. To support their alarming statements about the decline of American education and the need for academic reform, the policy reports detailed a host of gloomy trends and statistics. These weaknesses as summed up by this author from a—I must add magnificent—book Curriculum Foundations, Principles and Issues 3nd edition. This report stated the following:

Schools and colleges had shifted away from requiring students to take what had 20 years ago been the standard academic core curriculum for graduation. Grade inflation was on the rise; students were required to complete less home work; 75% of high school students completed less than one hour of homework a night; average achievement scores demonstrated a virtually unbroken decline and mathematics scores dropped nearly 20 points; international comparisons of student achievement revealed that a Mr. and Miss America were the last. Other indicators included the fact that some 23 to 25 million adults were functionally illiterate by the simplest test of everyday reading and writing; about 13% of all 17 year old youths were considered functionally illiterate and this illiteracy rate jumped to 40% among minority youth; (and that's not all).

Business and military leaders complained that they were required to spend millions of dollars annually on costly remedial education and training programs in the basic skills. (And then concludes the report that): "All these sordid figures pile up and stare at us, despite high expenditures for education (notice also that) these deficiencies came to light at a time when the demand for highly skilled military personnel and workers in labor and industry was accelerating rapidly and amid growing concern that the United States was being overtaken...in commerce science and technology."[103]

Did America need transformation? You bet she did!

If we can momentarily focus on Tanzania, consider the following facts: Ours is a very low-rated reading and writing culture. Quick fix pervades our youth—and the society as a whole. The number of senior executives managing top organizations here at home or internationally, or even performance of our youth in Olympics or regional tournaments does more than illustrate low self-esteem in our society today.

Low ambition is behind poor performances. In 2010, in every two secondary school graduates, one failed. In 2012, out of three, two failed. In every hundred students in Kigoma North constituency, 98 scored zero in 2012! The problem isn't only regional but national. A research by UWEZO indicated that in 2010, 8 out of 10 among 42,000 primary school students from 38 districts, could not read English or Kiswahili. Average score in numeracy was only about 30%. In the year 2012, a number of forgeries and thus dismissed or disqualified candidates has more than doubled as compared to the past years.[104]

It is not anymore a surprise that after 53 years of independence from Britain, we remain poor? Growing at 6%, our GDP doesn't reflect in the lives of the masses. In 2010, only 14% of people had access to electricity (Issis Gaddis). Majority doesn't access flowing water. Youth unemployment is already a crisis with only 14% having formal wage-earning jobs (globalpost.com). Traditional education—marketing, engineering, bookkeeping, auditing, hotel management—leaves thousands unemployed since we don't generate employment—only for which they are prepared. The rich grow fewer and richer. The poor get poorer and in masses.

For 53 years, conventional education hasn't addressed how we can conquer poverty or corruption. We identified poverty, diseases and ignorance as our major national challenges since independence. But with overstretched resources, we cannot and shouldn't expect to triumph an iota. Battling ignorance—but in a different way—will heal poverty and diseases altogether. But traditional approaches and business-as-usual methodologies can't address innovation we need and self-employment we crave. And these challenges aren't the author's, or mere speculations by a growing number of cynics in the country. Can we validate the foregoing assertion? Should we? Certainly, yes!

The government has come up with BIG RESULTS NOW as an effort to address such challenges. By itself BRN is an admission by the government that our past strategies didn't succeed. That's why we see students and many adult people rebelling and getting out of the box the superstructure has imposed on them. They want solutions. This author is an exemplar.

On his own accord, the author resigned from work in 2007, to write and create programs addressing these weaknesses our society is faced with.

With injection of new ideas into our education, reorientation of our people's mindset, and incentives along with even greater disincentives to promote certain specific ideals and values, we will address the challenges our education in general, and the curriculum and the people in particular are facing. We must change the focus from the mastery of the subject matter to mastery of one's person.[105]

That's the kind of an education that ought to get entry into mainstream education. That's why we ought to teach how to study and teach innovatively, providing the youth with unbiased picture of faults and virtues required to make a big difference between success and failure. That's why we ought to focus on the situation at home and the needs of now.

That's why we ought to focus on the human factor. And that's the source of the failure we face under the present conventional education. We must learn therefore from our past mistakes if we should comprehensively redress the situation—and once again help the nation rise to the heights we were destined under Mwalimu Nyerere to achieve academically, socially and economically, thereby reclaiming class and dignity that is innate to us as a Tanzanian people—or any other worthy nation across the globe.

Again, our schools should be agents of social change and institutions for social reform. George Counts and I believe that if education had to count, or rather, if it had to be progressive, it had to encompass consideration of the social and economic problems of the era, and to use the schools to help reform the society.[106]

Accordingly, George Counts wrote: *"If progressive education is to generally be progressive, it must...face squarely and courageously every issue, come to grips with the life in all its stark reality, establish an organic relation with the community, develop a realistic and comprehensive theory of welfare, fashion a compelling and challenging vision of human destiny, and become less frightened than it is today by the bogeys of imposition and indoctrination."*[107]

What then are these social issues? The social issues of today include poverty, unemployment and demand for social welfare. They include mastery of the youth, time and computers or technology.

They also include political instabilities, income inequality, environmental degradation, hunger, moral collapse, HIV and AIDS, insecurity, mass emigration of people from the south to the northern hemisphere, etc. you wouldn't forget to add tribal wars and growing distrust near the magnitude that ended in the genocide but now especially the religious radicalism in Asia on one hand and deregulation of religion in the west on the other and conflicts raging throughout the world today from all its curves in Myanmar to our vicinity in Middle East and West Africa, and now right here in East Africa?

Are all these concerns baseless? No sir! Where's the arrogance of the ancient emperors and societies who were less futuristic—the Roman Empire, the Ottoman, Hitler and Mussolini? The USSR? Yugoslavia? Ukraine? Libya? Somalia? Saddam Hussein? Haiti? Where is the might of the ancient Greece, or the Great Britain? Where is the Massai triumph or that of the Hinda kingdom? Can we ignore the rising might of the Chinaman or the Indian-man in the contemporary world of economics or politics?

BUILDING THE PERSONAL AS WELL AS NATIONAL EQUILIBRIUM

Now the question is: is there a solution to the problems we have discussed—problems leading to a sick nation situation as well as the death of a nation? No one—in light of the death of Yugoslavia, the Soviet Union, the collapse of Roman Empire, collapse of the Ottoman Empire as well as both the ancient and the modern Greece, the weakening of the Great Britain—can heal such a malady in a South African, Somalian or Haitian situation today "by hacking at the leaves," as wrote Anwar Sadat in his autobiography.

Let us recall what Margaret Thatcher said in chapter one and our conclusion concerning a society: "There is no such a thing as society," so aptly said Margaret Thatcher. "There are individual men, and women, and families." By addressing the problems and mindset of these individual men and women, we transform them and their families. By transforming their families, we transform the whole society.

When Sadat had this note at the back of his mind at the time or not the author has no way of knowing. But what we know is that Sadat worked on the root of his problem by drawing upon his inner strength before he could heal himself and his nation before the downfall we saw under Mubarak following the coup. "It was then (that) I drew, almost unconsciously, on the inner strength I had developed in Cell 54 of Cairo Central Prison," he records in his autobiography, "I drew, almost unconsciously, on the inner strength I had developed in Cell 54 of Cairo Central Prison—strength, call it a talent or capacity, for change. I found that I faced a highly complex situation," he continued, "and that I couldn't hope to change it until I had armed myself with the necessary psychological and intellectual capacity. My contemplation of life and human nature in that secluded place had taught me that he who cannot change the very fabric of his thought will never be able to change reality, and will never, therefore, make any progress."

CRITICAL ISSUES EDUCATION HAS TO ADDRESS—WITH SIMILE TO TANZANIA

Having thus arrived this far, we hope you realize we have staked the future of a nation on education. For that future to be bright and its brightness safeguarded, *"Education therefore (1) has to critically examine the cultural heritage of the society as well as entire civilization, (2) is not afraid to examine the controversial issues, (3) is deliberately committed to bring about social and constructive change, (4) cultivates a future planning attitude that considers the realities of the world, and (5) enlist teachers and students in a definite program to enhance cultural renewal and interculturalism."*[108]

Talk of the needs of now, what about education—focused curriculum—pertinent to our society and its needs? We have enviable rich natural resources such as gold and diamond; we have recently discovered rich bowels of oil and gas that now slumberously lie under our feet: How do we equip our people to be able to take charge of their country's rich natural resources? How are we focusing on the education in the areas of land use including the use of the Sea, Rivers and Lakes we have in no less than abundant?

How does the curriculum we have today address patriotism: national unity, peace or harmony and cohesion when sectarian and in particular the religious sentiment and nepotism seem to be on the rise today? No community can impose domination on another one forever. My fears are in the dash—the time during which the disadvantaged or even the persecuted decide to say: *No. Enough is enough.* This is my greatest fear, and should it come to pass, those in charge of the country and of education sector in particular have a responsibility—and a bad one—to stomach. And mind you, I wouldn't say so before this book was published. For now I have reason to, after having placed all reasons on your laps.

And mark you: I am not suggesting all this simply as something conceived in my own imaginations or radical emotions. No sir! Ornstein and Hunkins in their great book, Curriculum Foundations, Principles and Issues 3rd edition (pp.66-67) went on record saying that: As long as we don't transform our education, economic as well as political independence "beyond rudiments" was wishful thinking. In a new country, in which the chief task was to explore and develop natural resources as well as to promote democracy, education should be functional to these concerns. Under these circumstances to spend four or five years in learning...dead (subjects) is to turn our backs upon the gold mine in order to amuse ourselves catching butterflies. If the time spent...were devoted to sciences, the human condition would be much improved..." That's certainly why Noah Webster called passionately upon his fellow Americans to "unshackle (their) minds and act like independent beings. You have been children long enough subject to control and subservient to the interests of a haughty parent...you have an empire to raise...and a national character to establish and extend by your wisdom and judgment," reasoned Noah Webster. "Unquestionably educational aims and especially school reform must be relevant or meaningful to our times. If the schools are not adaptable to changing conditions and social forces, how can we expect them to produce people who are (Ornstein and Hunkins 1998 p.167)?"

THE RIGHT ATTITUDE IN THE FACE OF CHANGE

For most of us, change is quite disconcerting. But it is foolish to cling to something that is not only useless, but something which is also detrimental to your wellbeing. With reference to the recommendations we are attempting to bring to the fore in as far as education is concerned: Consider educational needs of a society whose major tasks for survival were catching fish to eat, clubbing horses, and frightening away saber tooth tigers.[109] The school in this society set up a curriculum to meet its needs teaching courses in these three areas of survival. Eventually conditions changed; streams dried up, and the horses and tigers disappeared. Social change necessitated learning new tasks for survival, but the school curriculum continued to feature courses in catching fish, clubbing horses, and to frighten saber tooth tigers.

Today we live in a highly technical, automated, and bureaucratic society; we are faced with pressing social and economic problems—an increasingly diverse ethnic population, aging cities, the effects of centuries of racial and sexual discrimination, an aging population, unemployment, and displaced workforce, exhaustion of natural resources and the pollution of the physical environment. These trends and forces are highly interrelated; they mutually reinforce each other, and they are accelerating…in an era of space technology, telecommunications, computers, and robots…we must have schools that teach the kinds of skills and information and develop the kinds of attitudes requisite for success in a knowledge society. We need curricula that go beyond just having us well informed; we need education that contributes to the further evolution of our consciousness that will enable us to speculate, imagine, appreciate, emphasize.[110] We need dispositions developed in school and in general society that allow us to have successful participation with our diverse fellow citizens. Future successes…will depend to a large extent on how well Curricularists draw from the social foundations and create curricula of relevance and educational aims of significance. In doing so they can decide on appropriate aims and curricula and they can thus prepare students for the world of tomorrow by providing them with the knowledge and values they need to make wise decisions…[111]

What are we doing to prepare our people to become innovative and competitive—rather than evasive—in the ever emerging competition from ever emerging regional blocks such as East African Cooperation? What are we doing about the fast changing trends, ICT and globalization?

"I am concerned," wrote Conant, "we are allowing the social dynamite to accumulate in our (society and especially) large cities…Leaving aside human tragedies. I submit that a continuation of this situation (youth out of school and out of work) is a menace to the social and political health of the (society and especially) large cities. The improvement of slum conditions is only in part a question of improving education. But the role of schools is of utmost importance… added responsibility however requires additional funds. Indeed the whole question of financing public education…is a national concern.[112]

Using Conant's phraseology, this author is concerned that we are allowing the indolent and religious dynamite to accumulate in our society: *in the school, at work,* in the household, *in the churches,* in the mosques or synagogues—and in the government; that we are allowing social and economic dynamite to accumulate in our mining towns and cities; that we are allowing social and economic dynamite to accumulate in our oil and gas industry and faculties; that we are allowing the dynamite caused by

ICY and globalization and East African community to accumulate in our classrooms and workplaces and among our youth leaving aside human tragedies.

That's why I submit that a continuation of this situation; youth out of school and out of work; escalating religious radicalism and sectarian fanaticism; and alienation of the citizens from the mineral rich land among the local communities alongside environmental tragedies and unpreparedness of our human resources and our academic faculties to render such needed educational services in oil and gas, besides deficiency in the social economic infrastructures; I am afraid that as long as we are allowing spiritual, social and economic dynamite to accumulate in the social media, a menace to the spiritual, social economic and political health of our society is around the corner unless we act—and act now. Engagement of the people, reformation of our education and social revolution together are a national emergency—an emergency that evokes urgent attention.

Our curriculum should necessarily be relevant to our circumstances and needs. It shouldn't be one and the same as the Kenyan curriculum or that of the UK for that matter. Whereas Kenya has for instance to deal with fragmented nature of its society, and therefore the challenge to address the sense of 'patriotism' in order to combat 'regionalism' and tribalism; or the UK to have a curriculum that assesses and addresses where she went wrong as to why she is no longer the world superpower, with high scale of indolent people and low self-esteem; a nation with soaring mania to leave the country to SA or USA;
with towering culture of cohabiting couples, multiplicity of secret matrimonies and secret children, widespread single mothers and unprecedented boycott against marriage and soaring divorces and generally collapse of family institution; with the mushrooming of bar-culture and ubiquitous bars and unlicensed lucrative quickie-guest-houses, and emerging commercial sex, drugs, and unparalleled nepotism and corruption as industry; with female mutilation, gender and sexual—hard and soft—violence[113] among couples and persistently growing religious sentiment, with lack of, or low, attention to innovation and lack of thinking out of the—music, art, beauty and modeling—box, we are faced with the challenge to have courage to face up to the truth rather than hiding our problems and weaknesses under carpet—or hiding the head in the sand when these concerns are chatted out.

We are faced with the challenge to face up to the extent of the problem and how deep and wide these problems pervade the society, we are faced with the challenge of addressing the same through the national curriculum if we have to redress the situation—urgently and practically—notwithstanding the use of every other possible platform available to us in our streets, in the homes, the media houses, the churches and mosques, the parliament and the presidency.

Finally, but not least, we must recognize that we cannot eliminate poverty, or emancipate our youth, and reform our society, bringing this country from its knees and put it once again back on its feet and gain active existence one by one as individuals and together as a nation, unless we think and work not only really hard as individuals, but also together and smart. When I say getting this country or people from its knees and once again back to work and indeed active existence, one by one as individuals and together as a nation, I refer to any nation with symptoms I highlighted in the preceding chapters.

You notice I write this book in a century where we are much the same—and our societies no longer impermeable with the influence from the outside. When I say getting a people from its knees and get it once more, again, back to work and indeed active existence one by one as individuals and together as a nation, I mean to be self-respecting, to be a people respecting others and therefore above all, to be a people respected by others.

And this change doesn't suddenly fall from the sky, or come by ordination from God anymore. Gone are those days when angels descended the skies with tidings of good joy—and presents from the generous Deity! We have a God who believes we all are equal before him. He is a loving God. Here is also another word of caution. Being considered top today is a result of being actively involved in your own affairs, as well as in the affairs affecting others. And this is impossible without appropriate education. And not only that, but also an education that is provided—well, no—that's not the word. The right word is *shared*. Thus we need an education that is *shared* in the correct and relevant manner.

When we say *shared*, we mean there are lots of shared interests at stake. The work on education should be democratic because we are all affected by its effects. Ornstein and Hunkins sum it up this concern thus:

"Because our knowledge is changing so rapidly we must continuously ask ourselves what is the most worthwhile knowledge, and we must continuously reappraise what we mean by worthwhile…We need to organize a curriculum that is conducive to change and that enables scholars and practitioners to work together and test their ideas in the context of changing problems and issues of the society.[114]

Besides isolation in the preparation of and authorizing the curriculum, we realize that there is a great need for a national curriculum notwithstanding flexibility on localization or customization of local or new ideas that are yet to be national. Developing national standards allows access of advantageous ideas to all. The drive for national curriculum and national standards was made evident in President Bush's American 2000. President Clinton participated in the creation of American 2000 as…governor of Arkansas. Clinton carried his interest in national standards into his administration and pushed for legislation that would make these goals official throughout the land.[115]

There is one more critical area we must address if we should have a responsive curriculum, which the reader, with his vast knowledge and experience in educational and human affairs cannot miss, can he? That is to say the reader recognizes that no single group of select people is responsible for this change. Yes, the academics can, and ought to, take the leadership role, but dialogue from all four corners of the wind across the nation is pivotal, with an eye on new needs and new ideas is pivotal. This, in summary, is not a burden that we should load on the broader shoulders of the traditional academicians, conventional schools or to the politicians only as it seems to be right until as I write. Yet exclusion of the masses from this process has never been, it is not, and it will never be a privilege to the masses, don't you think so?

Ornstein and Hunkins couldn't be more right when they wrote thus concerning social foundations of curriculum: "Ideally, new knowledge should be integrated into a moral legal context. Whose morality? The standards of that society which is governed by constitutional process (that protects people from other people and provide people's basic rights) and promotes worthwhile and just consequences."[116]

Talk about new knowledge, there is nothing this country and the human community of this century needs like new ideas. The old school textbooks and technocrats seldom work to inspire change but preserve the status quo, to resist change.

Diane Ravitch couldn't be more correct: [117] *The need for publishers, and now textbook authors, is to be "politically correct," to reflect...all.* Indeed Mwalimu Nyerere once said: "Tanzania is for all Tanzanians," said Mwalimu. "And when I say Tanzanians," he continued, "When I say Tanzanians, I mean all. No one single person has the right to say *I am the people* (or say *I and I alone speak for the people).* And there is no one single Tanzanian who has the right to say *I know what is good for Tanzanians, and so therefore the rest should do as I say.* All Tanzanians must discuss, and together, decide what is good (or bad) for Tanzanians."[118]

LESSONS FROM TANZANIA

Talking about xenophobia in South Africa may create a feeling that that is the only country where this crime is rooted. Nay! We have seen xenophobia in Africa as we see it in America, Europe and Asia.

To narrow down the field, we have experienced, yes on different scale, xenophobia here at home in Tanzania. Let's speak the truth and shame the devil! We have experienced a number of cases where the local boys fear the Ugandans—and Kenyans especially—are taking their jobs. So what's a big deal about South Africa—excepting of course the scale?

Now, since we discussed the matter in the book *How Universities Under Develop You*, this book is not going to dwell on that topic. However we are going to borrow from the book the mention that was made on how to heal it, as an introduction to healing xenophobia as one of the maladies of nations.

Now, can we really heal xenophobia? The book *How Universities Under Develop You*, confirms that it can be done—that it can be done from both the part of the people and that of the government. It suggests that to heal this malady, the individual citizens can study what makes the employers hire foreigners. They can study why the foreigners run big businesses, why they work hard?

The government should and can always learn from the programs that are run by foreign governments—programs that make their citizens hardworking and industrious. And in the end, "Tanzanian people are fast learning to gain these key attributes and capabilities. They are learning investors don't give a damn about nationality and citizenship but productivity, innovations, and output.

They are as well fast learning from a healthy competition with neighbors who are aggressive, hardworking and committed to results. We are fast learning actions speak louder. We are fast learning the world is becoming a village or a nation without borders. And truly here the Darwinic principle of survival of the fittest is in application. You either par or perish! The leadership is learning it can be done, too."[119]

Indeed it all goes down to a new kind of education—an education with a different DNA—a DNA which controls the structure and purpose of each member of the society and transmits the generic genetic information. This information must, of necessity, help to transmit a certain particular way of thinking, doing and living.

Though I may not love the wording, but the essence of his argument is bona fide. That's why I had to bring Herbert Spencer to the show. Who's he?

Herbert Spencer was an English social scientist who based his ideas of education on Charles Darwin's theories of biological evolution and survival of the fittest. Spencer maintained that social development takes place according to the process by which…Because of the laws of nature only intelligent and productive populations would adapt to environmental changes. Less intelligent people would slowly disappear.[120]

It's no wonder that transforming our people's lives is like to wake them up from darkness and rising once again to see the sun behind a bank of thunderous dark clouds and beaming rays.

Yet, like infants, oftentimes men welcome strife without intentions or knowledge of how catastrophic it can be. The experiences of pre genocide Rwanda, or post 1997 election Kenya, or even what we see and hear happening today in Ukraine or Nigeria, Somalia, CAR etc., prove that truly we humans are naïve to the fact that:

"Our life is an apprenticeship to the truth that around every circle another can be drawn and that there's no end in nature…," said Emerson. "Every end," he continued, "Every end is the beginning. And under every deep, a lower deep opens!"

WORD OF COUNSEL

Recalling our discussion about the symptoms of a sick nation, make reference to the above analysis to see if you are still okay with who you are. However as you make this analysis, notice that not one symptom can lead to the conclusion that a person, organization or a nation is sick. A great good number of individuals, organizations and nations have one or a couple of the symptoms. However, nothing can be far from the truth that a nation is no longer safer when most of these symptoms pervade her systems—and especially her people.

When that happens, you must really halt and ponder about what future a nation chooses for itself—if there is any left. And I say if any because really for such a society there is no future. Such a mediocre society gives way and will soon perish if its illness is not well reported and diagnosed so that the right medication or prevention of such maladies is discharged. But sadly, *"Health is not valued,"* rightly said Thomas Fuller, *"Health is not valued till sickness comes."*

Because of the significance of what we have just laid down through the foregoing chapter, we have found that it is a matter of great importance to make additional counsels to individual readers concerning the imminent dangers they, their families and the nation as a whole face, in the face of the sick nation status.

For instance, just like some of the diseases—communicable and non-communicable—such as sickle-cell anemia or asthma are genetic; as others are endemic—a condition, regularly found and very common among a particular group or in a particular area such as Malaria is endemic in many of the hotter regions of the world, as others are airborne or waterborne epidemics—particular diseases affecting a large number of people at the same time such as influenza or dysentery; while others are more subject of what man chooses to or not to do such as is the case of HIV/AIDS or Ebola.

The only or best remedy against diseases that are genetic, is to be aware of the diseases and probably scanning the potential spouses before marriage. That is how we can prevent sickle-cell anemia or asthma aside from prescription of medication that provide relief to the patients.

For water or airborne diseases, we can control them by keeping our environment clean and of course keeping an eye on hygiene and sanitation. We can also use drugs to heal ourselves when we contract such diseases as dysentery or malaria. But there are some of the diseases a nation contracts just like how we human beings contract HIV/AIDS or Ebola.

For such a disease like HIV/AIDS, the only and best long term remedy, as I write, is abstaining from sex.

As for Ebola, we must stop eating monkeys and bats. And this seems easy to me. We can redirect our appetites to other kinds of dignified meat such as beef or chicken—excepting of course the Hindu—while working hard to eradicate the diseases by discovery of preventive medication.

But there is still one more caution that I have to make. Whereas the mentioned are a few ways we can use to heal such diseases, I mean once we contract them, but as a human society, we have learned that the recent pandemics—such as Ebola, or even insecurity from both sectarian conflicts such as we have experienced in the Arab world, Nigeria, Somalia etc., much as we have grieved over xenophobia in South Africa or genocide anywhere else—are best combated with international forces coming together. It is important that nations must come together to combat such infirmities because they transcend household or regional borders. The international community must therefore, learning from the foregoing analysis, begin working together to combat maladies of nations such as extreme religious philosophies, xenophobia, corruption and nepotism, extreme poverty, hopelessness, etc.

Sadly, like infants, oftentimes grown men and women—no matter whether they are highly educated, black, brown or white—tend to entertain problems unaware how catastrophic that can be.

That's human nature. That's indeed in the nature of the beast, the nature that is still in the human DNA of modern man! Such is how Congolese men and women were recently aired by BBC swearing upon their dead bodies that they will never stop hunting and eating monkeys and baboons—come what may, with or without Ebola or how in West Africa traditionalists invaded Ebola treatment camps to steal back their sick men and women away from medication—the human society seems to entertain jihadists, xenophobia, exploitation of one society by another, extreme poverty, corruption and nepotism without realizing that we all pay the price.

The recent disquieting cases such as economic crisis, terrorist attacks and mass emigration into Europe and drowning of masses from Africa and Asia into the Mediterranean across Lampedusa and Malta running away from extreme poverty, failed states and islamists back home have helped to put that assertion into perspective!

Finally, I am certain you realize that I have made my tale so long. What I have done is whistle blowing. I have blown a whistle to forewarn the nation but especially the immediate reader that he is not any safer unless he became objective, remaining alert and diligent, for indeed: "Like species, humans, business organizations, institutions and nations, if they don't evolve and adapt to changing environment, they become extinct!"

I wrote this chapter and book because I don't want that fate to happen to you, your family or posterity, your business, community or the nation and humanity as a whole![121]

A GLIMMER OF HOPE
Recognizing that what I write for Tanzania, so I write for any worthy people, finally, now that we have placed before you the weaknesses that almost ban a nation from growing, almost outlawing that country from prosperity, we have placed before you the reasons why we should change direction—only if you want to prosper as an individual or society—or close your eyes and ears to what we have told you grounding yourself in the sand and ground in permanent misery!

As a final point, despite the prevalent gloom that pervades a true analysis of our society like this one, you the reader, and the nation as a whole, shouldn't despair an iota if we have found the reason to change direction. Mo Kamilagwa, a onetime author's co-worker, is such an optimistic and inspirational leader. Here's a note he sent to his mail list—a mail list in which the author was a member—on December 9, 2009 at 09.23.33 P.M, the time the nation celebrated her 48th anniversary.

He wrote thus beautifully:

"We are a 48 years (now 53) *nation. Yes we have a long march ahead. Yes we still have many challenges. But more importantly, we are a young nation with youthful population. Once nurtured and unleashed, the energy of the youth will drive on to a new growth path.*

"Yes we need to change some of our attitudes: we complain too much, play blame games and point fingers, but iff in their places we will start working hard and support one another, and of course if we confidently begin to aim higher, as individuals, families, schools, organizations and the nation as a whole, we shall surely make it if we can learn from our past, identify our goals, and focus on the challenges ahead, while maintaining our steadfast resolve to keep marching forward. But we must capitalize on the people: the youth, the farmers, the labor force, the business sector and the middle class.

"Indeed, as aptly said President Kikwete, 'Tanzania Yenye Neema Yawezekana' (A dream for a prosperous Tanzania is not a dream any more, it is real,)" concluded Mohammed Kamilagwa.

LAST WORD

As we end the book let me point out one more important thing: We are positive that you realize we have placed before you a book that is going to be instrumental in changing your performances as individual students, employees, schools, governmental and nongovernmental organizations, the private as well as public sector and performances among all worthy peoples or nations.

We know this education is going to bring about revolution. Revolution? Well, if it doesn't bring revolution, then it will bring about evolution of, and in the reader or trainee and all about him. It will bring about evolution first to the person himself; and then he will impart the same evolution to his household, his business, his neighborhood, his community, the environment and humanity as a whole. This is the ideal citizen our training builds—the ideal scholar and employee we as parents, teachers, employers and the government aim to build. That we are sure of! And it's not from personal emotions or feelings only. We have testimony from more credible sources.

In his book The Promise, Professor Maliyamkono wrote thus: "Education has no boundaries. Anything can be taught and anything can be learnt," said the good Professor, "It is a weapon against poverty, it a weapon against poor health; and when used wisely, can be a weapon against exclusion and discrimination. It can enable understanding, acceptance and integration. The easiest way to achieve this is to use schools to bring together different and disparate sections of young community…under one roof to study can only help understanding."[122]

Ornstein and Hunkins suggested *that we must nurture all types of intelligence and all types of excellence that contribute to the worth of the individual and the society."*[123] We present this book and training hoping one day it will be respectively integrated into civics and development study programs for lower and higher learning institutions. Now that we have done our part as we inch to the end, we need you on board. We need you on board because we need each other. That is obvious! Arif Billah was incredibly right. No one becomes someone on his own. We all need one another. For anyone who doubts that we all need one another, let him consider his own daily lives. Take the case of a pilot for example. You and I recognize that airplanes are flown by pilots excepting of, of course the American drones.

Yet pilots need air-hostesses—besides copilots. You are the pilot; we are air hosts and air hostesses in your air plane. Yes—you are driving the bus—or even a Dala dada—or a Matatu, but you need the services of the bus conductors—us! There is a referee or an umpire in almost every game but there is an assistant referee.

Trucks have helpers besides their drivers—we are the truck helpers. In athletics, for splinters to perform at their top, even Usain Bolt himself—have pace-Makers.

Today we can no longer live in an island or isolation like Robinson Crusoe. Yet even Robinson had Friday to give him company only a little while later just like how Adam had Eve. Parents are two—excepting of Jesus of course—Christians believe so—but even so, the services of Joseph were inevitable—even in the upbringing of the messiah!

It is tick-bird and rhino relationship; it is complementarily between butter and bread. Indeed we need each other—in all circles of life. We need better schools for the better future of our children and nation.

We need work and workplaces. We need schools. Corporations need schools. Schools need corporations. We need families. Families need schools and corporations. We need your support. And you need us! We need everybody in the field—on the ground—playing!

Here's a big opportunity to make a major difference in your own life and the lives of your countrymen and women. From here an opportunity has spread before you to enhance long term change of attitude among our students and employees.

By change of attitude, you will help uplift schools' performances, and guarantee the students with the great future, leading free self-reliant and more meaningful lives for themselves their families and their posterity and people and environment around them. In simple terms think of a nation where every son and every daughter; a country where every employee and every manager; every parent and every public and corporate leader was ideal or at least have ideals, what would this country be like? We know with the consciousness and realization of difference this program will make to you personally, your family, your business and the whole nation and humanity as a whole, you will not let this opportunity slip through your fingers.

Again you must not forget—for this change to happen and happen now—it all begins with you: the immediate reader and leader. Indeed ultimately, "A leader has an obligation to do whatever is in his or her power to protect and prolong a healthy life of a family, community, or for that matter, the school or organization; and in this specific case the nation as a whole. We believe that, "one bold idea can transform a company, an industry or an entire nation." We believe that it takes "only one man or woman—one person—to make it happen. And what's more, that person could, and should be you, sir or madam!"[124]

My good friends, as we seal this book, together, tonight, we have turned the page. Tonight you are set on a new journey. By beginning to read, and thereupon finishing this very book, today you have embarked on a journey—a journey to a new destination into which you now have just entered—at least in the domain of the psyche or on the psychological level. The journey is not yet over though? This is just a new beginning as you draw out your path to transform yourself first—and your life thereafter.

You have only begun a journey of transforming everything about you, making everything about and around you more and better—better persons, better households and environment around you, better institutions, better organizations, better communities, and a great nation. That's why thanking you, we plead that you give us another chance to be of service to the needy individual persons, families, organizations and nations again soon, confident that if you do so, not only will the opportunities conspire to make you highly successful both in those areas you consciously choose and those unthought-of , but also the people will discover, and reward you to the degree unthought-of!

Finally, farewell! Do keep my admonition. Grace be with you.[125] Heed my appeal, agree with one another, live in peace...Whatever is true, whatever is honorable, whatever is just, whatever is pure, whatever is lovely, whatever is gracious, if there is any excellence, if there is anything worthy of praise, think about these things. What you have learned and received and heard and seen in me, do; and God of peace will be with you!"[126]

—————————To be continued—————————

—Author,

Dar es Salaam, Tanzania, EA

November 11, 2015[127]

EPILOGUE:
HOW TO BUILD THE IDEAL CITIZEN, UPLIFT SCHOOL PERFORMANCES, RAISE EMPLOYEES PRODUCTIVITY AND ATTRACT PROSPERITY

"Faith is taking the first step even when you can't see the whole stair case."—Martin Luther King Junior

We've finally come to the end of this book. You must realize I'm more than delighted to accomplish this mission. It is for this reason that I suggest we now calm down a little. Yes, we need to calm down for a few seconds and ponder about what we have managed to accomplish so far. It is not a bad idea. Sometimes if we don't sit back and evaluate what we have accomplished, we run the risk of finding ourselves having overspent or misused our energies or resources unawares. And really any overuse or misallocation of resources is unwise anyway. A little reflection on what we have done already is more than a wise decision. Those who succeed in anything they do, do so not because they put in more energy than anyone else. Nay! Oftentimes, all it takes is just a little grace—a little grace of reflection between what you have already accomplished, and what is yet to be done. A little reflection helps to connect you and your work or goal with the *Infinite Intelligence,* or God , if you are a man of religion. No one has ever failed when he had at his disposal this kind of connection. That's why I decided to dedicate this chapter for that course.

I began writing this book reasonably long time ago. When I began, I was hoping to finish swiftly. But when I started working on it that first day in November, 2010; it suddenly became day and then night. It was the first day! It was until yesterday when I penned off exhausted in the heart of the night when again it was day, and it was night and then I woke up. It was another day four years down the line since that first day. I am a happy man today because we have finally managed to put before you a *Pot of Gold*—I trust.

Did I say *Pot of Gold*? Well, yes it is, since this book shapes a person in such a way that it makes him attract whatever prosperity or path to whatever destination the reader chooses. It is a *Pot of Gold* in that, with this tool—the book now and in your hands and its twin i.e., Volume Two—you the reader or any other individual persons, households, schools, corporations and nations can now choose and arrive at any future stations of their choice.

With this book or program, we "breathe" new life into the human society. How do we do it?

We do mentoring, we inspire people to choose and pursue the big dreams they were born to serve, we give vocational guidance and guidance on how to study for success, choosing career and employer, mindset and behavior change how to relate and prosper etc., offering you a self inventory that will help to keep you on the right track in your pursuit for the desired goal in your life.

You recognize that this is only Volume One of the same book series. You will find some more insights in Volume Two and Three and four of this same series—series that is itself interpreted in a training program addressing the same common goal.

I am a happy man today because we finally can reclaim that hero in every child, and equally, the potential champion in every failed person in our society. And how ubiquitous they are!

I am a happy man today because with this book and training thereof, you and I can impart to our people superior character: discipline and self-confidence, purpose in life and obsession to excel, among others.

I am a happy man today because we have finally presented the society with tools to fill gaps pervading work-skills-based curriculum we have now in place.

I am a happy man today because we have finally presented the society with solutions to the problems the majority poor face—solutions which made Michael John, a senior human resources director and at the time acting principal secretary at the ministry of health to declare that: "Finally, I've stumbled upon a book that bespeak what I consider as right solutions to our problems."

We have mentioned that the major victims in the present state of affairs are mainly the folks from the poor families. Why? Most children among the poor are sent to the deprived community schools which lack facilities. This is not all. The poor of the poor also lack the real feel of affluence, inspiration and role models in their respective communities, and thereupon, in their community schools. These children have experienced nothing but failure. That's why they never fight back because they consider failure as fate, and therefore accept whatever life throws at them as destiny—and vice such as thievery and prostitution as industry.

Consequently, there's high rate of school dropouts among the community schools, especially girls because of early childhood pregnancy, teenage marriage, child labor and truancy which rose by about 30% in 2007.[128] Besides, because of unique setbacks due to our history: colonialism, slave trade and partly the Ujamaa policy—that latter of which didn't work to encourage hard work and industriousness—our society weeps for a program that imparts ideals and values necessary for growth in the contemporary global economy.

Again, our society weeps for such a training program because of communication barrier in terms of English language we have grown to have because of the nature of our education structure aside from the mentioned historical reasons, and as a result there is prevalence of low self-esteem and timidity among our people.

Ours is a very low-rated reading and writing culture. Quick fix pervades our youth—and the society as a whole. The number of senior executives managing top organizations here at home or internationally, or even performance of our youth in Olympics or regional tournaments does more than illustrate the extent of self-esteem in our society today.

Low ambition is behind poor performances. In 2010, in every two secondary school graduates, one failed.

In 2012, out of three, two failed. In every hundred students in Kigoma North constituency, 98 scored zero in 2012! The problem isn't only regional but national.

A research by UWEZO indicated that in 2010, 8 out of 10 among 42,000 primary school students from 38 districts, could not read English or Kiswahili.

Average score in numeracy was only about 30%.

Misinformation, methodology and lack of the right orientation are behind this failure besides lack of facilities at which everyone else's fingers point. Yet, there's more to failure than lack of facilities. On their own, work skills are inadequate when education ignores the *Human Factor*: his calling and aspirations. Education isn't knowledge. It is action. It's a tool that helps to identify and crack the life's ever mounting challenges.

"In basic terms," analyzed Professor Maliyamkono in his book The Promise: "Education is… not only (a tool of) infusing knowledge but also …equipping citizens with ability to understand and unravel problems within the society caused by the ever changing economic, technological, and social environment..."

Through this program, students reap self-respect, family values and the spirit of self-reliance or self-employment: qualities that help a person to learn and succeed in making life better and the world a better place—with or without university degrees.

On the other hand, compared with the focus of the conventional education's general knowledge where facilities can be an impediment, our program transcends traditional disciplines of basic mathematics, economics, medicine or tax. We emphasize specialized knowledge and self-training. We sow superior character and develop purpose in a student's life, and desire to think, do, and become more and better! Teaching them how to identify and pursue their calling; we sow self-confidence, passion for results, loyalty, cooperation, productivity, self-reliance, and perseverance in whatever one chooses to have, do or be.

Did we talk about the children from poor families as the most disadvantaged? They lack the desire to excel, to be top. They have no role models back home while schools teach them Russian Revolution or to dissect frogs or work-skills such as engineering they don't relate to.

We teach them about themselves first: their aspirations and virtues that make a difference in their lives—something we no longer have since dissolution of schools affiliated to religions—religions that taught virtues such as good self-conduct, cooperation, peace and harmony and desire to lead decent lives, among others. To the disadvantaged, we demonstrate that they have equal chances to prosper, if they work hard and persevere in their studies or work, focusing on transforming their lives. Our program builds the inner compass that not only guides, but also acts as a catalyst, and pressures a person to achieve nothing but the highest of his or her true potential by thinking and doing nothing but only the best.

We build the mind-set that compels the child to exceed expectations at school, work or home, and meet God's hopes in him or her as is humanly possible. We reinforce quality and the finest spirit of self-conduct viz., how to relate with others advantageously and family values which traditional education tends to take no notice of.

We focus on an individual's *Human Factor* because we know successes of any dynasty or country such as India or China have their roots in the strong family institution. Besides: "Even in such technical lines as engineering, only about 15% of someone's success is due to one's technical knowledge whereas 85% is due to skills in human engineering—personality and ability to lead and serve others.[129]"

With insights into personal leadership, we transform students into responsible people; who pursue their calling; make right decisions about career; able to manage themselves and their families, people and environment around them; learn to build advantageous relationships, respect one another; master and muster self-esteem; respect another sex; gain self-control; manage HIV/AIDS and themselves as a whole; have a big goal in life and obsession to excel and live longer meaningful and impactful lives; and in turn, transform their families, neighborhood, the nation and humanity as a whole.

Responsible people we build, become and raise innovative and productive children; better and responsible future leaders; they enhance good governance; widened middle class and tax-base and build a self-reliant society willing and able to support itself and others. In short, we pluck thorns from the disadvantaged children's lives, and put roses in their places.

NEW NEEDS

We all know that the world has gone through sweeping challenges—socially and economically. One of these challenges is the economic crisis. Because of the crisis, people are not anymore seeking short term answers. They need long-term solutions to their problems in their own lives and lives of their families, schools, business and public service. The old solutions don't work anymore.

If they do, they don't produce adequate or sufficient output or results compared to efforts we put in. That's why we need new solutions. Individual youth have so many questions about their future. Education—however questionable it has become—is so expensive even when graduates don't get jobs. Parents don't get appropriate support from their own children even after they have spent fortunes on their education.

The people are taxed highly and prices are on the rise even when the government institutions cannot provide required social services. Employers and business owners are lamenting in distress and helplessness, while agriculture as an industry is almost lifeless.

They invest but they don't get returns. As a result there is rampant surrender and return to the weed among the youth especially, and insanity is once again on the rise as a result. We can't anymore leave the responsibility to find solution to our problems to the West. We need home grown initiatives—initiatives created and supported by the local people themselves. Indeed as wrote Tom Sharpe in Vintage Stuff, initiatives like this one will help to prove that really: "It is a functional fact that the under developed nations of the world have much to contribute on social, cultural and spiritual basis to modern thinking!"[130]

And when we talk about change, it isn't about the government or schools alone. As parents we need to rise to the occasion. Very soon you will need your children to give you the support you need and deserve. Employers want their employees to work hard. They expect them to be innovative and productive—to meet and exceed their goals. That will be impossible as it stands today. The International Monetary Fund magazine of February to March 2012 files the same fact about irrelevant material or education among our graduates, and reveals that in India for instance organizations have managed to address the gap by establishing in-house schools for its employees after they have even graduated from top schools and the benefits are so tremendous.

RESPONSIBLE PARENTS DESPERATELY CRAVE TO TRANSFORM THEIR CHILDREN

I've chosen to include a testimony on how parents are desperate to give insight on what people experience and say about this program. Because it is a new initiative, you demand and certainly deserve evidence to come on board.

Here's the event that I experienced recently in that cold region of Mbeya, Tanzania. I was scheduled for a training session at Lutengano High School when I met a couple of elderly but strong persons. The man introduced himself as an auditor—but that's what he said. Moments later, I had reasons to doubt his word.

And here is how:

We were seated in the same hotel lounge in town, when he began auditing people around him. And I was "those people!" He began asking questions about me. They were plenty and nonstop—I mean the questions. I'd thought he could do better not as an auditor but as an agent for the Scotland Yard, M26, National Investigation Agency or FBI.

But since I'd my laptop on my lap, and was writing and revising my training for the morrow, I thought it was not a bad idea to sell what I was doing. So I simply chose to tell him what I was doing both in Mbeya city and generally what I did for a living.

So I simply showed him the "books of accounts!" I told him I was a writer and showed him my previous books and hinted on the training with Lutengano High School.

I did this not intending to brag of course, but in the main because that was the only language the auditor would understand and thus shorten my description of "The people" around him! How some vocations can make you suspicious is unspeakable and that's why quite frankly I don't fancy such jobs as auditing or policing.

After he had read through some of my book back covers, he did something that shocked me! He shut the computer down! I trembled! I was certain a tragedy was in the vicinity! I thought my passage to the hereafter would commence at once.

But I also sensed I would die very unconventionally, and at the hand of an elderly couple who hated writers—as corrupt executives and politicians tend to hate journalists—unfortunately! It is very unfortunate that in the world of humanity, we tend to love what we should hate and hate what we should love! And there was nothing I could do about it.

As I was hastily preparing to make my final payers—setting myself ready for the kingdom come before this couple strangulated me—I glanced at the man's face. It predicted menace.

Then he opened up a small bag. I closed my eyes. I hate to look at guns. But silence—deafening silence—followed. I threw him a quick glance one more time.

And I saw it—a phone in his hands! Thank God it wasn't a revolver! But his anger was still there. His wife's situation didn't help much! She was mesmerized too! I had to pray very quickly, quickly before I meet my Maker.

In my bewilderment, my memory failed me. Not *Hail Mary* or *Our Father Who Art in Heaven* was forthcoming.

I tried to concoct one but I failed.

And there was no time to summon a "high priest" from the nearby parish considering the anger of an old man with the blood of Mkwawa flowing in his veins. Mkwawa was a king of the Hehe in the southern Tanzania whose fury made him pull a trigger between his own eyes.

And since then, coupled with some of the animal meat they eat down in Iringa, a region where the rate of fury and suicide is unprecedented. I had learned that that's where he hailed from. Some traditional think-tank suggests it could also have something to do with the curse of the Germans.

A very humble Mkwawa had humbled a whole garrison of German army during the early days of colonization of Tanganyika, and it didn't sit well with the proud white men—people among whom related by blood to the Fuhler.

Well, concerning his anger, I didn't understand it one bit. I was innocent. So why worry? I told myself on the second thought. But that's not what would save my neck. How many innocent people rot behind bars as the criminals are let off the hook to continue their business as usual? That thought made me tremble.
Probably I looked like a drug dealer to this retired police officer? He certainly was an army man. His anger, his disposition and suspicion wouldn't suggest otherwise. And his voice too! I knew he was calling the FBI or Scotland Yard. No!

He was probably calling his own gang to avenge me for reasons about which I didn't know though. I was a wrong person! "Can I speak to Jimmy?" he shouted at his phone!

Well—Jimmy isn't the actual name—and it isn't the Jimmy in the famous old Indian Mithun Chakraborty movie! He went on—and on—in his mixed Swahili and some Kihehe vernacular! I didn't understand what he ordered. Then he commanded—and I obeyed like a sacrificial lamb—a black little innocent lamb prepared for offering!

He commanded hoarsely: "Wait there, you hear me!" I nodded obediently! He led his hands in his pockets and expecting this time to see a gun, I saw a card that resembled the old-time call box account cards.

I was not myself! I was certain he was calling Scotland Yard—or some gang!

Though we are a peaceful people in this country, but you know these borders! In Malawi, the presidential race had just begun, and a smoking gun wasn't abnormal in some other borders. The DRC border was just nearby. M23 and the Rwandan Interahamwe genociders across the border in D.R Congo heightened the tension in this region.

And the upcoming elections across the borders didn't do much to help the situation— with Kabila and Nkurunziza plotting for their extra terms in office. Then, as he left, in a fleeting moment, I wanted to take cover. But I asked myself why worry? I was innocent in my dealings! I'd not robbed or been convicted for any crime! I was in Mbeya to add value to the people—and the region. So why worry. I'd not wronged anyone not him, not God.

I had not even transgressed against my own wife. I had spent many nights alone, reading and writing—like a Pope—Pope Kambarangwe. That cannot warrant death, can it? God cannot surely sign a death warrant for such a man. He cannot sign a document allowing his death squad to pull a trigger on such an innocent person. No.

Now this is the account of events that followed! I kept my eyes on his back and saw him not toward the Scotland Yard offices but to an ATM machine—and that was NBC Bank, to be specific!

I also learned through his wife that Jimmy is their son! A prodigal son—if you know what I mean! He had left school while in Form Two; he had impregnated a girl and brought a child to his parents without even running a DNA test.

He then ran away with another girl after dumping a couple of them in between! Weed wasn't taboo to him!

To him hard liquor was juice! School fees paid for his pleasures, not his boarding school or tuition. Several times without number he had been caught in lodgings and restaurants drinking his school fees staying with a different woman every couple of days. With his school fees, he purchased trendy cloth lines to please ladies and his peers. To be brief, he put his school fees where his mouth and the zipper were.

To him, the word of God was a vocabulary! With those few moments, out of their desperation, they were positive that I was a messiah. Yet I wouldn't blame them to have pleaded with me to lay my hands on their prodigal son! They were desperate. I'm narrating this for the sake of the others! I hope this couple will understand as they read this and be proud of their efforts and love they have accorded their family—if the children know. They have gone to a great deal of trouble to do the best for the children. They even were proud grandparents to a baby conceived in the unspeakable love affair between two teenagers—and a baby who calls its own grannies papa and mama! To realize how great and noble this couple was, evaluate what you and I would do in their position. What would you do? We would add a street child to the already bulging number! As you read I can see you already find pride in this great couple! (And you can contact them through the author—if you may wish to help or meet them—for they are real people).

Now, we made arrangements and within the next two days, I was scheduled to be "bagged" with this prodigal son to—well, to my "clinic!" This clinic is this program! I was like, ooops! I witnessed for first time in my writing and training life mountains of roasted meat—my best—and a sea of drinks! It took me time to recover. And when I did—I was drunk? Well in Mbeya—as in Moshi, Ngara, Karagwe or Arusha even the liquor drinkers don't—it is too cold! Jimmy's clinic didn't materialize though, for I didn't finalize the business in Mbeya and untimely left the municipality.

From this couple, I learnt how critical we truly ought to stop our youth becoming antisocial crooks who only seek to squander the money on pleasure. We ought to transform them into ideal or model youth, graduates and workforce. We must help the youth in schools to bear image of the ideal youth for others to emulate. Today youth believe the ideal youth are those outside schools. Why? They make money, and are popular even without wasting many years in the classrooms. If we don't change the situation we are blessing quick fix and undermining education and industry! This is a catastrophe. It is indeed a buzzing detonated bomb that is about to explode.

Of late, we experience almost on every day basis students' boycotts. Yes the allowances are meager but they should prove what they do with whatever they get today. We must change this attitude. We cannot force them to study or spend the little money rationally on meals and books rather than phones and credits and some music or non-educational fancy gadgets if they don't know why. This is what I want to hear.

I want to hear somebody say when I'm president—whether president of a nation state, president of the church or religion, business organization, governmental or nongovernmental organization or even the president of the family unit—I'll put an end to this trend.

At work we want to see people who work hard to get results first among , adding value to the employer, the society and to themselves before thinking about promotion or pleasure every evening where they spend longer hours in ubiquitous pubs and clubs in the neighborhood.

Our schools and workforce should present the image of ideal youth or persons for others to emulate for otherwise we are soon going to experience an about-turn in the opposite direction away from a freer, wealthier, peaceful and healthier society. We need youth in the schools to be finished products. First installment! Ready for use. That is why we created this program—that's why we wrote this book.

And this isn't about the government or schools alone. As parents and corporations we need to rise to the occasion.

CHANGE IS POSSIBLE

But the question is this: Can really a person change? Can we—individual persons, households, schools, corporations and nations—shine and be true stars? Can we? Definitely! I mean we can change. Though it is believed that stars just be, but there must be work behind it.

There must be his or her own parent, guardians or circumstances and environment surrounding the person that propel him to success—or throw him into grand failure. I have said this earlier on, but let me emphasize the point of change one more last time.

I can say this with all conviction because I've experienced transformation happening. And mark you, I have not seen it happening a distance away. Not even near. But within me! I've been transformed myself. I am that transformation itself! It is within me and I am within it.

You and I need someone to guide us—as Serena Williams revealed. Earlier on, my mother—like Martin Lawrence's mother—used to tell me that "the world is yours, son. So don't sleep."

Get to work, she was saying, with a twinkle in her eye. I did not transform myself, didn't work as would please my mama.

In class, I was in the permanent weak students, a group of failures and mediocre students led by Kamisha Zibonera (you may read about it in "What Makes People Rich and Nations Powerful"). I didn't concentrate with my studies and remained the same hopeless dumb until when I was in class five. It was then when Domina became the messenger of peace (and reformation). Domina is my sister. She tossed this idea of excellence to me more than 20 years back now—confiding her confidence in something within me that was uniquely splendid in the domain of intellect. (You may read more about it in the book "What Makes People Rich and Nations Powerful"). I finally changed. She had plucked a thorn in me and in its place planted a rose. With her guidance, with my transformation, a real Festo Michael Kambarangwe began to form. One astonishing fact from that humble transformation is that, that year I shot to a second place in my class of around 60 students. In doing so, she had reclaimed me back from a group I didn't belong to. She had built in me a deep desire for success and indeed confidence and want to distinguish myself.

Then, like what John Nash was told by his professor on cracking the original idea he regarded as a breakthrough in modern mathematics in a movie *A Beautiful Mind*, I heard a small voice telling me that "Now Mr. Kambarangwe, with breakthrough of this magnitude you will get any place you want in life!" As I narrate this tale, remember it is not about me, it is about you and any worthy reader—like you! It is about our youth: our children, students and employees. But what is so amazing is that I went on to be top in most of rest of my classes through secondary school and high school and among them regional exams and national essays competition. Then I joined the university where I became an all faculties top student in the first ever exam we did there: communication skills— and general knowledge! Imagine! Top among tops! Looking back, I realize a failure in my boyhood-self had risen to fame in rather a splendid fashion—thanks to my sister.

What's the point? We can—and must—learn from others. No one becomes someone on his own," said Arif Billah, a re-known Islamic Scholar, adding that "No iron becomes a sharp dagger alone!" Recalling how I was a failure and how I managed to change and reverse the situation, I can't but agree with Professor William James of Harvard. In his observation on human capabilities, he concluded thus: "Compared with what we ought to be, we are only half awake. We are making use of only a small part of our physical and mental resources. Stating the same thing broadly," he continued, "the human individual thus lives far within his limits. He possesses powers of various sorts which he habitually fails to use..." Yes you and I possess powers of various sorts which we habitually fail to use. I have become a walking billboard of that testimony over the years! And so can you!

YOU CAN CHANGE AND HELP OTHERS TO CHANGE

Through this and the previous chapters in this and preceding titles, I've placed before you how in a very short meeting with my sister I changed into a completely different person. So I trust Bill Clinton when he says he met President Kennedy and when they shook hands, he decided then and there that he should be president. George W. Bush happened to be with President Bush in the White House.

That's how his dream to be president began.

Martin Lawrence met a criminal judge in the court of law on charges about drugs and street fight. It was this very judge who on asking him why he didn't use his talent to make something worthwhile—something within him than fight in the streets or smoke weed in frustration—he changed from a drug addict to a film start and billionaire.

Martin Luther went to Vatican and Vatican changed him and he started his own church. Saul was a killer and a proud anti-Christ crusader until when he met the Light—then he became Paul apostle—the greatest messenger of peace and the greatest writer.

Personal transformation—which is the beginning of the transformation at family, organization and national level—therefore begins with some kind of enlightenment we happen to chance upon. It was Gideon Mkama who introduced me to my new self when I worked at the brewery in Tanzania.

He told me I was rather still intelligent to allow my brains to decay in the beer bottle. He pleaded with me to leave before I was forty. Why? He said otherwise I would never leave.

I can recall that meeting. When I promised him hand on heart that I would do so after two years he didn't like it. He emphasized that I should leave before the two years.

That's how I emerged from acting as regional sales manager in the upcountry to be the national brand manager of bigger brand in the capital city.

I met Amani Mworia, my former workmate at Celtel. He had made his decision earlier on and had chosen his career path. He was so fond of his personal liberties. He was always happy.

He used to come to the office happy and went back all smiles because he had a goal in life. Recalling his enthusiasm at the time when many wore wrinkled faces out of despair, desperation and hopelessness, *I'd always wished I could catch the absolute joy that spread across his face and bottle it forever.*[131] And I, yes, I realized—through him—that life was in my hands. I resigned from my job at Celtel in my mid-thirties. For better or worse, people we meet help us to change. You can do the same, for better or worse.

Eve met a serpent, and then she met Adam and both were cursed! Therefore choose who you meet. Think about it—think of those you met and their influence on you—for better or worse. Lucky was Adrian Mutu. He met Jose Mourinho as his coach at Chelsea. What did he learn? Let's learn from him: "I told (Adrian) Mutu," Jose Mourinho reported, "you are already a rich boy, you won a lot of money, you are still in a big contract. So no problem with your future about money, no problem about prestige in your (little) home country (and in fact) when you go back to Romania you will be one of the kings. But five years after you leave football nobody remembers you—only if you do big things. This is what makes history."

It is worth repeating here that, born in a log cabin and working as a grocery store clerk, a young unlearned American citizen found himself in the presence of a burglar with a set of unclaimed items among which lay some law books. He devoured these books with the vengeance of a hungry nursing lioness. A few years later he qualified as a licensed lawyer.

His upward journey didn't end there. He became president of the United States of America a few years later—and probably a philosopher. You must have heard about him—I am sure. For his name is Abraham Lincoln.

I began this chapter by stating that I am a happy man. I am because I have accomplished a dream I had for longtime. In addition, it gives me pleasure to realize that I've at least shared a mission of not simply being a writer, but indeed a noble duty of dedicating my time and meager resources, sacrificing my salaries for the past eight years and pleasure of clubbing or partying or even living a more worldly life to offer my contribution in elevating humanity, making life better, and the world a little bit better—for many. Truly I may never see cash filling my bank account in my lifetime as a result of such dedication. I know that.

I know you may never see the world changing in my lifetime. I may never witness new peace and harmony in the world today because of my dedication.

I may never live or endeavor to be appointed in any worldly high office or even to be conferred with an honor of tutoring among any prestigious universities within and without, but whoever, whenever, however, wherever and for whatever reasons this very statement will be quoted, let it go down on record that this book being read and put to use by the reader thereupon passing down the lessons thereof to his family, schools , corporations and in the public sector, that's the greatest windfall—a piece of fruit blown down from a tree I could ever dream of.

That is what I should ever demand!

A TRANSFROMED ME

Virgil said: *Believe in one who has proved it*. With the transformation we have illustrated, you can rest assured that we can transform the mediocre children, the poor performing students, your average employees, your weak departments and commonplace community into top performers. Furthermore, associating with people who strive against all odds and still accomplish whatever they set out to achieve is an inspiration and advantageous to any person or institution. *Associating with people who choose to reject circumstances they don't like and choose their own path is a great advantage to others.*[132]

Indeed your faith in us isn't baseless. With us you see the possibility. You hear it echoing in your mind. In his great book The Science of Getting Rich, Wallace D. Wattles wrote thus: *The poor don't need charity. They need inspiration.*

The author, in particular, chose the vocation of his own choice putting an end to the status quo rejecting to put up with business as usual. That is how he resigned from what was considered a lucrative job to pursue his own calling. Being so close to this person, this author, than anyone else, I can say with certainty that he chose the spouse of his choice without being bound by hearsay, traditions, religion or tribal background.

We have chosen places of domicile for long, for long we chose the future we wanted. We also chose the friends, the vocation, a higher station in life and society etc., and have placed life in our own hands.

We are certain, you realize now what we are capable of doing in breathing new life into individual trainees and the society as a whole. We must emphasize that to progress we have only to learn from the past but not cling to it.

We all know that to progress we have got to keep astride with technology and world trends. This is however not enough. We know students and employees who remain very, very ordinary despite their amazing potential! To excel you need to be a pioneer of these trends—trends that can be found within you.

And if you do so, it will not be long before we click our glasses in a toast celebrating a new you—yes you—the immediate reader (and what's more, we may not only be celebrating only a new you, but along with a new you, we may be celebrating a noble family, a world class business organization and generally a dignified nation)!

No wonder when installed president at Harvard, Lawrence Summers said: "In this new century, nothing shall matter most like education of future leaders and development of new ideas."

If you discover that academic excellence on its own cannot help anyone advance his life to his potential station in life before you finish this book, then certainly you are heading for a bigger future. How do I know? I began this section by a subtitle that says that you are not a chicken.

I stated that you can fly—like me. Indeed. I have narrated how I was a mediocre person on the bottom of almost everything I was engaged in.

Yet only a few years after my transformation, referring to my achievement, a many years schooling friend and a close associate of the author who was then the commercial director at Lafarge Tanzania and now CEO at Mwananchi communications limited—Francis Nanai—sent the author a note saying thus:

"Congratulations." I replied saying *I am trying to move ahead*. He said in response:

"No. You are not simply moving. You are actually leaping!" He was saying, in other words; you are jumping—covering spaces in one leap—flying! And he couldn't be more right!

By changing you become more resourceful, more influential, more powerful, and more helpful; you raise happier children, capable students and employees and a prosperous nation! And indeed to this, the author sings praises—not prays—saying: "Honor and glory be unto God forever." That's why often when I recall where I have come from in this shorter period of time, like Marvin Sapp, the American gospel singer, I can't help but sing along stating that: "I'm stronger, I'm wiser, and I'm better—(far) much better. I have made it...!" You, yes, you the reader, can sing the same song! With this book on your lap, you should by now be singing the same song.

YOU: THE DISPLACED EGG

Here now comes an important message—a message that may illustrate to the reader that with this book on his lap, he should, by now, be singing the same song asserting that he is stronger, wiser, and better—(far) much better. And that he has made it…!"

And this message goes to all those who are grounded in chaos and aggravation. Don't lose hope. Many of the people you meet today may not be different from you. Many of those you see as successful may have gone through the life you are going through now. Many may have had to rediscover themselves and retrace their feet back to where they began losing track. Many may have had to pick themselves up after they had fallen and displaced—displaced in the wrong vocation or station in life.

Long time ago, an egg rolled the wrong way only to find itself on the wrong side of the nest. As a result of its displacement, after 21 days, it was hatched among chicken eggs nearby. Therefore, on being hatched, this bird found itself on the ground—crawling, walking—instead of flying! One afternoon, this "chicken" watched with admiration and abandonment at how an eagle was flying past in the high blue skies. Then as the eagle cruised near the ground, the "chicken" shouted at the top of its voice in sheer approbation and wonder. The eagle came down and the pair started conversing. "What can I do to fly like you do?" asked the chicken. The eagle looked closely at his admirer—and felt deep compassion.

After a profound thought, the eagle replied—and as the eagle told the chicken, I'm telling you now:
"Look at my face. You look just like me. Look at my beak; you look just like me! Look at my wings; you look just like me! Friend you are not a chicken; you are an eagle. Flap your wings and fly like an eagle you were born to be!"[133]

And lo! The chicken did flap the wings and did fly even far more gracefully and farther away into the deep high blue skies like no other eagle had ever done before. Why? On one hand it was a great privilege to the chicken to fly. He enjoyed every part of it while birds that are born eagles took it for granted! It was so exciting. It was his long time passion and thus he did fly with great enthusiasm.

On the other hand eagles didn't know the troubles chicken faced on the ground: the dangers from vultures, dangers from predators, danger from man etc.

THE TRAINER'S PROFILE AND TESTIMONY

We have backers! On finishing one of his books, Laurean Rugambwa Bwanakunu, a former director with a number of international agencies and now director for MSD—he had purchased all 3 titles—sent a note saying, "I've read a book I can relate to!"

Dr. Alawi Shaaban Swabury, a countryman based in Germany Member of the UN Business Sector Steering Committee on Finance for the Development-New York; CEO of ESSB Berlin sent a note saying: "I congratulate you for a book with so much useful insights."

Michael Ogwari John, a senior government human resource director and at the time acting principal secretary ministry of health—he had purchased all my book titles—said that; "Finally, I've stumbled upon books that bespeak what I consider as right solutions to our problems."

Respicius Didace, a prominent lawyer in Dar es Salaam said, "I'm proud of your achievement. Thank you for this gift," he wrote. "Given the response I see," he continued, "I suggest that the priority now should be to make these books available in the country."

On launching of the books in this series and program thereof, and the interview that we had with Mlimani (University) Television a year back, the show was repeated a couple more times following the incessant requests by the viewers and listeners at this station.

Referring to the original idea of this book series in a letter dated June 28, 2008 from Phillip Parham, at the time when he was a British High Commissioner to Tanzania, said , "I like your emphasis on common sense—a commodity which is often short in supply!"

But lastly, as a testimony and tribute to our brand of training, I told the students from the higher learning institutions in Tanzania—students funded by the UN—that if they come out feeling the same after the training, "I would with pleasure accept myself as one of the greatest idiots that Africa has produced." After the training, five days later, S. Ndikubagabo, a higher education student from Burundi approached me and extending his hand—which I received of course—he said, "Thank you and congratulations. You were right.

You are not an idiot," and, holding my right hand in his, he shook it for a very, very, very long time! Now forget the testimonies above. Asides from whatever worldly accomplishments you or I can have, the author believes that among human qualities, moral obligation is the noblest of all. The author, previously working as a training development and business consultant at INNOVEX, and now a writer and published author, resigned to write and create training programs that address challenges we face today, the idea from which this book series was conceived.

Graduate of economics, the author, who is also the founder and principal trainer at KI, has recently trained students from Kyambogo University in Uganda alongside University of Dar es Salaam students at Nkrumah Hall.

He has also sampled our training program among such schools as Lutengano Secondary School, Lutengano High School, St. Ann's Primary and Secondary School, etc. He has trained the UN and DAFI sponsored students from Universality of Dar es Salaam, University of Dodoma, St. John's University, Institute of Finance Management, Dar es Salaam University College of Education, Institute of Social Works, and College of Procurement among whom were refugee students from Somalia, Congo DR, Ethiopia, Burundi etc.

He has trained staff and management for Upeo Education, Tanzania Broadcasting Corporation and President Mkapa Foundation's Mkapa Fellows, among others. He also previously trained and managed staff, distributors and budgets while serving among different organizations in the country among them Smithkline Beecham, Tanzania Breweries Limited, and Celtel (now Airtel).
He coordinated Tanzania and the principals in Copenhagen serving in the capacity of the national brand manager and Carlsberg representative for Tanzania.

As for the real work on the ground, at KI, we have got other advantages. We are experienced trainers. We have been recently running and mentoring programs among students from top universities, colleges and schools in the country.

Our principal trainer is a researcher, writer and is privileged to be a published author of a number of books covering a set of topics on improving education and learning, family institution, children, gender, culture, patriotism, self esteem, how to get results, promoting the culture of reading and writing, leadership, creativity and innovation etc. We, as trainers are so diverse a team—in expertise, talents and professions.

We, as practitioners draw our training, consultations and facilitation from our broad team of associates who are always willing to share their unique experiences in different fields of study. We further—in providing this fundamental support—possess such noble distinctiveness as innovativeness, knowledge sharing, excellence, partnership and cooperation, integrity, constancy, confidentiality and commitment to growth for our stakeholders—besides customizing our programs to suit the client's needs.

Here's another reminder about us, something you would not want to miss. You are engaged with exemplary people who have chosen their lives. We are the people who began from the least in the class, lived like any poor persons but made it to university and later landed themselves in the top world class organizations rising to senior positions.

Did we stop here? No! We resigned. Why? To pursue new career, vocations or calling. We are literally self made and self trained in areas of writing, training, and coaching. Why is this remark important? "I believe that close association with one who refuses to compromise with circumstances he does not like," recommended Napoleon Hill, in Think and Grow Rich, "is an asset that can never be measured in terms of money—(and money alone)!" That is why this is a big moment for you.

When Sir. Winston Churchill was called to lead up the world war preparations of the Great Britain, in his "acceptance speech"; he remarked that, "All my life had prepared me for this hour." Like Churchill, I, the author, bear testimony to the truth that all my life has prepared me for this hour—the hour of role-playing and transforming lives of the poor, the mediocre and hopeless; the hour of uplifting performances and future potential among schools, families and corporations.

THE GREATEST CONTRAVERSY OF OUR TIME
After reading testimonies for, and tributes, to the author, we know there are many amongst our readers who will say, "Mhh! surely he doesn't have solid academic or experience to stir, and enhance, anything significantly meaningful to me, or my organization, let alone the country. Some academicians will doubtlessly question credentials of a self-declared one-degree "seer!" And such a claim is vindicated—by all academic conventional standards. In no uncertain terms I want to go on record refusing to accept that all praiseworthy ideas or innovations come from the highly classed people. No. You probably are also disappointed that the author is not necessarily highly instructed.

Don't be. Doubtless you have read about or heard of Ralph Waldo Emerson. He is probably the most influential person who transformed and transcended the American minds and education of the 19th century to those of this day. His works on transcendence and self reliance are certainly among the rarest works from which most prominent writers and academics have drawn inspiration and assembled the groundwork for their works until as I write. His was considered to be a thorough mind that was a true *think-tank*.

To many, any of his suggestions was perfect and his ideas simply foolproof. And to be fair, his ideas generally transcend time and space. People believed he could not be beaten or humbled by anyone even the greatest intellectuals of the times before him. But one day, only one day changed that code of belief.

Dale Carnegie, among others, writes so well about him especially the story I am adapting hereafter. This is how it began.

On that evening, he, Emerson, and his son, endeavored to see a calf into its barn when the others had long since entered willingly. Then in his urgency, Emerson pushed, and his son pulled. This infant of a calf was unfortunately in no way connected to Emerson's reasoning, or intentions, and no wonder it stubbornly stiffened its legs and refused to leave its pastures. After they had pushed and pulled for a significant duration of time, beads of perspiration glistened on their brows.
Emerson and his son licking their lips, took a break. They then wiped the perspiration off their faces with the back of their hands and dried their palms with their trousers, and then rolled their sleeves and went back to work. It was all to no avail, unfortunately. The calf simply scaled up her resistance as defiance in it now only mounted to so much as insurmountable.

Now Emerson's own humble, unlearned, immigrant Irish housemaid, watching the whipping her own boss had been enduring at the hand of an infant, and evidently unschooled beast; unprepared, instantly put away the salt she had in her hands, and for a moment forgetting the stew she was preparing, without even changing her kitchen apron and sleepers into more appropriate wear like jeans and sneakers or sportswear such as shin guards, she traced her feet toward the scene in urgency to rescue her boss she genuinely admired.

When she arrived at the scene, she paid no attention to the rest, giving her whole undivided attention to the calf. Then looking the calf into the eye, she put her soft, warm, salty maternal finger in the calf's mouth, and without much ado, began walking toward the barn.

The calf? Sucking the soft, warm, salty motherly finger now in full obsession, she followed the Irish housemaid into the barn as she gently reclaimed the finger.

Caressing the calf, she gently reclaimed her finger, turned locking the barn behind her, strode back to her kitchen chores leaving Emerson and his son in total shock, shocked out of their minds, stunned, humbled.

You recognize that this maid was in no way nowhere near Emerson's own scholarly or masculine genius or credibility. It was in one and only one way that she was superior. And that was her strength. She knew how to connect with the calf, the calf's own needs.

She knew what the calf desired and interpreted her goals or desires into the calf's own point of view. Yes, you are right; I am not as intellectually credible as Emerson. Yes I am not a person as experienced and gifted and in limelight like someone you would ordinarily have wished to have as your mentor, life coach or role player. The author is not anywhere near J.K. Nyerere or Mandela.

Yes you are right he may not be Einstein or one of the greatest inspirational and successful authors and billionaires like Robert Kiosaki, Donald Trump, Ngugi wa Thion'go, Wole Soyinka, Richard Branson, Dr. Ben Carson, or Barrack Obama.

And yes, let me the author, admit publicly. I am not any of these men even if I may have wished to be one of them. Indeed I am playing the role of that unlearned, humble Emerson's Irish housemaid.

Now, concerning the standing of the author, notice that however evil was the economic crisis, it has helped create new perspectives that are advantageous to the traditionally disadvantaged folks and societies like ours today.

Economic crisis has drawn out new battle lines. It has made the terrain level for all of us: poor or rich, big or small, learned and not learned.

And this isn't my own conception! It is by the greatest thinker of the last century—Napoleon Hill—a man who witnessed and wrote about life before, during and after the great depression—a situation very close to ours today. Indeed the economic crisis has changed the way we defined credibility. It has changed success factors as well as growth drivers—and thereof credibility.

On the international stage, it has brought a new balance of power where young economies have major role to play. Anyone who aspires to get to the top will get there provided he abides by the principles we have laid down in this very book. As a result—as observed Napoleon Hill—out of this experience, there will arise a new breed of leaders in business and industry, people who will enjoy the greatest following ever known in history of mankind. These leaders will come from the rank and file of unknown men and women who now labor in the steel plants, the coal mines, the automobiles factories and in the small towns and cities of America, (or Tanzania for that matter)," he concluded.

"For behold," says the bible in *Isaiah 3:1-4*, "the Lord God of hosts is taking away from Jerusalem and Judah (from the ruler) support and supply. He is taking his support away from the mighty man and the soldier, the judge and the prophet, the diviner and the elder, the captain of fifty and the man of rank, the counselor and skillful magician and the expert in charms. And I will make boys their princes, and infants shall ruler over them."

The testimony we have given is true and just a drop in the bucket. And it doesn't matter. Garry Spence said: I would rather have a mind opened by wonder than one closed by belief. Now since the training we offer accords you a chance to open up and see the opportunities within your reach, we believe now the ball lies in your court. Yes, we cannot choose for you, but we know that if you join our world you can only gain: you, your family, your business and the community as a whole.

Talk is cheap. Kindly, give us appointment to meet you in person and present the case if it is necessary or helpful in affirming that you have made the right decision by choosing to work with us in adopting this program into your own.

In words of Muhammadu Buhari March 2015, "Allow me prove to you that in your lifetime you and your children can be proud of this country."

Finally, you recognize it all boils down to you, yes you the immediate reader, we hope you realize you don't have to be the president of the nation state, organization or even a household to make things happen. That's why they do better those of you who don't sit there and lament of the problems they, their families, community or business and the nation as a whole are facing. These are of the company of well guided. When they see a problem, they do something about it—by their hands, their words of mouth, pen—or prayer. And that—the latter is the weakest of them all![1134] Abu Sa'eed al-Khudree narrated thus: the Messenger of Allah said, "Whoso-ever of you sees an evil, let him change it with his hand; and if he is not able to do so, then (let him change it) with his tongue; and if he is not able to do so, then with his heart—and that is the weakest of faith."

That's why I am going to end by a poem developed and extended by this author from a Kiswahili poem by Kahabi G. Isangula from a Kiswahili Newspaper, Raia Tanzania of Tuesday December 23, 2014, a poem that illustrates that you can do something in your present position—and yes you can have and be anything you want in life—much as you or Isangula can even be the president of the United Republic:

IF ONLY I WERE PRESIDENT

It is but daydreaming, me in the state house?

A malnourished weakling, voters me to refuse,
Since a child and crawling, leadership me didn't choose,
But if I were president, quick fix down would close,

The idler and robber, victims of my presidency!
Would be a sharp razor, corruption I'd slice,
Turn each youth into a farmer, or work in factories,
We would export mangoes, and coconut juice,

Refine coffee and tanzanite, build infrastructure and create real jobs,
Put'n an end to begging *to-nite*, would end budget aid grants,
In schools to innovate, new mindset in sports, science and industry,
To lift productivity and quality, till produces spill over the borders,

D'smash down the classroom padlocks, drag youth back into classes,
D'reform education and discount gas, protect elephants and vegetations,
Health and flowing water access, back to village movements,

Would end Machingas and slums, turn EA Federation into a paradise!

With smaller government, d'light the horizon,
Evergreen turn the semi-desert, build values and ideals of a nation,
End gender and religious concert, challenge female mutilation,
In place of tribal war songs, they'd sing Psalms among Tarime tribes,

If and only if I were president ooo![1135]

NINGALIKUA RAISI

By Kahabi G. Isangula

Ni ya alinacha ndoto, kutamani uraisi,
Msoto bin msoto, mtu wa lishe nyepesi,
Toka nikiwa mtoto, uongozi sijihisii,
Ila nikiwa raisi, wazembe wangenikoma.

Wangenikoma wazembe, wezi na wahalifu,
Ningalikua kiwembe, kuchanja wabadhilifu,
Wangalishika majembe, wenye nguvu timilifu,
Tuexport maembe, na juice ya madafu.

Maembe *tuexport*, tuze vito vya madini,
Sio kuomba supoti, ya bajeti marekani,
Ningagawa pasiport, kwa watu wa vijijini,
Ili wauze chapati, hadi nchi za jirani.

Nchi hizi za jirani, ziwe soko la mazao.
Makumbusho ya zamani, yang'ae kama farao
Kila darasani, asiwepo wa pumbao
Ningenunua mashini, umeme sio mgao

Sio umeme mgao, uwake kwenye mapori,
Sehemu zenye ukame, mabwawa ya kifahari,
Zile mbuga za machame, ziproduce sukari,
Ndugu wa Tarime, wangaliimba zaburi.

THE IDEAL SCHOLAR
By Festo Michael Kambarangwe
(Coming Soon)

If after 50 years of education GDP growth doesn't echo in improved lives of the average citizen i.e. access to electricity, flowing water, housing, health and education; when a nation remains dependent; when produced scholars aren't productive as employees, or successful as self-employed, and therefore remain unemployed vs. persistent low performances in schools, at workplace, or in Olympics; when preferring quick fix our scholars cease reading after graduation amidst rising rates of school dropouts, corruption, religious sentiments, environmental degradation and poverty as the rich families and nations grow richer but fewer and the masses ground in abject poverty while the country is loaded with natural resources; when outsiders fill senior positions locally and internationally as the natives slave in their own country, certainly there's miseducation in this society —an indicator that there's more to mediocrity than lack of resources or degree papers.

That's why we have made no significant headways for 50 years now. And we can't make significant headways marshalling meager resources toward many battle lines leaving only overstretched resources directed towards education—education which is itself focused on the mastery of the subject matter e.g. botany, bee-keeping or even rocket-science instead of focusing on the mastery of one's person. Introduction of BRN in Tanzania is an admission that skills-based curriculum has failed. Skills-based education is barren when it pays no attention to the Human Factor i.e. a learner's calling or aspirations, culture and history e.g. colonialism, slave trade and socialism which helped to erode a nation's self- esteem, ambition and industry. This explains why we produce illiterate graduates and educated slaves. It explains why a nation is weeping for ideal scholars!

To illustrate the Human Factor: Take two persons or teams and give them same-same tools. One will exceed expectations as another will complain of poor tools; one team will be crowned champions and another will sit at the bottom of the table! Likewise, two companies endowed with equivalent resources in selling similar products or services: One will have a constant flow of loyal, patient customers lining-up in queues like ants willing to pay top dollar for its products or services, while next door products decay on the shelves from lack of customers. Take two graduates of finance or economics; give them a million dollar each. One will make a fortune as the million dollar, like water, will, in a twinkling of an eye, filter through the fingers of another fellow! Interesting, isn't it? This illustrates the individual person, school, organization or a nation often makes use of only a small fraction of its physical and mental resources, living far within its limits. It illustrates we possess a variety of powers which we ordinarily fail to use.

This is the handicap of our education—the gap the conventional education has failed to fill. This, Sir, is the gap we fill! This, Madam, is the difference we make.

A WORD FROM THE AUTHOR

As the New Beginning unfolds, and beckons you, we would love to hear from you! For training, support, cooperation or enquiries about this and other books or find more exciting insights into the training opportunities we offer please call us or contact us now!

FESTO MICHAEL KAMBARANGWE

Cell 1: +255 715 11 11 06
E-mail: author.tanzania@gmail.com

REFERENCES AND ENDNOTES RETRIEVED DURING THE WRITING PERIOD UP TO JULY 2015

[1] Ornstein and Francis P. Hunkins, Curriculum: Foundations, Principles and Issues 3rd Edition P. 154
[2] Ibid. P. 51
[3] Taken from An Exercise in World Making page 56
[4] Adapted from Identifying Causes of State failure: The Case of Somalia Failed States in Sub-Saharan Africa by Ahmad Rashid Jamal
[5] http://www2.webster.edu/~corbetre/haiti/misctopic/leftover/whypoor.htm?
[6] Transcript of Haiti the Failed State by: Elsa Chase, Avery Ortega, Tyler Varley, and Dan Dabkowski
[7] Adapted from Transcript of Haiti the Failed State by: Elsa Chase, Avery Ortega, Tyler Varley, Dan Dabkowski
[8] Adapted from Transcript of Haiti the Failed State by: Elsa Chase, Avery Ortega, Tyler Varley, Dan Dabkowski
[9] (http://www.lib.utexas.edu/maps/americas/haiti_rel99.jpg).
[10] http://mettyz-bongoland-reflections.blogspot.com/2007/11/bba-may-be-u-but-im-not-proud.html
[11] https://en.wikipedia.org/wiki/Unus_pro_omnibus,_omnes_pro_uno
[12] https://www.facebook.com/kamaleki.mutalemwa?fref=nf
[13] Ubuntu is a Bantu word for "Humanity," a South African philosophy on humanity advocated by Despond Tutu
[14] Source: Immigration Department diary of 2010; also available http://www.blackwoodconservation.org/where.html
[15] https://en.wikipedia.org/wiki/The_Rise_and_Fall_of_the_Great_Powers#cite_note-1
[16] https://books.google.co.tz/books?id=wX5eAAAAcAAJ&pg=PA644&lpg=PA644&dq=The+warlike+states+of+antiquity,+Greece,+Macedonia,+and+Rome
[17] https://en.wikipedia.org/wiki/Slavery_in_the_Ottoman_Empire
[18] www.hurriyetdailynews.com (retrieved on 23 July 2015)
[19] Adapted from http://www.hurriyetdailynews.com/african-slaves-in-the-ottoman-empire.aspx?pageID=238&nID=69858&NewsCatID=438 (retrieved on 23 July 2015)
[20] https://www.ricksteves.com/watch-read-listen/read/understanding-yugoslavia
[21] https://en.wikipedia.org/wiki/Breakup_of_Yugoslavia
[22] https://www.foreignaffairs.com/reviews/review-essay/1995-07-01/titos-last-secret-how-did-he-keep-yugoslavs-together
[23] Allan C. Ornstein and Francis P. Hunkins, curriculum: Foundations, Principles and Issues 3rd Edition p.44

[24] Adapted from *What Makes People Rich and Nations Powerful*
[26] Adapted from http://www.economist.com/node/13315108?zid=309&ah=80dcf288b8561b012f603b9fd9577f0e
[27] http://www.arushatimes.co.tz/2007/29/local_news_6.htm; https://books.google.co.tz/books?id=n-tlo3KPcgMC&pg=SA6-PA71&lpg=SA6-PA71&dq=leading+tanzanite+exporting+countries&source;
[28] http://evankawishe.blogspot.com/2014/11/kenya-india-zaipiku-tanzania-mauzo-ya.html
[29] 2002 Rebecca Fine & Certain Way Productions www.scienceofgettingrich.net; www.scienceofgettingrich.net/
[30] Allan C. Ornstein and Francis P. Hunkins, curriculum: foundations, principles and Issues 3rd edition p. 375
[31] Adapted from What Makes People Rich and Nations Powerful
[32] www.uwezo.net/
[33] Allan C. Ornstein and Francis P. Hunkins, curriculum: Foundations, Principles and Issues 3rd Edition P. 50
[34] http://www.thecitizen.co.tz/News/national/700-fake-certificates-seized-this-year/-/1840392/1913364/-/icnbpm/-/index.html
[35] Allan C. Ornstein and Francis P. Hunkins, Curriculum: Foundations, Principles and Issues 3rd Edition P. 46
[36] Ivan Pavlov experimented with a dog to explore the power of stimulus to our responses. *In* this experiment a dog learned to salivate at the sound of a bell. The bell a biologically neutral or inadequate stimulus was being presented simultaneously with food a biologically non-natural or adequate stimulus. So closely were the two stimuli associated by the dog that the bell came to be substituted for the food and the dog reacted to the bell as originally had to the food.
[37] Allan C. Ornstein and Francis P. Hunkins, Curriculum: Foundations, Principles and Issues 3rd Edition p.103
[38] Ibid p. 355
[39] Source: This concept is an adaptation rooted from the Greek concept of Paideia and The Chicago School also quoted from Allan C. Ornstein and Francis P. Hunkins, Curriculum: Foundations, Principles and Issues 3rd Edition P 2
[40] Allan C. Ornstein and Francis P. Hunkins, curriculum: Foundations, Principles and Issues 3rd Ed, p. 3
[40] Ibid p. 3
[41] Ibid p. 5o
[42] Ibid p. 123
[43] What Is Education For? Six myths about the foundations of modern education, and six new principles to replace them by David Orr

[44] Adapted from Allan C. Ornstein and Francis P. Hunkins, curriculum: foundations, principles and Issues 3rd edition pp: 46 -50
[45] Allan C. Ornstein and Francis P. Hunkins, curriculum: Foundations, Principles and Issues 3rd Edition P. 46-48
[46] Ibid p. 47
[47] Ibid p. 47
[48] Ibid p. 49
[49] Put here your own country
[50] What Is Education For? Six myths about the foundations of modern education, and six new principles to replace them by David Orr
[51] From the play The Tragic History of the Life and Death of Doctor Faustus by Christopher Marlowe
[52] An Exercise in World Making 2007 page 28
[53] What Is Education For? Six myths about the foundations of modern education, and six new principles to replace them by David Orr
[54] Allan C. Ornstein and Francis P. Hunkins, curriculum: Foundations, Principles and Issues 3rd Edition P. 397-398
[55] You may find more insightful information from Brands and Branding and End users and Consumers' Satisfaction chapters in What Business Leaders Should Know but They Don't!
[56] Ibid p 27
[57] Please read What Business Leaders Should Know But They Don't
[58] Allan C. Ornstein and Francis P. Hunkins, curriculum: Foundations, Principles and Issues 3rd Edition P,53
[59] Ibid p. 145
[60] Ibid pp: 48- 49
[61] Allan C. Ornstein and Francis P. Hunkins, Curriculum: Foundations, Principles and Issues 3rd Edition p. 19
[62] Cathy Williams in *Wife for Hire*
[63] *Please be advised to read the book: How Universities Under Develop You!*
[64] Adapted from Mark McCormack, *What They Can't Teach You at Harvard Business School (P.13)*
[65] Lincoln in his 2nd inaugural address
[66] http://www.jamiiforums.com/habari-na-hoja-mchanganyiko/209675-upasuaji-tata-wa-binadamu-tz-imo-juu.html; http://news.bbc.co.uk/2/hi/africa/7084615.stm
[67] http://well.blogs.nytimes.com/2007/11/28/when-surgeons-cut-the-wrong-body-part/?_r=0
[68] Adapted from how universities under develop you
[69] http://www.jamiiforums.com/jukwaa-la-siasa/254104-utamu-uchungu-wa-kimombo-ubunge-a-mashariki.html
[70] What Makes People Rich and Nations Powerful

[71] Adapted by the author from 2 Samuel 23:10
[72] Dale Carnegie, How to Stop Worrying and Start Living
[73] BBC - A History of the World - Object _ The Magna Carta.html; http://www.softschools.com/timelines/the_british_empire_timeline/166/; https://en.wikipedia.org/wiki/Declaration_of_the_Rights_of_Man_and_of_the_Citizen
[74] Adapted from https://en.wikipedia.org/wiki/Roger_Boisjoly
[75] http://www.tzaffairs.org/1996/09/tanzanias-titanic-disaster-%E2%80%93-mv-bukoba/; https://en.wikipedia.org/wiki/MV_Bukoba
[76] en.mwikioedia.org/wiki/mv_bukoba
[78] Adapted from André Labuschaigne PEP MD in Pep case study
[79] *Allan C. Ornstein and Francis P. Hunkins, Curriculum Foundations, Principles and Issues 3rd edition p.35*
[80] Think and Grow Rich Unabridged Edition p. 250
[81] Source: Quran Translation by Abdullah Yusuf Ali
[82] www.goal.com/
[83] https://en.wikipedia.org/wiki/Mass_in_C_major_(Beethoven) http://mesocosm.net/2012/02/17/dies-irae-mozarts-requiem/ %20Wikipedia,%20the%20free%20encyclopedia.html https://en.wikipedia.org/wiki/Mass_in_C_major_(Beethoven
[84] Dies Irae Mozart Requiem_Mesocosm.html; https://en.wikipedia.org/wiki/Mass_in_C_major_(Beethoven); http://mathcs.holycross.edu/~groberts/Courses/Mont2/2012/Handouts/Lectures/Mozart-web.pdf; http://www.americanscientist.org/issues/pub/did-mozart-use-the-golden-section
[85] http://compasstech.com.au/ARNOLD/davinci/davinci2.htm; https://en.wikipedia.org/wiki/Mass_in_C_major_(Beethoven); http://mesocosm.net/2012/02/17/dies-irae-mozarts-requiem/
[86] Think and Grow Rich, Unabridged Edition p.244
[87] Ibid pp: 242-3
[88] Julius Nyerere in Nyerere of Tanzania by William Edgett Smith, 19
[89] Napoleon Hill in Think and Grow Rich the unabridged edition page 250
[90] Napoleon Hill in Think and Grow Rich the unabridged edition page 241
[91] Wayne Dyer in www.Motivatingqouotes.com
[92] John O Miller in How to Lead, How to Manage Executives by James C. Sarros, 991 p. 181
[93] Source: What Makes People Rich and Nations Powerful
[94] Adapted from What Makes People Rich and Nations Powerful
[95] Please make reference to the chapter on the principled universe, or in the book A Sick Nation in this very series
[96] The Promise, Maliyamkono and Mason p138
[97] The phrase was in the original document of the constitution drafted by Thomas Jefferson which was amended into the final document

[98] https://en.wikipedia.org/wiki/Paul_Kennedy
[99] Genesis 1:27-28 (Gideon's International)
[100] The quotation is the author's and therefore unofficial translation
[101] http://www.voanews.com/MediaAssets2/learningenglish/2006_06/audio/mp3/se-nation-roaring-twenties.mp3
[102] This is the comparison between the time spent on labor or work and leisure. The higher the ratio, the more the productive is the society. The lower the ratio, the higher the leisure and the less is the productivity and economic activity in general
[103] Adapted from Allan C. Ornstein and Francis P. Hunkins, Curriculum: Foundations, Principles and Issues 3rd Edition P 162
[104] http://www.thecitizen.co.tz/News/national/700-fake-certificates-seized-this-year/-/1840392/1913364/-/icnbpm/-/index.html
[105] Derived from the Greek concept of Paideia
[106] Adapted from Allan C. Ornstein and Francis P. Hunkins, Curriculum: Foundations, principles and issues
[107] Allan C. Ornstein and Francis P. Hunkins, curriculum: Foundations, Principles and Issues 3rd Edition pp. 50-51
[108] Adapted from Ornstein and Hunkins, 3rd edition p.51
[109] This issue is pointedly illustrated in a satire on education entitled the Saber Tooth Curriculum
[110] Stephen L. Talbott, The Future Does Not Compare in Ornstein and Hunkins 1998,
[111] Adapted from Allan C. Ornstein and Francis P. Hunkins, curriculum: foundations, principles and Issues 3rd edition P167- 168
[112] Adapted from Allan C. Ornstein and Francis P. Hunkins, curriculum: foundations, principles and Issues 3rd edition p.157
[113] Hard violence is mainly physical in nature and it has the female as its victim. The male folks aren't safer either. They are subject of the soft violence: mental and spiritual abuse by the female folks especially in the household which is normally a by-product of hard violence—and vice versa.
[114] Allan C. Ornstein and Francis P. Hunkins, Curriculum: Foundations, Principles and Issues 3rd edition p. 152
[115] Ibid p. 352
[116] Ibid p. 152
[117] Ibid p. 356
[118] Adapted from Raia Mwema a Swahili paper of 11 to June 17, 2014 page 11
[119] *How Universities Under Develop You!*
[120] Allan C. Ornstein and Francis P. Hunkins, Curriculum: Foundations, Principles and Issues 3rd Edition P.71
[121] *How Universities Under Develop You!*

[122] The Promise Maliyamkono and Mason p. 445
[123] Allan C. Ornstein and Francis P. Hunkins, Curriculum: Foundations, Principles and Issues 3rd Edition p.112
[124] Adapted from City Group's corporate slogan
[125] Adapted: anonymous New Year wish
[126] Adapted from traditional farewell from epistles of Apostles Peter and Paul
[127] The events in the book overlap the date as the author endeavored to capture any important developments even during the publication process

www.ingramcontent.com/pod-product-compliance
Lightning Source LLC
Chambersburg PA
CBHW071648090426
42738CB00009B/1453